Mencius and Early Chinese Thought

Mencius and Early Chinese Thought

Kwong-loi Shun

Stanford University Press
Stanford, California

Stanford University Press
Stanford, California
© 1997 by the Board of Trustees of the
Leland Stanford Junior University

Printed in the United States of America

CIP data appear at the end of the book

Publication of this book was underwritten in
part by a grant from the Chiang Ching-kuo
Foundation for International Scholarly Exchange (USA).

To Wai-kuen

Acknowledgments

This book is the first of three projected volumes that examine the nature of Confucian-Mencian ethical thought. The first two volumes are textual studies of Mencius's thinking and its development by later Confucian thinkers, and are directed to understanding the perspectives of Mencius and of Confucian thinkers influenced by his thinking. The third volume will provide a more philosophical discussion of the spirit of Confucian-Mencian ethical thought; although it will build on the first two volumes, it will be directed less to a faithful representation of the perspectives of these thinkers, and more to drawing out the implications of their ideas for contemporary practical and philosophical concerns. I have deliberately separated the more philosophical discussion from the textual studies, because their different goals call for different approaches. For example, developing these thinkers' ideas in a way that is philosophically appealing to a contemporary investigator may help address certain contemporary practical and philosophical concerns, but it may not contribute to an understanding of the perspectives of the thinkers themselves since they might not have developed their thinking in this manner.

Because of the separation of the textual studies from the more philosophical discussion, this book does not attempt to relate its discussion to Western philosophical thought or to develop and assess ideas in Mencius's thinking; these tasks will be deferred to the third volume. For this reason, readers with more philosophical interests may find the book comparatively unphilosophical in nature. On the other hand, because the book is part of a larger project leading to a more philosophical discussion of the spirit of Confucian-Mencian thought, its content is shaped by this further goal. For example, it focuses more on the analysis of concepts that have philosophical implications to be explored in the third volume and does not consider philological details that do not bear on these further explorations. As a result, readers with more philological interests may find that the book pays less attention to philological details than they would expect.

My work on the book has taken several years, and I have incurred numerous debts in the process. I have been influenced by David Nivison both in methodology and in the way I interpret various aspects of early Chinese thought, such as my interpretation of Mo Tzu's thinking and of Mencius's disagreement with his contemporaries Kao Tzu and Yi Chih. I have benefited from numerous discussions with him, and his own writings on the subject have been a constant source of inspiration. I am also grateful to him for letting me consult and use his previously unpublished papers, which will soon be published in revised form in *The Way of Confucianism: Investigations in Chinese Philosophy* (La Salle, Ill.: Open Court Press).

Besides David Nivison, the writings of a number of scholars have also helped to shape my work. I have learned from A. C. Graham's methodology, and T'ang Chün-i's work has helped shape my overall interpretation of Mencius. I have also been helped by the writings of Ch'en Ta-ch'i, Hsü Fu-kuan, and Mou Tsung-san in my interpretation of various aspects of Mencius's thinking, and I have regularly consulted D. C. Lau's translation of the *Meng-tzu*, which I have often followed with occasional modifications. Although I sometimes express disagreement with these scholars, I would not have arrived at the conclusions I draw without having thought through their writings.

I have benefited from discussions and correspondence with a number of people, including Roger Ames, Irene Bloom, Chan Sin-yee, Cheng Chung-ying, Chong Kim-chong, Antonio Cua, Chad Hansen, Huang Chün-chieh, Craig Ihara, John Knoblock, Joel Kupperman, Whalen Lai, Lee Ming-huei, Liu Shu-hsien, Thomas Metzger, Jeffrey Riegel, Bryan Van Norden, and David Wong. Several of them have read and commented on parts of an early draft of the book or papers related to the book, and I am particularly grateful to Chong Kim-chong, Craig Ihara, and Joel Kupperman for taking the time to read most of the draft and provide me with comments on it. There are also people with whom I have had less frequent interaction, but from whose work I have benefited, including Lin Yih-jing, Donald Munro, Tu Wei-ming, Yang Rur-bin, and Lee Yearley.

I have received help from several graduate research assistants and participants in graduate seminars in which I presented related materials. They include Derek Hertforth, Jiang Xinyan, Michael Millner, Sang Tzu-lan, Eric Schwitzgebel, and Ted Slingerland. Undergraduate research assistants who have contributed to the project include Angelina Chin, Jasmin Chiu, Fan Wei-chun, Charles Huang, Esther Lin, Mimi Mong, and Amanda Shieh.

Over the years during which I worked on the book, I have received support from the Stanford Humanities Center and from the following programs at the University of California at Berkeley: Faculty Research Grants from the Center for Chinese Studies, Research Grants from the Committee on Research, a Humanities Research Fellowship, and several Humanities Research Assistantships. Parts of Chapter 4 are based on previously published papers, and I am grateful to the editor of *Philosophy East and West* for permission to use previously published materials. I am indebted to John Ziemer for his meticulous copy-editing and efficient handling of the book manuscript, and to Imre Galambos for assistance with the index.

K.-L. S.

Contents

Abbreviations

The following abbreviations are used in the Text and the Notes; for complete publication data, see the Bibliography, pp. 269–80:

Early Texts

CT	*Chuang-tzu*	LY	*Lun-yü*
HFT	*Han-fei-tzu*	M	*Meng-tzu*
HNT	*Huai-nan-tzu*	MT	*Mo-tzu*
HT	*Hsün-tzu*	SC	*Shih-ching*
KT	*Kuan-tzu*	SCS	*Shang-chün-shu*
KY	*Kuo-yü*	SPH	*Shen-pu-hai*
LC	*Li-chi*	SS	*Shang-shu*
LiT	*Lieh-tzu*	ST	*Shen-tzu*
LSCC	*Lü-shih ch'un-ch'iu*	TC	*Tso-chuan*
LT	*Lao-tzu*		

Commentaries on the *Meng-tzu* (by commentators with two or more commentaries included in the Bibliography)

C	Chao Ch'i, *Meng-tzu chu*
CC	Chao Ch'i, *Meng-tzu chang-chih*
MTCC	Chu Hsi, *Meng-tzu chi-chu*
MTHW	Chu Hsi, *Meng-tzu huo-wen*
MTKC	Yü Yüeh, *Meng-tzu ku-chu tse-ts'ung*
MTPI	Yü Yüeh, *Meng-tzu p'ing-i*
MTTI	Yü Yüeh, *Meng-tzu tsuan-i nei-wai p'ien*
TMHP	Yü Yün-wen, *Tsun-meng-hsü-pien*
TMP	Yü Yün-wen, *Tsun-meng-pien*
YL	Chu Hsi, *Chu-tzu yü-lei*

Mencius and Early Chinese Thought

1   *Introduction*

1.1   The Subject Matter

In what follows, I discuss Mencius's ethical thinking and, to some extent, its relation to the ideas of other thinkers in early China (by "early China" I refer to China before and during the third century B.C.). Our main access to Mencius's thinking is through the *Meng-tzu*, which was probably compiled by disciples or disciples of disciples and subsequently edited and shortened by Chao Ch'i in the second century A.D. To be more exact, rather than Mencius's thinking, my subject matter is the thinking of Mencius as it can be reconstructed from this text as it has been transmitted by compilers and editors.[1] The same qualification applies to my subsequent references to other early Chinese thinkers. In each case, although for convenience I speak of the way a certain thinker viewed things, I am referring to the ideas of the thinker as they can be reconstructed from the relevant text(s) as transmitted by their compilers and/or editors.[2]

In discussing the ethical thinking of Mencius and other early Chinese thinkers, I make a number of assumptions. One is that such thinking existed in early China. By "ethical thinking," I mean thinking concerned with how one should live, and I refer to an answer to this question as a conception of the ethical life or ethical ideal. The scope of "one" is supposed to extend considerably beyond the thinker addressing this question, but how far it extends may vary from thinker to thinker; it may, for example, encompass only people of certain social classes in what was China at that time. I believe that different conceptions of the ethical life were put forward in that period and were rooted in such practical concerns as how best to restore social order or to conduct oneself given the chaotic and in other ways problematic situation of the times.[3] More specifically, I believe that the thinkers of the period referred to retrospectively as Confucians, Mohists, Taoists, or Yangists did share an ethical concern in this sense, even though they had different conceptions of the ethical life.[4]

Even if these thinkers had different conceptions of the ethical life, it does not follow that they were competing conceptions, since they may well have been different conceptions of the ethical life for different individuals. Another assumption I make is that there was a considerable overlap in the scope of the individuals to whom these conceptions were supposed to apply and hence that they were indeed competing conceptions. I use the term "human beings" to refer to those individuals with whose way of life the so-called Confucian thinkers were concerned; to the extent that there is an overlap between these individuals and those to whom other conceptions of the ethical life were supposed to apply, the other conceptions were also concerned with some or all human beings. Introducing the term "human beings" in this way leaves open the question whether the term is applicable to all human beings as a biological species, since at this stage of my discussion it is an open question whether Confucian thinkers regarded their conception of the ethical life as applicable to all biological human beings or even whether they had a conception of human beings as a biological species (see §6.1.2).

Having a conception of the ethical life requires some degree of reflectivity, but ethical thinking can also be reflective in ways that extend beyond having such a conception, such as having a defense of that conception and, as part of such a defense, a picture of the way human beings are constituted. A further assumption I make is that many early Chinese thinkers were reflective in these additional ways, including both Mencius and other thinkers who came before and after him, such as Mo Tzu and Hsün Tzu.

I have so far used the term "Confucian" with qualification. Although the term appears in the subsequent discussion without qualification, I want to make explicit both my use of the term and the picture underlying this usage. It is generally agreed that by the sixth century B.C. there existed in China a social group consisting of professional ritualists who performed rituals in such ceremonial contexts as funeral rites, sacrifices to ancestors, and marriages. In addition, they were often professional teachers, not just of rituals but also of other disciplines such as music. Many scholars believe that members of the group were already referred to as "ju[a]" at that time, although there is disagreement on this issue as well as on the origins of the group—whether its members were descendents of the enslaved Shang people or descendents of Chou nobles who had lost their hereditary official positions.[5]

According to one view, certain individuals who were members of this group by virtue of being professional ritualists and teachers, including Confucius, Mencius, and Hsün Tzu, came to develop concerns that were no longer restricted to rituals or to their own economic sustenance. Instead, they directed their attention to finding a remedy for the chaotic social and political situation of the times and to establishing the ideal way of life for humans beings in such a situation. They believed that the remedy lay with the maintenance and restoration of certain traditional norms and values, including but going beyond rituals, and proposed that, ideally, people should follow a way of life that embodies such norms and values. They sought to effect the desired changes by seeking political influence and by promulgating their conception of the ethical ideal. They were reflective not just in having such a conception but also in being concerned with the proper spirit behind the observance of rituals and other traditional norms and, at least in the case of Mencius and Hsün Tzu, with the grounds for observing these norms and values. In addition to sharing a common ethical ideal and these broader and more reflective concerns, they also shared the use of certain key terms in elaborating on their thinking. Their reflectivity warrants our describing them as thinkers, and the broad similarities in their views warrant our regarding them as members of the same school of thought, which has traditionally been referred to by Chinese scholars as *ju^a chia*.[6]

There is no standard English expression unambiguously referring to this school of thought. The closest English expression is "Confucianism," but, as a number of authors have noted, this term can be used to refer to various phenomena related to the *ju^a*.[7] For example, the expression "Confucian way of life" can refer to the way of life of the *ju^a* as a social group or the way of life advocated by the thinkers just described, and the term "Confucian" can refer to someone who lives like a *ju^a* or someone who aspires to the way of life defended by these thinkers. Even when used to refer to the school of thought under consideration, "Confucianism" can have misleading connotations, such as the suggestion that the norms and values these thinkers upheld originated with Confucius. In this regard, the term "ju^a chia" in modern Chinese has an advantage since it refers unambiguously to the school of thought under consideration. Although it would be possible to use the term "ju^a chia" or variant forms in the subsequent discussion, in practice it is awkward to do so. For this reason, I will use "Confucianism" to refer specifically to the school of thought traditionally referred to as *ju^a chia* and to phenomena associated with that school.

Having laid out my assumptions, I will not attempt to defend them explicitly since this would involve a full-scale investigation of early Chinese thought. The assumptions that competing conceptions of the ethical life existed in early China and that their proponents were reflective in ways that went beyond merely advancing these conceptions are not too controversial. To the extent that I succeed in making plausible my presentation of Mencius and of other early Chinese thinkers as having reflective ethical concerns, the following discussion is a partial defense of these assumptions. The picture of early Confucian thought just described is widely accepted, and to the extent that I succeed in making plausible my presentation of Mencius (and to a lesser extent also Confucius and Hsün Tzu) as having reflective ethical concerns, I also regard the following discussion as a partial defense of that picture.[8]

Mencius (fourth century B.C.) proclaimed himself a follower of Confucius (sixth to fifth century B.C.) and presented the teachings of Mo Tzu (fifth century B.C.) and Yang Chu (fifth to fourth century B.C.) as the two major intellectual challenges to which he was responding. In Chapter 2, I discuss those aspects of the teachings of Confucius and of the two opposing schools that bear on the subsequent discussion of Mencius. In Chapter 3, I present Mencius's conception of the ethical ideal; parts of this discussion build on the discussion of Confucius. In Chapter 4, I consider Mencius's conception of the relation between *yi^a* (propriety) and *hsin^a* (heart/mind) in the context of his disagreement with two contemporary adversaries, Kao Tzu and Yi Chih; part of this discussion concerns Mencius's response to the Mohist challenge. In Chapter 5, I deal with Mencius's conceptions of self-cultivation, the restoration of political order, and the sources of ethical failure. Finally, in Chapter 6, I consider his views on *hsing^a* (nature, characteristic tendencies) and his claim that *hsing^a* is good; part of this discussion concerns his response to the Yangist challenge as well as the differences between his views on *hsing^a* and those of Hsün Tzu (third century B.C.).

1.2 Some Methodological Issues

Although I will not be able to defend the larger assumptions just described, I will discuss some specific considerations related to these assumptions that are discussed in the literature. These considerations, which bear on the legitimacy and methodology of the present study, are of two kinds. The first concerns the legitimacy of approaching early Confucian thought by making its constitutive ideas an object of intellectual inquiry. The second grants the legitimacy of such an approach but instead bears on the proper way to conduct such a study.

1.2.1 *Early Confucian Thought as an*
Object of Inquiry

The first group of considerations take as their starting point an observation about the predominantly practical concern of the early Confucian thinkers. Their primary concern was to live the way of life they advocated by embodying its outlook and cultivating the character it requires, as well as to convert and guide others to such a way of life through teaching and political participation. Their main concern was not to treat such a way of life as an object of intellectual inquiry — to understand it through careful analysis or to justify it with detailed argumentation. Given their predominantly practical concerns, they were not interested in presenting their ideas clearly and systematically. When conversing with others, their primary purpose was to induce the audience to have a personal feeling for the way of life they advocated and to motivate them to live that way. They sought to accomplish this through whatever utterance would serve this purpose, given the specific audience being addressed; since aspects of the ethical life often cannot be described adequately in language, they sometimes resorted to paradoxical utterances as a way of stimulating the appropriate outlook in their audience.[9]

Although this general sketch may need to be qualified in certain ways, for example, to accommodate the differences between the kinds of discourse engaged in by Mencius and Hsün Tzu, it does seem plausible as a rough statement of certain features of early Confucian thought.[10] That early Confucian thinkers were moved by predominantly practical concerns can be seen from their political endeavors and their devotion to the personal cultivation of themselves and their disciples, and the records we have of their teachings often lack a clear and systematic character. But, as various authors have pointed out, this observation is compatible with their having a body of ideas with a coherence and connectedness that warrants our making the ideas and their interconnections an object of study.[11] Individuals moved primarily by practical concerns can still have a reflective view of the relevant subjects that they seek to convey in their discourse, and although their practical concerns might lead to unsystematic presentation of their ideas, this does not preclude the possibility of interesting interconnections among such ideas. Hence, the predominantly practical concern of early Confucian thinkers does not by itself render illegitimate a study that focuses on such ideas and their interconnections.

The observation about practical concerns may be linked to the conclusion about the illegitimacy of such a study by at least three lines of thought. The first proposes that since the Confucian thinkers were moved primarily by practical concerns, they had no interest in, or were perhaps even impatient about, developing a body of ideas with coherence and interesting interconnections. They had no concern for, or might even have been hostile toward, maintaining the coherence of the ideas they expressed or establishing connections between such ideas. If so, we cannot legitimately ascribe to these individuals ideas with a reasonable degree of coherence and connectedness, and any study that focuses on these ideas and their interconnections is misguided.[12]

It is not clear, however, how such a claim might be substantiated. There is, as far as I know, no evidence outside the relevant texts for such a claim. And the texts do not seem to exhibit the kind of explicit and pervasive contradictions and discontinuities that one would expect to follow from such a claim; at least, it is not obvious that there is more evidence for a lack of concern for coherence and connectedness than for the presence of some such concern.[13] The resolution of this question should, it seems, depend on the outcome of an attempt to extract the ideas and their interconnections from the relevant texts. The investigation may reveal that coherence and connectedness are not really present, or present only in such a minimal form as to make the ideas uninteresting. But there is, prior to the investigation, no clear evidence that this is the case, and the attempt at such an investigation cannot be regarded as doomed to failure at the outset.

A second line of thought challenging the legitimacy of making the ideas of Confucian thinkers an object of study does not deny the possibility that the relevant texts may contain a body of ideas with some reasonable degree of coherence and connectedness. However, it proposes that since such ideas were the product of practical concerns rooted in the social and historical contexts of the times, it would be misguided to focus attention on their content and interconnections. Instead, the appropriate approach should focus on their sources, and this involves a careful examination of the social and political contexts in which these practical concerns were rooted.[14]

However, even if these ideas were products of practical concerns rooted in certain social and political contexts, it does not follow that it is misguided to attend to the content of the ideas.[15] Instead, whether one should focus on the content of the ideas or their source appears to be a function of the interests of those engaged in the study. Those more interested in the sociological and historical explanation of the emergence of such ideas attend more closely to the relevant practical concerns and their social and historical contexts. Those more interested in understanding how the ideas present themselves to these individuals, the nature of the ethical experiences reflected in these ideas, and the relevance of such ideas to one's own ethical experiences devote more attention to the content of the ideas. The second kind of investigation can benefit from appropriate historical and sociological studies, since such studies help reveal the concerns that engaged these individuals and thereby also help one better understand the ideas they expressed in addressing such concerns.[16] However, the relevance of historical and sociological studies does not render a close study of the content of the ideas misguided, and it seems more appropriate to view the two kinds of studies as complementary in that together they yield an understanding of the object of study that is more comprehensive than either can accomplish on its own.

A third line of thought proposes that since Confucian thinkers were not themselves primarily concerned with the ethical ideal as an object of intellectual inquiry, it is illegitimate to treat it as an object of such inquiry. Instead, what is needed is the kind of devotion to the Confucian ideal displayed by Confucian thinkers, as well as a readiness to employ nonstandard uses of language such as paradoxical utterances in order to stimulate the audience to aspire to that ideal. To treat the Confucian ideal as an object of intellectual inquiry, with emphasis on such qualities as clarity or textual evidence, is to "objectivize" it in a way that leads to a distorted understanding of the ideal.[17]

This line of thought emphasizes that treating early Confucian thought as an object of intellectual inquiry is a different kind of activity from that early Confucian thinkers engaged in. Unlike the Confucian thinkers, who were guided by the kind of practical concerns described earlier, such studies are directed instead toward understanding the Confucian thinkers' view of the ethical life, their defense of it, and the picture of the human constitution that underlies that defense. This difference in goals leads to a difference in emphasis; for example, a study of this kind emphasizes clarity and textual evidence in a way that the Confucian thinkers themselves would not. And, from the perspective of someone committed to the Confucian ideal, a study of this kind will likely have less importance and urgency; it is of greater importance to personally live up to the Confucian ideal and to guide others in that direction than to attempt to arrive at a clear understanding of the content of the ideal and its defense.

Although this line of thought helps us better understand the place of this kind of study, it does not show that such a study is misguided. This conclusion would follow only if it could be shown that the goal of such a study, which is to understand the Confucian perspective on the ethical life, is not worth pursuing or cannot be achieved by such a study. But, to the extent that it is possible to achieve this goal, it seems that it is worth pursuing even if it is less important than other goals of more direct practical relevance. Whether one is committed to the Confucian ideal or not, achieving this goal will help us understand an ethical ideal that has shaped the development of a whole culture as well as those aspects of the culture shaped by the ideal. And, for one committed to the ideal, such an understanding will enable one to better understand the way of life one endorses and its grounds. Even someone committed to the ideal can benefit from such an understanding, since it can help strengthen one's commitment and put one in a better position to convert others or to combat opposing influences. And to the extent that one is also prepared to critically assess the way of life to which one is committed, such an understanding will also help one conduct such an assessment and to reshape one's life accordingly.

The question of the legitimacy of this kind of study hinges, then, on whether it is possible to achieve its goals—whether the study can further our understanding of the Confucian perspective on the ethical life. Now, such a study probably cannot by itself achieve such an understanding, because that may depend on one's sharing to some extent the ethical experiences constitutive of the Confucian way of life, and perhaps also on having some degree of sympathy for the Confucian ideal.[18] But what this shows is only that such a study needs to be supplemented with relevant ethical experiences, imagination, and sympathy. There is no obvious reason why, when appropriately supplemented, such a study cannot contribute to the goal of furthering our understanding of the Confucian perspective.

1.2.2 *Studying Early Confucian Thought*

Even if we grant the legitimacy of a study of early Confucian thought that focuses on the constitutive ideas, the question of the proper way to conduct such a study remains. One main difficulty often mentioned in methodological discussions is the problem of how to avoid imposing on early Chinese thought certain presuppositions and frameworks alien to it that appear natural because one is accustomed to certain ways of thinking.[19] And, as some have noted, this is as much a difficulty for contemporary Chinese as well as Western scholars; since the modern Chinese language also embodies presuppositions and frameworks alien to early Chinese thought, even a contemporary Chinese can be intellectually quite distant from early Chinese thinkers.[20] In what follows, I describe some steps I have taken to address this difficulty.

The mere fact that an account of an early Chinese thinker's views goes beyond the relevant text does not by itself render the account problematic. To the extent that the account is more than a reorganization of the text, it will discuss the thinker's views in a contemporary language that already embodies conceptual apparatus alien to the early thinker. Furthermore, to help us understand the thinker's views, the account presumably presents such views with more clarity than the original text and draws connections between ideas where such connections are not explicit. This in itself does not render the account problematic; instead, the plausibility of the account depends on a variety of considerations internal or external to the text. Considerations internal to the text include the extent to which the account makes sense of different parts of the text, the degree of simplicity of the account, its lack of ad hoc elements, and perhaps also the plausibility of the thinker's views as presented by the account.[21] Considerations external to the text include our understanding of the relevant language based on the corpus of texts from that period, the kind of practical concerns that probably moved the thinker as evidenced by historical records, and the kind of intellectual concerns and approaches that thinkers of the period shared as evidenced by other texts recording ideas likely to be known to the thinker under consideration.

Hence, whether an account has imposed alien presuppositions and frameworks on the views of a thinker cannot be decided solely on the basis of whether the account has gone beyond the relevant texts in its presentation. One common concern often raised in this connection, however, is the employment of terminology that embodies alien presuppositions and frameworks. This concern is particularly likely to arise in the case of a study conducted in a contemporary Western language, and it can be directed at the way key Chinese terms get translated or at the use of Western terms not as translations but as part of the presentation of a thinker's views. This is a legitimate concern, and I have taken the following steps to address the difficulty.

The danger arising from a translation carrying alien presuppositions is that the translation can mislead not just readers but also the person engaged in the study; having adopted a certain translation, one may conduct the discussion in a way that assumes the extraneous element introduced by the translation is actually present in the term being translated. Since any translation of a key term is unlikely to match the term's connotations exactly, one possible strategy is to leave all key terms untranslated. This strategy, however, can result in such pervasive use of romanized Chinese terms that it makes reading extremely awkward. Another strategy is to continue to use translations for key terms, while preempting misunderstanding by carefully examining the actual use of the terms, including both the structure of the idioms in which they occur and the framework of thought providing the background for their use.[22] Although this strategy makes the discussion more readable without sacrificing accuracy, there are some terms whose use I will discuss extensively and that are better left untranslated.

I have tried to strike a balance between these two alternatives. For certain key terms whose interpretation makes a significant difference to the substance of my discussion, I basically leave the terms untranslated, although I sometimes provide one or more tentative translations in parentheses to help identify the terms. These include, for example, such terms as "hsing[a]" (nature, characteristic tendencies) and "ch'ing[a]" (fact, what is genuine); the translations are tentative and are here provided solely for the purpose of identifying the terms, and they have no substantive significance. For key terms that occur frequently in my discussion but whose interpretation is less crucial for my purpose, I adopt a translation after introducing the term, although I may revert to the romanized form from time to time. On occasion, I will provide two possible translations, both to capture different connotations of the term and to serve as a reminder of the tentativeness of the translations; one example is my translation of "hsin^a" as "heart/ mind."

There are also important terms in early Chinese thought that would require extensive discussion in a project with a different purpose and emphasis, but reference to which is more of an incidental nature in the following discussion; for example, such a term may occur in a line that I am translating in the context of discussing another term or topic. To avoid excessive use of romanization, I provide a translation after introducing the term and then use the translation whenever the term recurs in the discussion; one example is my translation of "min" as "common people."

As for contemporary Western terms used not as translations but as part of the discussion, the concern about introducing alien connotations may be directed at terms specific to Western philosophical discussions, terms that have acquired technical uses in philosophical discussions while also having a non-philosophical usage, or terms that have not acquired a technical use. Examples of terms of the first kind are "deontology," "consequentialism," and "practical reasoning." Although a project with a different purpose, such as an attempt to compare the Chinese and the Western tradition or to reconstruct Confucian thought using Western philosophical categories, might use such terms legitimately, it does seem advisable to avoid them in an attempt to understand the Confucian thinkers' own perspectives. Accordingly, I have avoided such terms in my discussion.

Examples of terms of the second kind are "morality," "reason," and "autonomy." Even though these terms have an ordinary, non-philosophical usage, they are also used in philosophical discussions and have sometimes been associated with presuppositions alien to early Chinese thought. While it is possible to use these terms after giving a careful explanation that avoids the alien presuppositions, I have minimized the use of such terms to avoid possible misunderstanding. For example, I have avoided the use of the term "reason" altogether and have instead used related terms like "grounds," "in support of," and "defense," which are less loaded with philosophical presuppositions. It is not always possible, however, to express what I want to say without using terms that appear regularly in philosophical discourse, unless I invent new terms for such purposes. In these cases, I will continue to use such terms, but only after explaining how I use them (see, e.g., my explanation of "ethical" in §1.1).

Examples of the third kind of terms are "human beings" and "natural." Although these terms do not typically carry philosophical presuppositions, their use may nevertheless introduce connotations alien to early Chinese thought. While I have tried to minimize their use, I again find it difficult to avoid their use altogether without having to invent new terms, thereby making the reading awkward. One example is the term "human beings," which can carry the connotation of a biological species. Since it is not clear at this stage of the discussion that the early Chinese had a conception of human beings as a biological species or that the Confucians regarded the way of life they advocated as applicable to all members of a biological species, it seems advisable to avoid the term. But I do need a term to refer to the individuals to whom the way of life the Confucians advocated is supposed to apply, and "human beings" is the closest English expression for this purpose. My strategy is to use the expression after introducing it in a way that makes explicit that its scope need not be co-extensive with human beings as a biological species (see §1.1).

The danger of imposing alien presuppositions on early Chinese thought can also arise from allowing certain preconceptions to shape one's interpretation of key terms or parts of the relevant texts. To address the difficulty, I have adopted the following strategies to deal with key terms and passages in the *Meng-tzu*. I often review the use of a key term in various early Chinese texts before considering its use in the *Meng-tzu*. Mencius's use of the term may have deviated from its use in other early texts, or Mencius may even have deliberately tried to steer his audience toward a new use of the term. Often, there was a fluidity in the use of early Chinese terms that allowed a thinker to appropriate them in a somewhat novel way that fit the thinker's own position.[23] However, even when this happened, the novel use of a term was often not entirely severed from existing usages. Accordingly, examining the use of the term in other early texts helps determine the range of possible connotations in preparation for examining the connotations of the term as it occurs in the *Meng-tzu*. By looking closely at the use of key terms in both the *Meng-tzu* and other early texts, we can reduce the danger of letting a preconceived understanding shape our interpretation of these terms.

Sometimes, in discussing key terms, I may invoke certain distinctions when it is unclear that the thinkers who used the term had a clear conception of those distinctions. For example, in discussing the use of "ming[a]" (decree, destiny), I distinguish between a normative and a descriptive dimension of its use as a heuristic device for talking about certain differences in the use of the term in early texts. But early thinkers may well not themselves have drawn such a distinction, and there may be many occurrences of the term for which it would be inappropriate to expect a definite answer as to which dimension of its use is being emphasized. When this happens, I make it explicit that the distinctions are introduced merely for heuristic purposes and are not ascribable to early thinkers.

In discussing passages from the *Meng-tzu*, I often refer to commentaries and translations, in connection with both the ideas in the passages and the grammatical issues that bear on the understanding of such ideas. It would be a huge task to do this for every passage of the *Meng-tzu*, and I do it only for those passages or parts of passages that play a particularly important role in my discussion. Consulting commentaries and translations helps reveal possible interpretations of a passage, or possible considerations in favor of a certain interpretation, that may not have occurred to oneself working independently. Having highlighted the possible interpretations, I often defend a particular interpretation on the basis of a comparative assessment of these interpretations; when it is practically difficult to consider all the possible interpretations, I focus attention on those that have been more common or influential. By comparing and adjudicating between the major alternative interpretations, I seek to provide some reason for accepting a proposed interpretation, rather than merely presenting it as my own preferred interpretation. Although some may disagree with the proposed interpretation, I hope to have at least put forward considerations in its favor to which they can respond, thereby providing the starting point of a dialogue to resolve such disagreements.

Sometimes, for a certain passage or part of a passage, there may be no clear textual evidence favoring one interpretation over another. Indeed, in distinguishing between different possible interpretations, we may again be drawing distinctions not clearly drawn by the thinker under consideration; if so, there is no reason to expect evidence favoring one interpretation over another. When this happens, I make clear that, based on my reflections on the passage, I see no clear evidence favoring a particular interpretation. For this reason, my discussion is occasionally open-ended.

2 Background

2.1 From Pre-Confucian Thought to Confucius

This discussion of certain developments in Chinese thought from before to around or shortly after the time of Confucius is based on the *Shih-ching*, *Shang-shu*, *Tso-chuan*, *Kuo-yü*, and *Lun-yü*. There is scholarly agreement that most of the materials in the *Shih-ching* date to a period before Confucius's time, down to the seventh or sixth century B.C. The *Shang-shu*, on the other hand, probably contains interpolations added after the time of Confucius. Although its "Chou shu" portion probably includes genuinely pre-Confucian documents, there has been disagreement over which ones those are.[1] In my discussion, I use the *Shih-ching* and the parts of the *Shang-shu* that scholars generally agree to be pre-Confucian as sources for understanding the pre-Confucian use of certain terms. The *Tso-chuan* and the *Kuo-yü* may have been compiled as late as the third century B.C. and contain ideas from different periods, extending from before to after the time of Confucius. I use these texts as sources for tracing the evolution of certain key terms by or shortly after Confucius's time.[2]

The *Lun-yü*, although purportedly a record of statements by Confucius and his disciples, probably contains elements composed and incorporated at different times.[3] The text thus might contain internal inconsistencies, although some scholars see a general homogeneity in the ideas expressed in the text.[4] Given the uncertainties about the authorship and dating of the different parts of the text, I regard the *Lun-yü* as a source for understanding certain ideas associated with a movement of thought centered on Confucius and datable to a period extending from Confucius's time to maybe a few generations after his death, without committing myself to viewing it as an authentic and consistent report of the teachings of Confucius and his immediate disciples.

2.1.1 *Evolving Attitude Toward t'ien (Heaven) and ming^a (Decree, Destiny)*

In the early Chou, *t'ien* was thought to be responsible for various natural phenomena, to have control over human affairs, and to have emotions and the capacity to act. The "Shao kao" of the *Shang-shu* and parts of the *Shih-ching* (e.g., *SC* 260/1, 241/1) present *t'ien* as just and loving. *T'ien* is also the source of political authority: the king retains the authority to rule only if he retains *t'ien ming^a*, and his retention of *t'ien ming^a* depends on his *te^a* (virtue, power). In its earliest use, the connotations of "*te^a*" probably were primarily religious and implied an attitude leading to the king's communion with *t'ien*.[5] But the word eventually came to refer in addition to qualities such as generosity, self-sacrifice, humility, and receptiveness to instruction, as well as certain powers associated with these qualities, including a compulsion to respond on the part of the recipient of generous or self-sacrificial acts and a noncoercive power of attraction and transformation.[6] The king can cultivate and make more evident his *te^a*; *t'ien* and the spirits can discern this and respond to it. Since preserving *t'ien ming^a* depends on *te^a*, it follows that *t'ien ming^a* is not constant and not easily preserved (see, e.g., *SC* 235/1, 5–7; 267), and that the king has to watch over and cultivate *te^a* cautiously to retain *t'ien ming^a* (e.g., *SC* 235/6, 236/3, 288, 299/4–5). This conception of political authority fits the view of *t'ien* as loving and just: *t'ien* continues to bestow *ming^a* on a king only if he cares for the people and properly fulfills his responsibilities.

Along with the increasing social and political disorder and the resulting miseries in the middle Chou period, there gradually emerged a sense of dissatisfaction with *t'ien* for allowing the miserable conditions to persist. The critical tone can be detected in the *Shih-ching*, and it is more conspicuous in the "Hsiao ya" than the "Ta ya" sections of the text; the former probably belongs to a later period than the latter.[7] In the "Ta ya," a number of odes ascribe the miserable conditions to *t'ien* and describe *t'ien*'s failure to intervene (e.g., *SC* 254/2, 4–5; 257/1, 3–4, 7; 258/1, 3, 5–6; 265/1, 2).[8] In the "Hsiao ya," the dissatisfaction takes the form of explicit complaints about the injustice of *t'ien* (e.g., *SC* 193/8, 197/1, 198/1) and its unkindness as well as injustice (e.g., *SC* 191/5-6, 9; 192/4; 194/1).

Further change in the attitude toward *t'ien* can be discerned in the *Tso-chuan* and the *Kuo-yü*. In the political context, *t'ien* came to be seen as being concerned not just with the Chou king's authority to rule but also with the preservation and destruction of states (e.g., *TC* 189/1–2).[9] The view of *t'ien* as rewarding the good and punishing the evil and as assigning the authority to rule on the basis of *te^a* is still retained (e.g., *KY* 2/10b.1-3, 12/5b.2-9), and *t'ien* is still thought to be guided by a concern with the well-being of the people in assigning political authority (e.g., *TC* 462/11-12). But there also emerged the view that the will of *t'ien* is identical with that of the people; that is, to retain from *t'ien* the authority to rule, a ruler has to care for and gain the allegiance of the people (e.g., *KY* 2/15a.8; cf. *KY* 3/5b.2-3). In addition, *t'ien* also came to be regarded as the source of norms of conduct, as reflected in the use of the combination "t'ien tao" to refer to the observance of *li^a* (*TC* 270/11-12) or the proper relation between rulers and subordinates (*TC* 493/13).

Although parts of these texts continue to portray *t'ien* as assigning political authority on the basis of *te^a*, more pervasive is a view of *t'ien* as assigning political authority in a way independent of a ruler's quality. There are numerous instances in which *t'ien* is presented, independently of the *te^a* of the ruler, as allowing a state to perish or continue to thrive.[10] Of particular interest are the descriptions of *t'ien* as depriving a ruler of proper perception (*KY* 8/5a.10, 16/5a.1) and thereby making him lose *te^a* (*KY* 3/19b.7-8) or as having predetermined how long the Chou rule should last and therefore allowing it to continue despite the decline of *te^a* in the Chou kings (*TC* 292/7). This conception of *t'ien* as assigning political authority independently of merit reflected an awareness that the contemporary retention of political authority had nothing to do with the ruler's merit. Related to this conception of *t'ien* is the use of "t'ien tao" to describe, not norms of conduct, but certain brute facts about changes in political fortune (e.g., *TC* 624/13, 631/4, 823/10).

The use of "ming^a" also evolved in a number of ways in the *Tso-chuan* and the *Kuo-yü*. *T'ien ming^a* is still linked to political authority and to *te^a* (*KY* 3/9b.2-3), and there is reference to the idea that it is *t'ien ming^a* for the good to replace the bad (*TC* 547/14). Also, the notion of *ming^a* is used in connection with obligations or norms of conduct; for example, we find a ruler observing that *ming^a* has to do not with the span of one's life but with nourishing the people, this being *t'ien*'s purpose in establishing the position of ruler (*TC* 263/1–7). In addition to these usages, however, "ming^a" has come to be used to refer to certain brute facts that obtain independently of human effort. Examples in the political context include the use of "ming^a" to describe the fact that the Chou rule should last seven centuries despite the decline of *te^a* in the Chou kings (*TC* 292/7) and the subordination of one state to another (*KY* 19/14a.4–6, 20/4a.4–6, 21/6b.5–7). Examples outside the political context include its use in connection with the termination of one's life (*TC* 583/7, 686/3). The use of "ming^a" to refer to occurrences not within human control is so pervasive that some have suggested that this is its more prevalent use in the *Tso-chuan*.[11] Such a use is already present in the *Shih-ching*, as when it describes as the *ming^a* of *t'ien* something brought about by *t'ien* that is not necessarily desirable (e.g., *SC* 193/8, 255/1; cf. 21/1–2).[12] But, in the *Shih-ching*, this use of "ming^a" is much less pervasive than the use of "t'ien ming^a" in connection with the bestowal of political authority on the basis of *te^a*.

These considerations suggest that it might be a useful heuristic device to distinguish two dimensions in the use of "t'ien" and "ming^a": a *normative* dimension that carries implications about what should be done or should happen, and a *descriptive* dimension implying that certain things are not due to human effort or not fully within human control. Both dimensions have to do with certain constraints on human conduct, one normative and the other causal. The distinction allows us to say that one dimension is highlighted more in certain occurrences. For example, the normative dimension is emphasized in contexts portraying *t'ien* as the source of norms of conduct or the use of "ming^a" to refer to one's obligations. On the other hand, the descriptive dimension is stressed in contexts portraying *t'ien* as predetermining certain events without regard to their desirability, or in the use of "ming^a" to refer to the termination of life.

In introducing this distinction, I am not suggesting that it is clearly drawn by the authors or editors of the texts; on the contrary, both dimensions may well be present and not clearly distinguished in certain occurrences. Indeed, in many instances in which one dimension is highlighted, the other may also be present to some degree. For example, whereas the ascription of certain political occurrences to *t'ien* as a brute fact highlights the descriptive dimension of "t'ien," the normative dimension may be present if there is the implication that one should further that event or at least not oppose it, and that failure to do so can lead to ill-fortune (e.g., *TC* 222/10, 325/6–8). And when "t'ien" or "ming^a" is used in connection with one's obligations, thereby stressing the normative dimension, the descriptive dimension may also be present in that these obligations are viewed as something given and over which human beings have no control. However, despite the intimate link between the two dimensions, the distinction is a useful heuristic device for highlighting differences in the use of the characters and for making certain general observations about the evolution of their use. For example, it allows us to make the general point that the descriptive dimension is more conspicuous in the *Tso-chuan* and the *Kuo-yü* than in the *Shih-ching*, probably as a result of an increasing awareness of the undesirable conditions of life over which human beings have little control. For convenience, I will say that the use of the characters is primarily descriptive or primarily normative depending on whether the descriptive or the normative dimension is emphasized.

Both dimensions of "t'ien" can be discerned in the *Lun-yü*. The normative dimension is highlighted in passages emphasizing the loving and just nature of *t'ien*, such as those implying that improper conduct offends against *t'ien* (*LY* 3.13), that *t'ien* rejects one for improper conduct (*LY* 6.28), or that *t'ien* protects one who has *te^a* (*LY* 7.23). The descriptive dimension can be discerned in passages ascribing to *t'ien* things over which human beings have little control, such as wealth and honor (*LY* 12.5), death (*LY* 11.9), and even the preservation or destruction of culture (*LY* 9.5).

Unlike the "Hsiao ya" section of the *Shih-ching*, the *Lun-yü* does not express dissatisfaction with *t'ien* even in contexts touching on the apparent personal misfortune of Confucius. For example, through the mouth of a border official, the point is conveyed that although Confucius did not succeed in his political mission, this was because *t'ien* had other plans for him—namely, to be the propagator of the Way (*LY* 3.24). Confucius similarly observed that although not appreciated and employed by people, he did not complain against *t'ien* but regarded himself as appreciated and employed by *t'ien* (*LY* 14.35).[13] Thus, the text retains the conception of a loving and just *t'ien* and, in contexts dealing with apparent personal misfortune, expresses faith that the apparent misfortune is part of a larger plan of *t'ien*.[14] At the same time, Confucius is portrayed as not discussing the way *t'ien* operates (*LY* 5.13), showing his tendency to avoid speculating about supra-human affairs (e.g., *LY* 11.12).

Two controversies have arisen concerning the use of "t'ien" in the *Lun-yü* — whether it refers to a personal deity, and whether it carries a transcendent (*ch'ao yüeh*) as opposed to an immanent or inner (*nei tsai*) dimension. Since similar controversies arise in connection with its use in the *Meng-tzu*, I defer discussion of these issues till §6.2.3. For now, let us turn to the use of "ming[a]." The character occurs several times in the *Lun-yü*, twice in the combination "t'ien ming[a]." There has been extensive scholarly disagreement concerning the interpretation of its use. In one view, most occurrences are primarily descriptive and refer to what is not fully within human control.[15] Some even take its use to reflect a general fatalistic attitude, which Confucius advocated in order to discourage attempts to introduce revolutionary economic measures.[16] A second view sees the use of "ming[a]" in the combination "t'ien ming[a]" as primarily normative, and its use in other contexts as primarily descriptive.[17] In this view, "t'ien ming[a]" refers to one's obligations, and "ming[a]" in isolation refers to what is not fully within human control. A third view holds that a few occurrences of "ming[a]" might refer to what is not fully within human control (e.g., *LY* 6.10, 12.5), but most occurrences are primarily normative, referring to *yi[a]*, or propriety of conduct.[18] That "ming[a]" could have come to refer to *yi[a]* is explained on the grounds that when one realizes that acting in a certain way is *yi[a]*, one also feels that the propriety of acting in this way comes from a source independent of oneself and so is due to the *ming[a]* of *t'ien*.[19]

To put aside for the moment the issue of adjudicating between these views, we should note that even if some or most occurrences of "ming[a]" are primarily descriptive, it does not follow that the text conveys a fatalistic belief in predetermining forces that human beings cannot resist or fathom. The reason is not just that Confucius is presented as urging effort in certain areas of life, such as cultivating one's character and ability, since this observation is compatible with Confucius's having a fatalistic view about some though not all areas of life.[20] Rather, even when "ming[a]" is used in a primarily descriptive manner to convey the thought that certain things are not fully within one's control, its use need not reflect a belief that things are predetermined but might well serve to express an attitude one has toward occurrences that go against one's wishes and to which one attaches importance. Such occurrences might concern outcomes, such as making the Way prevail (*LY* 14.36), that do not happen despite one's efforts or events, such as serious illness (*LY* 6.10) or death (*LY* 12.5), that are undesirable and could have been otherwise. The attitude expressed may be one of acceptance — no longer being worried by the outcome and not blaming *t'ien* or other human beings for its occurrence (*LY* 14.35). Furthermore, it may involve not engaging in improper conduct to alter things and redirecting attention toward other pursuits, such as Confucius's accepting the failure of his political mission and redirecting his attention to teaching.[21]

Another point worth noting is that it is often possible to move from one dimension of *ming*ᵃ to the other. Any occurrence of "ming*ᵃ*" that can be interpreted as carrying a normative dimension stressing one's obligations can also be viewed as having a descriptive dimension in that the use of "ming*ᵃ*" to refer to one's obligations highlights the fact that such obligations cannot be avoided through human efforts. Conversely, any occurrence that can be interpreted as carrying a descriptive dimension can be seen as having a normative dimension in that it highlights the point that when confronted with conditions of existence outside one's control, one is subject to certain normative constraints in dealing with such conditions. For example, one should not try to achieve one's goals or avoid certain outcomes by improper means and should not complain against *t'ien*.[22]

The possibility of such transitions reinforces the earlier point that the two dimensions might not have been clearly distinguished in early texts. For this reason, it is difficult to adjudicate between the competing interpretations of the use of "ming*ᵃ*" in the *Lun-yü*. It is possible to make some general observations, however; for example, in light of the fact that "t'ien ming*ᵃ*" and "ming*ᵃ*" are used in the same kind of construction in the text, as in "chih*ᵃ* ming*ᵃ*" (*LY* 20.3) and "chih*ᵃ* t'ien ming*ᵃ*" (*LY* 2.4, 16.8), it is unlikely that there is a clear distinction between the use of the combination "t'ien ming*ᵃ*" and the use of "ming*ᵃ*" in isolation, with the former being primarily normative and the latter primarily descriptive. And we can say that a certain dimension is emphasized if that dimension is more directly linked to an occurrence of "ming*ᵃ*" in the sense that interpreting that occurrence as carrying that dimension does not require first introducing the other dimension, whereas the reverse is not the case. On this basis, we can say that the occurrences of "ming*ᵃ*" in such observations as that there is *ming*ᵃ in death and life (*LY* 12.5) or that the illness of a disciple is *ming*ᵃ (*LY* 6.10) emphasize the descriptive dimension more — the further thought that one should respond to such conditions in certain ways presupposes the recognition that such conditions are not fully within human control. However, there are still a number of instances in which it is not possible to decide whether the normative or the descriptive dimension is being emphasized; since the two dimensions are probably not clearly distinguished in early texts, there is no reason to expect a definite answer to such a question. Because the present discussion is largely a preparation for a discussion of Mencius, I will not examine the occurrences of "ming^a" in the *Lun-yü* one by one; it suffices for my purpose to note the presence of both the normative and the descriptive dimensions in texts earlier than the *Meng-tzu*.

2.1.2 *Emerging Ethical Concern: te^a (Virtue, Power), jen^a (Benevolence, Humaneness), li^a (Rites), and yi^a (Propriety)*

The evolution of another group of terms — *te^a*, *jen^a*, *li^a*, and *yi^a* — reflects the emergence of a broader ethical concern by the time of Confucius. I have already considered the use of "te^a" in the political context in connection with the idea of *t'ien ming^a*. Even in the *Shih-ching*, "te^a" had come to be used not just of the king but also of worthy officials (*SC* 260/2; cf. 240/5) or good persons generally (*SC* 253/3). It was also used in the sense of favor or goods bestowed (*SC* 201/3), such as those bestowed by parents (*SC* 202/4). In the *Tso-chuan* and the *Kuo-yü*, *te^a* is ascribed even to the common people (*KY* 1/2b.4; *TC* 391/2, cf. 247/17). It still has the connotation of kindness or favor, often directed toward one in a lower social position, as when it is paired with "hui" (favor) (e.g., *TC* 391/1, 512/8; cf. *KY* 1/11a.6–7). But it was linked with various desirable attributes such as filial piety (*hsiao*), respectfulness (*kung*), conscientiousness (*chung^a*), trustworthiness (*hsin^b*), and yielding to others (*jang*; e.g., *KY* 15/4b.2–4; *TC* 228/14–15).

The *Lun-yü* continues to emphasize *te^a* in the political context, as when it observes that the transformative power of *te^a* should ideally be the basis of government (*LY* 2.1, 2.3, 12.19). But *te^a* is also ascribed to the ordinary person, for example, the *te^a* of Confucius (*LY* 7.23), the superior person and petty person (*LY* 12.19), and the common people (*LY* 1.9). Confucius emphasized the cultivation of *te^a* in himself (*LY* 7.3) and others (*LY* 9.18, 15.13; cf. 14.5), and this illustrates a concern with cultivating the self, a major focus of the early Confucians.

Besides first-person pronouns such as "wo" (I, me), the classical Chinese language has two characters with the meaning "oneself." "Tzu" is used in reflexive binomials to refer to one's doing something connected with oneself, such as people's examining themselves (*LY* 4.17), bringing disgrace upon themselves (*LY* 12.23), or labeling themselves in certain ways (*LY* 16.14). "Chi[a]" is used to talk about one's doing something connected with oneself such as conducting oneself in a certain way (*LY* 5.16, 13.20), others doing certain things connected with oneself such as appreciating oneself (*LY* 1.16, 4.14, 14.30, 14.39, 15.19), or oneself doing certain things connected with others such as helping others to establish themselves (*LY* 6.30). The difference between the two characters is that *tzu* emphasizes reflexivity, and *chi[a]* oneself as contrasted with others (*jen[b]*).[23] In addition, another character "shen[a]," which refers to the person or the body, can be used in combination with the appropriate possessive pronoun to refer to oneself or one's own person (e.g., *LY* 13.6, 13.13).

These linguistic observations show that the early Chinese had a conception of the way people relate to themselves. In early Confucian texts, the characters just mentioned are often used to talk about one's turning back to examine oneself (e.g., *LY* 1.4, 4.17; cf. 5.27, 12.4) and cultivating oneself (e.g., *LY* 13.13, 14.42). This shows that not only did the early Confucians have a conception of the relation of people to themselves, but they also had a conception of people being related to themselves in a self-reflective manner, with the capacity to reflect on and examine oneself and to bring about changes in oneself. In ascribing a conception of the self to Confucius and other early Confucians, I am crediting them with conceiving of persons as having a capacity of this self-reflective kind.[24]

According to the *Lun-yü*, although material well-being is something one desires, one's concern with self-cultivation should be independent of such material concerns (*LY* 4.5). The point is put in terms of what one should worry or be concerned about (*yu*); the proper object of worry or concern is the Way and not poverty (*LY* 15.32; cf. 7.3), and one can take joy (*le*) in the Way even if materially deprived (*LY* 6.11, 7.16). Similarly, although one desires appreciation by others, self-cultivation should be undertaken for the self (*wei[a] chi[a]*) and not for others (*wei[a] jen[b]*) (*LY* 14.24). The proper object of worry or concern (*huan*) is not appreciation by others, but one's own character and ability as well as one's appreciation of others (*LY* 1.16, 4.14, 14.30; cf. 15.19). The idea of not worrying about material well-being or others' appreciation is related to the attitude of acceptance expressed in the use of "ming[a]," since accepting an adverse outcome involves being no longer worried by the outcome.[25] And since the proper object of worry is the Way, one who realizes that he or she is in accord with the Way has no worries (*yu*) (*LY* 12.4; cf. 9.29, 14.28).

As for the ideal guiding self-cultivation, the *Lun-yü* characterizes it in terms of *jen^a*. The character "jen^a" was probably cognate with "jen^b" (human beings, persons); the latter originally referred not to biological human beings as such but to members of certain tribes or aristocratic clans.[26] There are two main scholarly views concerning the early use of "jen^a." In one view, it originally referred to the desirable attributes making one a distinctive member of certain tribes or aristocratic clans; its two occurrences in the *Shih-ching* (*SC* 77/1, 103/1) have been cited in support of this view.[27] Others argue that the character originally referred to love or the tender part of human feelings, especially the kindness of a ruler toward his subjects.[28] Along with these competing views, scholars have also suggested ways in which one meaning could have led to the other.[29]

For the purpose of explicating the content of Confucius's ethical ideal, it is not necessary to adjudicate between these competing views. It suffices to note that in the *Lun-yü* "jen^a" is used both in a broader sense to refer to an all-encompassing ideal for human beings that includes such desirable attributes as courage (*LY* 14.4) and in a narrower sense to refer to one desirable attribute among others, such as wisdom and courage (*LY* 9.29, cf. 14.28). In the broader sense, *jen^a* includes wisdom, courage, filial piety, conscientiousness, trustworthiness, a reverential or serious attitude, or even caution in speech and the ability to endure adverse circumstances. In the narrower sense, the term probably emphasizes the part of the ethical ideal having to do with affective concern for others; on one occasion, it is explained in terms of love for fellow human beings (*ai jen^b*) (*LY* 12.22). When used in a political context in early texts, it often refers to kindness directed toward those in a lower position; for example, *jen^a* is linked to protecting the people (*KY* 2/1b.10) or a weaker state (*TC* 812/10). The *Lun-yü*, while also emphasizing kindness to those below oneself (e.g., *LY* 3.26, 5.16, 17.6), probably takes the love involved in *jen^a* to extend not just to those in a lower position. This can be seen from the contrast between "ai jen^b" (loving fellow human beings) and "shih min" (employing the common people) (*LY* 1.5); whereas the latter attitude is directed downward to the common people, the former is probably directed more generally to fellow human beings.[30] Furthermore, *jen^a* in the *Lun-yü* is not restricted to those in office. For example, Yen Hui, known for his avoidance of official position, was described by Confucius as not deviating from *jen^a* for three months (*LY* 6.7).[31]

"Jen^a" is used more frequently in the broader sense of the all-encompassing ideal, an important part of which involves the observance of *li^a* (e.g., *LY* 12.1, 12.2).[32] The character "li^a" originally referred to rites of sacrifice, but later came to be used of rules of conduct governing ceremonial behavior in various social contexts. This broader use of the character can already be discerned in the *Shih-ching*; although "li^a" is used in connection with sacrifices on some occasions (e.g., *SC* 279, 290), it is also related to *yi^b* (good form) (e.g., *SC* 209/3, 5; cf. 52/1, 3) and used in contexts other than sacrifices (e.g., *SC* 193/5). Subsequently, its scope of application expanded even further to include not just ceremonial behavior but behavior appropriate to one's social position; sometimes *li^a* was distinguished from *yi^b* (good form). For example, in the *Tso-chuan*, rules governing polite behavior such as ways of presenting a gift are described as a matter of *yi^b* (good form) but not *li^a* (*TC* 601/8–12, 704/8–9). And, in both the *Tso-chuan* and the *Kuo-yü*, "li^a" is used in connection with rules governing conduct between those in different social positions (e.g., *TC* 704/16, *KY* 17/1b.4–5), proper ways of governing a state (e.g., *TC* 521/10–12, 601/8–12), and the proper relation between rulers and ministers, fathers and sons, older and younger brothers, husbands and wives, and mothers and daughters-in-law (e.g., *TC* 715/12–17). Furthermore, *li^a* is described as having its source in *t'ien* (*TC* 270/11–12, 704/9–10; cf. 537/7), and proper observance of *li^a* is presented as the basis for an orderly society and the ideal basis for government (e.g., *TC* 31/13, 158/8, 554/1, 601/9, 715/11–12; *KY* 10/3b.7–10). However, although "li^a" came to have a broader scope of application, it continued to be used frequently to refer to rules of conduct governing·ceremonial behavior. For example, although the *Hsün-tzu* occasionally uses "li^a" interchangeably with "li^a yi^a" (*HT* 19/1–15), where "li^a yi^a" is often used to refer generally to social distinctions and norms (*HT* 4/72–77, 9/17–18, 9/64–75), it continues to use "li^a" mostly in connection with ceremonial behavior.

In the *Lun-yü*, observance of *li^a* with the proper spirit, such as *ching* (reverence, seriousness), is highlighted (*LY* 3.26; cf. 3.8, 17.11, 19.1). Many scholars think that "li^a" is used in the text to refer generally to rules governing behavior in all kinds of social and political contexts.[33] This point is not entirely obvious, since the examples of *li^a* in the text have to do largely with ceremonial behavior (*LY* 3.4, 3.15, 3.17, 9.3, 17.11). Certain occurrences can be taken to have a broader scope, as when *li*^{a} is described as the ideal basis for government (*LY* 2.3, 4.13), the substance of filial piety (*LY* 2.5), something one should learn in order to take a stand (*LY* 8.8, 16.13, 20.3), and something that one should use to mold one's behavior (*LY* 6.27) and follow in all one's actions (*LY* 12.1). However, although interpreting "li^a" in a broader sense might make these observations more plausible to us, there is no clear textual evidence that the scope of "li^a" in these occurrences goes beyond the ceremonial.[34]

Another issue of disagreement concerns the extent to which the attitude toward *li*^{a} displayed in the *Lun-yü* is conservative. On the basis of passages such as 12.1, which describes an intimate link between *jen*^{a} and *li*^{a}, some scholars have suggested that the text advocates an extremely conservative attitude that opposes any revision of or departure from existing rules of *li*^{a}.[35] And the text does seem to display a generally conservative attitude, as seen from passages in which Confucius presented himself as an advocate of traditional Chou *li*^{a} (*LY* 3.14) and as someone who loved and transmitted ancient culture (*LY* 7.1, 7.20). However, other scholars have pointed to passages like 9.3, in which Confucius proclaimed he would follow the multitude in departing from a rule of *li*^{a}, as evidence that the text does allow room for departing from existing rules of *li*^{a}.[36] And the observation that the text does not advocate unconditional observance of *li*^{a} is often linked by scholars to the notion of *yi*^{a}.

According to some scholars, the character "yi^a" was probably a near relative of, if not derived from, "wo" (I, me).[37] As I will show in §3.2.2, the early use of the character was often related to *ju*^{b} (disgrace), suggesting that the character probably had the meaning of a proper regard for oneself or a sense of honor, involving such things as not brooking an insult. By the time of Confucius, it had come to be used more generally in connection with proper conduct, such as the proper way of obtaining things for oneself (e.g., *LY* 7.16, 14.13). *Yi*^{a} is something with which one should always accord (*LY* 4.10), and it is often contrasted with *li*^{b}, or profit (e.g., *LY* 4.16, 14.12). Some scholars have suggested that "yi^a" in the *Lun-yü* applies primarily to actions and only derivatively to persons.[38] Probably, the character is used in the text to refer both to a quality of actions and to an attribute of persons. For example, "yi^a" probably refers to a quality of actions in 2.24, which describes *yi*^{a} as something one discerns and enacts. On the other hand, it probably refers to an attribute of persons in 17.23, which pairs *yi[a]* with courage (*yung*), the latter being an attribute of persons. Many other occurrences of "yi[a]" can be interpreted either way, and the claim that it is primarily applied to actions cannot be defended in terms of the frequency with which it is so used. It is possible, however, that the claim is based on an analysis of *yi[a]* as an attribute of persons: if we take the attribute to be basically a commitment to proper conduct, then *yi[a]* as an attribute of persons presupposes a conception of *yi[a]* as the propriety of conduct. There appears to be insufficient textual evidence for such an analysis in the case of the *Lun-yü*. However, as I show in §3.2.2, there is some plausibility to this analysis in the case of the *Meng-tzu*.

In an interpretation that highlights the more creative dimension of the *Lun-yü*, *yi[a]* provides the basis for assessing and possibly departing from *li[a]*. Even when *li[a]* should be observed, *yi[a]* underlies the appropriateness of observing *li[a]*; this provides an interpretation of 15.18 that presents *yi[a]* as the substance practiced by observing *li[a]*. Various authors have proposed this conception of the relation between *yi[a]* and *li[a]* in the *Lun-yü*.[39] Again, the lesser prominence of the notion of *yi[a]* in the *Lun-yü* makes it difficult to fully substantiate this conception, although the conception is probably already emerging in that text and becomes more explicit in the *Meng-tzu*.[40]

Having considered some of the key terms in the *Lun-yü*, let us turn to its conception of government. Passage 12.17 explains government (*cheng[a]*) in terms of rectifying (*cheng[b]*), and 13.13 links government to rectifying people through rectifying oneself. This explanation leaves open the question whether the goal of government is to transform the character of people through moral example or to make people conform to certain standards through the use of legitimate force; some have suggested that the latter option captures the earlier meaning of "cheng[a]" (government).[41] Whether the latter is the earlier meaning or not, it is a possible meaning of "cheng[a]" and one still found in the *Lun-yü* (2.3). However, there is also evidence the text idealizes the form of government that emphasizes transforming people through moral example. The point is made explicitly in 2.3, which advocates government through *te[a]* (virtue, power) and *li[a]* (rites) rather than government by edicts and punishment. Passage 2.21 even extends the notion of *cheng[a]* beyond taking office to exerting influence by being a good son and friendly to one's brothers.[42] Other passages also advocate *te[a]* (*LY*

2.1, 12.19) and *li*[a] (*LY* 4.13) as the ideal basis for government and high-light the transformative power of a good character (*LY* 8.2; cf. 12.18, 13.4). On one occasion (*LY* 15.5), there is even a reference to Shun's government by non-action (*wu wei*[a]).

One obvious question raised by this conception of government is how it can be reconciled with the discussion of actual policies in the text.[43] Part of the answer is that although good character is the primary basis for government, it has to be supplemented by actual policies carried out by able officials. Herrlee G. Creel, citing He Yen's commentary, suggests that what enables the ruler with good character to govern by non-action is that, having appointed able and worthy officials, all the ruler needs to do is to set a moral example and leave the functions of government to the officials.[44] This proposal fits the emphasis on *chih*[a] *jen*[b] (know and appreciate a person), which is explicated in terms of appreciating and employing able officials (*LY* 12.22).[45] In addition, the text mentions specifics such as the need for proper taxation (*LY* 12.9), always acting in accordance with one's position in the state or family (*LY* 12.11, 13.3), and educating, feeding, and benefiting the common people (*LY* 5.16, 6.30, 12.7, 13.9, 20.2). Despite the need for policies, a good character is still the primary basis for government in at least two senses. A ruler with good character cares for the people, and proper policies that serve this purpose are themselves a manifestation of a good character. Furthermore, government serves not just to provide materially for the people but also to transform them, and the latter function has to be achieved through the moral example of those in power.

Another way the emphasis on good character can be reconciled with the need for actual policies is that since it takes time for government to achieve its goal of transforming the people, interim measures are needed, although such measures will eventually become dispensable. For example, although the text idealizes government that dispenses with punishment (*LY* 2.3) and litigation (*LY* 12.13), it also says that proper punishment depends on first establishing rites and music (*LY* 13.3). And even though it downplays the significance of military affairs (*LY* 15.1), it also speaks of the need for military preparedness (*LY* 12.7; cf. 13.29–30) and holds that military expeditions should originate from the king (*LY* 16.2). These different aspects of the text can be reconciled by the observation that since it takes time to establish the ideal form of government (*LY* 13.10–12), punishment and military expeditions might be necessary as interim measures until the people become transformed and the king fully commands their allegiance.

The discussion in this and the previous sections illustrates how a broader concern with the ideal human life had emerged by the time of Confucius. Some scholars have described this development as the growth of humanism, but to avoid any unintended connotations of that term, I will simply speak of a broadening ethical concern.[46] This broader ethical concern is reflected in the way te^a came to be ascribed to ordinary people and linked with various desirable attributes, as well as in the broadening of the scope of "li^a" beyond religious sacrifice to rules governing human conduct in other social and political contexts. In the *Lun-yü*, this broader ethical concern is reflected in the emphasis on jen^a as an ideal encompassing all kinds of desirable attributes, as well as in the attitude toward *t'ien* and $ming^a$. We have seen that Confucius tended to avoid speculations about things outside concrete human affairs and that there was an increasing sense of the external conditions of life outside human control, which were ascribed to *t'ien* and described as $ming^a$. By contrast, jen^a is something that one can attain with sufficient devotion, and ethical pursuits should be guided by a concern with the self rather than with externals. The implication is that one should devote oneself fully to ethical pursuits, which are within one's control, and not worry about the attainment of externals, which are not within one's control. I will return to this idea in §3.5 in connection with Mencius.

Although a broader ethical concern had emerged by this time, certain dimensions of early Chinese thought describable in some intelligible sense of the word as "religious" had also been retained and transformed. For example, the *Tso-chuan* and the *Kuo-yü* retain the conception of *t'ien* as the source of political authority and ascribe li^a to *t'ien*, and the *Lun-yü* retains the idea of *t'ien* as an object of reverence and regards it as the source of the ethical life. Just as the observance of rites of sacrifice was supposed to be accompanied by *ching* (reverence, seriousness) and to lead to certain responses from the spirits, observance of li^a, whose scope had by now broadened to include one's interactions with other human beings, was also supposed to be accompanied by *ching* toward others and to bring about certain responses from them. Likewise, just as te^a in the king was thought to lead to certain responses from *t'ien* and the spirits, te^a in an ordinary person would have a noncoercive transformative effect on others. So, the broader ethical concern not only reflects a shift of attention to the human realm but also involves the permeation of the human realm by the religious attitude, construed in some broad sense.[47]

2.2 The Mohist Challenge

In discussing the Mohist challenge to the Confucian ideal, I will consider Mo Tzu's conception of the relation between yi^a (propriety) and li^b (profit, benefit), his views on *yen* (words, doctrines), and his implicit picture of human psychology. The discussion will be based primarily on chapters 8–37 of the *Mo-tzu*, which I take to contain ideas ascribable mostly to Mo Tzu. Although different chapters may present different versions of a doctrine, I will not discuss these variations, which for the most part concern the application of Mo Tzu's ideas to the political realm and have less bearing on the topics I focus on.[48] Also, I sometimes draw upon ideas from other chapters on the assumption that these ideas bear some affinity to, or are later developments of, Mo Tzu's teachings.

2.2.1 *Yi^a (Propriety) and li^b (Profit, Benefit)*

Although the *Lun-yü* contains the notion of yi^a (propriety), which differs from that of li^a (rites), it still regards proper conduct as to a large extent determined by li^a. Mo Tzu drew a distinction between yi^a and custom (*su*); he described different customs of disposing of the dead found in various lands and observed that people continued such practices as elaborate funerals and lengthy mourning only because they were customary, not necessarily because they were yi^a (*MT* 25/75–81; cf. *LiT* 5/5a.5–9). The examples of elaborate funerals and lengthy mourning have to do with li^a, and although the *Mo-tzu* does not explicitly link li^a to custom, the link is made in other texts (e.g., *ST* 276, no. 74). Hence, Mo Tzu's observation that what is customary is not necessarily yi^a is probably directed against the Confucian advocacy of li^a.

For Mo Tzu, a practice is yi^a if it brings li^b (profit, benefit). The character "li^b," which probably had the earlier meaning "smooth" or "unimpeded," had by this time acquired the meaning profit or benefit.[49] Often, Mo Tzu regarded what is yi^a as what benefits human beings (li^b jen^b) or the common people (li^b *min*) (e.g., *MT* 46/30). When criticizing the Confucians and defending his own alternative proposals, he often appealed to what benefits the public. Such benefits include enriching the poor, increasing the population, and bringing about order (*MT* 25/11-12, 35/1-2). Also, according to Mo Tzu, disorder arises from discrimination (*pieh*), which leads to harming others to benefit oneself, one's family, or one's state; the remedy lies with replacing discrimination by indiscriminate concern for each (*chien*ª *ai*) (*MT*, chaps. 14-16). The kinds of benefit invoked in these arguments probably appealed generally to people of that time, although Mo Tzu set aside considerations that a Confucian would regard as also relevant. He emphasized primarily what benefits the common people, including such things as food, warmth, and rest, but not sensory pleasures (*MT* 32/5-13). Although such things as buildings, clothing, food, and transportation could provide for basic needs, other purposes they serve, such as aesthetic appreciation and sensory pleasures, were regarded as irrelevant (*MT*, chap. 6). This emphasis on basic material needs can probably be explained in terms of Mo Tzu's humble social background, but it also led to Hsün Tzu's subsequent criticism that Mo Tzu had ignored other relevant and important considerations (e.g., *HT* 21/21).

Besides the appeal to public benefit, the Mo Tzu also defended an indiscriminate concern for each on the grounds that its practice profits oneself or those (such as one's parents) to whom one stands in a special relation. One line of thought appeals to *t'ien*; *t'ien* has indiscriminate concern for each, desires people to practice indiscriminate concern, and brings fortune or misfortune accordingly; hence, it is to one's interest to practice indiscriminate concern (*MT*, chaps. 4, 26-28). Another line of thought argues that others treat oneself or one's parents the way one treats others or others' parents; if one wants others to benefit oneself (*MT* 15/15-19, 15/27-28) or to have concern for and benefit one's parents (*MT* 16/64-72), one should benefit others and have concern for and benefit others' parents.

There might seem to be a tension between a defense of indiscriminate concern on the grounds that discrimination leads to disorder and a defense that argues its practice will benefit oneself or those to whom one stands in a special relation. It seems that the former argument regards a concern for oneself and those to whom one is specially related as problematic, and yet such a concern provides the starting point for the latter argument. But, in fact, there is no genuine conflict here. At the beginning of the "Chien ai" chapters, disorder is presented as resulting not just from a concern for oneself or one's family and state.

Rather, it results from such a concern coupled with a disregard for others; indeed, the attitude toward others is described in such strong terms as disliking and robbing them. Such an attitude leads to one's benefiting oneself or one's family and state at the expense of others, thereby resulting in disorder; the remedy is to be as concerned for others as one is for oneself. Hence, a concern for oneself or one's family and state is not by itself problematic; the third "Shang t'ung" chapter makes the point that a concern for one's family and state is desirable as long as this is not coupled with a disregard for other families and states (*MT* 13/22–42).

Probably, the appeal to benefit to oneself or those to whom one is specially related is a way of addressing a difficulty arising from a potential conflict between benefit to oneself and benefit to others. When the two kinds of benefit conflict, an ordinary person is likely to opt for the former over the latter. And if such conflicts are frequent, the practice of indiscriminate concern will be practically difficult if not impossible. In the context of responding to this challenge, Mo Tzu appealed to benefit to oneself (*MT* 15/15–19, 15/27–28) and to one's parents (*MT* 16/64–72). His proposal is that not only is the practice of indiscriminate concern compatible with benefiting oneself or those to whom one stands in a special relation, but its practice will actually result in such benefit. Showing that the interests of oneself and those to whom one is specially related coincide rather than conflict with the interests of others helps remove an obstacle to the practice of indiscriminate concern.

The objection to indiscriminate concern on grounds of its impracticality also has to do with Mo Tzu's implicit picture of human psychology, which I discuss in the next section. For now, let me comment briefly on my translation of "chien^a ai." A. C. Graham proposes translating the term as "concern for everyone" rather than as "universal love."[50] He argues that "chien^a" implies "for each" rather than "for all," and "ai" for the Mohist refers to an unemotional will to benefit and avoid harming people. Since *ai* in *chien^a ai* is supposed to be directed indiscriminately, I have followed Graham in translating it as "concern" rather than "love," because "love" often connotes an attitude restricted to those to whom one stands in a special relation. It is not entirely obvious that indiscriminate concern cannot also engage the emotions; for example, it may involve reacting affectively in response to negative conditions of the objects of concern. As for "chien^a," Graham's observation that it implies "for each" seems well taken. But since "chien^a" also has the connotation of being indiscriminate, and since Mo Tzu held that one's concern should be indiscriminate whether directed at individuals or at families and states, I have opted for the translation "indiscriminate concern for each" rather than "concern for everyone," where "each" can refer not just to individuals but also to families and states.[51]

2.2.2   *Doctrines (yen) and Mo Tzu's Picture of Human Psychology*

Given the task of challenging the Confucian ideal and defending an alternative way of life, a more reflective concern with doctrines emerged in the *Mo-tzu*. The *Lun-yü* contains occurrences of the character "yen" that may plausibly be interpreted as referring to a teaching or doctrine, such as the observations that one with *te*^a will also have *yen* (*LY* 14.4) and that *shu*^a (reciprocity) is a *yen* that one follows throughout one's life (*LY* 15.24). The *Mo-tzu* frequently uses "yen" to refer to teachings or doctrines, such as teachings about burial and mourning practices (*MT* 25/57), the teachings of one who believes in *ming*^a (*MT* 35/3, 5, 18, 42, 47), and the teachings of those advocating non-discrimination or discrimination (*MT* 16/21–28). The frequent link between *yen* and *tao* (*MT* 9/44; 25/25, 34, 38) or *yi*^a (*MT* 35/18, 36/1, 46/55–60, 47/3, 48/81, 49/50–54, 49/83) shows that a *yen* is often a teaching about *tao* or *yi*^a. Also, the character "yi^a" itself is often used in the *Mo-tzu* to refer to a conception of what is proper. For example, the "Shang t'ung" chapters speak of different people with different *yi*^a and advocate having everyone share the same *yi*^a. Mo Tzu referred to as *yi*^a Wu-ma Tzu's view of hurting others to benefit oneself and subsequently referred to Wu-ma Tzu's expression of this view as a *yen* (*MT* 46/52–60). There are also references to one's *yi*^a of not killing others (*MT* 50/3) and to the fact that killing another over a *yen* is to value *yi*^a more than the person (*MT* 47/3). In these examples, "yi^a" refers to a conception of what is proper, whose verbal expression is a *yen*.[52]

Mo Tzu's more reflective concern with doctrines can be seen not just in his attempt to defend various doctrines but also in his explicit discussion of three ways of assessing *yen* (*MT* 35/7–10). Of the three, the most frequently used and probably most basic is the assessment of a *yen* in terms of whether its practice benefits the people.[53] But sometimes the focus in assessing a *yen* is not the consequences of endorsing and practicing it but the consequences of promulgating it. For example, one of Mo Tzu's objections to those who oppose indiscriminate concern in words is that they themselves would prefer one who practices indiscriminate concern when selecting a ruler or a person to entrust their parents to, and hence that their deeds do not conform to their words (*MT* 16/23–46). The immediate implication of such an objection is not that one should endorse and practice indiscriminate concern but only that one should promulgate or at least not oppose it. A later chapter has Mo Tzu arguing against Wu-ma Tzu's *yen*, on the grounds that if the *yen* were made known, it would lead to disastrous outcomes for Wu-ma Tzu (*MT* 46/52–60). Again, this is an objection to promulgating a certain *yen* but not a direct objection to endorsing and practicing it. The fact that part of the assessment of *yen* has to do with the consequences of promulgation probably reflects an assumption that any plausible conception of the ethical life is one whose general promulgation is also beneficial.[54]

One probable explanation of Mo Tzu's concern with doctrines and their assessment is the need to combat rival doctrines — not only Confucian teachings, but also the teaching that one is incapable of treating a friend like oneself (*MT* 16/23–25) or Wu-ma Tzu's view that he would kill others to benefit himself but not vice versa (*MT* 46/52–55).[55] Another probable explanation is that Mo Tzu viewed the problems of his times as in part arising from doctrines. For example, at the beginning of the "Shang t'ung" chapters, he depicted disorder in a state of nature as due to each person's having a different view of what is proper (*yi*[a]), with strife resulting from one's approving of one's view and disapproving of others' views.[56]

Some have proposed on the basis of this description of a disorderly state of nature that Mo Tzu regarded human beings as basically self-seeking.[57] If each individual viewed pursuing his or her own interests as what is proper, this observation will be substantiated, although it is of interest to note that the ensuing strife stems from each person's having a reflective view about what is proper, rather than stemming, as in the picture portrayed in the *Hsün-tzu*, from seeking unreflectively to satisfy his or her own self-regarding desires. However, it is not obvious that the disorderly state results from everyone's seeking his or her own interest. That each person has a different view of what is proper makes it likely that each individual's view of what is proper makes a reference to that individual. However, it does not follow that these individuals are concerned only for their own interests, since they may well be like Wu-ma Tzu in having a concern for others that diminishes as the object of concern becomes more distant from oneself.

David S. Nivison has proposed that, for Mo Tzu, human beings have no fixed moral nature.[58] I will avoid the use of the word "nature" since it is often used as a translation of "hsing[a]," a term I consider in the next section. However, we can restate the observation by saying that Mo Tzu did not regard the way of life he advocated, especially indiscriminate concern, as the realization of certain inclinations that human beings already share. When so stated, the observation gains support from several parts of the text.

If Mo Tzu had believed that human beings share inclinations realized in the practice of indiscriminate concern, we would expect him to appeal to such inclinations in certain contexts, when in fact he did not. For example, when defending indiscriminate concern, he did not characterize it as a realization of certain shared inclinations. When discussing the measures those in office can adopt to move people to practice indiscriminate concern, Mo Tzu mentioned only reward and punishment, which appeal to the self-regarding motives of human beings (*MT*, chaps. 8–13). In response to the challenge that it is difficult to practice indiscriminate concern, he again made no appeal to any predisposition to do so (*MT*, chaps. 15–16). And, in debating with Wu-ma Tzu he did not dispute Wu-ma Tzu's observation that one feels the suffering of oneself but not of others unrelated to oneself (*MT* 46/55–60).

Besides the absence of appeals to such inclinations, there is also positive evidence for the observation that Mo Tzu did not believe human beings share inclinations toward indiscriminate concern. When describing what human beings are like, he frequently referred to self-regarding desires, such as desires for life (*MT* 9/72) and for wealth and honor (*MT* 10/32–33, 10/37–38); when discussing what human beings are like after *t'ien* has given birth to them, he presented them as lacking affection for others, even for immediate family members (*MT* 11/1–4, 12/1–5, 13/8–11). Also, when describing one's transition to the way of life proper to human beings, he compared it to the processes of dyeing silk (*MT*, chap. 3; cf. *LSCC* 2/12a–16b) and building walls (*MT* 47/29–30). These analogies suggest that he regarded the transition as a matter of imposing something onto one's inclinations rather than a realization of inclinations one already has.

One implication of the view that human beings do not have predispositions that are realized in the proper way of life is that one learns what the proper way of life is not by attending to one's predispositions but by some other means, such as by endorsing a doctrine (*yen*) on the basis of supporting considerations.[59] But if the proper way of life is not a realization of one's predispositions, this raises the question of how the transition to that way of life is possible. The problem was raised by Mo Tzu's opponents; Wu-ma Tzu (*MT* 46/52–60) and others (*MT* 15/15–16, 16/45–46, 16/71–72), for example, highlighted the difficulties of practicing indiscriminate concern. Mo Tzu's response was basically to insist that it is easy to practice indiscriminate concern and that this will become clear when one sees that such practice is in one's interest; furthermore, indiscriminate concern was practiced in the past, and people were able to do even more difficult things (*MT* 15/16–42, 16/46–63, 16/72–86). Probably, Mo Tzu thought that the difficulty one sees in the practice of indiscriminate concern arises from regarding it as being in conflict with one's own interest; once one properly sees its link to one's own interest, one is moved to practice it, even though one lacks predispositions in that direction. This response, however, does not fully address the worry. Even if one regards the practice of indiscriminate concern as in one's interest, its practice still requires a restructuring of one's motivations, given Mo Tzu's implicit assumption that human beings do not share predispositions toward indiscriminate concern. And this restructuring of motivations is not easy to accomplish, a point made in Wu-ma Tzu's observation that he lacked the ability (*neng*) to practice indiscriminate concern because his concern for people diminished as they became more distant from him, and in the observation by those who advocate discrimination that they lack the ability (*neng*) to view their friends as being like themselves. As Nivison has observed, this restructuring of motivations requires an elaborate process of self-cultivation, something not discussed by Mo Tzu.[60] I will take up this issue in §4.5 in connection with the debate between Mencius and the Mohist Yi Chih, and in §6.3.2 in connection with the use of "neng" (ability) in the ethical context.

2.3 *Hsing*ᵃ (Nature, Characteristic Tendencies) and Yangist Thought

Mencius described the movements of thought associated with Mo Tzu and Yang Chu as influential during his time and presented his own position as a response to their challenge (*M* 3B:9, 7A:26). Following A. C. Graham, I refer to as "Yangism" the movement of thought of which Yang Chu was one representative thinker. There is little evidence that Yangist teachings were influential during Mencius's time, and this has led some scholars to suggest that Mencius exaggerated the movement's influence and restructured the intellectual scene of the time so as to present Confucian teachings as lying between Mohist and Yangist teachings.[61] For example, by describing Mohist and Yangist teachings as denying, respectively, one's father and one's prince (*M* 3B:9), he highlighted that the two together undermined the family and the state, which the Confucians regarded as the foundation of human society. Although this suggestion may capture part of Mencius's motivation in presenting his own position as a response to these movements, it is also likely that Mencius had thought through Yangist and Mohist teachings and genuinely saw himself as responding to their challenge.

That Yangist thought played a role in the development of his thinking can be seen in part from Mencius's concern with *hsing*[a], which is presented in the *Huai-nan-tzu* as a key term in Yang Chu's teachings (*HNT* 13/7b.10–11). If we follow Fung Yu-lan, himself followed by Graham, in regarding chapters 1/2, 1/3, 2/2, 2/3, and 21/4 of the *Lü-shih ch'un-ch'iu* as a source for reconstructing Yangist thought, we can discern close parallels between ideas in these chapters and ideas in the *Meng-tzu*.[62] For example, the Yangist chapters advocate nourishing (*yang*) *hsing*[a] (*LSCC* 1/7a.3, 1/14b.8), and the *Meng-tzu* likewise advocates nourishing *hsing*[a] (*M* 7A:1) and *hsin*[a] (heart/mind) (*M* 7B:35; cf. 6A:14). The Yangist chapters caution people against injuring *hsing*[a], expressing the idea of injury with the characters "hai" (*LSCC* 1/8a.3), "shang" (*LSCC* 1/8a.5–6), and "fa*[a]*" (*LSCC* 1/10a.4); the *Meng-tzu* uses similar terms to describe injury to *hsin*[a], such as "hai" (*M* 6A:14, 7A:27) and "fa*[a]*" (*M* 6A:8). And just as the Yangist chapters hold that sensory pursuits and external possessions should be subordinated to the nourishing of *hsing*[a] and that it is a loss of proper balance to live otherwise (*LSCC* 1/8a.3–4, 1/7a.3–8), similar ideas about subordination and loss of balance are found in the *Meng-tzu* (*M* 6A:10–15). It is possible that the Yangist chapters of the *Lü-shih ch'un-ch'iu*, compiled after Mencius's death, represent only a later development of the Yangist movement. Still, on the assumption that this later development bears an affinity to the movement as it existed in Mencius's time, the parallels just described suggest that Mencius probably had thought through Yangist ideas and attempted to respond to them. To prepare for the subsequent discussion of Mencius's views on *hsing^a*, I first consider the use of "hsing^a" in early Chinese texts and then examine the Yangist conception.

2.3.1 *Use of "hsing^a" in Early Chinese Texts*

In my discussion, I take for granted two observations on which there is general scholarly agreement: that "hsing^a" derived from "sheng^a" (life, growth, give birth to) and that, contrary to Fu Ssu-nien's suggestion, "hsing^a" and "sheng^a" were already distinguished in pre-Han texts and, more specifically, before Mencius's time.[63] There is also agreement that the early use of "hsing^a" bore a close relation to that of "sheng^a," and that "hsing^a" probably referred to the direction of *sheng^a* of a thing — that is, the direction that a thing develops in its process of growth.[64] It is likely, however, that the use of "hsing^a" also evolved in early texts to refer to other things related to the life of a thing, such as the tendencies or desires that a living thing has.

The "Shao kao" of the *Shang-shu* contains a reference to regulating (*chieh^a*) *hsing^a* (SS 429/3), and the *Shih-ching* contains references to fulfilling (*mi*) one's *hsing^a* (SC 252/2–4). Some have taken these occurrences of "hsing^a" to refer to the desires that arise in the process of living.[65] However, it is still possible to regard "hsing^a" in these occurrences as referring to the direction of the life process as a whole; for example, Graham translates "chieh^a hsing^a" as "live a regular life" and "mi hsing^a" as "fulfil one's term of life."[66] As far as these two texts are concerned, there is insufficient evidence that "hsing^a" refers to anything other than the direction of the life process.

In the *Tso-chuan* and the *Kuo-yü*, however, there is evidence that "hsing^a" sometimes takes on other related meanings. For example, "hsing^a" in connection with enriching (*hou*) the *hsing^a* of the common people (*min*) occurs twice in the *Kuo-yü*. One passage says that early kings made correct the *te^a* and enriched the *hsing^a* of the common people, increased their riches, and sharpened their weapons and agricultural tools (KY 1/2b.4–5); another speaks of having ample riches, sharpening weapons, and illuminating *te^a* in order to enrich the *hsing^a* of the common people (KY 10/13b.11–14a.1).[67] This use of "hsing^a" in the *Kuo-yü* parallels the use of "sheng^a" in a number of passages in the *Tso-chuan* that refer to enriching (*hou*) the *sheng^a* of the common people; with one exception (TC 243/17–18), these passages also speak of enriching *sheng^a* in connection with making *te^a* correct and sharpening agricultural tools (*TC* 247/17, 391/1–2, 539/5). The parallel shows that "hsing^a" in the two *Kuo-yü* passages and "sheng^a" in the *Tso-chuan* passages probably refer to the same thing. Since some of these passages explicitly talk about attending to the material well-being of the common people (e.g., *KY* 10/13b.11–14a.1; *TC* 539/3–6), and since the way to enrich the *sheng^a* of the common people is also described as the way to enable the common people to live (*TC* 243/17–18), it is likely that the *hsing^a* or *sheng^a* of the common people has to do with their livelihood.

Further evidence comes from other parts of the *Tso-chuan*. In one passage (*TC* 674/6–9), *hsing^a* is again linked to *te^a*, and the common people's joy in *hsing^a* is contrasted with a situation in which they are materially deprived. In another passage (*TC* 620/3–4), material deprivation is presented as a situation in which there is failure to preserve or protect (*pao*) the *hsing^a* of the common people. A. C. Graham acknowledges the use of "hsing^a" to refer to livelihood, and other scholars such as Hsü Fu-kuan, Mou Tsung-san, and T'ang Chün-i take the further step of explaining it in terms of the basic needs and desires of the common people.[68] This last move seems plausible since the reference to the material well-being of the common people shows that their *hsing^a* has to do not just with living out their term of life but with their basic needs and desires.

Besides referring to livelihood in the sense of basic needs and desires, "hsing^a" probably referred as well to certain tendencies characteristic of a thing. A passage in the *Tso-chuan* refers to certain aggressive tendencies as the *hsing^a* of the petty person (*shao jen^b chih hsing^a*; *TC* 522/9–10). A passage in the *Kuo-yü* speaks of the *hsing^a* of those who enjoy fat meat and millet (*KY* 13/2b.11); another passage refers to the desire to rise to a higher position as the *hsing^a·* of people (*KY* 2/14a.10). In these passages, "hsing^a" is more than the biological desires that one has by virtue of being alive, and includes certain tendencies characteristic of the things under consideration. Another interesting aspect of this use of "hsing^a" is that, in referring to these tendencies as *hsing^a*, one is not necessarily endorsing such tendencies. The point can also be seen from the use of "hsing^a" in other texts to refer to undesirable tendencies, such as the reference in the *Kuan-tzu* to the depraved or erroneous *hsing^a* of the common people (*KT* 1/45.6–7).[69] This feature of the use of "hsing^a" leaves room for subsequent debates about whether the *hsing^a* of human beings is something that should be followed or something to be molded by external norms of behavior.

It has been suggested that some occurrences of "hsing^a" in the *Tso-chuan* refer to certain "inherent moral tendencies" or "inborn moral propensities."[70] In one passage, it is said that *t'ien* (Heaven) institutes the ruler to guide the people to whom *t'ien* has given birth, so that people do not lose their *hsing^a*; also, the ruler is remonstrated by subordinates because *t'ien* loves the people and would not allow a ruler to indulge in his lewdness and abate the *hsing^a* of Heaven and Earth (*TC* 462/7-12). In another passage, *li^a* (rites) is described as preventing lewdness, which would otherwise result in people's losing their *hsing^a*; *li^a* also serves to regulate the emotions so that one can conform to the *hsing^a* of Heaven and Earth (*TC* 704/9-16). In these passages, *hsing^a* is presented as something preserved through ethical means such as proper guidance by the ruler and regulation by *li^a*. Still, it is not entirely obvious that *hsing^a* itself involves ethical tendencies, since it might well be the livelihood of the common people that is supposed to be preserved through ethical means. It is also possible to interpret "hsing^a" in these two passages as Graham does, as referring to a proper balance of the six energies (*ch'i^a*).[71] Hence, it is not entirely clear that "hsing^a" in these two passages has ethical connotations, although this remains a possible interpretation.

This discussion shows that, in the *Tso-chuan* and the *Kuo-yü*, the use of "hsing^a" had evolved to refer not just to the direction of growth of a thing over a lifetime but also to needs or desires that a thing has by virtue of being alive or to certain tendencies characteristic of a thing, where such tendencies may or may not be ethically desirable. In all of these usages, "hsing^a" still retains a dynamic connotation, referring not to fixed qualities but to directions of growth, to desires, or to other tendencies. It is probably generally true of the use of "hsing^a" in early texts that it has a dynamic connotation. One possible exception is the reference in the *Lü-shih ch'un-ch'iu* to *ch'ing^b* (being clear, clear up) as the *hsing^a* of water (*LSCC* 1/6b.8), if we take "ch'ing^b" to refer to the quality of being clear. However, this reference to *ch'ing^b* as the *hsing^a* of water is immediately followed by the comment that water may, when disturbed, fail to attain *ch'ing^b*, showing that *ch'ing^b* is not a given quality of water but water's tendency to become clear when it settles, a tendency that can be interfered with. This reading gains support from the subsequent characterization of the *hsing^a* of human beings as living to an old age, which is again presented as a tendency

that can be interfered with (*LSCC* 1/7a.2–3). Other texts also cite tendencies rather than fixed qualities as the *hsing^a* of water, such as the
way water tends to flow (e.g., *M* 6A:2; *KT* 3/17.4–10).

In regard to the use of "hsing^a" as a key term in the thought of the
period, A. C. Graham proposes that it was first used as a philosophical
term by the Yangists; before that it had been used to refer to matters of
health and longevity.[72] "Hsing^a" occurs in two passages in the *Lun-yü*;
one says that Confucius did not discourse on *hsing^a* (*LY* 5.13), and the
other observes that people are close to each other by *hsing^a* but diverge
as a result of practice (*LY* 17.2). In addition, other passages (e.g., *LY*
6.21, 16.9, 17.3) seem to describe different grades of human beings.
Still, even when taken together, these passages do not give an elaborate account of *hsing^a*, and it is likely that the primary emphasis of
some of these passages (e.g., *LY* 16.9, 17.2–3) is on the ability of people
to change through learning and practice. Hence, there seems justifica-
tion for not regarding "hsing^a" as a prominent philosophical term in
the *Lun-yü*.

Disagreeing with Graham, Benjamin I. Schwartz believes some occurrences of "hsing^a" in the *Tso-chuan* have ethical connotations, and
suggests that Mo Tzu had a conception of the *hsing^a* of human beings
as basically self-seeking, although Mo Tzu avoided using the term
"hsing^a" to absolve *t'ien* of the responsibility of bestowing such a
hsing^a.[73] For reasons mentioned earlier, it is not obvious that the occurrences of "hsing^a" in the *Tso-chuan* have ethical connotations, and
even if they do, this still does not show that "hsing^a" was already used
as a key term in any notable movement of thought prior to the Yangists. As for Mo Tzu, we saw that he probably did have a certain implicit picture of human psychology. Even so, there is little evidence
that "hsing^a" was already a key term in movements of thought during
Mo Tzu's time, one that Mo Tzu deliberately avoided. Based on the
available evidence, there seems insufficient ground for thinking that
"hsing^a" was a key term in movements of thought before the Yangist
movement.

2.3.2 *The Yangist Conception of hsing^a and sheng^a (Life)*

Besides the *Meng-tzu*, there are occasional references in other early
texts to Yang Chu's teachings or to ideas possibly belonging to the
Yangist movement. Both the *Huai-nan-tzu* (*HNT* 13/7b.10–11) and the
Lü-shih ch'un-ch'iu (*LSCC* 17/30b.8), for example, contain a brief refer-

ence to Yang Chu and his teachings, and the *Han-fei-tzu* (*HFT* 50/4.4) describes, without mentioning Yang Chu, ideas characteristic of the Yangist movement. The *Lieh-tzu* contains a dialogue involving Yang Chu and a possibly Mohist opponent (*LiT* 7/4b.8–5a.5), and A. C. Graham has argued that the dialogue probably has a Mohist origin.[74] In addition, Graham, following Fung Yu-lan, who identifies chapters 1/2, 1/3, 2/2, 2/3, 21/4 of the *Lü-shih ch'un-ch'iu* as representing Yangist teachings, and adding chapter 30 to chapters 28, 29, and 31 of the *Chuang-tzu*, which Kuan Feng identified as Yangist, takes these chapters to represent a body of Yangist literature, probably from a later stage of the movement.[75]

It is difficult to tell to what extent these chapters from texts compiled in a later period can be relied on to reconstruct the Yangist movement of thought as it existed by Mencius's time; it is not even clear that one single coherent view of *hsing*[a] can be reconstructed from these chapters. Although the basis for identifying these chapters as Yangist is the similarity between the ideas they contain and the brief references to Yang Chu's thinking found in other texts, it is quite possible that the chapters together contain different trends of thought despite exhibiting some overall similarity. For example, Hou Wai-lu, Chao Chi-pin, and Tu Kuo-hsiang distinguished an earlier and a later trend of Yangist thought in these chapters, with the former having a more positive attitude toward sensory desires.[76] Still, given the parallels between the Yangist chapters of the *Lü-shih ch'un-ch'iu* and the *Meng-tzu* noted earlier, it is likely that these chapters present ideas belonging to later developments of a movement of thought that existed by Mencius's time. I will therefore use these chapters as the basis for reconstructing a rough outline of that movement.

There are close parallels between the use of "*hsing*[a]" and of "*sheng*[a]" in these Yangist chapters. There are references to making complete (*ch'üan*[a]) *hsing*[a] (*LSCC* 1/8a.4) and *sheng*[a] (*LSCC* 1/6b.1–2, 2/7a.4), nourishing (*yang*) *hsing*[a] (*LSCC* 1/7a.3, 1/14b.8) and *sheng*[a] (*LSCC* 2/6b.1), injuring (*hai*) *hsing*[a] (*LSCC* 1/8a.3) and *sheng*[a] (*LSCC* 1/8b.1, 2/5a.5–6), and harming (*shang*) *hsing*[a] (*LSCC* 1/8a.5–6) and *sheng*[a] (*LSCC* 1/8b.1, 2/5b.3–4). Also, the text advocates subordinating satisfaction of sensory desires to *hsing*[a] and not letting it harm *hsing*[a] (*LSCC* 1/8a.3–4) and regards giving external possessions precedence over *hsing*[a] as a lack of proper balance (*LSCC* 1/7a.3–8), and makes similar observations about the relation between *sheng*[a] and the senses (*LSCC* 2/4b.4–6) and that between *sheng*[a] and external possessions

(*LSCC* 21/9a.1–10). These parallels suggest "sheng^a" and "hsing^a" are probably used interchangeably in certain contexts; this alternation may arise from an irregularity in later graphic standardization, an observation that gains some support from the fact that whereas both "hsing^a" and "sheng^a" occur in the first two Yangist chapters, only "sheng^a" occurs in the last three chapters. Still, the interchangeability of the two characters in some contexts does not show that they are not distinguished in pre-Han texts, as Fu Ssu-nien claims; indeed, there are contexts in which the two might not be interchangeable, such as the reference to the tendency of water to become clear as its *hsing^a* (*LSCC* 1/6b.8). What follows is only that with regard to human beings, *hsing^a* is regarded as being constituted at least in part by *sheng^a*, and hence that we may regard the things said about the *sheng^a* of human beings as also observations about their *hsing^a*.

On one occasion, *hsing^a* is related to living a long life (*LSCC* 1/7a.2–3), and longevity is emphasized elsewhere (*LSCC* 1/13b.3–8, 1/14a.5, 21/10b.6); this shows that the Yangist notion of *hsing^a* includes longevity. Passages about subordinating sensory satisfaction to *hsing^a*/ *sheng^a* (*LSCC* 1/7a.10–8a.6, 2/4b.4–10, 2/8a.8–8b.5) and subordinating external possessions, including possession of the empire, to *hsing^a*/ *sheng^a* (*LSCC* 1/7a.3–8, 2/4b.10–6b.1, 21/9a.1–10) and comments that acting otherwise represents a loss of proper balance (*LSCC* 2/6b.10–7a.4, 21/8a.3–4, 21/10a.5–6) can be read in a way that takes *hsing^a*/ *sheng^a* to be primarily a matter of living out one's term of life. The Yangist conception of *hsing^a*/*sheng^a* has often been interpreted in this manner, in terms of biological life.[77]

There is evidence, however, that at least for a certain trend in the later development of Yangist thought, *hsing^a*/*sheng^a* includes more than just living out one's term of life. That the Yangist valued things other than just living out one's allotted term can be seen from the emphasis on sensory satisfaction: living without sensory satisfaction is described as no different from death (*LSCC* 2/10a.3–7).[78] And although Tzu-hua Tzu is presented in one part of the text as being concerned with the body (*LSCC* 21/9b.2–10a.6; cf. *CT* 28/18–23), in another part he advocated sensory satisfaction as well as the avoidance of disgrace (*LSCC* 2/7a.4–8a.5). The second reference to Tzu-hua Tzu has important implications, and I will consider it more carefully.

Tzu-hua Tzu distinguished four kinds of existence: *ch'üan^a* (complete) *sheng^a* (life), *k'uei* (deplete, diminish) *sheng^a*, death, and *p'o* (oppress, force) *sheng^a*. The first, and highest, is characterized in terms of all six desires getting what is appropriate to them; the second in terms of the six desires partly getting what is appropriate; and the fourth, and lowest, in terms of the six desires not getting what is appropriate to them and getting what they dislike most, this being a state of servitude and disgrace (ju^b), a state worse than death.

Graham translates "ch'üan^a sheng^a," "k'uei sheng^a," and "p'o sheng^a" as "the complete life," "the depleted life," and "the oppressed life," respectively, showing that he takes "ch'üan^a," "k'uei," and "p'o" to be adjectival.[79] There is evidence, however, that the three are used verbally: *ch'üan^a*, *k'uei*, and *p'o* are things done to *sheng^a* rather than qualities of *sheng^a*. First, "ch'üan^a" when used in the Yangist chapters in conjunction with "sheng^a" or "hsing^a" is usually verbal: for example, it is said "that the offices of government were established was in order to *ch'üan^a sheng^a*" (LSCC 1/6b.1–2), and that regulating sensory pursuits "is the way to *ch'üan^a hsing^a*" (LSCC 1/8a.4). Also, in the reference to Yang Chu in the *Huai-nan-tzu* (HNT 13/7b.10–11), "ch'üan^a" in "ch'üan^a hsing^a pao chen" (complete *hsing^a* and preserve what is genuine) is used verbally, as seen from the pairing with "pao," which is used verbally. And, in the Tzu-hua Tzu passage, *ch'üan^a sheng^a* is also characterized in terms of *tsun sheng^a*, where "tsun" (to honor) is used verbally, as seen from the reference to one's "being able to *tsun sheng^a*" (LSCC 21/9a.8–9).[80] Second, "k'uei" is used verbally in the explanation of *k'uei sheng^a* in the Tzu-hua Tzu passage: "if k'uei sheng^a, then . . . ," "that which one *k'uei* is much and that which one *tsun* is little." In the second example, "k'uei" is used parallel to "tsun," which, as we have seen, is used verbally. Third, "p'o" is also used verbally elsewhere in the explanation of *p'o sheng^a*. For example, there is the reference to "pu yi^a p'o sheng^a," which reads more naturally as what is not *yi^a* doing something (viz., *p'o*) to *sheng^a*. If "p'o" were used adjectivally, the idea would have to be expressed by something like "pu yi^a chih^g sheng^a p'o sheng^a yeh."

The verbal use of "ch'üan^a," "k'uei," and "p'o" has an important implication. In the adjectival reading, we can still regard "sheng^a" as referring primarily to biological life and take *ch'üan^a*, *k'uei*, and *p'o* to be three possible qualities of such a life. But in the verbal reading, these are three things that one can do to *sheng^a*; since these three things have to do with the senses and with disgrace, it shows that *sheng^a* is not just biologically conceived but is regarded as life of a certain kind, involving sensory satisfaction and the absence of disgrace. The highest form of existence is to complete (*ch'üan^a*) a life of this kind, the next is to deplete (*k'uei*) it, and the lowest, even worse than death, is to oppress (*p'o*) it.

What, then, is the content of *sheng*^{a}? To complete *sheng*^{a}, all six desires have to get what is appropriate to them. Although the Tzu-hua Tzu passage mentions the aversions of the ear and eye as examples, it does not specify the six desires. In other parts of the *Lü-shih ch'un-ch'iu*, we find references to the eye, ear, nose, and mouth (*LSCC* 1/8b.6) and their desires (*LSCC* 2/4b.4–6, 5/9b.6–10a.1) as well as to the desires of human beings for long life, security, honor, rest, and their aversions to premature death, danger, disgrace, and hard work (*LSCC* 5/10a.7–8). Since the Tzu-hua Tzu passage refers to the aversions of the ear and eye and the aversion to disgrace, the six desires presumably include at least the desires and aversions of the four senses (ear, eye, nose, mouth) as well as the desire for honor and aversion to disgrace. Hence, the *sheng*^{a} that should ideally be completed is not just biological life, but one free from disgrace and from that to which the senses have an aversion.

For reasons mentioned earlier, it is difficult to tell whether the trends of thought presented in the Yangist chapters existed in Mencius's time or whether they were later developments. Given the pervasiveness in these chapters of the conception of *hsing*^{a}/*sheng*^{a} as constituted at least in part by biological life, it seems likely that this conception also characterizes the earlier form of Yangist thought. Things are less clear, however, with regard to the characterization of *hsing*^{a}/*sheng*^{a} in terms of sensory satisfaction and avoidance of disgrace. Even so, the presence in the Yangist movement of a (probably later) trend that conceived of *hsing*^{a}/*sheng*^{a} in a way that goes beyond biological life shows that Mencius's disagreement with Kao Tzu's explication of *hsing*^{a} in biological terms (*M* 6A:4) was probably part of a larger trend.

2.3.3   *Concern for Self and Concern for Others*

To complete this discussion of the Yangist view of *hsing*^{a}/*sheng*^{a}, we need to consider whether the emphasis on nourishing *hsing*^{a}/*sheng*^{a} demonstrated a concern for one's own self to the neglect of others. Even the Yangist who regarded *hsing*^{a} as including things like sensory satisfaction and avoidance of disgrace may have been concerned only with himself. It is true that the Yangist chapters do not advocate nourishing one's *hsing*^{a}/*sheng*^{a} at the expense of others, and this seems to show some minimal concern for others' well-being. Still, it is possible that a Yangist's active concern was only with himself, and he would not actively seek to benefit others, especially if doing so worked to his own detriment.

This view is reinforced by the sections of the Yangist chapters emphasizing the self over external possessions, including the empire (*LSCC* 1/11a.5–11b.1, 2/6a.4–6b.1, 2/10b.7–11a.3, 21/8a.3–4, 21/9b.10–10a.2), and passages idealizing those who resisted political involvement, even possession of the throne, to avoid injury to themselves (*LSCC* 2/5a.2–5b.4). There is now scholarly agreement that Mencius's characterization (*M* 7A:26) of Yang Chu as someone who would not give up a single hair to benefit the empire does not represent the basic tenets of Yangist teachings.[81] On the basis of a statement about Yangist teachings in the *Han-fei-tzu* (*HFT* 50.4.4) and the presentation of such teachings in the *Lü-shih ch'un-ch'iu*, it is likely that what the Yangist would refuse to do is to give up a single hair to gain possession of the empire; this observation fits in with the fact that the basic contrast in the Yangist chapters is not between self and others but between one's *hsing^a/sheng^a* and external possessions.[82]

It has been proposed that what Mencius ascribed to the Yangists is nevertheless implied by their teachings: on the assumption that gaining possession of the empire is a way to benefit the empire, the Yangist would not give up a hair to benefit the empire. D. C. Lau makes this point explicitly, describing the Mencian characterization as a corollary of Yangist teachings.[83] A. C. Graham sometimes makes the point that Mencius was exposing *what Mencius saw* as the selfish implications of Yangist thought.[84] But at times he seems to endorse the view that Yangist teachings do imply that one should not contribute to the good government of the empire at the cost of the least injury to oneself.[85] Indeed, for Graham, the Yangists were individuals who preferred the comforts of private life to the burdens and perils of political power, and Yangism was basically a philosophy entitling members of the ruling class to resist the moral pressures to take office.[86] Although the Yangist might not be opposed to helping others per se, his basic concern was still with himself, and he would not help others if doing so involved the slightest harm to himself. And even though political involvement might benefit others, the Yangist would not accept such involvement because doing so is likely to endanger himself.

The phenomenon of political withdrawal is described in the *Lun-yü* (e.g., 6.9, 14.37, 18.7) and so presumably existed during Confucius's time, but withdrawal is often presented as a consequence of viewing political participation as futile (*LY* 18.6; cf. 5.7, 8.13) and as causing unnecessary endangerment (*LY* 18.5) rather than as a matter of indifference to others. And, despite the Yangist advocacy of political withdrawal, it is quite possible that at least one trend in Yangist thought was still concerned for the *hsing^a/sheng^a* of others. The fact that the Yangist advocated nourishing *hsing^a/sheng^a* as a way of life for people in general itself shows a concern for other people. And, in the Yangist chapters, allowing people to complete *sheng^a* is presented as the purpose of government (*LSCC* 1/6a.8–6b.3). This concern for others is reflected in the story about the Great King, Tan-fu, who left his state because he would not let a means of nourishing do harm to what it nourishes (*LSCC* 21/8a.10–9a.9; cf. *CT* 28/9–14 and *M* 1B:15; also cf. *M* 1B:3 and 1B:5). That Tan-fu is characterized as one who was able to honor *sheng^a* and that he is said to have left his state because he was unable to bear having his subjects killed show that what is supposed to be nourished is the *sheng^a* of his subjects: the purpose of his rule was to nourish the *sheng^a* of the people, and he refused to rule if doing so defeated its purpose.[87] But if the Yangists were concerned with nourishing the *hsing^a/sheng^a* of people in general and regarded the offices of government as serving this purpose, why should the Yangist chapters idealize individuals who devoted themselves to nourishing their own *hsing^a/sheng^a* at the expense of political participation?

A possible answer is suggested by passages containing a negative assessment of current officeholders. Although the purpose of government is to complete *sheng^a*, the deluded lords of the time harmed *sheng^a* and could not avoid the destruction of their state (*LSCC* 1/6a.8–7a.9). Similar judgments of contemporary rulers can be found elsewhere (*LSCC* 2/8b.5–10a.4). The point seems to be that those currently in office were concerned primarily with possessions, including political power, and as a result brought disorder to society. If this was the source of the problem, then the remedy would be to have those who did not care about possessions rule. And this idea is present in the Yangist chapters. For example, although Tzu-chou Chih-fu is depicted as one who would not let possessing the throne harm his *sheng^a*, it is also said that this is exactly the kind of person who can be entrusted with the empire (*LSCC* 2/4b.10–5a.6; cf. *CT* 28/1–3). And although Prince Sou is described as one who tried to avoid being made a lord, it was because he would not allow ruling a state to harm his *sheng^a* that the people sought to make him a ruler (*LSCC* 2/5a.6–5b.4; cf. *CT* 28/15–18). Finally, in the dialogue with Ch'in Tzu in the *Lieh-tzu*, Yang Chu is reported to have said that it is by each person's not giving up a hair to benefit the empire that order in the empire can be achieved (*LiT* 7/4b.10).

The discussion shows that there probably was a trend of Yangist thought that exhibited a concern not just for oneself but also for others and for order in society. Diagnosing the current political disorder as a product of the concern with external possessions and political power, it proposed that order could be restored if each attended to his own *hsing*^{a}/*sheng*^{a} and did not compete with others for external possessions or for political power, and if government were conducted by one without a concern for power.[88] For this trend of Yangist thought, a concern for oneself was seen as instrumental to political order; that is, a Yangist of this kind was not indifferent to others or to political order but viewed each person's being concerned with himself as the way to attain order. This trend of Yangist thought would reject the assumption, shared by Confucians and Mohists, that attaining political power was the means to benefit the empire. While sharing the Mohist assumption that public and private interests converge, it regarded the public interest as served by attending to one's own interest, unlike the Mohists, who regarded one's own interest as served by attending to the public interest. Although this may represent only one trend of Yangist thought, it shows at least that the Yangist concern with *hsing*^{a}/*sheng*^{a} was not necessarily linked to an indifference to others.[89]

3 The Ethical Ideal

Mencius mentioned *jen^a* (benevolence, humaneness), *yi^a* (righteousness, propriety), *li^a* (observance of rites), and *chih^b* (wisdom) as four aspects of the ethical ideal and related them to *hsin^a* (heart/mind), the site of both affective and cognitive activities (2A:6, 6A:6). He did not refer to them as *te^a* (virtue, power), although at times he talked about *jen^a* (e.g., 1A:7, 2A:3, 2A:4) and *yi^a* (e.g., 7A:9) in relation to *te^a*. It is unclear that the use of "te^a" had evolved by Mencius's time to allow references to particular desirable attributes as different *te^a*. For this reason, I refer to them simply as ethical attributes rather than, as is sometimes done in the literature, as the four virtues, where "virtue" is often used as a translation of "te^a." In the *Lun-yü*, *yung* (courage) is sometimes mentioned along with *jen^a* and *chih^a* (knowing) as three desirable attributes (*LY* 9.29, 14.28). There are occasional references to *yung* in the *Meng-tzu*, and a discussion of *yung* occurs in the context of Mencius's explanation in 2A:2 of what it means for the heart/mind to be unmoved. The idea of the unmoved heart/mind has to do with a steadfastness of purpose that is also related to Mencius's attitude toward *ming^a* (decree, destiny). In this chapter, in addition to the four attributes just mentioned, I also consider Mencius's idea of the unmoved heart/mind and his attitude toward *ming^a* in discussing his conception of the ethical ideal.

3.1 *Jen*ᵃ (Benevolence, Humaneness) and *li*ᵃ (Rites, Observance of Rites)

3.1.1 *Jen*ᵃ

In §2.1.2, we saw that "jenᵃ" is used in the *Lun-yü* both in a broad sense to refer to the all-encompassing ethical ideal and in a narrow sense to refer to that aspect of the ideal having to do with affective concern. Mencius sometimes used "jenᵃ" in the broad sense (e.g., 7B:16), but, more often, he used it to emphasize affective concern. Even his references to *jen*ᵃ in a political context as the quality that enables a ruler to become a true king (*wang*ᵃ) often emphasize the ruler's concern for the common people (e.g., 1A:7).

*Jen*ᵃ as the aspect of the ethical ideal that emphasizes affective concern is characterized in terms of *ai* (love, concern) (4A:4, 4B:28, 7A:46, 7B:1). It is explained as a reluctance to cause harm to others (7B:31), for example, not killing the innocent (7A:33), as well as *ts'e yin* (2A:6, 6A:6), the capacity to be moved by the imminent or actual suffering of others. It is also related to *pu jen*, an inability to bear the pain and suffering of others (1A:7, 2A:6, 7B:31). Chao Ch'i (C 2A:6) explains "pu jen" as an inability to tolerate causing harm to others; many commentators, such as Chu Hsi (MTHW) and Hsü Ch'ien, take it to mean the same as "ts'e yin," being moved by the suffering of others. Chao probably takes his hint from 7B:31, where *pu jen* is linked to not desiring to harm others. But since *pu jen* is illustrated in 2A:6 by the example of being moved by the imminent danger to an infant crawling toward a well, it probably also includes the inability to bear the suffering of others whether caused by oneself or not.

The reference in 2A:6 (cf. 4A:1) to the heart/mind that does not bear (the suffering of) human beings (*pu jen jen*ᵇ *chih*ᵍ *hsin*ᵃ) and the government that does not bear (the suffering of) human beings (*pu jen jen*ᵇ *chih*ᵍ *cheng*ᵃ) may suggest that the attitude of *pu jen* is restricted to human beings (*jen*ᵇ). However, the use of "pu jen" in 1A:7 in connection with an ox and with animals generally shows that the attitude is also directed toward other animals. Probably, the specific mention in 2A:6 of human beings but not other animals as the object of *pu jen* is explained by the fact that the passage concerns government, which deals primarily with human beings.[1] Hence, *pu jen* includes a reluctance to cause harm to, and being moved to relieve the suffering of, human beings and other animals generally.[2]

This attitude may move one to act for certain objects but not others depending on circumstances. For example, one may be more moved to relieve the suffering of certain objects because their suffering is vividly presented (1A:7), and one may feel more urgency to help those in greater need, such as the widowed (1B:5). This differential treatment results from the different circumstances of the objects rather than from the different social relations in which one stands to them. But *jen*[a] also involves special attitudes directed toward those, such as parents, to whom one stands in special social relations.

The special attitude toward parents is described as "ch'in ch'in" (7A:15, 6B:3), literally "regarding and treating one's parents as parents." *Ch'in ch'in* partly involves concern for parents (*ai ch'in*; cf. 7A:15), and this concern goes beyond the concern one has for other objects, as seen from the gradation described in 7A:45: "ch'in ch'in, jen[a] min, ai wu[a]." The exact scope of "wu[a]" is unclear. Chao Ch'i (C) takes it to include anything that can be used to nourish human beings; Chu Hsi (MTCC) understands it as encompassing both animals and plants and takes *ai wu*[a] to involve being sparing in one's use of such things. In other passages, "wu[a]" is used to refer to living things including plants (e.g. 6A:8, 6A:9), as well as to things in general (e.g., 3A:4), including the senses and their ideal objects (e.g., 6A:15). As for "ai," "being sparing" is a possible reading, illustrated by the occurrence of "ai" in 1A:7. But another possibility is suggested by 7A:37, which restricts the objects of *ai* to certain kinds of animals, excluding those that one breeds for food. As it occurs in 7A:37, "ai" probably has the connotation of affective concern and not just that of being sparing.

The passage also suggests that *wu*[a], as the object of *ai*, probably includes certain kinds of animals but not all living things, not even animals one breeds for food. However, conflicting evidence comes from 1A:7, which describes King Hsüan's compassion on seeing an ox tremble with fear as it was being led to the sacrifice. The king's reaction involves an affective concern that goes beyond being sparing in the use of things, suggesting that the object of affective concern might include animals bred for specific purposes. A similar point is suggested by the reference in 1A:7 to being unable to bring oneself to see the death of and eat animals that one has seen alive and heard. Some commentators, such as Chang Shih and Hsü Ch'ien, even regard the king's reaction as an example of *ai wu*[a]; if this is right, then *wu*[a], as the object of *ai*, can have a broader scope than that suggested in 7A:37. As far as I can tell, there is no clear evidence for determining the exact scope of *wu^a*, although there is some evidence that *ai* involves affective concern at least when directed toward human beings and certain kinds of animals.[3]

Independently of how we interpret *ai* and what the scope of *wu^a* may be, 7A:45 shows that one's attitude toward parents should go beyond that toward the common people, and that one's attitude toward the common people should go beyond that toward other living things. The passage says that *ai* but not *jen^a* is directed to *wu^a* (living things), *jen^a* but not *ch'in* is directed to *min* (common people), whereas *ch'in* is directed to *ch'in* (parents). Since the text also speaks of *ai* being directed to human beings (*jen^b*) (4A:4, 4B:28, 7A:46; cf. 7B:1) as well as to parents (7A:15), presumably 7A:45 does not rule out *ai* being directed to the common people and parents. On the other hand, *ch'in* as an attitude is restricted to parents, whereas the scope of the objects to which *jen^a* may be directed is less clear. Since the text characterizes *ch'in ch'in* in terms of *jen^a* (7A:15; cf. 4A:27) and also describes as the method (*shu^b*) of *jen^a* King Hsüan's substituting a lamb (which he had not seen) for an ox (which he had seen and toward which he reacted with compassion), "*jen^a*" when used as a nominal probably concerns one's relation not just to the common people but also to parents and animals. However, 7A:45 shows that when "*jen^a*" is used verbally, its object includes the common people but not animals; I am not aware of any example in early texts in which the verbal use of "*jen^a*" takes parents as objects. As mentioned in §2.1.2, although *jen^a* as an attribute is not restricted to those in high positions, in the political context "*jen^a*" often has the connotation of kindness or favor directed toward human beings below oneself. Probably, the verbal use of "*jen^a*" carries similar connotations and hence is not used of parents and animals.[4]

Putting aside this special characteristic of the verbal use of "*jen^a*," 7A:45 illustrates the gradations involved in *jen^a* as an ethical attribute that emphasizes affective concern. One's concern for the common people takes a different form from one's concern for animals (cf. Chiao Hsün 27/21b.1-2), and one's relation to parents takes a different form from one's relation to the common people (cf. Chao Ch'i, C 7A:45; Chiao Hsün 27/21b.5-6). For example, whereas one's concern for animals is compatible with using them in certain ways, this is not true of one's concern for the common people. Also, one's special relation to parents involves honoring (*tsun*) them (5A:4), pleasing them (4A:12, 4A:28, 5A:1), providing for them with consideration (4A:19), and not endangering them (4B:30), as well as fulfilling various special obligations that one does not have toward other people. This special relation to parents is not a mere matter of giving more weight to their interests; if it were so, it would have been compatible with benefiting one's parents at the expense of others, the kind of attitude depicted as the source of disorder in the "Chien ai" chapters of the *Mo-tzu*. Rather, the special relation has to do with a network of social obligations that involves not just doing certain special things for one's parents but also not looking after their interests in certain socially unacceptable ways.

3.1.2   Li^a

In the *Meng-tzu*, "li^a" is used to refer to various rules of conduct, such as the proper ways to bury and mourn deceased parents (1B:16, 3A:2), to have an audience with a prince (5B:7), to see a wise person (3B:7), to present gifts (5B:4), to interact with one's host or guests (7B:24), to give or receive an object from a person of the opposite sex (4A:17), and to get married (4A:26, 5A:2). These are not merely rules of polite behavior, as their violation has much more serious implications.

On the other hand, li^a does not include all rules of conduct, but only those governing the way people interact in recurring social contexts; for example, the obligation to save a drowning person is not described as a rule of li^a (cf. 4A:17). Also, the rules of li^a are often (though not always) rules that govern the form such interactions take where the grounds for such interactions are independent of li^a; for example, they govern the manner of giving and receiving between men and women where the grounds for such acts are often independent of li^a. This feature of li^a is reflected in the description of li^a as a kind of adornment (4A:27); li^a is a way of regulating or beautifying interactions that people may engage in for reasons independent of li^a. Since li^a often involves minute details, especially in ceremonial contexts such as marriage or sacrifice, an ability to follow li^a is a skill that one can master to a greater or lesser degree, or exercise with more or less ease and grace.[5]

The attitude typically associated with the observance of li^a is *ching* (reverence, seriousness) (4A:4, 4B:28, 6B:14, 7A:8). In describing li^a as one of the four ethical attributes in 2A:6 and 6A:6, Mencius related it to *tz'u^a jang* (declining and yielding to others) (2A:6) as well as *kung ching* (respectfulness and reverence) (6A:6), and an interesting question concerns what these attitudes are and how they are related.

Ching, although often directed toward persons, can also be directed toward affairs and things. The *Shang-shu* speaks of *ching* in relation to one's *te^a* ("Shao kao"), and the *Shih-ching* of *ching* in relation to one's person (*SC* 194/3), good form (*yi^b*) (*SC* 196/2; cf. 253/3, 256/2, 256/5, 299/4), or official responsibilities (*SC* 276). It can qualify the way one deals with affairs such as listening to a poem (*SC* 200/7) or making clear one's *te^a* (*SC* 299/4), and it can be directed toward the anger of *t'ien* (*SC* 254/8) and to the spirits (*SC* 258/6). Also, it is paired with *shen^b*, a cautious and attentive attitude (*SC* 253/3, 256/2, 299/4), and with *chieh^b*, an attitude of being on guard (*SC* 263/1). The linking of *li^a* to *ching* appears in both the *Tso-chuan* (*TC* 158/8–10) and the *Lun-yü* (*LY* 3.26). *Ching* is again paired with *shen^b* in the *Tso-chuan* (*TC* 513/12–13) and, in the *Lun-yü*, *ching* is supposed to be directed at the spirits (*LY* 6.22), the employment of the people (*LY* 2.20), one's conduct (*LY* 15.6), and, on several occasions, *shih^a*, that is, affairs or probably official responsibilities (*LY* 1.5, 13.19, 15.38, 16.10).

In the *Meng-tzu*, although "ching" is used mostly to refer to an attitude directed toward a person (e.g., 2B:2, 4A:2, 5B:3, 6A:5, 6B:7, 7A:15), it can also be directed at such affairs as continuing the way of Yü (5A:6). Later, in the *Li-chi*, *ching* is presented as directed at one's body (*LC* 15/5b.8–10) or profession (*LC* 11/1b.10) and as qualifying the way one holds on to *yi^a* (*LC* 8/10a.1); it is also characterized in terms of fully devoting oneself (*LC* 14/19b.3–4). These examples show that *ching* is an attitude that involves caution, being on guard, devotion, and mental attention. It can be directed toward something one should be on guard against, but when its object is persons or affairs (such as official responsibilities) to which one should be devoted, or when it is an attitude that qualifies one's doing something to which one should be devoted, it also involves seriousness as well as devotion to and focusing attention on its object.[6]

As for *kung*, Chao Ch'i sometimes identifies it with *kung ching* (e.g., C 2A:9), presumably seeing no difference between *kung* and *ching*. Chu Hsi (MTCC 6A:6), on the other hand, explains *kung* as the outward manifestation of *ching*, and *ching* as the inner counterpart of *kung*. In objection to Chu Hsi, it has been pointed out that certain passages in the *Meng-tzu* speak of *kung* as something other than outward manifestation.[7] For example, 4A:16 distinguishes it from a pleasant outward appearance, and 7A:37 speaks of *kung ching* as what is there before the presentation of a gift, presumably implying that it is an attitude lying behind the outward manifestation. There is some substance to this objection, although Chu Hsi's proposal possibly still captures an important difference between *kung* and *ching*.

A survey of the occurrences of "kung" in the *Lun-yü* and the *Meng-tzu* shows that it is often used in connection with outward appearance or behavior. For example, it is linked to not insulting others (*LY* 17.6; *M* 4A:16), to a ruler's adopting a correct posture facing south (*LY* 15.5), to not accepting a gift from a superior when one does not have an official position (*M* 5B:6), and to appearances of various kinds (*LY* 5.25, 7.38). It is presented as the proper attitude in one's interaction with others (*M* 5B:4) but, unlike *ching*, it is not portrayed as an attitude directed at official responsibilities or other affairs. When used in contrast to *ching*, *kung* concerns the way one conducts oneself, and *ching* the way one serves superiors (*LY* 5.16); someone who is *kung* in dealing with others conforms to *li*^{a}, and someone who is *ching* does not err (*LY* 12.5); one should be *kung* in one's daily conduct and *ching* in carrying out one's responsibilities (*LY* 13.19); one should think of being *kung* in one's appearance and *ching* in affairs (*LY* 16.10).

These observations suggest that whereas *ching* is an attitude of caution, seriousness, and mental attention that can be directed toward people and affairs, *kung* is a more specific attitude probably having to do with attention to one's appearance, posture, and the manner one deals with others. Having *kung* is close to conforming to *li*^{a}, since one is then concerned with following *li*^{a} (*LY* 1.13), but the spirit of *li*^{a} also requires *ching*, which involves caution, seriousness, and attention to those with whom one is dealing. On this account, both *kung* and *ching* have to do with the way one's attention is directed, fitting in with the observation in 7A:37 that *kung ching* is an attitude that lies behind outward manifestation. Hence *kung* is not a mere matter of outward appearance, contrary to Chu Hsi. However, there is some truth to his proposal, since *kung* is an attitude concerned mainly with attention to externals, such as one's appearance, posture, and the way one deals with others.[8]

As for *tz'u*^{a} *jang*, *jang* is often linked in early texts to *li*^{a} (e.g., *TC* 456/7, 519/15, 582/16; *LY* 4.13) and to *ching* (e.g., *LC* 17/4a.5, 20/6b.3, 20/14b.10), and a failure to *tz'u*^{a} *jang* in response to a question from an elder is described as contrary to *li*^{a} (*LC* 1/3b.9). *Tz'u*^{a} involves politely declining, and *jang* letting others have something good or of honor to oneself. It has been argued on the basis of *Meng-tzu* 5B:4, which refers to a situation in which refusing (*ch'üeh*) something demonstrates a lack of *kung*, that *kung ching* and *tz'u*^{a} *jang* are different attitudes and hence that Mencius actually related *li^a* to two things that may conflict in certain situations.[9] But it is unclear that 5B:4 has this implication. In 2A:6 "tz'u^a" has the connotation of politely declining, and in 5B:4 "ch'üeh chih^g ch'üeh chih^g" has the connotation of an insistent refusal; although the latter may be disrespectful, it does not follow that the former can also be disrespectful.[10] Although *tz'u^a jang* and *kung ching* are different attitudes, they may well be two aspects of a more general attitude of putting others in a higher position; the *Li-chi* links *li^a* to "lowering oneself and elevating others" (*LC* 1/3a.1). The attitude involves attending to others and dealing with them cautiously and with seriousness, being attentive to one's posture and manner in dealing with them, and, when offered a good or an honor, politely declining it and letting others have it.

Certain passages in the *Meng-tzu* imply that it may be appropriate not to observe *li^a* in certain exigencies. One example is 4A:17, in which Mencius made the point that a man should exercise *ch'üan^b* (weighing, discretion) and save a drowning sister-in-law, even though pulling her out of the water with the hands violates the rule of *li^a* that men and women should not touch hands in giving and receiving. Chu Hsi takes the passage to say that *li^a* is completed in *ch'üan^b* (MTCC; cf. MTHW 6B:1), unlike Wang Fu-chih (607–8) who understands it as illustrating how *ch'üan^b* can lead to a breach of *li^a*. There has even been a debate whether one or the other way of viewing the relation between *ch'üan^b* and *li^a* might have a corrupting effect. Su Tung-p'o thinks that regarding *ch'üan^b* as involving a breach of *li^a* might lead people to arbitrarily depart from *li^a*, whereas Yü Yün-wen (TMHP 2/4a-6b) thinks that to regard saving the sister-in-law with one's hand as itself following *li^a* will undermine the rule of *li^a* governing giving and receiving. The way the example is described makes it more likely that Mencius took saving the sister-in-law to involve, if not a breach, at least a suspension of *li^a*. The passage refers specifically to the rule of *li^a* governing giving and receiving, and since rules of *li^a* typically concern conduct related to one's social position or to recurring social contexts, it seems unlikely that the consideration overriding this rule in this example can itself be described as a matter of *li^a*. Furthermore, the structure ". . . li^a yeh, . . . ch'üan^b yeh" suggests a contrast between *li^a* and *ch'üan^b*, contrary to Chu's suggestion that *ch'üan^b* serves to complete *li^a*.

The example in 4A:17 should be distinguished, however, from that in 4A:26 (cf. 5A:2) concerning Shun's failure to inform his parents before taking a wife, contrary to *li^a*. Although "li^a" and "ch'üan^b" do not occur in 4A:26, most commentators, including Chao Ch'i (C) and Chu Hsi (MTCC), take informing parents to be a matter of *li*ᵃ and Shun's omission to be an exercise of *ch'üan*ᵇ. Chiao Hsün, however, goes further and describes not informing parents as an instance of both *ch'üan*ᵇ and *li*ᵃ. Although this seems similar to Chu Hsi's interpretation of 4A:17, Chiao Hsün's comment on 4A:26 captures an aspect of the passage not present in 4A:17. Since Shun did not inform his parents for fear of not having an heir (the most serious way of being an unfilial son), Mencius observed in the passage that to the superior person this was as good as having informed his parents. The point seems to be that due to exigent circumstances, reverence for parents, which is typically expressed by informing them before getting married, was best expressed in Shun's case by not informing them because this is the only way Shun could avoid being unfilial through not having an heir. That is, although there seems to have been a breach of *li*ᵃ, this is not because the rule has been overridden by some other consideration (as in the case of 4A:17) but because the breach is itself a way of preserving the spirit behind the rule of *li*ᵃ.

That Mencius allowed for circumstances in which *li*ᵃ can be overriden by other considerations is also seen from 6B:1, which observes that although *li*ᵃ is generally weightier than other considerations such as eating and having sex, the latter may outweigh the former in exigent circumstances. On the basis of this discussion, we may characterize the ethical attribute of *li*ᵃ as involving a general disposition to follow *li*ᵃ and a mastery of the details of *li*ᵃ, enabling one to follow *li*ᵃ with ease. Furthermore, one should observe *li*ᵃ with the proper attitude and mental attention as described in the discussion of *kung ching* and *tz'u*ᵃ *jang*. At the same time, one should be prepared to suspend or depart from rules of *li*ᵃ in exigencies.

3.2   *Yi*ᵃ (Propriety, Righteousness)

3.2.1   *Yi*ᵃ *and li*ᵃ

Before considering *yi*ᵃ as an ethical attribute of a person, let us first look at *yi*ᵃ as a quality of actions and its relation to *li*ᵃ. As a quality of actions, "yiᵃ" refers to what is fitting or proper to do, and it is often related to a path (4A:10, 5B:7, 6A:11, 7A:33) or way (*tao*) (2A:2, 5A:7, 7A:9). It pertains to the relations between those who govern and those who are governed (3A:4) and between prince and minister (7B:24), as well as one's relation to parents and elder brothers (1A:3, 1A:7). Some examples of *yiᵃ* behavior in the *Meng-tzu* are instances of following *liᵃ*, such as pouring wine first for certain individuals in the ancestral temple (6A:5). Like *liᵃ*, *yiᵃ* is related to *ching* (6A:4–5). "Liᵃ" and "yiᵃ" sometimes occur in the combination "liᵃ yiᵃ" (1A:7, 4A:10, 6A:10), and the lack of *liᵃ* and the lack of *yiᵃ* are sometimes mentioned together (2A:7, 4A:1). This shows that there is a close relation between *liᵃ* and *yiᵃ*, and that many instances of *liᵃ* behavior are also *yiᵃ* behavior.

But some examples of *yiᵃ* behavior are not a matter of following *liᵃ*. Some such behaviors are still related to *liᵃ* in that they concern ways of responding to a breach of *liᵃ*, but the proper way of responding to a breach of *liᵃ* is itself often not a matter of following *liᵃ*. One common example is not having an audience with a prince when one is not summoned in accordance with *liᵃ*. Some such passages use the notion *yiᵃ* (e.g., 5B:7); others use related notions such as *tao* (way) and *hsiu* (regard as below oneself; e.g., 3B:1). In these examples, despite the breach of *liᵃ* involved, it is unclear that refusing to have an audience in such circumstances is itself a matter of following *liᵃ*. Other examples of *yiᵃ* behavior that are not a matter of following *liᵃ* include having those who use their heart/mind rule over those who use their muscles (3A:4), not imposing heavy taxation (3B:8), not taking inappropriately from the common people (5B:4), declining food given in an abusive manner (6A:10), and not taking what does not belong to oneself (7A:33).

Another difference between *yiᵃ* and *liᵃ* is that whereas the latter can be overridden by other considerations, the former cannot. Unlike 6B:1, which allows for a minor breach of *liᵃ* in order to get food in some circumstances, 6A:10 states without qualification that *yiᵃ* is always more important than life, showing that Mencius would not find a breach of *yiᵃ* acceptable in any circumstances. The same point can be seen in such observations as that one should always abide by *yiᵃ* (4B:11), or from the characterization of Po Yi, Yi Yin, and Confucius as refusing to do one single thing contrary to *yiᵃ* even if they could thereby gain possession of the empire (2A:2). It seems that whereas *liᵃ* concerns rules of conduct that it may be appropriate not to follow in exigencies, *yiᵃ* has to do with whatever is appropriate to a situation, whether that behavior is an instance of some general rule. Hence although behavior in accordance with *liᵃ* is often *yiᵃ* behavior, *yiᵃ* and *liᵃ* are not identical notions.[11] Rather, what we find in the *Meng-tzu* is the conception of *yiᵃ* considered in §2.1.2 in connection with the *Lun-yü*: *yiᵃ* underlies both the observance of and departure from li^a and governs one's behavior in contexts in which li^a does not provide guidance.

3.2.2 Yi^a

In 2A:6 and 6A:6, Mencius related the ethical attribute yi^a to *hsiu* (regard as below oneself) and wu^b (aversion). To better understand this attribute, I begin with a discussion of *hsiu* and wu^b, as well as the related notions ju^b (disgrace) and *ch'ih* (regard as below oneself).

Lack of yi^a is linked to ju^b in the *Mo-tzu* (*MT* 3/6) and in the *Lü-shih ch'un-ch'iu*, both in the "Tang jan" chapter, which reports Mohist teachings (*LSCC* 2/13b.7), and in the Tzu-hua Tzu passage of the Yangist chapters (*LSCC* 2/7b.5–9). In the *Meng-tzu*, we also find examples of yi^a that involve not subjecting oneself to insulting treatment, such as not having an audience with a prince who summons one in an improper manner (5B:7) or not accepting food given in an abusive manner (6A:10). Probably, the earlier use of "yi^a" has the connotation of an absence of ju^b. This provides one link between yi^a and li^a, since, although there may be instances of ju^b not involving a breach of li^a (such as defeat in war), someone who has been treated in violation of li^a and who is unable to respond appropriately typically suffers ju^b and thereby lacks yi^a.

One possible attitude toward ju^b is wu^b, or aversion, and early thinkers probably regarded the desire for honor (*jung*) and aversion to disgrace (ju^b) as general human characteristics. For example, such desire and aversion are presented in the *Lü-shih ch'un-ch'iu* as a fact about human beings (jen^b $chih^g$ $ch'ing^a$), like the desire for life and aversion to death (*LSCC* 5/10a.7–8, 8/4b.2–5), and they are described in the *Hsün-tzu* as shared by both the superior person and the petty person (*HT* 4/33) and by Yü and Chieh (*HT* 12/66). But wu^b can be directed at anything that one dislikes, such as death, unpleasant sights and sounds, or insecurity. Although all these things relate to oneself — it is one's own death or insecurity, and it is the unpleasant sights or sounds that one experiences, that one dislikes — ju^b is related to oneself in a more intimate way. The ju^b one suffers is not just something that one dislikes; it reflects adversely on oneself and results in a lowering of one's standing. One's attitude toward ju^b can therefore take on a special form, which is often referred to as *ch'ih* (regard as below oneself) and which can be directed toward something contemplated as well as toward what has already come about. Although both wu^b and *ch'ih* can be directed at the same occurrence, the focus of attention differs. Whereas *wu*[b] focuses on the occurrence as something that one dislikes, *ch'ih* focuses on it as something that is beneath oneself or lowers one's standing. Also, *ch'ih* often involves a resolution to remedy the situation; for example, in the political context, *ch'ih* arising from military defeat can move one to avenge oneself (1A:5), or from the presence of a corrupt ruler can move one to remove the ruler (1B:3). And just as *ju*[b] often results from being treated in violation of *li*[a], *ch'ih* often concerns such treatment. For example, the *Tso-chuan* contains a narrative about officials of one state deliberating whether to *ch'ih* another state by not treating its envoys in accordance with *li*[a], thereby bringing *ju*[b] upon them (*TC* 601/13–602/10).

Ch'ih involves a more reflective concern with the self: thoughts about the effect on oneself of certain events. Such a concern is arguably present in the *Lun-yü* in a way that it is not in the *Mo-tzu*— although both texts contain several occurrences of "wu[b]" and "ju[b]," the former but not the latter contains occurrences of "ch'ih." However, neither text refers to "hsiu," a character that is closely related to "ch'ih"; the only exception is one passage in the *Lun-yü* in which the character occurs in a quote from the *Yi-ching*. In this, they differ from the *Meng-tzu*, which contains several occurrences of "hsiu" in addition to occurrences of "ju[b]," "wu[b]," and "ch'ih."

A survey of the use of "ch'ih" and "hsiu" in early texts such as the *Tso-chuan* reveals one interesting difference between them: there are, by comparison, noticeably more instances of "ch'ih" used with a direct object and more occurrences of the combination "ch'ih chih[g]" (to *ch'ih* it) than similar uses of "hsiu." This suggests that *ch'ih* is probably focused more on the thing that reflects badly on oneself and involves a resolution to distance oneself from or remedy the situation. For example, one's focus of attention can be directed at such things as defeat in war (1A:5), being subordinate to others (2A:7, 4A:7), being in office and yet unable to put the Way into practice (5B:5), not being as good as others (7A:7), and so forth.

Hsiu, on the other hand, is focused more on the badness or the low standing of oneself as reflected in, or as likely to ensue from, the thing that occasions *hsiu*. In the *Meng-tzu*, we find such examples as the charioteer who *hsiu* teaming up with an archer who can catch birds only if the charioteer breaks the rules for proper driving (3B:1), or the Ch'i man's wife and concubine who *hsiu* when they discover that their husband feeds himself by begging for food used in sacrifices to the

dead (4B:33). In each example, a past or (as in the case of the charioteer) contemplated action by oneself or (as in the example of the Ch'i
man) by someone to whom one is intimately related occasions *hsiu* because the occurrence is regarded as beneath oneself. The focus is the
effect on the self rather than the thing that occasions *hsiu*. This is unlike *ch'ih*, whose focus is the thing that occasions *ch'ih* even though the
thing is still seen as something beneath oneself.

According to Chu Hsi, *wu*[b] is directed at the badness of others,
whereas *hsiu* and *ch'ih* are directed at the badness of oneself (MTCC
2A:6, YL 1286). Taken literally, this account cannot be correct since
wu[b] can also be directed at one's own actions or things that happens to
oneself, such as one's heart/mind falling short of others' (6A:12),
one's not following the Way in getting what one wants (3B:3), or one's
acting in a way contrary to *yi*[a] (6A:10). The difference seems to concern primarily the nature of the reaction and the focus of attention. To
wu[b] something is to dislike it, and it may involve wanting to alter the
situation so that the object of *wu*[b] no longer obtains. This attitude can
be directed at any object of dislike, including one's own or others' actions, or things that happen to oneself or others. *Hsiu* and *ch'ih*, on the
other hand, are directed at things that one regards as reflecting adversely on oneself. The focus of attention can be on the thing that occasions the reaction (*ch'ih*) or on the actual or possible lowering of one's
standing (*hsiu*); either way, the reaction can only be directed at things
that relate to oneself in some special way. Still, although Chu Hsi's account cannot be accepted as it stands, it has an element of truth: even
though *wu*[b] can be directed at one's own actions or things that happen
to oneself, the attitude involved in *wu*[b] when so directed is like the attitude that one has toward what one dislikes in others. This is unlike
the attitudes occasioned by *hsiu* and *ch'ih*, which cannot be directed at
what one dislikes in another person unless the other person stands in
some special relation to oneself.

At what kind of things may *ch'ih* and *hsiu* be directed? We saw that
ch'ih is often directed at *ju*[b] (disgrace), and probably the earlier use of
"ju[b]" had to do with certain publicly observable facts about a person,
such as defeat in war, being beaten in public, or not being treated in
accordance with *li*[a]. Correspondingly, the earlier use of "jung" (honor)
concerned such publicly observable facts as attaining high rank in
government. Suppose we call "social standards" those standards involving publicly observable facts that people ordinarily use to make
judgments about honor and disgrace. In the *Lun-yü* and the *Meng-tzu*,

we find references to objects of *ch'ih* that are not considered disgraceful by such social standards. For example, the *Lun-yü* refers to *ch'ih* directed at such things as receiving a salary as an official (*LY* 14.1) or being honored and wealthy (*LY* 8.13) in a state in which the Way does not prevail, clever talk and insincere appearance (*LY* 5.25), and one's words exceeding one's deeds (*LY* 14.27). The *Meng-tzu* refers to *ch'ih* directed at such things as having a reputation exceeding what one actually is (4B:18) or being in office without being able to put the Way into practice (5B:5). In these texts, what is regarded as reflecting adversely on oneself has to do with standards that need not coincide with ordinary social standards and common notions of honor and disgrace. There are overlaps between the two kinds of standards; for example, the texts still regard not being treated in accordance with *li*[a] as an appropriate object of *ch'ih*. But the two kinds of standards can also diverge, as when *ch'ih* is directed toward honor and wealth or toward occupying an official position in certain circumstances, even though such things are regarded as honorable by ordinary social standards.

This distinction is reflected in the contrast in *Meng-tzu* 6A:16 between the ranks of *t'ien* and the ranks of human beings, which parallels a contrast in 6A:17 between what is truly worthy of esteem and esteem that is conferred by others. The contrast is between the ethical attributes and official ranks in government, a contrast also found in 2B:2. Although the former is supposed to lead to the latter (6A:16), and although a lack of *jen*[a] in the political context is supposed to lead to disgrace (*ju*[b]) in the ordinary sense of being dominated by others (e.g., 2A:4), the implication of 6A:16 is that the former should be one's primary object of concern.

A similar contrast is found in the *Hsün-tzu* in the context of opposing Sung Hsing's proposal not to regard an insult as a˙ disgrace (*ju*[b]) (*HT* 18/93–114). Sung Hsing is presented in the *Chuang-tzu* as being indifferent to social opinion (*CT* 1/18–19), and in the *Hsün-tzu* as advocating not regarding an insult as a disgrace as a way of putting an end to fighting. Hsün Tzu disagreed on the grounds that fighting stems from disliking insults rather than from viewing insults as a disgrace, and hence that fighting ends when one lacks concern for insults even though one may still regard them as a disgrace. Hsün Tzu went on to distinguish between propriety honor (*yi*[a] *jung*) and propriety disgrace (*yi*[a] *ju*[b]) on the one hand and social honor and social disgrace on the other; the superior person's main concern is with the former rather than the latter, where the former is a matter of one's ethical qualities and the latter is measured by ordinary social standards (*HT* 18/104–11). Similarly, other parts of the *Hsün-tzu* explain honor (*jung*) in terms of putting propriety (*yi^a*) before profit (*li^b*) and disgrace (*ju^b*) in terms of putting profit before propriety (*HT* 4/22–23). The superior person is said to *ch'ih* the lack of appropriate character and ability rather than the lack of such external things as employment (*HT* 6/40–42). Like Mencius, Hsün Tzu regarded as the proper object of concern certain standards that are not identical with ordinary social standards.

Let us call such standards "ethical standards." For Mencius, *yi^a* as an ethical attribute of a person has to do with a firm commitment to such standards. The commitment involves having disdain for, and regarding oneself as being potentially tainted by, what falls below these standards. For example, in 6A:10, the *yi^a* reaction of the beggar toward accepting food given with abuse is described as *pu hsieh* (disdain); similarly, the idea that there are things one just would not do (*pu wei^a*) is both related to *yi^a* (e.g., 7B:31) and to *pu hsieh* (7B:37). "Pu hsieh" is used to describe Po Yi's attitude toward accepting office in a corrupt government, an attitude linked to regarding oneself as being tainted by so acting (2A:9; cf. 5B:1). In addition, that *ch'ih* is related to a sense of being tainted can be seen from the reference to "washing off" one's *ch'ih* in early texts (e.g., *M* 1A:5; *HFT* 47.4.1–24).[12]

Hence, the attribute *yi^a* involves disdaining and regarding as potentially tainting to oneself what falls below ethical standards, as well as an insistence on distancing oneself from such things, even if gravely undesirable consequences may result. Presumably, it also involves to some degree a capacity to judge in accordance with such standards, since a person committed to doing what he judges to be proper but who regularly misjudges is unlikely to be described as a *yi^a* person. The ethical standards involved can concern one's conduct, in which case they are expressed in terms of what a person will do (*wei^a*) or not do (*pu wei^a*) (e.g., 4B:8, 6A:10, 7A:17, 7B:31, 7B:34). They can also concern one's character; for example, there are references to *wu^b* (6A:12) and *ch'ih* (7A:7) directed at one's failure to be as good as others. This account of the ethical attribute *yi^a* allows us to make sense of the suggestion considered in §2.1.2 in connection with the *Lun-yü* that application of the notion "yi^a" to conduct is in some sense prior to its application to persons. In this account, *yi^a* as an attribute of a person involves a commitment to certain ethical standards, and *yi^a* as a quality of action is itself defined in terms of such standards. Hence the notion of yi^a as an attribute of a person, in presupposing such standards, also presupposes the notion of yi^a as a quality of actions.

3.2.3   *Jen^a and yi^a*

Mencius contrasted *jen^a* and *yi^a* by saying that the former concerns the heart/mind of human beings (6A:11) and is that in which one resides (4A:10, 7A:33; cf. 2A:7), and the latter is the path for human beings (6A:11, 4A:10) and is that which one follows (4A:10, 7A:33). In 7A:33 he gave the killing of the innocent as an example of what is contrary to *jen^a*, and the taking of what does not belong to oneself as an example of what is contrary to *yi^a*. Passage 7B:31 describes *jen^a* as having to do with what one cannot bear (*pu jen*), and *yi^a* as concerning what one would not do (*pu wei^a*). As examples of the latter, it cites getting a wife by improper means (cf. 3B:3, 6B:1) and accepting insulting treatment (cf. 6A:10); although it does not give an example of what one cannot bear, 2A:6 mentions being unable to bear the sight of an infant crawling toward a well. And, as we will see in §5.1.2, although the terms "jen^a" and "yi^a" are not used in that passage, the references in 7A:17 to not doing what one does not do (*pu wei^a*) and not desiring what one does not desire (*pu yü^b*) probably refer to *yi^a* and *jen^a*, respectively.

On the basis of these contrasts, we may infer that *jen^a* emphasizes an affective concern for others, both not wanting to harm others (7B:31, 7A:33) and not being able to bear the suffering of others (7B:31; cf. 1A:7, 2A:6). On the other hand, *yi^a* emphasizes a strictness with oneself, a commitment to abide by certain ethical standards that involves both not acquiring things by improper means and not accepting others' improper treatment of oneself. *Jen^a* and *yi^a* are also contrasted in the familial context. *Jen^a* has to do with loving (7A:15) and serving (4A:27) parents; *yi^a* with reverence for elder brothers (7A:15) and obeying them (4A:27). The contrast again illustrates the point that *jen^a* has to do more with affective concern and *yi^a* more with a strictness with oneself.[13]

Despite these differences, *jen^a* and *yi^a* are intimately related. The affective concern involved in *jen^a* can lead to *yi^a* behavior; for example, one's love for parents may lead one to serve parents in ways that are *yi^a*. Chu Hsi (YL 1334) suggests that Mencius did not describe serving parents as *yi^a* behavior because it is something that one is inclined to do and does not require being strict with oneself. Although this may be right, Mencius presumably still regarded serving parents in certain ways as *yi^a* behavior since he spoke of *yi^a* in connection with being filial to parents (1A:3, 1A:7). On the other hand, it seems that the affective concern involved in *jen^a* may also lead to improper behavior. This point is often made in Legalist writings, in criticism of the Confucian idea of *jen^a* government. Legalist thinkers drew a distinction between impartiality and partiality (e.g., *HFT* 49.10.1–5; cf. *SPH* 358, no. 8) and regarded the Confucian emphasis on *jen^a*, *ai* (love), and *hui* (favor) in government as leading to partiality, whereas government by *fa^b* (standards, laws) ensures impartiality (e.g., *ST* 268, nos. 62–63, and 276–78, nos. 75–78; *HFT* 14.7.1–53, 47.1.1–35, 47.6.26–56). The Confucian could respond that anyone whose affective concern leads to improper behavior does not really have *jen^a*. Although Mencius probably used "jen^a" in this manner, more needs to be said about what prevents the affective concern involved in *jen^a* from leading to improper behavior.

In his dialogue with King Hsüan in 1A:7, Mencius reminded the king of an incident in which the king unexpectedly saw an ox being led to the slaughter so that its blood could be used to consecrate a new bell. The king was moved by compassion and ordered the ox to be spared. When asked whether the ceremony should be abandoned, the king answered in the negative and ordered a lamb to be used instead. In connection with the substitution of the lamb for the ox, Mencius observed that this is the *shu^b* of *jen^a* — it took place because the king had seen the ox but not the lamb. Mencius then observed that the superior person stays away from the kitchen because, having seen animals alive and heard their cries, he cannot bear to see them killed and eat their flesh. Given the context of this example, it presumably was intended as another instance of the *shu^b* of *jen^a*.

In the case of King Hsüan, the *shu^b* of *jen^a* concerns the king's way out of the dilemma between compassion for the ox and his responsibility to ensure the consecration of the bell. Commentators disagree about the interpretation of "shu^b" in this context. Chao Ch'i (C 1A:7), Chiao Hsün (3/9a.2–3), and Wang Fu-chih (509) explain it in terms of *tao* (way); a similar explanation is found in the *Shuo-wen*. Chu Hsi (MTCC 1A:7; YL 1223) understands it in terms of skill (*ch'iao*), and Hsü Ch'ien links it to the exercise of discretion (*ch'üan^b*) in unusual situations. Yü Yüeh (MTKC), on the other hand, argues against Chu Hsi and in support of Chao Ch'i that "shu^b" in early texts does not carry the connotation of skill. Chu Hsi was probably led to his interpretation by passages like 6B:16, which gives as an example of *shu^b* a way of teaching that is devious, and 4A:1, which compares the *jen*^{a} heart/mind to skill (*ch'iao*) and the *jen*^{a} government of ancient kings to compasses and squares. A survey of the occurrences of "shu^b" in early texts shows that it probably has the more general meaning of *tao*, a way things happen or a method of doing things. For example, we find reference to *shu*^{b} as the method of defending a state (*KY* 5/3b.8), the way corrupt rulers perish (*KY* 4/12a.3), the method of judging water (*M* 7A:24), or the way political changes come about (*TC* 531/3).

The reference to the *shu*^{b} of *jen*^{a} in 1A:7 shows that Mencius regarded *jen*^{a} as involving not just affective concern but also an ability to act properly even in the presence of an affective response that potentially leads to improper behavior. A similar point is illustrated by the kitchen example, if we assume that it would be improper for the superior person not to eat meat. One difference, however, is that the case of King Hsüan involves a way out of a dilemma posed by an unusual situation, whereas the kitchen example illustrates a general policy geared to avoiding a similar dilemma (cf. Wang Fu-chih, 511–12). Since the ability to adjust one's behavior in the manner described is regarded as the *shu*^{b} of *jen*^{a}, *jen*^{a} is, for Mencius, not just a matter of affective concern but also an ability of this kind. This point can be seen from the fact that the *jen*^{a} person is characterized in terms of not killing the innocent rather than not killing (7A:33). This implies that even the *jen*^{a} person may order the execution of the guilty, and hence that the *jen*^{a} person is not only moved by affective concern but also sensitive to what is proper. Hence a person cannot be said to be *jen*^{a} unless his affective concern is regulated at least to some extent by *yi*^{a}. This point is also found in the *Hsün-tzu*; having explained *jen*^{a} in terms of love, it makes the point that such love has to be regulated by *yi*^{a} before one can truly be said to have *jen*^{a} (*HT* 27/20–24).[14]

The discussion shows that the ethical attributes *jen*^{a} and·*yi*^{a} are related, and the same is true of the attributes *li*^{a} and *yi*^{a}. A person with *li*^{a} is not only skilled in and disposed to follow the rules of *li*^{a} but is also prepared to depart from such rules when appropriate. This preparedness involves the operation of *yi*^{a}, a commitment to propriety. Even when a rule of *li*^{a} should be followed, *yi*^{a} still has a role to play in that one should ideally follow the rule with an awareness of its appropriateness to the situation and, in that sense, make the observance of the rule not a mechanical action but a display of one's own assessment of the situation.[15]

3.3   *Chih^b* (Wisdom)

Besides references to *chih^b* as one of the four ethical attributes (e.g., 2A:6, 6A:6, 7A:21), the *Meng-tzu* also discusses the exercise of *chih^b* in political contexts (e.g., 1B:3, 2B:9, 5A:9). Passage 5B:1, which discusses *chih^b* in connection with political behavior, throws light on how Mencius understood *chih^b*. In that passage, Po Yi, Yi Yin, and Liu Hsia Hui are described as sages; the three are also mentioned in 2A:2, 2A:9, and 6B:6, where they are described as *jen^a* (6B:6) and as never doing what is not *yi^a* (2A:2) and hence presumably as also having the attribute *yi^a*. But, in 5B:1, they are said to fall short of Confucius. Unlike these three, who adhered to fixed policies concerning when to serve in government, Confucius was a sage who was timely — he took or stayed in office, hastened or delayed his departure, all according to the circumstances. The passage then discusses the relation between sageness and *chih^b*, presumably with the implication that Confucius alone possessed *chih^b*, although all four individuals had sageness. The relation between *chih^b* and sageness is compared to that between skill (*ch'iao*) and strength in archery; strength suffices for the arrow to reach the target but not to hit the mark (*chung^b*). This passage highlights two important features of *chih^b*.

First, just as hitting the mark in archery requires skill and strength, proper human conduct requires proper aims and sufficient motivation to carry out the aims. And, just as skill in archery both guides strength and requires its support, proper aims in human conduct both guide motivational strength and require its support.[16] Since Mencius compared the relation between *chih^b* and sageness to the relation between skill and strength in archery, we may infer that *chih^b* involves having the proper aims to guide one's motivation, whereas sageness involves having sufficient motivation to carry out one's aim so that proper conduct flows easily.[17]

A similar picture of human behavior is found in 2A:2 in terms of the relation between *chih^c* and *ch'i^a*, and *chih^c* is also linked to archery in some early texts (e.g., LC 20/9a.5–6, 20/11a.9–11b.1). "Chih^c," often translated as "will," is linked to "hsin^a" (heart/mind) in the *Meng-tzu*. For example, there are references to working *hsin^a chih^c* hard (6B:15) and focusing one's *hsin^a* and devoting one's *chih^c* (6A:9); also, the moving of *chih^c* is linked to the moving of *hsin^a* (2A:2). "Chih^c" can refer to general aims in life, such as aiming at the Way (7A:24; cf. *LY* 4.9,

7.6) or *jen^a* (4A:9, 6B:8, 6B:9; cf. *LY* 4.4), or to more specific intentions, such as residing in a state for a long time (2B:14) or departing from a state (2B:14, 2B:12). It can also refer to the underlying goals or motives behind one's actions, such as traveling from state to state with the goal of acquiring sustenance (3B:4) or the motive behind an official's exiling an unworthy ruler (7A:31). In early texts, *chih^c* is regarded as something that one can establish (*M* 5B:1, 7B:15), observe (*LY* 1.11), talk about (*LY* 5.26, 11.26), nourish (*M* 4A:19), seek (*LY* 16.11), fulfill (*KY* 8/3a.7), and attain (*M* 3B:2, 4B:1, 7A:9, 7B:34). Others can assist one in one's *chih^c* (*M* 1A:7), and *chih^c* can become more ambitious (*KY* 8/1a.5) and be illuminated (*KY* 17/1b.4), altered (*KY* 8/2a.6), lost (*KY* 14/10a.4), or swayed (*LY* 14.36).

These occurrences show that *chih^c* has to do with certain directions of the heart/mind; these can include general aims in life as well as more specific intentions, and they can be established, nourished, altered, and attained. "Chih^c" occasionally means "to record something" or "to bear in mind" (e.g., *CT* 1/3; *TC* 189/5, 638/16), a point noted in the *Shuo-wen*. A. C. Graham has observed that in pre-Han texts the character is not yet graphically distinguished from the character "chih^d" (to record, remember, or bear in mind), and that there might not be a clear line between aiming at something and bearing the thing in mind.[18] Probably, the kind of general aims or specific intentions referred to as "chih^c" to some extent involves bearing in mind the objects of the aims or intentions. For this reason, there might not be that much difference between Chao Ch'i's (C 2A:2) explanation of "chih^c" in terms of what one bears in mind and deliberates about and Chu Hsi's (MTCC 2A:2; YL 1238) explanation in terms of the direction of the heart/mind. Henceforth, I will translate "chih^c" as "direction of the heart/mind" rather than "will," since the latter may misleadingly suggest that *chih^c* is a faculty of the heart/mind.

Ch'i^a is described in the *Kuo-yü* as something that fills Heaven and Earth, and its proper balance is linked to order in both the natural and the human realms (*KY* 1/10a.3–5, 3/4b.10–5a.10).[19] The *Tso-chuan* mentions that the six *ch'i^a* are generated in human beings by Heaven and Earth and are responsible for the five tastes, the five colors, the five sounds, and the six emotions (*TC* 704/10–16). The *Kuo-yü* describes *ch'i^a* as growing when the mouth takes in taste and the ears take in sounds, with *ch'i^a* in turn generating speech in the mouth and sight in the eyes (*KY* 3/13a.7–13b.6). A person needs a proper balance of *ch'iᵃ* for physical and psychological well-being (*TC* 573/17–18), and the lack of proper balance eventually leads to disorder in the human realm (*KY* 3/13a.7–13b.6). Thus, in human beings, *ch'iᵃ* is something that fills the body and is responsible for the operation of the senses as well as the emotions. This matches the characterization in *Meng-tzu* 2A:2 of *ch'iᵃ* as what fills the body, an idea also found in the *Kuan-tzu* (*KT* 2/66.10). Henceforth, I will translate "ch'iᵃ" as the "vital energies."

In 2A:2, Mencius described *chihᶜ* (directions of the heart/mind) as commander over *ch'iᵃ* (vital energies); the military analogy suggests that *ch'iᵃ* is conceived as something guided by, and also providing support to, *chihᶜ*.[20] This view of the relation between *chihᶜ* and *ch'iᵃ* matches Mencius's description in the same passage of *chihᶜ* as *chihᵉ* (extreme, arrive) and *ch'iᵃ* as *tz'uᵇ* (secondary, follow), whether this is interpreted to mean that *chihᶜ* is primary and *ch'iᵃ* secondary (e.g., Chao Ch'i, C; Chu Hsi, MTCC) or that where *chihᶜ* arrives, *ch'iᵃ* follows (e.g., Chang Shih; cf. Chu Hsi, YL 1238).[21] A similar view of the relation between *chihᶜ* and *ch'iᵃ* is expressed in other early texts such as the *Tso-chuan*, which describes *ch'iᵃ* as that which consolidates (*shihᵇ*) *chihᶜ* (*TC* 624/18). Mencius's view of the relation between *chihᶜ* and *ch'iᵃ* shows that he regarded human behavior as involving directions of the heart/mind guiding and being supported by the vital energies that fill the body. In light of his comparison of *chihᵇ* (wisdom) to skill in aiming, we may conclude that *chihᵇ* has to do primarily with forming proper directions of the heart/mind.[22]

The analogy with archery in 5B:1 also highlights a second feature of *chihᵇ*. In archery, proper aim is not a matter of following rigid rules but requires an ability to adjust one's aim according to the circumstances, such as wind direction. The comparison of *chihᵇ* to skill in archery thus suggests that forming proper directions of the heart/mind requires an ability to adjust one's behavior according to circumstances. Confucius, described as timely, had this ability, and hence had both *chihᵇ* and sageness. The other three individuals had sageness in that they had sufficient motivation to carry out their policies on political participation, but they lacked *chihᵇ* since they abided by fixed policies and were therefore not sufficiently sensitive to circumstances.[23] Indeed, the description of their policies shows that they held to certain extremes. Po Yi would serve only the right prince and only when there was order; Yi Yin would serve any prince whether there was order or disorder. Po Yi was constantly alert to the danger of being tainted; Liu Hsia Hui did not regard himself as vulnerable to this danger.

That proper conduct requires an ability to adjust one's behavior to circumstances might be part of the point of 4B:11, which stresses the flexibility of the great person's words and actions (cf. *LY* 4.10, 13.20).[24] This point is also highlighted in the use of "ch'üan^b," which has both the earlier meaning of weighing objects and the derived meaning of weighing the circumstances to arrive at an appropriate decision. The character occurs in 4A:17, in which the exercise of *ch'üan^b* is supposed to lead a man to extend a hand to save a drowning sister-in-law contrary to the rule of *li^a* that forbids touching hands when giving and receiving. It also occurs in 7A:26, in which Yang Chu, Mo Tzu, and a certain Tzu Mo are criticized for holding on to certain views without *ch'üan^b*, and in 1A:7, in which Mencius urged King Hsüan to weigh things. And, as Chu Hsi (MTHW 12/1a) has noted, the notion is implicit in 6B:1, which, in discussing the comparative importance of *li^a* and eating or having sex, refers to the relative weight of these considerations (see §3.1.2 for a discussion of the relation between *ch'üan^b* and *li^a* in 4A:17). To better understand Mencius's view of *ch'üan^b*, let us consider 7A:26 in relation to 4B:29.

In 7A:26, after criticizing Yang Chu and Mo Tzu, Mencius went on to say that Tzu Mo held to *chung^b* (middle), presumably a middle position between the Yangist and Mohist extremes. Even though this was closer to the Way, Tzu Mo still did violence to the Way by holding to *chung^b* without *ch'üan^b*. To understand Mencius's criticism, it helps to consider his criticism of Mo Tzu and Yang Chu in light of 4B:29. Passage 4B:29 describes Yü's and Chi's devotion to public service in a time of peace and Yen Hui's life of withdrawal in a time of disorder. The Way they follow is described as the same, and it is said that in a time of peace Yen Hui would behave as Yü and Chi did, and vice versa. As Chu Hsi (MTCC 7A:26; YL 1447–8) and Chang Shih (4B:29) have noted, 4B:29 probably contains an implicit criticism of Mo Tzu and Yang Chu. Mo Tzu resembled Yü and Chi and Yang Chu resembled Yen Hui in their way of life; Mo Tzu went out of his way to benefit the empire, and Yang Chu shunned political participation. However, unlike Yü, Chi, and Yen Hui, who behaved differently in different circumstances, Mo Tzu and Yang Chu held on to their way of life regardless of circumstances. This illustrates their lack of *ch'üan^b*.

Mencius's criticism of Tzu Mo for holding to *chung^b* may seem puzzling in light of his favorable view of *chung^b* in other contexts. For example, the superior person is described as *chung^b tao erh li* (7A:41), Confucius is said to desire the company of those who *chung^b tao* (7B:37), *chung^b li^a* is one of the highest achievements of *te^a* (7B:33), and *chung^b* is desirable in archery (Mencius sometimes used archery as an analogy to describe the ethical ideal; see 2A:7, 5B:1). Mencius's favorable comments on *chung^b* probably use *chung^b* in the sense of hitting the mark; *chung^b tao* and *chung^b li^a* refer to being able to "hit," or accord with, *tao* and *li^a*. *Chung^b* in this sense is not to be understood as something fixed that lies between two extremes, but as something dependent on circumstances. In the example from 4B:29, passing one's door three times without entering is *chung^b* for Yü and Chi but not for Yen Hui, whereas living in a mean dwelling is *chung^b* for Yen Hui but not for Yü and Chi, given their respective circumstances. A similar point is implicit in 5B:1, which depicts *chung^b* as requiring skill (*ch'iao*). On the other hand, since Tzu Mo is described as holding to *chung^b*, "*chung^b*" here probably refers to some fixed middle position lying between the Yangist and Mohist extremes (cf. Chang Shih, 7A:26). Tzu Mo still had a fixed policy of conduct, and although the policy might not be as objectionable as the extreme positions of Yang Chu and Mo Tzu, holding to such a policy without *ch'üan^b* was still objectionable.

From this discussion, we may conclude that *chih^b* (wisdom) involves having proper directions of the heart/mind, which in turn requires *ch'üan^b*, an ability to weigh circumstances without adhering to fixed rules. *Ch'üan^b* may lead one to depart from established rules of *li^a*, as in the example from 4A:17, or it may guide one's behavior in situations in which no general rule is applicable, as in the case of the political behavior of Confucius described in 5B:1 and that of Yü, Chi, and Yen Hui described in 4B:29. Other possible examples of the exercise of *ch'üan^b* include adjusting one's behavior according to one's relation to the parties affected (e.g., 6B:3) and the social or official position one occupies (e.g., 2B:5, 4B:31); Mencius's own conduct is involved in some cases (e.g., 1B:16, 2B:3).[25] What follows from the emphasis on *ch'üan^b* is not that general rules of conduct are dispensable, but only that one should not hold to them rigidly. Having general policies to follow in government is especially important, a point emphasized in 4A:1. In government, one needs both policies transmitted from the past and the heart/mind of *jen^a* (cf. 2A:6), just as in the crafts one needs both squares and compasses as well as skill (*ch'iao*; cf. 7B:5).

If *chih^b* (wisdom) enables a person to tell what is proper, how does it differ from the ethical attribute *yi^a* (propriety, righteousness)? The difference cannot be that *chih^b* is not motivational. In 2A:6, the heart/mind of *shih^c* (approve) and *fei* (disapprove) is described as the starting point for cultivating *chih^b*. *Shih^c* and *fei* are more than just knowing what is proper or improper; they also involve approving of what is proper and disapproving of what is improper. Also, in 4A:27, *chih^b* is linked not only to knowing to serve parents and obey elder brothers (or knowing *jen^a* and *yi^a*, depending on interpretation) but also to not letting go of them. Thus, *chih^b* involves a motivational component going beyond just knowing what is proper.

According to Donald J. Munro, both *chih^b* and *yi^a* involve a sense of what is proper and what is improper, as well as a positive feeling of obligation to act accordingly; *yi^a*, however, involves evaluations of events or activities in which the evaluator can be involved, whereas *chih^b* involves those in which the evaluator may not be involved.[26] This proposal captures the fact that *yi^a* is more closely related to oneself; as we saw in §3.2.2, since *yi^a* is linked to a sense of what is beneath oneself, it often has to do with events or activities involving oneself. However, there is probably another difference between *chih^b* and *yi^a*. Although Yi Yin and Po Yi are described as lacking *chih^b* (5B:1), they are also said to be committed to never doing what is not *yi^a* (2A:2); they would thus probably not be described as lacking *yi^a*. Since they lack *chih^b* but not *yi^a*, and since their lacking *chih^b* is a matter of their own political behavior rather than their evaluations of others' behavior, there seems more to the difference between *chih^b* and *yi^a*.

Probably, the difference lies in what the two notions emphasize. *Yi^a* emphasizes a firm commitment to proper conduct. Although *yi^a* might not be compatible with a persistent failure to know what is proper, and hence involves to some degree a capacity to tell what is proper, it is the firmness of the commitment rather than the ability to tell what is proper that is emphasized. On the other hand, *chih^b* emphasizes the ability to tell what is proper in accordance with circumstances. And although *chih^b* might not be compatible with a persistent failure to do what one recognizes as proper, it is the ability to tell what is proper rather than the commitment to proper behavior that is emphasized.

3.4   The Unmoved Heart/Mind (*pu tung hsin*[a])

The idea of the unmoved heart/mind (*pu tung hsin*[a]) is introduced in
2A:2, in the context of a query by Kung-sun Ch'ou whether Mencius's
heart/mind would be moved in a certain political context. The nature
of the context is not entirely clear, because of the different possible
interpretations of the line "sui yu tz'u pa wang[a] pu yi[c] yi," which follows a reference to the scenario of Mencius's attaining a certain rank
in government.[27] One interpretation punctuates the line as "sui yu tz'u
pa wang[a], pu yi[c] yi" and takes "yi[c]" (different, surprise) to mean "surprising." In this interpretation, Kung-sun Ch'ou was asking whether
Mencius's heart/mind would be moved given that it would not be
surprising for Mencius to achieve the accomplishments of an overlord
(*pa*) or a true king (*wang*[a]) in the described scenario, presumably by
successfully helping the king of Ch'i become an overlord or even a
true king (e.g., Chu Hsi MTCC; Lau; Legge; Yang).

A second interpretation punctuates the line as "sui yu tz'u, pa
wang[a] pu yi[c] yi" and takes "yi[c]" to mean "different." In this interpretation, Kung-sun Ch'ou was asking whether Mencius's heart/mind
would be moved given that he can achieve accomplishments not different from that of an overlord or a true king in the described scenario,
again presumably by successfully helping the king of Ch'i to achieve
such accomplishments (e.g., Chao Ch'i, followed by Sun Shih; Chu
Hsi, YL 1231). The two possible interpretations are noted by Chiao
Hsün; in either interpretation, Kung-sun Ch'ou's query concerns
whether Mencius's heart/mind would be moved if he could achieve
certain political accomplishments.

A third interpretation, proposed by Jeffrey Riegel, takes Kung-sun
Ch'ou's query to be an implicit criticism of Mencius.[28] Like the second
interpretation, it punctuates the line after "tz'u" and takes "yi[c]" to
mean "different." But it takes Kung-sun Ch'ou to be referring to Mencius's having achieved a certain rank in government and to be asking
whether Mencius's heart/mind was moved, since he had failed to
distinguish between an overlord and a true king in that although he
thought he could encourage the king of Ch'i to become a true king, the
king ended up acting like an overlord. Although I am drawn to this
interpretation, the following discussion does not depend on it.

Mencius explained the idea of the unmoved heart/mind by discussing three forms of courage (*yung*), the two exhibited by Po-kung

Yu and Meng Pin and the one advocated by Confucius (as reported by Tseng Tzu). Po-kung Yu always fought back and never accepted defeat or insult in any circumstances. Meng Pin looked upon defeat as victory and was without fear. According to Tseng Tzu, Confucius said that one would not cause even a lowly person to be afraid if one discovers one is not *so* (straight, upright) upon self-examination, but would go forward even against people in the thousands if one discovers one is *so*. Mencius compared Po-kung Yu to Tzu-hsia, and Meng Pin to Tseng Tzu. He described Meng Pin as holding to *yüeh*[a] (simple, what is important or essential) by comparison to Po-kung Yu, and as holding to *ch'i*[a] (vital energies), which was not comparable to Tseng Tzu's holding to *yüeh*[a].

Chao Ch'i takes "so" to mean propriety (*yi*[a]); Chu Hsi to mean straight (*chih*[f]). With a few exceptions, most commentators and translators adopt one or the other of these readings.[29] In the *Li-chi* (LC 2/8b.9–10, 2/22b.3), "so" occurs contrasted with "heng" (horizontal), showing that it can have the meaning of straight (Chu Hsi's reading), which in turn can lead to the metaphorical meaning of being upright, or *yi*[a] (Chao Ch'i's reading). This interpretation of "so" in the context of Tseng Tzu's description of the supreme courage advocated by Confucius gains some support from the fact that Confucius did relate courage to *yi*[a] (LY 2.24, 17.23) and that Mencius subsequently related the unmoved heart/mind, which the supreme courage reported by Tseng Tzu is supposed to illustrate, to *yi*[a].

The description of Meng Pin as holding to *yüeh*[a] in one instance and as inferior to Tseng Tzu, who held to *yüeh*[a] in another, may seem puzzling. Chao Ch'i (C) explains "yüeh[a]" in terms of *yao*, what is important or essential, and Chu Hsi (MTCC; MTHW 3/1b.5–11; YL 1234–35) elaborates further by saying that "yüeh[a]" does not refer to a specific thing that one holds to (since otherwise it would be odd to say that Meng Pin held to *yüeh*[a] in one context but not in the other) but is used to make the comparative observation that one attains what is more important or essential. Most commentators follow this reading, although a few commentators (e.g., Hu Yü-huan) and translators (e.g., Yang) take "yüeh[a]" to mean what is simpler. In early texts, "yüeh[a]" can mean "poverty" (e.g., LY 4.2, 7.26) or "restraint" (e.g., LY 6.27, 9.11, 12.15). On a number of occasions, it is contrasted with what is extensive, broad, or elaborate (e.g., M 4B:15, 7B:32; HT 3/38, 9/82, 11/55, 16/67). In such contexts, while carrying the connotation of being simple, "yüeh[a]" probably also connotes what is important or essential. For example, in *Meng-tzu* 7B:32, to bring peace to the empire via cultivating the self is described as an instance of holding to *yüeh*[a] while having an extensive application; here, "yüeh[a]" probably has the connotation of not just what is simple but what is important or essential. The use of "yüeh[a]" to describe one's words (*yen*) probably has a similar meaning (e.g., *TC* 316/15–16; *LC* 11/4b.5–6, 15/16a.5). This makes possible Chao's and Chu's interpretation of "yüeh[a]" in 2A:2.

As for the difference between the three forms of courage described in 2A:2, Po-kung Yu's concern was not to accept insult and defeat, and hence to avoid social disgrace. His reaction to potential social disgrace was to fight back, regardless of circumstances; this emphasis on fighting back is probably the point of comparison to Tzu-hsia, whose followers are described in the *Mo-tzu* as holding the view that the superior person does fight (*MT* 46/22–24).[30] For Mencius, this is a lower form of courage since it concerns outward behavior rather than one's inner state and since it is guided by considerations of social disgrace rather than by *yi*[a], which can diverge from social standards in regard to what is disgraceful. Meng Pin's courage is an improvement in that it involves fearlessness and thus is concerned more with not being affected by things than with outward behavior; in Huang Tsung-hsi's interpretation (1/14b.3), Po-kung Yu was concerned more with overcoming others, whereas Meng Pin was concerned more with overcoming the self. Furthermore, Meng Pin exhibited a loosening of concern with social standards; he is described as regarding defeat, a form of social disgrace, as victory. Still, his form of courage is insensitive to circumstances in that he was always without fear, whatever the situation might be. Mencius described Meng Pin's courage as like Tseng Tzu's, presumably in those respects in which Meng Pin surpassed Po-kung Yu, showing that Tseng Tzu's form of courage is more concerned with one's inner state. Still, Meng Pin's form of courage involves holding to *ch'i*[a] (vital energies), since it is a matter of ensuring that one is without fear, whatever the circumstances. On the other hand, Tseng Tzu's form of courage is sensitive to considerations of *yi*[a]; it involves a lack of fear only when one is in accord with propriety, an idea also found in the *Lun-yü* (*LY* 12.4).

That Mencius regarded as the superior form of courage that guided by *yi*[a] can also be seen from 1B:3, in which he distinguished between small courage and the great courage of King Wen and King

Wu. The former is just a matter of competing with others and not accepting defeat, like the courage of Po-kung Yu. The latter is not concerned with social disgrace; although there is a reference to *ch'ih* (disdain, regard as below oneself), the object of *ch'ih* is not social disgrace but a situation one regards as improper, and courage involves one's correcting the situation.[31] The Mencian conception of ideal courage was not uncommon in early Chinese thought. A similar distinction between higher and lower courage is found in the *Hsün-tzu* (*HT* 23/82–86): lower courage is insensitive to propriety and has to do with overcoming others; higher courage involves following the Way without fear. In other texts, ideal courage is related to *yi[a]* (e.g., *LY* 2.24, 17.23; *KY* 2/14b.11–15a.1, 3/3b.3; *LSCC* 11/10b.7–9, 11/11a.2–3; *TC* 844/13), to an absence of fear (e.g., *LY* 9.29, 14.28; *HNT* 10/8b.7), and to an absence of uncertainties (e.g., *KY* 19/11b.3–4; *LSCC* 8/10b.4–5).

To return to the idea of the unmoved heart/mind, Mencius probably also allowed for ideal and non-ideal ways in which the heart/ mind can be unmoved, since he described Kao Tzu as having attained an unmoved heart/mind although not of an ideal kind. The discussion of the ideal form of courage suggests that unmoved heart/mind of the ideal kind is related to *yi[a]*. Further support comes from the subsequent discussion in 2A:2 in which Mencius related the unmoved heart/mind to nourishing the flood-like *ch'i[a]* (vital energies), and said that *ch'i[a]* should be nourished with rectitude and that it would shrivel up if not properly related to *yi[a]*.[32] Also, *ch'i[a]* will shrivel up if one's conduct is not satisfying to the heart/mind or does not measure up to its standards.[33] Since 6A:7 says that the heart/mind takes pleasure in *li[c]* (pattern, principle) and *yi[a]*, the point of the observation is probably that *ch'i[a]* will shrivel up if it is not in accord with *yi[a]*.[34] So, ideally, for the heart/mind to be unmoved, *chih[c]*, which guides *ch'i[a]*, should accord with *yi[a]*, and *ch'i[a]* has to be cultivated to provide adequate support to *chih[c]*. This accounts for Mencius's explanation of his strong points (by comparison to Kao Tzu, who also attained an unmoved heart/mind) in terms of his knowing *yen* and nourishing *ch'i[a]*; as I will show in §4.4.3, "yen" as it occurs in 2A:2 probably refers to teachings about *yi[a]*.

It follows from this discussion that the moving of the heart/mind can involve fear, but Chu Hsi proposes that it can involve uncertainty as well (*MTCC*; *MTHW* 3/1a.11–12). In discussing the relation between *chih[c]* and *ch'i[a]*, Mencius said that if *chih[c]* is *yi[d]* (one), this will move *ch'iᵃ*; conversely, if *ch'iᵃ* is *yiᵈ*, this will move *chihᶜ*. The interpretation of "yiᵈ" is unclear; Chao Ch'i (C) takes it to mean "being blocked," and Chu Hsi takes it to mean "concentrate." Both interpretations are found among translators.[35] But, however we understand "yiᵈ," the observation shows the mutual influence between *ch'iᵃ* and *chihᶜ*. A failure to nourish *ch'iᵃ* adequately will not only result in insufficient motivation to execute *chihᶜ* but may in turn affect *chihᶜ*. This gives some support to Chu Hsi's proposal that the unmoved heart/mind involves the absence of uncertainty as well as of fear. Chu adds the interesting observation that Mencius's reference to his attainment of an unmoved heart/mind at the age of 40 probably refers to Confucius's remark about his being free from *huoᵃ*, or perplexity, at the same age (*LY* 2.4); "huoᵃ" is sometimes related to *chihᶜ* in early texts (e.g., *LY* 14.36; *TC* 573/14) and probably has to do with a moving of *chihᶜ*.

Thus, the ideal form of unmoved heart/mind involves following what is proper without being influenced by fear or uncertainty. It is related to, though not the same as, the ethical attributes *chihᵇ* (wisdom) and *yiᵃ* (propriety, righteousness). Whereas *chihᵇ* emphasizes the proper directions of the heart/mind and *yiᵃ* a firm commitment to proper conduct, the idea of the unmoved heart/mind, although involving both ideas, emphasizes the cultivation of *ch'iᵃ* to ensure freedom from fear, uncertainty, or other influences that might lead one to depart from what is proper. That is, unlike *chihᵇ* and *yiᵃ*, which emphasize more positively the proper directions of the heart/mind and a firm commitment to what is proper, the unmoved heart/mind emphasizes more negatively the absence of distortive influences that may affect the directions of the heart/mind or the ability to execute such directions. Ideas similar to that of the unmoved heart/mind are found in other passages. For example, 3B:2 concerns not being "led into excesses by wealth and honor, deflected by poverty and obscurity, or bent by superior force."[36] Passage 7A:9 enjoins one to be contented "whether appreciated by others or not" and "not to abandon *yiᵃ* in adversity or to depart from the Way in success." Such steadfastness of purpose is also illustrated by examples such as a beggar's declining food given with abuse even though it meant starving to death (6A:10), or the gamekeeper who would rather die than respond to improper summons (5B:7).[37] Since these ideas are related to Mencius's views about the proper attitude toward *mingᵃ*, I turn now to a discussion of that term.

3.5   Attitude Toward *ming*[a] (Decree, Destiny)

3.5.1   *Use of "t'ien" (Heaven) and "ming*[a]*"*

In 5A:6, Mencius observed: "What is done without having been done is due to *t'ien;* what comes about without having been brought about is *ming*[a]." Ch'en Ta-ch'i takes the first half of the line to be saying that *t'ien* does things without actually doing them, in the sense that *t'ien* does things through the agency of something or someone else.[38] A few commentators also take the first half to refer to *t'ien*'s doing things without actively acting. For example, Huang Tsung-hsi (2/46a.3-6) understands it as saying that natural processes are due to *t'ien*, even though there is no sign of its activity, and Sun Shih cites the phrase "wu wei[a] erh wu pu wei[a]" (not acting and yet nothing not accomplished) from the *Lao-tzu* to describe the activity of *t'ien*.[39] This differs from the interpretations of most commentators (including Chu Hsi [MTCC] and others) and translators (including Dobson, Lau, Legge, Lyall, Ware, and Uchino), who take the first half to say that what human beings do not (or cannot) do but is nevertheless done is due to *t'ien*.

The second interpretation is more likely than the first, since it is difficult to read the second half of the line, which concerns *ming*[a], in a way parallel to the first interpretation of the first half. The second half makes better sense if interpreted, as it is by most commentators and translators, to say that what comes about, but not through human effort, is *ming*[a]. Another consideration in favor of the second interpretation is that right before the line under consideration, Mencius was talking about things that are not done by human beings but are due to *t'ien*. That the context concerns what human beings do not do, rather than what they do without wanting to, also speaks against Chao Ch'i's (C) interpretation of the first half, which, as elaborated by Chiao Hsün, takes it to mean that what human beings do without wanting to are things they are made to do by *t'ien*. Thus, what the line shows is that Mencius regarded things not due to human effort as due to *t'ien* and as a matter of *ming*[a]; the difference between "t'ien" and "ming[a]" is probably that the former emphasizes the source of such things and the latter the outcome (cf. Huang Tsung-hsi, 2/46a.3-46b.4).[40]

What are ascribed to *t'ien* in the *Meng-tzu* include not only natural phenomena but also the success and failure of political endeavors (1B:14, 1B:16), the transferal of political power (5A:5), and whether order (2B:13) or the Way (4A:7) prevails in the empire. As in the *Lun-yü*, there is a tendency to ascribe to *t'ien* things which one regards as important but over which one has little control, and hence things with regard to which one feels a sense of dependence on some higher authority. *T'ien* is also regarded as the source of the ethical life. The ideal way of life is described as the Way of *t'ien* (4A:12, 7B:24), and *jen*[a] as the rank of *t'ien* (2A:7, 6A:16). Also, *t'ien* is the source of the heart/mind (6A:15) and its ethical predispositions (3A:5, 6A:7); fully developing and preserving the heart/mind is the way to know and serve *t'ien* (7A:1). Thus, "*t'ien*" has both a descriptive dimension, referring to the source of what is not within human control, and a normative dimension, referring to the source of the ethical ideal. As in the case of the *Lun-yü*, there have been controversies over whether *t'ien* is a personal deity and whether it has a transcendent dimension. Since these issues relate to Mencius's views on *hsing*[a], I defer their discussion to §6.2.3.

As for "*ming*[a]," it probably also has both dimensions, referring to occurrences not within human control as well as to propriety (*yi*[a]). *Ming*[a] has to do with, so to speak, both the causal and normative constraints on human activities.[41] There has, however, been scholarly disagreement on this point. Some scholars, such as A. C. Graham and Fu Ssu-nien, think the use of "*ming*[a]" in the *Meng-tzu* has both dimensions.[42] Some, such as Ch'en Ta-ch'i, Hsü Fu-kuan, and Lao Ssu-kuang, emphasize the descriptive dimension.[43] And some, such as T'ang Chün-i, emphasize the normative dimension.[44]

For the reasons mentioned in §2.1.1 in connection with the *Lun-yü*, it is often difficult to decide of a particular occurrence of "*ming*[a]" which dimension it emphasizes. Take, for example, 5A:8, which links *ming*[a] to *yi*[a] (propriety) and in which Confucius is reported as saying that *ming*[a] resides in one's attainment (*te*[b]) or non-attainment (*pu te*[b]) of political office.[45] On the one hand, the reference to *ming*[a] is introduced in a discussion of whether one should proceed in a certain manner to attain political offices, and it is possible to interpret "*ming*[a]" as having a descriptive dimension, referring to the fact that the attainment of political offices is not fully within human control. This reading gains further support from the contrast in 7A:3 between things whose attainment is up to oneself and things in whose attainment *ming*[a] resides. On the other hand, the *Meng-tzu* frequently mentions *yi*[a] in connection with the proper way to attain things, and this, along with the fact that the expression "*wu yi*[a] *wu ming*[a]" (to be lacking in *yi*[a] and in *ming*^{a}) links *ming*^{a} and *yi*^{a}, makes it possible to interpret "*ming*^{a}" as having a normative dimension, referring to the proper way of attaining things. Furthermore, even if we grant that "*ming*^{a}" has a descriptive dimension, it is possible to take it as also having a normative dimension, referring to the proper way to respond to the fact that the attainment of political offices is not fully within human control.[46]

Since the distinction between the two dimensions is largely a heuristic device and might not have been drawn clearly in early texts, there is no reason to expect one dimension to be present to the exclusion of the other. The possibility that both dimensions are present and not clearly distinguished is reflected in the way some commentators interpret the passage. For example, Chiao Hsün (19/9b.3–10) cites the view of Chang Erh-ch'i that the passage makes the point that *ming*^{a}, in the sense of limitations on what one can attain, is not knowable, and the superior person regards *yi*^{a} as *ming*^{a} in the sense that whatever *yi*^{a} forbids he regards as a limitation on what one can attain. Unlike other people who recognize *ming*^{a} only after having tried everything possible to attain their goals, the superior person and the sage do not try all means possible but just do what is *yi*^{a}, and regard the non-attainment of their goals as *ming*^{a} when it is contrary to *yi*^{a} to attempt other means to attain their goals. In this way, they identify *ming*^{a} with *yi*^{a} and reconcile themselves to *ming*^{a} while taking comfort in *yi*^{a}. Huang Tsung-hsi (2/47b.6–48a.2) has a similar reading, and Chang Shih likewise brings in both dimensions in interpreting 5A:8 — many people do not know *ming*^{a}, understood in the sense of limitations on human efforts, and therefore make futile efforts to attain their goals; Confucius, on the other hand, took *yi*^{a} and *ming*^{a} to be one, regarding *li*^{a} *yi*^{a} (rites and propriety) as that in which *ming*^{a} resides.

However we interpret the use of "*ming*^{a}" in 5A:8, it seems clear that the passage conveys the attitude that, with regard to the attainment of political offices, one should proceed in accordance with propriety and then just accept the outcome even if it is unfavorable, without making efforts contrary to propriety. A similar attitude is reflected in 7A:1–3, in which the character "*ming*^{a}" also occurs.

3.5.2   *Passages 7A:1–3*

Passage 7A:1 contains the observation: "being not *erh* [two] with regard to premature death and long life, cultivating oneself to await [*ssu*^{a}] it [*chih*^{g}], this is the way to stand on *ming*^{a}." The context of the remark concerns self-cultivation, and different interpretations are made possible by different readings of "erh," "chih§," and " minga."

Chao Ch'i (C) takes "not *erh*" to mean not being of two minds and changing one's way. Chu Hsi (MTCC; YL 1429) understands the observation as paralleling the preceding remark about knowing and serving *t'ien* and interprets its first half to be about knowing and the second half about cultivating oneself. Thus, according to Chu Hsi, "not *erh*" means not doubting, that is, not being of two minds with regard to what one knows. Most commentators and translators follow Chao's and Chu's interpretations, but Huang Tsung-hsi (2/76a.5–76b.1), citing the views of Liu Tsung-chou, has proposed a third possibility: one regards premature death and long life as one (not two) in that having understood clearly and followed what is proper, one is no longer concerned about whether one lives or dies.[47] Despite their different emphases, the three interpretations are not that much different in substance; they all emphasize the point that a person should not be led to deviate from what is proper by considerations of life and death.

There is also disagreement concerning what "chih§" (it) refers to. Chu Hsi (MTCC) takes it to refer to death, and he is followed by Legge, who takes "chih§" to refer to premature death or long life. On the other hand, Chao Ch'i (C) and Chang Shih see it as referring to *minga*. It is likely that "chih§" refers to *minga*, since 7B:33 contains the combination "ssua minga" (await *minga*), which parallels "ssua chih§" (await it) in 7A:1. Still, this leaves open the possibility that the content of what is being awaited has to do with life and death, since life and death are themselves a matter of *minga*.[48] In fact, Chao Ch'i (C 7B:33) himself explains "ssua minga" ("await *minga*") in 7B:33 in terms of awaiting premature death or long life, presumably reading 7B:33 in light of 7A:1.

The occurrence of "minga" can be interpreted as primarily descriptive or primarily normative. In the first interpretation, to await and stand on *minga* is to await the occurrence of what is not within human control, without making futile efforts to change things. Chu Hsi (MTCC) and Chang Shih read "ssua minga" in 7B:33 in this way, taking what is not within human control to include such things as fortune or misfortune, wealth or poverty. In the second interpretation, to await and stand on *minga* is to be fully prepared to follow *yia* and not be swayed by such considerations as premature death or long life. Fu Ssu-nien and T'ang Chün-i both read "ssua minga" in this manner.[49] Considering this passage by itself, we have no clear way of adjudicating between the two interpretations, although a consideration of 7A:2 may give some support to the first interpretation of "ming^a."

Passage 7A:2 begins with the observation that there is *ming^a* in everything and that one should willingly accept *cheng^b* (correct) *ming^a*.[50] It is less easy to interpret the use of "ming^a" in this passage as primarily normative, referring to *yi^a*, since it would then be difficult to make sense of the contrast between *ming^a* that is *cheng^b* and *ming^a* that is not *cheng^b*. Chu Hsi (MTCC; YL 1429, 1434–35) takes "ming^a" to refer to what is not within human control, including such things as fortune or misfortune, life or death. *Ming^a* that is not *cheng^b* is what comes about as a result of one's improper behavior, whereas *ming^a* that is *cheng^b* is what comes about but not as a result of one's improper conduct. For example, that one gets an official position is *ming^a* (decree from the ruler) and that the term of the office is terminated is also *ming^a* (decree from the ruler); whether the latter is *cheng^b* depends on whether the termination comes about simply because one's term of office has expired or because one is being dismissed for a fault. Chang Shih has a similar interpretation of the passage, and the fact that the descriptive dimension of "ming^a" is emphasized more in this passage reflects back on 7A:1. Since both passages concern life and death and one speaks of awaiting *ming^a* while the other speaks of willingly accepting *ming^a*, the occurrences of "ming^a" in 7A:1 probably also emphasizes the descriptive dimension.

Thus, 7A:1 emphasizes that one should cultivate oneself to await whatever is to come without being swayed in one's purpose, and 7A:2 similarly emphasizes that one should act in accord with propriety and then willingly accept what happens. Passage 7A:2 probably goes beyond 7A:1 in emphasizing that truly knowing (*chih^a*) *ming^a* involves awaiting and willingly accepting only *cheng^b* *ming^a*, that is, outcomes that follow upon one's having followed the Way. This attitude toward *ming^a* is related to the unmoved heart/mind in that both concern one's attitude toward actual or expected unfavorable conditions of life. The idea of the unmoved heart/mind highlights the absence of distortive effects due to such unfavorable conditions, whereas the idea of accepting *ming^a* highlights the willing acceptance of such unfavorable conditions, given the assurance that one has conducted oneself properly.

The character "ming^a" also occurs in 7A:3. T'ang Chün-i takes the occurrence of "ming^a" here to be primarily normative, referring to considerations of propriety that constrain what one does to attain one's goals.[51] However, the contrast in the passage between things within one's control and things in whose seeking *tao* resides and in whose obtaining *ming^a* resides favors interpreting the use of "ming^a" as primarily descriptive. Further support comes from the fact that the observation that *ming^a* resides in the obtaining of such things is immediately followed by the observation that seeking does not contribute to obtaining. Indeed, if we take "tsai" as it occurs in the contrast between "tsai wo" and "tsai wai" to mean "lie with" or "up to," the point of the passage is a contrast between the pursuit of things whose attainment is up to oneself and the pursuit of things whose attainment depends on outside factors. Chao Ch'i (C; CC) and Chu Hsi (MTCC) adopt this reading of "ming^a," taking 7A:3 to be contrasting ethical pursuits, which are within one's control, with attaining such things as wealth and honor, which are outside one's control.[52] More specifically, Chao Ch'i (C), followed by Sun Shih, takes the contrast to be one between the ranks of *t'ien* and the ranks of humans beings (cf. 6A:16); since attainment of the latter is dependent on others' conferring the ranks on oneself, it is not within one's control (cf. 6A:17). It is likely that the reference in 7A:3 to things whose attainment is not within one's control has to do at least in part with political office. Passage 5A:8 describes Confucius as going forward in accordance with *li^a* (rites) and withdrawing in accordance with *yi^a* (propriety) with regard to political office, and as saying that there is *ming^a* in matters of attainment or non-attainment. This seems a clear example of something with regard to which there is *tao* in seeking and *ming^a* in attaining.[53]

Of the two kinds of things contrasted, it is said of the former that seeking will contribute (*yi^e*) to getting and of the latter that seeking will not contribute to getting.[54] In 2A:2, it is said of the flood-like *ch'i^a* that it is misguided to regard efforts as not contributing (*yi^e*) to its nourishment; the implication is that efforts do make a contribution. This further confirms that the first of the two kinds of pursuits contrasted in 7A:3 concerns self-cultivation. However, the observation that seeking does not contribute to getting with regard to the second kind of pursuits may seem puzzling, since even if things like life, wealth, and honor are not fully within one's control, it seems that one's seeking these things can at least make a difference. But the observation can be made intelligible if we follow Chao Ch'i and take 7A:3 to concern the contrast between the ranks of *t'ien* and the ranks of human beings. To attain the ranks of human beings, one should seek the ranks of *t'ien* without aiming at the ranks of human beings (there is *tao* in seeking), and one should just let the ranks of human beings come on their own. Whether one gets them or not is outside one's control (there is *ming*[a] in getting), and seeking does not contribute to getting in that aiming at the ranks of human beings is precisely what prevents one from getting them (cf. 6A:16).

Passages 7A:1 and 7A:2 concern one's cultivating oneself so that one follows what is proper and willingly accepts unfavorable conditions of life that are not within one's control or are of such a nature that altering them requires improper conduct. This implies that one should devote effort to ethical pursuits and not worry about external conditions of life. This idea is highlighted in 7A:3, which contrasts things whose pursuit contributes to getting and things whose pursuit does not. The contrast implies that one should devote effort to the former, which has to do with ethical pursuits.

4 *Yiᵃ (Propriety) and Hsinᵃ (Heart/Mind)*

4.1 General

The ethical attributes considered in the previous chapter are intimately related to *yiᵃ* (propriety) as a quality of actions. The attribute *yiᵃ* (righteousness) is a commitment to live in accordance with *yiᵃ*, and the attribute *chihᵇ* (wisdom) involves an ability to tell what is *yiᵃ*. The unmoved heart/mind has to do with making the directions of the heart/mind (*chihᶜ*) conform to *yiᵃ* and with cultivating the vital energies (*ch'iᵃ*) to support these directions, thereby putting *yiᵃ* into practice without being swayed by distortive influences. One should follow *yiᵃ* and, knowing that one has done so, willingly accept any unfavorable outcome as an instance of *mingᵃ* (decree, destiny).

The attributes *jenᵃ* (benevolence, humaneness) and *liᵃ* (observance of rites) have to do with affective concern and reverence for others, respectively, but such affection and reverence have to be regulated by *yiᵃ*, with regard to both the form they take and the actions they lead to. It is *yiᵃ* to have more reverence for one's eldest brother than for a person from one's village even if the latter is older by a year; yet, although it is *yiᵃ* to have reverence for one's uncle rather than for one's younger brother generally, it is *yiᵃ* to have reverence for the latter when the younger brother is impersonating an ancestor at a sacrifice (6A:5). And although one's reverence for others generally leads one to follow *liᵃ*, it may be proper to depart from *liᵃ* in exigencies. Similarly, although not put explicitly in these terms, it is presumably also *yiᵃ* that one's affective concern for others should depend on their relation to oneself and on circumstances. And, as we saw in §3.2.3, one should also regulate one's behavior by *yiᵃ* when acting out of affective concern.

Given the significance of *yiᵃ*, an obvious question is how to tell what is *yiᵃ*. Since *yiᵃ* is determined by standards that do not necessarily coincide with ordinary social standards, *yiᵃ* does not originate in prevailing social opinion. In response to the Mohist proposal that *yiᵃ* is determined by *liᵇ* (profit, benefit) of the kind that the Mohists emphasized, there is evidence that Mencius regarded *yiᵃ* as in some sense deriving from the heart/mind (*hsinᵃ*). I will defend this interpretation through an examination of passages 6A:1–5, 2A:2, and 3A:5, all of which involve Mencius's debating with or distinguishing himself from philosophical opponents.

These passages make references to Yi Chih and Kao Tzu, two of Mencius's adversaries. The affiliation of Yi Chih is not problematic, since he is explicitly described in 3A:5 as a Mohist and he defended the Mohist doctrine of indiscriminate concern for each. Accordingly, in discussing 3A:5, I will assume that Yi Chih was a Mohist and endorsed certain ideas characteristic of the Mohist school. The affiliation of Kao Tzu, who debated with Mencius in 6A:1–4 (6A:5 contains a debate not involving Kao Tzu but concerning a subject matter similar to 6A:4) and whose ideas are reported in 6A:6 and 2A:2, is unclear. There are three references to an individual with the same name in the *Mo Tzu* (*MT* 48/81–87), but whether the two are the same individual is unknown. Nor is the affiliation of Kao Tzu mentioned in either text. Hence any claim about his affiliation has to be based on the interpretation of his position as presented in the relevant passages. Accordingly, I will defer consideration of the question of his affiliation until after I have discussed these passages.

In §1.1, I mentioned that, since our main access to Mencius's views is the *Meng-tzu*, my references to "Mencius's views" are an abbreviated way of referring to Mencius's views as represented by the editors of the text. For similar reasons, my references to the views of an adversary of Mencius refer to the adversary's views as represented by the editors of the text. Even with this qualification, however, it is important to draw a distinction between the position held by an adversary of Mencius and the position that Mencius ascribed to him. Whereas the former can be discerned from the things the adversary is reported to have said, the latter can be seen not just in what the adversary said but also in Mencius's comments on what the adversary said. The two can differ given the possible difference between a reconstruction based only on what the adversary is reported to have said and one also based on Mencius's comments. The difference need not amount to a conflict; it may be that a consideration of Mencius's comments allows us to say something more specific about the adversary's position as it was understood by Mencius. And even if the difference amounts to a conflict, it does not follow that Mencius misunderstood the adversary's position; his alternative construal of his adversary's position may have been an argumentative strategy geared to converting the adversary to a different view. Since my main goal is to understand Mencius's thinking, my focus is primarily on the way Mencius understood his adversaries. Still, the distinction is important, and it will come into play when I return to the question of Kao Tzu's affiliation.

Given my primary focus, I will take into account both the things said by an adversary and Mencius's comments. In defending my proposed interpretation of what is at issue in a debate between Mencius and an adversary, I will do so on the grounds that it makes sense of all stages of the debate in a way that other interpretations do not. This strategy may lead to the worry that since Mencius's understanding of an issue might differ from that of his adversary, it would be misguided to seek to make sense of all stages of the debate. However, even if there is such a divergence in understanding, it remains the case that there is a way of viewing what is at issue that is both the way Mencius himself looked at things and the way he took his adversary to look at things. Since my primary goal is to understand Mencius's thinking, it will further this goal to attempt to capture this view of things even if, in doing so, I may not capture the actual position of Mencius's adversary. What is needed to capture this view of things is an interpretation that makes sense not only of Mencius's comments but also those of his adversary.

Sometimes, different readings of a part of a debate may be grammatically possible, and my interpretation may require adopting one of these readings. In doing so, I do not assume that this reading is the only one grammatically possible or is to be preferred on grammatical grounds alone. My claim is only that taking into account all the grammatically possible readings of each stage of a debate, my proposed interpretation of what is at issue in the debate is the only one that makes sense of each stage of the debate in a way that all stages cohere. This strategy does not require that I show of each stage of the debate that my reading is to be preferred on grammatical grounds alone; rather, the choice is also a function of what I regard as the more plausible interpretation of what is at issue in the debate as a whole.[1]

4.2   The Debate with Kao Tzu About *hsing ᵃ* (Nature, Characteristic Tendencies) in 6A:1–3

4.2.1 *Passages 6A:1–2*

Passages 6A:1–3 are primarily about *hsingᵃ* rather than about the relation between *yiᵃ* (propriety) and *hsinᵃ* (heart/mind). However, the disagreement between Mencius and Kao Tzu about *yiᵃ* is probably related to their disagreement about *hsingᵃ* — the debates about the two topics are placed together in the text, and there is a reference to *yiᵃ* in the debate about *hsingᵃ* in 6A:1 as well as a reference to *hsingᵃ* in the debate about *yiᵃ* in 6A:4. For this reason, I begin with a discussion of 6A:1–3, using as background the statement in 6A:6 of Mencius's and Kao Tzu's views on *hsingᵃ*: Mencius regarded it as good (*shan*), whereas Kao Tzu believed that there is neither good (*shan*) nor bad (*pu shan*) in *hsingᵃ*. To facilitate discussion, I divide the passages into sections.

6A:1

a. Kao Tzu said, "*Hsingᵃ* is like the *ch'i* willow; *yiᵃ* is like cups and bowls. To make *jenᵃ yiᵃ* out of the *hsingᵃ* of human beings is like making cups and bowls out of the *ch'i* willow."

b. Mencius said, "Can you follow the *hsingᵃ* of the *ch'i* willow and at the same time make cups and bowls out of it? Or do you have to do violence to the *ch'i* willow before you make cups and bowls out of it? If you have to do violence to the *ch'i* willow to make cups and bowls out of it, then do you also have to do violence to human beings to make them *jenᵃ yiᵃ*? Surely, it will be your *yen* [words, teachings] that lead people of the world to *huoᵇ* [bring disaster upon, regard as a disaster] *jenᵃ yiᵃ*."

6A:2

a. Kao Tzu said, "*Hsingᵃ* is like whirling water [*t'uan shui*]. Give it an outlet in the east, and it will flow east; give it an outlet in the west, and it will flow west. That the *hsingᵃ* of human beings does not show a preference for either good or bad is just like water's not showing any preference for east or west."

b. Mencius said, "Water certainly shows no preference for either east or west, but does it not show preference for high or low? That the *hsingᵃ* of human beings is good is just like the tendency of water to flow downward. There is no human being who is not good; there is no water that does not flow downward. Now in the case of water, by splashing it to leap up, one can make it go over one's forehead, and by damming and leading it, one can force it up a hill. But is that the *hsingᵃ* of water? It is the circumstances being what they are.

> Although human beings can be made to become bad, their *hsingᵃ* is
> also like this."

I will leave "hsingᵃ" untranslated for now and will discuss its use
in §6.1.1. In 6A:1b, "yen" can mean "words" or, more likely, "teachings," and "huoᵇ jenᵃ yiᵃ" can mean either "bringing disaster upon *jenᵃ
yiᵃ*" or "regarding *jenᵃ yiᵃ* as a disaster." In 6A:2a, I follow Chao Ch'i
(C) in taking "t'uan shui" to mean "whirling water" (Lau's translation); Chiao Hsün is probably correct in pointing out that Chao Ch'i
takes *t'uan shui* to be not just rapidly running water (cf. *Shuo-wen*) but
water running in a circle because this fits better with Kao Tzu's further
observation about its lack of preference for east or west. In both 6A:1
and 6A:2, a comparison of Mencius's response with Kao Tzu's presentation of the analogies shows that Mencius construed the terms of
the analogies somewhat differently from Kao Tzu.

If we take "hsingᵃ" to be short for "jenᵇ hsingᵃ" in these two analogies, Kao Tzu is comparing making *jenᵃ yiᵃ* out of the *hsingᵃ* of human
beings to making cups and bowls out of the *ch'i* willow and the non-
preference of the *hsingᵃ* of human beings for good or bad to the non-
preference of water for east or west. Mencius's response, however,
shows that he took the analogies to be comparing human beings
(rather than the *hsingᵃ* of human beings) to the *ch'i* willow and to water, and the *hsingᵃ* of human beings to the *hsingᵃ* of the *ch'i* willow and
of water (rather than to the *ch'i* willow and water). For example, in
6A:1b, he compared doing violence to human beings to doing violence
to the *ch'i* willow and introduced a reference to the *hsingᵃ* of the *ch'i*
willow absent from Kao Tzu's presentation of the analogy. In 6A:2b,
although the earlier part of Mencius's response follows Kao Tzu in
comparing the *hsingᵃ* of human beings to water, Mencius immediately
went on to compare human beings (rather than the *hsingᵃ* of human
beings) to water—there is no human being who is not good just as
there is no water that does not flow downward. This is followed by a
comparison of the *hsingᵃ* of human beings to the *hsingᵃ* of water. Thus,
whereas each of Kao Tzu's analogies compares the *hsingᵃ* of human
beings to a certain thing (*ch'i* willow or whirling water), Mencius construed the terms of the analogy in such a way that human beings are
being compared to the thing and the *hsingᵃ* of human beings to the
hsingᵃ of the thing.

Before we discuss whether anything of significance hinges on the
different ways of construing the analogies, let us first consider how
Mencius probably viewed the debates. From his perspective, since

Kao Tzu believed that there is neither good nor bad in the *hsingᵃ* of human beings, Kao Tzu was committed to the possibility that human beings can follow *hsingᵃ* and at the same time (a) develop in the direction of goodness, (b) not develop in the direction of badness, (c) develop in the direction of badness, or (d) not develop in the direction of goodness. If possibility (b) [or (d)] does not obtain, human beings cannot follow *hsingᵃ* without becoming bad (or good), and in this sense there is badness (or goodness) in *hsingᵃ*. If possibility (a) [or (c)] does not obtain, it means that human beings cannot follow *hsingᵃ* and at the same time become good (or bad), and in this sense there is again badness (or goodness) in *hsingᵃ*. From Mencius's perspective, which takes Kao Tzu to be comparing the *hsingᵃ* of human beings to the *hsingᵃ* of the *ch'i* willow, Kao Tzu's analogy fails to allow for possibility (a).[2] Presumably, the objection is that it is the *hsingᵃ* of the *ch'i* willow to grow into a flourishing plant and that making the willow into cups and bowls requires doing violence to the willow. The observation that Kao Tzu's *yen* (words, teaching) will lead people to *huoᵇ jenᵃ yiᵃ* can be interpreted as saying that his words or teaching about *hsingᵃ* will lead people to regard *jenᵃ yiᵃ* as a disaster (e.g., Legge), or to bring disaster on *jenᵃ yiᵃ* by not practicing it (e.g., Lau) because they regard doing so as doing violence to themselves.

In this way of viewing Kao Tzu's position, the shift to the water analogy in 6A:2 bypasses the problem with the *ch'i* willow analogy. Whirling water has a tendency to flow outward and downward, and it can follow this tendency and at the same time (a) flow east, (b) not flow west, (c) flow west, or (d) not flow east. Thus, in comparing goodness and badness to these two directions, this analogy seems to illustrate Kao Tzu's position that there is neither good nor bad in the *hsingᵃ* of human beings. In his response, Mencius altered the terms of the analogy to illustrate his own position. Water has a tendency to flow downward, and although it can be made to go upward by being splashed or dammed, its tendency to flow downward remains. Similarly, human beings have a tendency to become good, and although they can become bad, this is due to circumstances; the inherent tendency to goodness remains despite such deviation.[3]

At the beginning of his response in 6A:1b, Mencius posed the alternatives—either one can follow the *hsingᵃ* of the *ch'i* willow and at the same time make cups and bowls out of it or one has to do violence to the *ch'i* willow to make cups and bowls out of it. This reveals his assumption that if one cannot both follow the *hsingᵃ* of a thing and accomplish something, then the accomplishment requires doing violence to the thing. This assumption fits in with the use of "hsingᵃ," discussed in §2.3.1, to refer to certain tendencies characteristic of a thing; if such tendencies are characteristic of a thing, to go against them is to change the thing radically and in a sense do violence to it. It need not follow that in ascribing such tendencies to the thing, one is at the same time endorsing the tendencies. For example, the reference in the *Tso-chuan* to certain aggressive tendencies as the *hsingᵃ* of the petty person does not have this implication. Still, from the perspective of one whose *hsingᵃ* is under consideration, one might resist anything that goes against one's *hsingᵃ* and involves a radical change in oneself. This probably explains why, according to Mencius, if people view *jenᵃ yiᵃ* as going against their *hsingᵃ*, they will regard *jenᵃ yiᵃ* as a disaster, or resist practicing them, thereby bringing disaster on *jenᵃ yiᵃ*. And, in making this point, Mencius was presumably assuming that Kao Tzu did want to uphold the practice of *jenᵃ yiᵃ*.

Let us bracket Mencius's response and try to understand Kao Tzu's position solely from his own presentation of the analogies. Contrary to Mencius's construal of his analogies, Kao Tzu was comparing the *hsingᵃ* of human beings to the *ch'i* willow and to whirling water, rather than to certain tendencies characteristic of the *ch'i* willow or of water. Probably, Kao Tzu viewed the *hsingᵃ* of human beings as a raw material that can be shaped in certain directions, in the way that the *ch'i* willow or water can be shaped.[4] In 6A:4, Kao Tzu cited eating and having sex as the content of *hsingᵃ*, and this fits in with such a view of *hsingᵃ*, since these activities can be shaped in the direction of *jenᵃ yiᵃ* or in the opposing direction. In this way of viewing *hsingᵃ*, *hsingᵃ* is not a direction of human life as a whole, but tendencies that pertain to human life and can be shaped according to the direction human life takes.

Although from Mencius's perspective the water analogy probably represents Kao Tzu's position more accurately than the willow analogy, this may not be true from Kao Tzu's perspective. Since he was comparing the *hsingᵃ* of human beings to the *ch'i* willow and not, as Mencius represented him, to certain characteristic tendencies of the *ch'i* willow whose violation involves violence to the *ch'i* willow, he might not have seen any force in Mencius's criticism. Kao Tzu might well have viewed the shift to the water analogy not as an improvement but as an attempt to avoid Mencius's construal of his willow analogy. Furthermore, on the basis of what is said in 6A:1a and 6A:2a, it is not clear, although it is possible, that Kao Tzu wanted to uphold the practice of *jenᵃ yiᵃ*. Although the view that *jenᵃ yiᵃ* is something imposed onto the *hsingᵃ* of human beings is compatible with an advocacy of *jenᵃ yiᵃ*, it is also compatible with an opposition to *jenᵃ yiᵃ* on the grounds that they are alien to human beings. As far as 6A:1–2 is concerned, there is little in Kao Tzu's own presentation of his position to tell us his attitude toward *jenᵃ yiᵃ*.

4.2.2   Passage 6A:3

In 6A:3, Kao Tzu explicated *hsingᵃ* in terms of *shengᵃ* (life, growth), and Mencius then drew an analogy between this explication and the explication of *pai* (white) in terms of *pai*. In discussing the passage, I will take into account Kao Tzu's statement at the beginning of 6A:4 that "eating and having sex are *hsingᵃ*."

> 6A:3
> a. Kao Tzu said, "Shengᵃ chihᵍ weiᵇ hsingᵃ."
> b. Mencius said, "Is 'shengᵃ chihᵍ weiᵇ hsingᵃ' like 'pai chihᵍ weiᵇ pai'?"
>   (Kao Tzu) said, "Yes."
> c. (Mencius said,) "Is *pai* feather *chihᵍ pai* like *pai* snow *chihᵍ pai*, and *pai* snow *chihᵍ pai* like *pai* jade *chihᵍ pai*?"
>   (Kao Tzu) said, "Yes."
> d. (Mencius said,) "Is it then that hound *chihᵍ hsingᵃ* is like ox *chihᵍ hsingᵃ*, and ox *chihᵍ hsingᵃ* like human being *chihᵍ hsingᵃ*?"

Yü Yüeh (MTPI), taking into account the derivation of "hsingᵃ" from "shengᵃ," suggests that "shengᵃ chihᵍ weiᵇ hsingᵃ" in 6A:3a probably read like "hsingᵃ chihᵍ weiᵇ hsingᵃ" to the disputants, and this explains the comparison to "pai chihᵍ weiᵇ pai." However, the interchangeability of "shengᵃ" and "hsingᵃ" in this context has been disputed, and I will not make that assumption in my discussion.[5]

Shengᵃ has been interpreted in different ways in this context. Dobson translates the line as "what I mean by nature is the thing that gives life." One way to derive this reading is to take "shengᵃ" as verbal, referring to what gives life. But this reading is unlikely since grammatically it requires "shengᵃ chihᵍ chihᵍ weiᵇ hsingᵃ" and, as far as I know, there is no instance of the ". . . chihᵍ chihᵍ weiᵇ . . ." structure being abbreviated to ". . . chihᵍ weiᵇ . . ." in early texts.[6] However, even if we take "shengᵃ" as a nominal, it can still be interpreted in a number of ways, one of which yields Dobson's translation. Some translators (e.g., Giles, Legge, Lyall, Ware, Kanaya) translate "shengᵃ" as "life," and

Graham takes it to refer to the living process.[7] T'ang Chün-i understands it as what gives life, an idea that he relates to Kao Tzu's specification of the content of *hsingᵃ* in terms of eating and having sex—
eating is what continues life in an individual, and having sex is what
continues life from generation to generation.[8] This interpretation fits
with Dobson's translation. Another possibility is to take "shengᵃ" to
refer to tendencies one has by virtue of being alive—namely, biological tendencies—and this interpretation also accords with viewing the
content of *hsingᵃ* in terms of eating and having sex. Finally, some
translators (e.g., Chai and Chai, Lau, Uchino, Yang) take "shengᵃ" to
refer to qualities one has by birth, and some commentators (e.g., Chiao
Hsün, Hu Yü-huan) explicitly take the line to be making the same
point that Hsün Tzu makes in explicating *hsingᵃ* in terms of what is
given at birth.[9]

Given the structural parallel between "shengᵃ chihᵍ weiᵇ hsingᵃ" in
6A:3a and "pai chihᵍ weiᵇ pai" in 6A:3b, the interpretation of the two
phrases has to be parallel. At least three readings of the structure "pai
N chihᵍ pai" in 6A:3c, where "*N*" is a nominal, are possible, each of
which treats the second occurrence of "pai" as a nominal. First, the
initial occurrence of "pai" may be read as adjectival, qualifying "*N*";
the whole expression then refers to the whiteness of white *N*. Second,
we can regard the initial occurrence of "pai" as verbal with "*N*" as its
object; the expression then refers to the whiteness that makes *N* white.
Third, we can regard the initial occurrence of "pai" as verbal with "*N*
chihᵍ pai" as its object; the expression then refers to treating as white
the whiteness of *N*, or treating as white the white ones among *N*.
Given the parallel between 6A:3c and 6A:3d, we may regard "*N* chihᵍ
hsingᵃ" as an abbreviation of "shengᵃ *N* chihᵍ hsingᵃ," and interpret
this expression similarly to "pai *N* chihᵍ pai."

Of the three possible readings of "pai *N* chihᵍ pai," the third is unlikely since there is no plausible parallel reading of "*N* chihᵍ hsingᵃ,"
even if we regard that phrase as an abbreviation of "shengᵃ *N* chihᵍ
hsingᵃ."[10] The way to read "shengᵃ chihᵍ weiᵇ hsingᵃ" and hence "pai
chihᵍ weiᵇ pai" has implications for the reading of "pai *N* chihᵍ pai." If
we take "shengᵃ" to refer to the life process, to the tendencies one has
by virtue of being alive, or to the qualities one has by birth, the first
reading of "pai *N* chihᵍ pai" becomes more likely; in this reading, we
can regard "*N* chihᵍ hsingᵃ" as short for "shengᵃ *N* chihᵍ hsingᵃ,"
where "shengᵃ *N*" refers to an *N* that is alive. On the other hand, if we
take "shengᵃ" to refer to that which gives life, the second reading of

"pai N chih^g pai" becomes more likely; in this reading, we can regard "N chih^g hsing^a" as short for "sheng^a N chih^g hsing^a," where "sheng^a N" refers to that which gives life to N.[11]

I am less inclined to take "sheng^a" to refer to the inborn, or the qualities one has by birth. It is not clear that "hsing^a" had acquired the meaning of the inborn at this time, and if we adopt this interpretation, it would be unclear why Mencius believed it follows from Kao Tzu's explication of *hsing^a* that the *hsing^a* of a hound, an ox, and a human being are the same. One possible suggestion is that Mencius was objecting not to Kao Tzu's explication of *hsing^a* in terms of *sheng^a* but to his accepting the comparison of "sheng^a chih^g wei^b hsing^a" to "pai chih^g wei^b pai."[12] On this proposal, that the *hsing^a* of an ox is the same as those of a hound and of a human being is not a direct consequence of the statement "sheng^a chih^g wei^b hsing^a," but a consequence of viewing "sheng^a chih^g wei^b hsing^a" as an analog of "pai chih^g wei^b pai." Although this proposal explains how Mencius could have derived the consequences that he did from Kao Tzu's position, it does so by regarding Mencius as not being opposed to Kao Tzu's explication of *hsing^a*, thereby leaving it unclear what Mencius's purpose was in 6A:3 in debating with Kao Tzu.

As for the interpretations that regard "sheng^a" as referring to the life process, to what gives life, or to the biological tendencies one has by virtue of being alive, each allows us to see why it follows from Kao Tzu's explication of *hsing^a* that the *hsing^a* of a hound, ox, and human being are the same—the biological life process, the biological tendencies that continue life or that one has by virtue of being alive, are similar in an ox, a hound, and a human being. The last two interpretations have the additional advantage that they fit better with Kao Tzu's specification in 6A:4 of the content of *hsing^a* in terms of eating and having sex; there is, as far as I can tell, insufficient textual basis for adjudicating between these two interpretations. These interpretations also allow us to see why Mencius opposed Kao Tzu's explication. As we saw in §§2.3.1–2.3.2, the Yangist conception of *hsing^a* or *sheng^a* emphasizes biological life, and the references to enriching the *hsing^a* or *sheng^a* of the common people in the *Kuo-yü* and the *Tso-chuan* have to do with people's biological needs and desires. Probably, Mencius realized that "sheng^a" when used in connection with "hsing^a" was often understood in biological terms; Kao Tzu himself cited biological tendencies like eating and having sex as the content of *hsing^a*.[13] Mencius, on the other hand, wanted to redirect attention to a way of viewing *hsing^a* that does not emphasize the biological. Instead, as seen from his query that ended the debate, he viewed the *hsing^a* of human beings as something that distinguishes them from other animals, rather than as biological tendencies common to all.[14]

4.3   The Debate with Kao Tzu About *yi^a* (Propriety) in 6A:4–5

4.3.1   *The Text*

Passages 6A:4–5 of the *Meng-tzu* contain debates about whether *yi^a* (propriety) is internal (*nei*) or external (*wai*); the debates were between Mencius and Kao Tzu (6A:4) and between Kung-tu Tzu and Meng Chi-tzu (6A:5). Mencius and Kung-tu Tzu defended the position that *yi^a* is internal, and Kao Tzu and Meng Chi-tzu that it is external. Kung-tu Tzu, who solicited Mencius's help in the debate, was probably a student of Mencius's who was defending a Mencian position. In what follows, I focus attention primarily on the way Mencius viewed the nature of the disagreement and argue that, from his perspective, to regard *yi^a* as internal is to hold the view that *yi^a* can be derived from certain features of the heart/mind. I begin by translating 6A:4–5, dividing the passages into sections (a, b, . . .) and subsections (1, 2, . . .). Where the original text can be read in different ways and where the choice between alternative readings bears on the assessment of competing interpretations, I provide alternative translations (indicated by roman numerals) to capture the different readings.

> 6A:4
> a1. Kao Tzu said, "Eating and having sex constitute *hsing^a*.
> 2. *Jen^a* is internal, not external; *yi^a* is external, not internal."
> 3. Mencius said, "Why do you say that *jen^a* is internal and *yi^a* external?"
> b1. (Kao Tzu) said, "It is old and I treat it as old;
>> (i)   *it is not that there is elderliness in me.*
>> (ii) *it is not that it gets its elderliness from me.*
> 2. This is like: it is white and I treat it as white;
>> (i)   *it is a matter of following, on the outside, its whiteness.*
>> (ii) *it is a matter of following the fact that it is made white by outside factors.*
> 3. So I call it external."
> c1. (Mencius) said,
>> (i)   *"Treating as white a horse's whiteness is not different from treating as white a person's whiteness.*

(ii) *"Treating as white the white ones among horses is not different from treating as white the white ones among people.*

(iii) *"A white horse's whiteness is not different from a white person's whiteness.*

(iv) *"The whiteness that makes a horse white is not different from the whiteness that makes a person white.*

2. I wonder if

(i) *treating as old a horse's elderliness is not different from treating as old a person's elderliness?*

(ii) *treating as old the elderly ones among horses is not different from treating as old the elderly ones among people?*

(iii) *an old horse's elderliness is not different from an old person's elderliness?*

(iv) *the elderliness that makes a horse old is not different from the elderliness that makes a person old?*

3. Moreover, do you say that it is

(i) *an old person* who is *yiᵃ*, or *one who treats him as old* who is *yiᵃ*?"

(ii) *elderliness* that is *yiᵃ*, or *treating as old* that is *yiᵃ*?"

d1. (Kao Tzu) said, "If it is my younger brother, I love him; if it is a Ch'in person's younger brother, I do not.

2. (i) *In this case, I am the one who is pleased.*

(ii) *This is to take pleasure in myself.*

(iii) *In this case, the motivating factor lies in me.*

(iv) *In this case, the explanation lies in me.*

That is why I call it internal.

3. I treat as old an old person from the Ch'u people; I also treat as old an old person from my (family).

4. (i) *In this case, the old people are the ones who are pleased.*

(ii) *This is to take pleasure in elderliness* (or: *the old people*).

(iii) *In this case, the motivating factor lies in elderliness* (or: *the old people*).

(iv) *In this case, the explanation lies in elderliness* (or: *the old people*).

That is why I call it external."

e1. (Mencius) said, "My liking a Ch'in person's roast is not different from my liking my own roast.

2. Even with mere things there are such cases; so, is there also externality in liking a roast?"

6A:5

a1. Meng Chi-tzu asked Kung-tu Tzu, "Why do you say that *yiᵃ* is internal?"

2. (Kung-tu Tzu) said, "I enact my respect. That is why I say it is internal."

b1. (Meng Chi-tzu said,) "If a person from your village is a year older than your eldest brother, whom do you respect?"

(Kung-tu Tzu) said, "I respect my eldest brother."

2. (Meng Chi-tzu said,) "In filling their cups with wine, whom do you give precedence to?"
(Kung-tu Tzu) said, "I first fill the cup of the person from my village."
3. (Meng Chi-tzu said,) "The one you respect is this; the one you treat as old is that.
· 4. So, after all, it is on the outside, not from the inside."
5. Kung-tu Tzu was unable to reply and told Mencius about this.
c1. Mencius said, "(Ask him,) 'Do you respect your uncle, or your younger brother?' He will say, 'I respect my uncle.'
2. Say, 'If your younger brother is impersonating a dead ancestor at a sacrifice, whom do you respect?' He will say, 'I respect my younger brother.'
3. You say, 'Where then is your respect for your uncle?' He will say, 'It is because of the position my younger brother occupies.'
4. You likewise say, '(In the case of the person from my village,) it is because of the position he occupies. Ordinarily, my respect is rendered to my eldest brother; on occasion, it is rendered temporarily to the person from my village.'"
d1. (Meng) Chi-tzu heard this, and said, "When you respect your uncle, it is respect; when you respect your younger brother, it is (also) respect.
2. So, after all, it is on the outside, not from the inside."
e1. Kung-tu Tzu said, "In winter one drinks hot water, in summer one drinks cold water.
2. Does that show that even drinking and eating are on the outside?"

Alternative translations have been given for 6A:4 b1, b2, c1, c2, c3, d2, d4. The problematic line in b1 is:

fei   yu   chang   yü^a   wo
not   have   *chang   yü^a*   me

I take "chang" to be a nominal, meaning "elderliness." If we interpret the structure "yu N yü^a N'" (where "N" and "N'" are nominals) to mean there being N in N', we get translation (i).[15] If we interpret it to mean getting N from N', we get translation (ii).[16]

The problematic line in b2 is:

ts'ung   ch'i^b   pai   yü^a   wai
follow   its   *pai   yü*   outside

If we interpret "pai" as a nominal meaning "whiteness," "yü^a wai" to mean "being on the outside," and the structure "V yü^a N" (where "V" is a verbal expression and "N" a nominal) to mean V-ing in/on N, we get translation (i).[17] If we interpret "pai" as a verb meaning to make white, and "*V* yü^a *N*" in the sense of being *V*-ed by *N*, we get translation (ii).[18]

The problematic line in c1 is:

yi^c yü^a pai ma chih^s pai yeh wu yi yi^c yü^a pai jen^b chih^s pai yeh

There are at least four ways of punctuating the line:

(A) *yi^c. yü^a pai ma chih^s pai yeh, wu yi yi^c yü^a pai jen^b chih^s pai yeh.*
(B) *yi^c yü^a. pai ma chih^s pai yeh, wu yi yi^c yü^a pai jen^b chih^s pai yeh.*
(C) *yi^c yü^a pai. ma chih^s pai yeh, wu yi yi^c yü^a pai jen^b chih^s pai yeh.*
(D) *yi^c yü^a pai ma chih^s pai yeh, wu yi yi^c yü^a pai jen^b chih^s pai yeh.*

None is entirely satisfactory. In (A), we get a redundant "yü^a." In (B), it is difficult to make sense of "yi^c yü^a." In (C), we lose the expected parallel between "pai ma chih^s pai" and "pai jen^b chih^s pai." (D) says that there is something different from *pai ma chih^s pai* yet not different from *pai jen^b chih^s pai*, and it is difficult to make sense of this in the context. Different proposals have been made to resolve the problem, but the general consensus of commentators is to read the line as saying that *pai ma chih^s pai* is not different from *pai jen^b chih^s pai*.[19] In light of the agreement, we need not concern ourselves with the problem of punctuation.

The other problem with c1 concerns the translation of "pai ma chih^s pai" and "pai jen^b chih^s pai." Translations (i) and (ii) read the first occurrence of "pai" in each as verbal, taking "ma chih^s pai" and "jen^b chih^s pai" as objects, and read the second occurrence of "pai" to mean whiteness and the white ones (among *ma* and *jen^b*), respectively. Translations (iii) and (iv) take the second occurrence of "pai" in each to refer to the whiteness of *pai ma* and *pai jen^b*, and read the first occurrence of "pai" as adjectival and verbal, respectively.

The problematic line in c2 is:

chang ma chih^s chang yeh wu yi yi^c yü^a chang jen^b chih^s chang

The grammatically possible translations are analogous to those for c1.[20] In the parallel structure "chang Ch'u jen^b chih^s chang" in 6A:4d3, the first occurrence of "chang" has to be read as verbal, taking "Ch'u jen^b chih^s chang" as object, and this favors adopting translation (i) or (ii).[21] However, we also saw in §4.2.2 that the parallel structure "pai *N* chih^s pai," which occurs in 6A:3c, has to be read as referring to the whiteness of *pai N*, where "pai" is interpreted either adjectivally or verbally, and this favors adopting translation (iii) or (iv). Given the conflicting evidence, I have included all four translations to accommodate all possibilities.

The problematic structure in c3 is:

chang che . . . chang chihᵍ che . . .

If we interpret ". . . che" as "one who is . . . ," we will have to interpret the first occurrence of "chang" as adjectival, and this yields translation (i).[22] If we interpret the structure ". . . che . . . che . . ." as posing alternatives, we will have to interpret the first occurrence of "chang" as a nominal, and this yields translation (ii).[23]

Finally, the problematic lines in d2 and d4 are:

shihᶜ yi wo weiᵃ yüehᵇ che yeh

and

shihᶜ yi chang weiᵃ yüehᵇ che yeh.

The natural reading yields translations d2(i) and d4(i).[24] But the structure "yi N weiᵃ yüehᵇ che yeh" can also mean one's regarding N as what is pleasurable, or one's taking pleasure in N, and this reading yields translations d2(ii) and d4(ii).[25] Although many translators have translated "yüehᵇ" as "pleasure" or "feeling," some have observed that this makes it difficult to make sense of d2 and d4.[26] One alternative is to take "yüehᵇ" to have the meaning of being moved or motivated, and this reading yields translations d2(iii) and d4(iii).[27] Another alternative is to emend "yüehᵇ" to "shuo" (explanation), and this yields translations d2(iv) and d4(iv).[28]

4.3.2   Three Major Interpretations

Of the different interpretations of the nature of the disagreement whether *yiᵃ* is internal, three are particularly common. The first takes the internality of *yiᵃ* to be the claim that an act is *yiᵃ* only if it is performed not just because it is proper, but because the agent is fully inclined to so act. Something like this interpretation has been proposed by Chu Hsi and David S. Nivison.[29] The second regards the internality of *yiᵃ* as the claim that *yiᵃ* is part of *hsingᵃ*, in the sense that human beings already share *yiᵃ* as one of the four desirable attributes or are already disposed to *yiᵃ* behavior. Chang Shih, Chiao Hsün, Tai Chen, and D. C. Lau have interpreted the idea along these lines.[30] The third regards it as the claim that one's knowledge of *yiª* derives from certain features of the heart/mind. This view has been suggested by Chiao Hsün, Wang Yang-ming, Huang Tsung-hsi, Mou Tsung-san, Hsü Fu-kuan, and T'ang Chün-i.[31] These three interpretations assign different contents to the idea that *yiª* is internal. They take it as, respectively, a claim about the agent's motivation for *yiª* behavior, a claim about shared human dispositions to *yiª* behavior, and a claim about the source of one's knowledge of *yiª*. These are different claims, even though they are related and Mencius may have subscribed to all three.

Before we assess these interpretations, let us first consider Kao Tzu's statement of his position in 6A:4a1-2. His reference to *hsingª* in 6A:4a1 suggests that his disagreement with Mencius about *yiª* is related to their disagreement about *hsingª* in 6A:1-3. Further evidence comes from the reference to *yiª* as like cups and bowls in the debate about *hsingª* (6A:1a) and from the fact that their debate about *yiª* is placed immediately after their debates about *hsingª*. We therefore have grounds for suspecting a link between Mencius's and Kao Tzu's views about *hsingª* and their views about *yiª*. The second interpretation can make sense of this link. In this interpretation, Kao Tzu's view that *yiª* is external amounts to the claim that *yiª* is not part of *hsingª*, and Mencius's view that *yiª* is internal amounts to the claim that *yiª* is part of *hsingª* and hence that *hsingª* is good. The third interpretation can also account for this link. Kao Tzu's analogy in 6A:1a illustrates his view that *hsingª* is neutral and that *yiª* is something imposed on *hsingª*, and this view fits with the externality of *yiª* understood as the claim that one has to learn *yiª* from the outside.[32] On the other hand, if *yiª* is internal in the sense that there are features of the heart/mind from which one derives knowledge of *yiª*, the presence of such features provides a sense in which *hsingª* is good, which is Mencius's position. It is less clear how the first interpretation can account for this link: that an act is *yiª* only if the agent is fully inclined to so act appears unrelated to the claim that *hsingª* is good.

The reference in 6A:4a2 to the internality of *jenª* and externality of *yiª* occurs in two other texts. The "Chieh" chapter of the *Kuan-tzu* has: "*Jenª* comes out from [or following] the inside; *yiª* is done/made from [or following] the outside [*jenª ts'ung chungᵇ ch'u, yiª ts'ung wai tso*]. *Jenª* and so one does not use the empire for one's benefit [*liᵇ*]; *yiª* and so one does not use the empire for one's reputation" (*KT* 2/16.2-3). The *Mo-tzu* has: "*Jenª* is love [*ai*]; *yiª* is benefit [*liᵇ*]. Loving and benefiting is this, the loved and the benefited is that. There is no difference between internal and external in loving and benefiting, nor in the loved and benefited. To claim that *jenᵃ* is internal and *yiᵃ* external is to pick loving and the benefited" (*MT* 43/88–90). The fact that the idea is mentioned in three texts and disputed in two of them (the *Mo-tzu* and the *Meng-tzu*) suggests that the idea was probably a common and yet controversial one. Furthermore, there was probably no agreement how the idea should be understood. The *Mo-tzu* gives one reading, and the presentation of the idea in the *Kuan-tzu* can be read in different ways. It can be interpreted as referring to a contrast between the nature of *jenᵃ* and *yiᵃ* as two ethical attributes: *jenᵃ* has to do primarily with having proper (inner) affective concern for others, whereas *yiᵃ* has to do primarily with a commitment to proper (outer) behavior.³³ It can be taken to concern what makes something a *jenᵃ* response as opposed to a *yiᵃ* response; a *jenᵃ* response has to stem from (inner) affective concern, whereas a *yiᵃ* response requires only proper (outer) behavior. And it can also be interpreted as a claim about how one tells what is *yiᵃ* as opposed to what is *jenᵃ*; whereas one's inner affective concern tells one that it is *jenᵃ* to respond in a certain way, it is by attending to external circumstances that one tells what the *yiᵃ* response is.

It may appear that the claim that *jenᵃ* is internal implies that *jenᵃ* is part of *hsingᵃ* and hence that *hsingᵃ* is good, which conflicts with Kao Tzu's position on *hsingᵃ*. However, it is unclear that Kao Tzu regarded *jenᵃ* as part of *hsingᵃ*. The claim that *jenᵃ* is internal comes immediately after his specification of eating and having sex as (at least part of) the content of *hsingᵃ*, and the fact that Kao Tzu did not also include *jenᵃ* in the content of *hsingᵃ* suggests that there is a difference between being internal and being part of *hsingᵃ*. Furthermore, even if *jenᵃ* is part of *hsingᵃ*, it still does not follow that *hsingᵃ* is good. This follows only if we assume that love of the kind described in 6A:4d1 is in the direction of goodness, but this assumption is not obvious. For example, the Mohists would regard such love as a form of discrimination that one should overcome in order to practice indiscriminate concern. Indeed, the definitions of "jenᵃ" and "t'i" (body) in the "Ching shang" and "Ching shuo shang" chapters of the *Mo-tzu* show that *jenᵃ* is viewed there as centered on the self in a way that is opposed to non-discrimination—*jenᵃ* is explained in terms of *ai* (love, concern) directed at the self (*MT* 42/4) and in terms of *t'i ai* (*MT* 40/2–3), whereas "t'i" is explained in a way that is contrasted with *chienᵃ* (non-discrimination; *MT* 40/1, 42/2) or as the part of a whole that remains after a part has been removed (*MT* 42/18–19; cf. *MT* 40/18).³⁴ Furthermore, even a Confucian would deny that *jenᵃ* as described by Kao Tzu is directed toward goodness, since it does not include concern for the brothers of others. As a number of commentators have noted, it is possible that love of the kind Kao Tzu described has no ethical content but is something that should be regulated by *yiᵃ*.[35]

The idea that *jenᵃ* is internal and *yiᵃ* external can be interpreted in different ways, depending on which of the three interpretations of the internality/externality of *yiᵃ* we adopt. The first interpretation can take the idea to claim that *jenᵃ* acts require one's being fully inclined to so act, unlike *yiᵃ* acts, which require only proper (outer) behavior. The second interpretation can understand it as the claim that human beings already share *jenᵃ* dispositions, although they do not share *yiᵃ* dispositions. In the third interpretation, it amounts to the claim that human beings do not have tendencies in the direction of *yiᵃ* and so can acquire knowledge of *yiᵃ* only from the outside, but they already share affective dispositions in the direction of *jenᵃ*.[36]

Having considered Kao Tzu's statement of his position in 6A:4a, I now turn to the actual arguments in 6A:4b–e and 6A:5a–e. I will defend the third interpretation on the grounds that it can make sense of all stages of the arguments, whereas the other two interpretations cannot.

4.3.3 *Two Major Interpretations Rejected*

Consider the first interpretation, which takes the internality of *yiᵃ* to be the claim that an act is *yiᵃ* only if one is fully inclined to so act. It cannot make sense of 6A:4b1, whether we translate "fei yu chang yüᵃ wo" as (i) or (ii). In this interpretation, what we expect Kao Tzu to say is that in performing the typical *yiᵃ* act of treating someone as old, it is not that I am inclined to treat him as old. But it is difficult to read the line in this way; to convey this idea, Kao Tzu would have to say something like "fei yu chang chihᵍ chihᵍ hsinᵃ yüᵃ wo" or "fei yu ching yüᵃ wo." As for b2, we may adopt translation (i) and take it to mean that I, in treating something as white, simply act in a way that meets some external (behavioral) criterion for treating it as white, without feeling inclined to so act. This will then illustrate the point that in performing the typical *yiᵃ* act of treating an old person as old, I similarly act in a way that meets some behavioral criterion, without feeling inclined to so act. Although this interpretation can make sense of b2, b1 still poses a problem for this reading of b2. The context of 6A:4b shows that "ts'ung ch'i^b pai yü^a wai" in b2 is supposed to be contrary to "yu chang yü^a wo" in b1, when "pai" is substituted for "chang" in the latter expression. However, this will not be the case if we adopt the reading of b2 just proposed, whether we translate "fei yu chang yü^a wo" as b1(i) or b1(ii).

This interpretation cannot make sense of d2 and d4 if we adopt translation (i) or (ii). Since d4, in this interpretation, is supposed to say that the *yi^a* act of treating an old person as old does not require the agent's being inclined to so act, it is difficult to see how the reference to the pleasure of the old person or the agent's pleasure fits. If we adopt translation (iii) or (iv), this interpretation can take d2 and d4 to be saying that a *jen^a* act is motivated/explained by the agent's love, whereas a *yi^a* act is not motivated/explained by the agent's inclinations but is compelled by external circumstances. That the interpretation can make sense of d2 and d4 only if it adopts the less literal translation (iii) or translation (iv), which involves an emendation, does not put it at a comparative disadvantage because the other two interpretations also need translation (iii) or (iv) to make sense of d2 and d4.

This interpretation also poses difficulties for understanding e2. In this interpretation, Mencius's objection to the claim that *yi^a* is external is not that it regards *yi^a* acts as requiring "external" behavior, but that it regards them as not requiring "internal" inclinations. Mencius's query "So, is there also externality in liking a roast?" (*jan tse ch'i chih yi yu wai yü*) is therefore puzzling. To make his point, Mencius would have to put his query by saying, "So, is there also no internality in liking a roast?" (*jan tse ch'i chih yi wu nei yü*). Finally, the interpretation poses a difficulty to making sense of Meng Chi-tzu's argument in 6A:5d and hence also Kung-tu Tzu's response in 6A:5e. In this interpretation, to hold that *yi^a* is external is to say that *yi^a* acts need not be accompanied by respect or other inclinations to so act. Meng Chi-tzu's observation in 6A5d, however, concerns how one's respect varies with circumstances. It is difficult to see how this fits with the first interpretation.

The second interpretation, which takes the internality of *yi^a* to be the claim that human beings already have the attribute *yi^a* or a disposition to *yi^a* behavior, also has difficulty making sense of 6A:4b1, whether we adopt translation (i) or (ii). In this interpretation, what Kao Tzu should have said is that, in treating an old person as old, it is not that one is already disposed to do so. However, it is not clear how the line "fei yu chang yüᵃ wo" can be read in this way. For reasons similar to those given for the first interpretation, the difficulty in making sense of b1 also poses a problem for the interpretation of b2.

This interpretation also has difficulty making sense of 6A:4c1–2. The first interpretation would adopt translation (i) or (ii), and Mencius would be insisting on a difference between treating an old horse as old and treating an old person as old. The difference is that the latter, but not the former, involves respect on the agent's part. In the present interpretation, however, it is difficult to see the point of c1–2. Even if it is granted that treating an old person as old involves something different from treating an old horse as old [or, if we adopt translations (iii) or (iv), that the elderliness of an old person is different from that of an old horse], this does not tell us whether human beings are already disposed to perform *yiᵃ* acts.

This second interpretation can adopt translation (iii) or (iv) to make sense of d2 and d4—it can take Kao Tzu to be saying that *jenᵃ* acts are internal because they are motivated/explained by something already in the agent, whereas this is not true of *yiᵃ* acts. It has difficulty making sense of e2, however. Since it takes Mencius to be arguing that human beings already have the attribute *yiᵃ* or a disposition to *yiᵃ* behavior, Mencius's query should have been expressed as "So, is there also no internality in liking a roast?" (*jan tse ch'i chih yi wu nei yü*). There is a similar problem with 6A:5b4 and 6A:5d2. In this interpretation, Meng Chi-tzu, in arguing for the externality of *yiᵃ*, was saying that *yiᵃ* is not already in human beings but is welded onto them from the outside. But, as seen by comparing "jenᵃ yiᵃ liᵃ chihᵇ, fei yu wai shuo wo yeh" in 6A:6, this point is more naturally expressed by saying that *yiᵃ* is "after all, from the outside, not in the inside" (*kuo yu wai, fei tsai nei*), rather than by saying, as in b4 and d2, that *yiᵃ* is "after all, on the outside, not from the inside" (*kuo tsai wai, fei yu nei*). Finally, this interpretation has difficulty making sense of Meng Chi-tzu's argument in 6A:5d, and hence also Kung-tu Tzu's response in 6A:5e. It is difficult to see how Meng Chi-tzu's observation in 6A:5d about the variation of respect with circumstances is related to the question whether *yiᵃ* is something already pertaining to human beings.

4.3.4   *A Third Interpretation Defended*

The third interpretation, which takes the internality of *yiᵃ* to be the claim that one's recognition of what is *yiᵃ* derives from certain features of the heart/mind, can make sense of all stages of the arguments in 6A:4–5. Consider 6A:4b1–2, where Kao Tzu compared two forms of behavior — treating as white something that is white, and treating as old something that is old. In the present interpretation, Kao Tzu was saying that what enables us to recognize the latter as proper resembles what enables us to recognize the former as proper. In the case of whiteness, b2 [adopting translation (ii)] makes two claims:

(p1) It is by virtue of the whiteness of a white object that we recognize the propriety of our treating it as white;

(p2) The whiteness of a white object is independent of us.

And b1 [adopting translation (ii)] claims that the same is true of our treating an old object as old:

(q1) It is by virtue of the elderliness of an old object that we recognize the propriety of our treating it as old;

(q2) The elderliness of an old object is independent of us.

By adopting options (ii) for both b1 and b2, we do justice to the fact that "ts'ung ch'iᵇ pai yüᵃ wai" is supposed to be contrary to "yu chang yüᵃ wo," when "pai" is substituted for "chang" in the latter. Since it is by virtue of the elderliness of an old object that we recognize the propriety of treating it as old, and since its elderliness is independent of us, it is by virtue of something independent of us that we recognize the propriety of treating an old object as old. And since treating an old person as old is a typical *yiᵃ* act, b3 concludes that *yiᵃ* is external in the sense that we recognize what is proper by appeal to something independent of us.

Mencius's response points to a difference between the behavior constitutive of treating an old person as old, and that constitutive of treating an old horse as old. The latter involves a mere acknowledgment of elderliness, whereas the former involves in addition respectful behavior. Adopting translation (i) or (ii), c1 says:

(p3) The way to treat a white horse as white is like the way to treat a white person as white.

Adopting translation (i) or (ii), c2 implies:

(q3)′ The way to treat an old horse as old is unlike the way to treat an old person as old.

But if we recognize the propriety of treating something as old solely by virtue of the elderliness in it, then, given that the same quality of elderliness exists in both an old horse and an old person, the same kind of behavior would be proper with regard to both. Hence, (q3)' implies that (q1) is false in either the case of a horse or that of a person. But since the behavior involved in treating an old person as old is in part (the part that constitutes the mere acknowledgment of elderliness) like the behavior involved in treating an old horse as old, it follows that we should reject (q1), although we may retain (q2), in the case of a person. That is, although we may accept that the person's elderliness is independent of us ("fei yu chang yü^a wo"), we have to deny that it is by virtue of the elderliness that we recognize the propriety of treating the old person as old (that is, deny "ts'ung ch'i^b chang yü^a wai"). Since, as Mencius suggested in c3 [adopting translation (ii)], *yi^a* pertains not to the old person's elderliness, which [according to (q2)] is independent of us, but to our treating the person as old, which has not been shown [contrary to (q1)] to be something we recognize as proper by appeal to facts independent of us, Kao Tzu had failed to show that *yi^a* is external in the sense under consideration.

Conceding that (q1) is not true in the case of an old person, Kao Tzu could still claim:

(r1) It is by virtue of the old-person-ness (that is, the quality of being an old person) of an old person that we recognize the propriety of treating the person as old;

(r2) The person's old-person-ness is independent of us.

Mencius's objection to (q1) does not work against (r1) since old-person-ness is exhibited only in old people, not in horses. To formulate a parallel objection to (r1), Mencius would need:

(r3)' The way to treat one old person as old is unlike the way to treat another old person as old.

But, in d3, Kao Tzu denied (r3)' and claimed instead:

(r3) The way to treat one old person as old is like the way to treat another old person as old.

The truth of (r3) provides support for (r1) since (r1) can explain why (r3) is true — if it is by virtue of the old-person-ness of an old person that we recognize the propriety of our treating the person as old, then, since the old-person-ness of one old person is like that of another, (r3) follows. Kao Tzu's contrasting of the case of old-person-ness with that of brotherhood reinforces his argument for (r1). Section d1 says that, in the case of brotherhood, we restrict our loving treatment to our own younger brothers. Section d3 says that, in the case of old-person-ness, we find it improper not to extend the same respectful treatment to all old people. Unless (r1) is true, there appears to be no other explanation for this. But if both (r1) and (r2) are true, then it is by virtue of something independent of us that we recognize the propriety of our treating an old person as old. The interpretation under consideration can make sense of d2 and d4 only if we adopt options (iii) or (iv). It takes d2 and d4 to be stressing the point that in recognizing the propriety of treating old people as old, that which moves us or that which explains the recognition has to do with their elderliness, which is external to us, unlike our love for our younger brothers, which is explained by, or which involves our being moved by, something in us.

Mencius's response in e1–2 was to deny that (r1) is needed to explain the observations Kao Tzu made in d1 and d3. We like a roast whether it belongs to us or to someone else, but we do not do so because we recognize it as proper to like a roast by virtue of its quality of being a roast, which is independent of us. This idea Mencius puts by saying that there is no externality in liking a roast, an observation that poses a problem for the other two interpretations. Rather, as Kao Tzu would presumably also agree, it is explained by the fact that we have a taste for roast in general, without regard to whether it belongs to us or to another. Likewise, in the case of treating old people as old, we recognize that it is improper not to extend the same respectful treatment to all old people because we are already inclined to treat old people in general with respect, whether they belong to our own family or not. Therefore we do not need (r1) to explain Kao Tzu's observations in d1 and d3.

Let us turn next to 6A:5. In the present interpretation of the internality of yi^a, one recognizes certain forms of behavior as proper by virtue of certain features of the heart/mind. One typical example Mencius gave for such features is respect for elders (7A:15), and a2 can be read as saying that the internality of yi^a is explained by the fact that one recognizes that one's respectful treatment of elders is yi^a by virtue of its being something one is inclined to do out of one's respect. The claim can be refuted by either of two observations:

(i)   Not all acts of respectful treatment of elders are acts out of respect; or

(ii)   Even if they are, respect for elders is not something people already share, but is something people regard as proper to have by virtue of circumstances independent of them.

Meng Chi-tzu deployed the first line of argument in b and the second in d.

In b, Meng Chi-tzu tried to convince Kung-tu Tzu that there are situations in which one respects one's eldest brother more, and yet the proper behavior is to treat another older person with greater respect by filling the latter's cup first. If this is right, then the act of filling the cup of the older person first cannot derive its propriety from our respect. From this, Meng Chi-tzu drew the conclusion that propriety lies on the outside in the sense that it is not something one derives from features of the heart/mind. This he put by saying in b4 that propriety is "on the outside, not from the inside," an observation that poses a problem for the second interpretation of the internality of *yi^a*.

To defend the internality of *yi^a* against this line of argument, one has to show that in filling the cup of the older person first, one in fact has more respect for him. This Mencius tried to do in c. One ordinarily respects one's uncle more than one's younger brother, but on certain ceremonial occasions, for example, when the latter is impersonating an ancestor, one has for the duration of these occasions greater respect for the younger brother because of one's greater respect for the ancestor the younger brother is impersonating. Likewise, one ordinarily respects one's eldest brother more than an older person from one's village. However, on certain ceremonial occasions, for example, when one is pouring wine at a gathering, one has for the duration of these occasions greater respect for the latter. Hence, contrary to Meng Chi-tzu's suggestion, the propriety of first filling the cup of the latter may well derive from one's greater respect.

In his response, Mencius made use of the fact that the object of one's greater respect may vary with circumstances. These circumstances are themselves independent of one's respect, and this allowed Meng Chi-tzu to resort to the second line of argument. In d, he argued that since the object of our greater respect varies with circumstances independent of us, it follows that whom we respect more is itself a function of external circumstances. But then it is from these external circumstances that we derive the propriety of our treating certain people with greater respect. Thus, it seems, propriety lies on the outside after all.

Kung-tu Tzu's response in e was to give what he took to be an example in which the objects of our preference vary with external circumstances and yet the variation itself is not something we recognize as proper by virtue of these circumstances. According to him, we just prefer to drink hot water in winter and cold water in summer; although our preferences vary with external circumstances, they are a matter of taste and not preferences we regard as proper to have by virtue of external circumstances. As commentators have pointed out, this analogy does not work well since, unlike Mencius's roast example in 6A:4e, it is more plausible to say of Kung-tu Tzu's example that the preferences involved are responses to external circumstances.[37] But Kung-tu Tzu took the example to illustrate the point that although the objects of our greater respect may vary with external circumstances, it does not follow that our greater respect is something we regard as proper to have by virtue of such circumstances. Rather, the variation may be a result of the way we ourselves are constituted, and hence Meng Chi-tzu's argument does not show that propriety lies on the outside.

The present interpretation thus allows us to make sense of all stages of the arguments in 6A:4–5. Furthermore, it shows how the arguments in 6A:4 and those in 6A:5 are related in an interesting way. In 6A:4, Kao Tzu defended the externality of *yiª* by pointing out that similarity in external circumstances calls for similarity in what counts as proper; if two people are both old, then propriety demands that we treat both respectfully. In 6A:5, Meng Chi-tzu defended the externality of *yiª* by pointing out that variation in external circumstances calls for variation in what counts as proper; although I ordinarily respect my uncle more, the position my younger brother occupies at a sacrifice may make it proper for me to respect my brother more. These two lines of argument complement each other by showing that what counts as proper is tied to circumstances independent of us. This is then supposed to show that we recognize what is proper by virtue of such circumstances.

In response, both Mencius and Kung-tu Tzu appealed to examples in which the same sort of tie obtains between our behavior and external circumstances, but in which it is less plausible to say that we recognize such behavior as proper by virtue of external circumstances. Both used examples of tastes to illustrate their point, and some have suggested that since Kao Tzu himself admitted in 6A:4a1 that eating is part of *hsingª*, the examples of tastes are particularly appropriate because Kao Tzu would have to admit that such tastes are part of *hsing^a* and are not mere responses to external circumstances.[38] But this is not an entirely satisfactory explanation of the choice of examples. Kung-tu Tzu used taste as an example in his debate with Meng Chi-tzu, even though the latter had not expressed any views about *hsing^a*. And although Kao Tzu admitted that eating is part of *hsing^a*, this does not commit him to saying that tastes for food or drink of certain specific kinds are also part of *hsing^a*.

An alternative explanation of the choice of examples is that they help illustrate Mencius's own position; in 6A:7, Mencius himself used the example of taste to illustrate his views. It is by virtue of the tastes we have that we can tell that certain kinds of food or drink are delicious; similarly, it is by virtue of certain predispositions of the heart/mind that we can tell that certain forms of behavior are proper. Furthermore, the examples help illustrate the point that this view about *yi^a* is compatible with the observations that similarity in response is called for by similar external circumstances (6A:4e), and variation in response is called for by varied external circumstances (6A:5e). Just as parallel observations are true of tastes without affecting the point that it is by virtue of our tastes that we regard certain kinds of food or drink as delicious, the view that *yi^a* is internal is compatible with these observations, which may well be explained by the fact that the responses stemming from the relevant predispositions of the heart/mind are themselves sensitive to external circumstances.[39]

4.3.5 *Further Comments*

My strategy in defending the proposed interpretation is to show that it makes sense of all stages of the debates in 6A:4–5, whereas the other interpretations cannot. It is obviously impossible to consider all possible interpretations, and I have chosen to focus on three common ones. To the best of my knowledge, none of the other interpretations found in the literature can account for all stages of the debates. For example, consider two other interpretations offered by Chu Hsi. He sometimes proposes that to regard *yi^a* as external (internal) is to lack (have) concern for *yi^a* (MTCC 2A:2, 6A:4; YL 1264). As an interpretation of Mencius's way of viewing the debate, this is unlikely to be correct, since it is difficult to see how it can make sense of the arguments in 6A:4–5.[40] In fact, Chu's attributing to Kao Tzu a lack of concern for *yi^a* is based on a debatable interpretation of a maxim of Kao Tzu's cited in 2A:2, which I will consider in §4.4, rather than on the actual text of 6A:4–5. Elsewhere, however, Chu proposes a different interpretation:

> If we just take *yiᵃ* to mean appropriateness, then *yiᵃ* appears to be on the outside. We need to follow Master Ch'eng's words that *yiᵃ* concerns our dealings with things, and that which deals with things is in the heart/mind rather than on the outside. . . . For although the appropriateness of things is on the outside, that with which we deal with them and make them appropriate is on the inside. (YL 1219)

Here, Chu is referring to the traditional explication of "yiᵃ" as appropriateness. He thinks that to claim that *yiᵃ* is internal is to say that "yiᵃ" refers not to such external things as appropriateness or to the objects of *yiᵃ* behavior (cf. MTCC 6A:5a2), but to proper behavior, which is internal in the sense that it originates from the heart/mind. A similar interpretation has been proposed by Chao Ch'i (CC 6A:4) and other commentators.[41]

There is some textual support for this interpretation. In 6A:4c3 [adopting translation (ii)], which Chu Hsi (YL 1378) regards as the crucial sentence explaining the internality of *yiᵃ*, Mencius appeared to be insisting that "yiᵃ" refers to the proper behavior of treating an old person as old, rather than to such external things as elderliness. Also, Kung-tu Tzu explained the internality of *yiᵃ* in terms of enacting one's respect in 6A:5a2, and Chu Hsi (MTCC 6A:5a2) takes this to mean that *yiᵃ* is internal in the sense that "yiᵃ" refers to enacting the respect in one's heart/mind, rather than to the object of one's respect.

However, although it can make sense of parts of 6A:4–5, there are three problems with this as an interpretation of Mencius's view of what is at stake in the debates. First, Mencius sometimes seemed to use "yiᵃ" to refer to a desirable quality of actions or relations, as, for example, when he spoke of *yiᵃ* as the standard of speech and behavior (*M* 4B:11), or a quality pertaining to the relation between the ruler and the ruled (*M* 3A:4). If so, it would be unlikely for Mencius to hold that "yiᵃ" does not refer to such external things as appropriateness. Second, in this interpretation, the internality/externality of *yiᵃ* concerns primarily the use of the term "yiᵃ." However, Mencius said in 2A:2 that Kao Tzu's view that *yiᵃ* is external had serious consequences for ethical development, and it is unlikely that endorsing a claim about the use of a term can have such consequences. Finally, this interpretation poses problems for making sense of all stages of the debates in 6A:4–5. For example, when Kao Tzu and Meng Chi-tzu defended the externality of *yiᵃ* in 6A:4b, d and in 6A:5b, respectively, both invoked certain observations about the paradigmatic *yiᵃ* behavior of treating an old person as old. It is difficult to make sense of this if what they are defending is the claim that the term "yiᵃ" refers to things other than proper behavior.

To sum up, I am not aware of any interpretation other than the proposed one that can make sense of all stages of the debates. This I take to provide support for the proposed interpretation and hence for believing that Mencius held the view that the recognition of *yiᵃ* derives from certain features of the heart/mind. In this interpretation, Mencius regarded his disagreement with Kao Tzu in 6A:4 as an argument whether our recognition of *yiᵃ* derives from circumstances that obtain independently of us or from the predispositions of our heart/mind. Since Mencius spoke as if Kao Tzu also acknowledged that it is appropriate to treat an old person as old in a way that goes beyond a recognition of elderliness, Mencius probably took Kao Tzu to have a concern for *yiᵃ* behavior as exemplified in respectful treatment of old people. As we saw in §4.2.1, his response to Kao Tzu in 6A:1 also shows that he believed Kao Tzu to have a concern for *jenᵃ yiᵃ*.

An interesting question is whether there might be room for Chu Hsi's interpretation of Kao Tzu's claim that *yiᵃ* is external as demonstrating a lack of concern for *yiᵃ* if we bracket Mencius's contribution to the debate and confine our attention to Kao Tzu's own presentation of his position in 6A:4. As far as I can see, the only comments of Kao Tzu that might pose a difficulty for such an interpretation are his references in 6A:4b1 to treating as elderly someone who is elderly and in 6A:4d3 to one's equal treatment of an old person from the Ch'u people or from one's family. Since respectful treatment of elders is a paradigmatic example of *yiᵃ* behavior, and since Kao Tzu spoke as if he was endorsing this kind of behavior, these parts of the passage seem to show a concern for *yiᵃ*.

To avoid this conclusion, one might, on the basis of Kao Tzu's comparison of treating an old person as old to treating a white object as white, suggest that Kao Tzu was talking about treating an old person as old in the sense of a mere acknowledgment of elderliness, without involving the kind of respectful behavior that Mencius regarded as part of a *yiᵃ* response.[42] Although this is an interesting suggestion, I am disinclined to accept it since I am aware of no instance in early texts in which a mere acknowledgment of some quality of an object is characterized as *yiᵃ* behavior. Furthermore, when Meng Chi-tzu defended the externality of *yiᵃ* in 6A:5, he mentioned pouring wine for someone first as an example of what is involved in treating someone as old, showing that treating someone as old involves more than a mere acknowledgment of elderliness. Since we do not know how Meng Chi-tzu and Kao Tzu were related, it remains possible that they had different conceptions of what it is to treat someone as old. But, given the way Kao Tzu's arguments in 6A:4 and Meng Chi-tzu's arguments in 6A:5 complement each other, it seems likely that the two shared a common understanding of *yiᵃ* behavior. Thus, even if we bracket Mencius's response, there is reason for thinking that Kao Tzu might in fact have a concern for *yiᵃ*. This observation will come into play when we consider the question of Kao Tzu's affiliation in §4.4.4; for now, I turn to Mencius's comments on Kao Tzu's position in 2A:2.

4.4   Mencius's Rejection of Kao Tzu's Maxim in 2A:2

4.4.1   *Kao Tzu's Maxim*

In 2A:2, after saying to Kung-sun Ch'ou that he had attained an unmoved heart/mind at the age of 40, Mencius added that Kao Tzu had attained an unmoved heart/mind before or at an earlier age than himself. When asked about the difference between his unmoved heart/mind and Kao Tzu's, Mencius quoted a maxim of the latter:

pu	*teᵇ*	*yüᵃ*	*yen,*	*wu*	*ch'iu*	*yüᵃ*	*hsinᵃ*
not	*teᵇ*	in	*yen,*	don't	seek	in	heart/mind
pu	*teᵇ*	*yüᵃ*	*hsinᵃ,*	*wu*	*ch'iu*	*yüᵃ*	*ch'iᵃ*
not	*teᵇ*	in	heart/mind,	don't	seek	in	vital energies

Mencius then expressed agreement with its second half but disagreement with its first half. He went on to talk about the relation between *chihᶜ* (directions of the heart/mind) and *ch'iᵃ* (vital energies) and methods of self-cultivation. In the course of doing so, he claimed that he knew *yen* (words, speech, doctrines) and criticized Kao Tzu for failing to know *yiᵃ* because he regarded *yiᵃ* as external.

Commentators differ in their interpretations of Kao Tzu's maxim. Crucial to its interpretation are the characters "yen" and "teᵇ," which I have left untranslated. Most commentators take "yen" to refer to words or speech, but they interpret "teᵇ" differently, as meaning "get," "do well," or "understand." Since 2A:2 contains only Mencius's comments on the maxim but not Kao Tzu's, I focus primarily on understanding Mencius's interpretation of it. Below I give reasons for rejecting a number of interpretations found in the literature and then defend the interpretation that, from Mencius's perspective, his disagreement with Kao Tzu had to do with their different views about the relation between *yiᵃ* and the heart/mind (*hsinᵃ*). More specifically, Mencius held and Kao Tzu rejected the position that one's recognition of *yiᵃ* derives from certain features of the heart/mind.

4.4.2 *Three Interpretations Rejected*

Chao Ch'i (C) interprets "teᵇ" to mean "get," and "pu teᵇ yüᵃ yen" and "pu teᵇ yüᵃ hsinᵃ" to mean that one fails to get good opinions of oneself from, respectively, the words and the heart/mind of others. Also, he takes "ch'iᵃ" to be short for "tz'uᵃ ch'iᵃ," meaning one's countenance and tone when speaking. According to him, Kao Tzu's maxim says:

> "If others have disapproving words for me, then I do not seek goodness (good opinions of me) in their heart/mind; I am just angry at them. . . . And if they have a disapproving heart/mind, then, even if they speak to me with good countenance and tone, I still am just angry at them."

Sun Shih basically follows Chao Ch'i's interpretation, with the following addition: if others have disapproving words (or heart/mind), then they will also have a disapproving heart/mind (or countenances and tone), and there is no point in seeking in them an approving heart/mind (or countenances and tone).[43] Chiao Hsün also follows Chao's interpretation, but justifies it by taking "teᵇ" to mean "do well," as in "pu teᵇ yüᵃ chün" (not doing well with regard to the ruler). Thus, "pu teᵇ yüᵃ yen" and "pu teᵇ yüᵃ hsinᵃ" refer to one's not doing well with regard to others' words and heart/mind; that is, not receiving good opinions from their words and heart/mind. In this interpretation, the disagreement of Mencius and Kao Tzu over the first half of the maxim concerns whether there may be good opinions of me in others' heart/mind should they speak disapprovingly of me.

Chu Hsi (MTCC; YL 1235) offers a different interpretation: if my words are in error, I should not worry about it or seek what is correct in my heart/mind; and if my heart/mind is dissatisfied, I should not seek help from my *ch'iᵃ*. Probably, Chu interprets "teᵇ" to mean "do well" and thus "pu teᵇ yüᵃ yen" and "pu teᵇ yüᵃ hsinᵃ" to mean that I do not do well, respectively, in my words (they are in error) and my heart/mind (it is dissatisfied). Unlike Chao Ch'i, Chu takes "yen" and "hsin^a" to refer to my words and my heart/mind, rather than the words and the heart/mind of others. Chang Shih has a similar interpretation. In this view, the disagreement between Mencius and Kao Tzu concerns whether one should worry about the correctness of one's speech. According to Chu Hsi (MTCC 6A:4), Kao Tzu constantly shifted positions in his debates with Mencius in 6A:1–4, and this shows that he was concerned only with winning debates and not with the correctness of what he said.

A different interpretation is found in D. C. Lau's translation of the maxim. Lau interprets "te^b" as "understand" and translates the maxim as "If you fail to understand words, do not worry about this in your heart; if you fail to understand in your heart, do not seek satisfaction in your ch'i^a." A similar interpretation can be found in Hattori and Uchino. Here, the disagreement between Mencius and Kao Tzu concerns whether one should worry about what one fails to understand. Both Lau's and Chu Hsi's interpretations regard Kao Tzu as having a lack of concern for understanding words or the correctness of one's own words; similar interpretations have been offered by, among others, Wang Fu-chih, Hsü Fu-kuan, and Lao Ssu-kuang.[44]

These three interpretations may appear to take the first half of Kao Tzu's maxim to express a rather uninteresting position, as saying that disapproval in speech implies disapproval in the heart/mind or as reflecting a lack of seriousness toward understanding or speech. If so, these interpretations would be unlikely, since there is reason to think that Kao Tzu's maxim has more substance to it. His defense of his position in 6A:1–4 and the fact that Mencius engaged in elaborate debates with him convey the impression that he was a serious thinker, and the fact that Mencius did not feel a need to explain the maxim suggests that it was probably a well-known teaching of Kao Tzu's.[45] Furthermore, after citing the maxim in the course of explaining the difference between his unmoved heart/mind and Kao Tzu's, Mencius then went on to discuss self-cultivation. This shows that their disagreement concerning the first half of the maxim is related to differences in their goals and methods of self-cultivation.[46] However, it is not entirely clear that these three interpretations are committed to construing the maxim as trivial. For example, in taking the first half of the maxim to reflect a lack of concern for correctness in understanding or speech, one may regard this lack of concern as stemming from a seriously thought-out position, such as that associated with the Taoist movement. Indeed, both Wang Fu-chih and Hsü Fu-kuan explicitly compare Kao Tzu's attitude toward words to the Taoist position.

Still, I think there are two considerations against these as interpretations of Mencius's views of the maxim. First, in his subsequent elaboration on his differences from Kao Tzu, he referred to Kao Tzu's view that *yiᵃ* is external, claiming that this explained why Kao Tzu did not know *yiᵃ*. This shows that there is a connection between the first half of the maxim (with which Mencius disagreed) and Kao Tzu's view that *yiᵃ* is external. One objection to these interpretations is that it is difficult to see how they can account for this connection. Chu Hsi sees the need to account for this connection, and his interpretation of the externality of *yiᵃ* is guided by his understanding of Kao Tzu's maxim. Thus, having interpreted the first half of the maxim to mean a lack of concern with the correctness of what one says, he goes on to interpret the externality of *yiᵃ* as an expression of a disregard for *yiᵃ* (MTCC 2A:2, 6A:4; YL 1264). However, as I discussed in §4.3.5, this is implausible as an interpretation of the way Mencius viewed the internality/externality of *yiᵃ*, since it cannot make sense of all stages of the debates in 6A:4–5.

Second, these interpretations have difficulty relating the second half of the maxim to Mencius's subsequent discussion of the relation between *chihᶜ* (directions of the heart/mind) and *ch'iᵃ* (vital energies). The placement of this discussion immediately after Mencius's comment on Kao Tzu's maxim shows that it was supposed to explain Mencius's position. Moreover, since *chihᶜ* is something pertaining to the heart/mind, the discussion is presumably intended to explain the second half of the maxim, which concerns the relation between the heart/mind and *ch'iᵃ*. In the three interpretations under consideration, the second half of the maxim is supposed to say that we should be angry at others' disapproving heart/mind even if they speak with good countenance and tone, that we should not ease our dissatisfied heart/mind with help from *ch'iᵃ*, or that we should not seek satisfaction in *ch'iᵃ* if our heart/mind fails to understand. It is difficult to see how, based on these interpretations, the discussion of *chihᶜ* and *ch'iᵃ* helps explain the second half of the maxim.

4.4.3 *An Alternative Interpretation Defended*

Each of these interpretations takes "yen" to refer to words or speech. But, as we saw in §2.2.2, "yen" is sometimes used in the *Lun-yü* and the *Mo-tzu* to refer to doctrines or teachings. It is also used in the *Meng-tzu* to refer to the teachings of Yang Chu and Mo Tzu (3B:9) and of Kao Tzu (6A:1). And, as David S. Nivison and T'ang Chün-i have independently observed, it is likely that "yen" is also used in this way in 2A:2.[47] When asked how he excelled Kao Tzu, Mencius said that he knew *yen*. He then explained what he meant by saying that he could tell the fault in different kinds of faulty *tz'u^a* (words, teachings), to which he ascribed serious consequences for government. A similar idea is found in 3B:9, where he discussed the *yen* (teachings, doctrines) of Yang Chu and Mo Tzu. This shows that "yen" and "tz'u^a" in these contexts probably refer to ethical doctrines, and to know *yen* is to be able to distinguish between correct and incorrect ethical doctrines. Knowing *yen* is important for two reasons. Faulty *yen* can lead to disastrous consequences—Kao Tzu's *yen* is said to bring disaster on *jen^a yi^a* or to lead people to regard *jen^a yi^a* as a disaster (6A:1), and the *yen* of Yang Chu and that of Mo Tzu are said to block the path of *jen^a yi^a* (3B:9). Knowing *yen* enables one to tell the faults in *yen* and thereby helps to oppose faulty *yen*. Furthermore, one's *yen* reflects what is in one's heart/mind; for example, the *Tso-chuan* notes in the political context that the direction of one's heart/mind determines one's *yen* (*TC* 624/18). Hence, by knowing a person's *yen*, one can also come to understand the person (cf. *LY* 20.3).

Given the link noted in §2.2.2 between *yen* and *yi^a*, it is likely that "yen" in the context of 2A:2 has to do with *yi^a*, which ethical doctrines are about. Support for this observation comes from the fact that after saying that he excelled Kao Tzu in knowing *yen*, Mencius criticized Kao Tzu for not knowing *yi^a*. Since Mencius used "yen" to refer to doctrines about *yi^a* in the context of 2A:2, it is likely that, at least from Mencius's point of view, "yen" in Kao Tzu's maxim also refers to teachings about *yi^a*.

As for "te^b," it is used in conjunction with "ch'iu" in several passages in the *Meng-tzu*, and each of the three senses of "te^b" described above can be found in these passages. First, "te^b" has the sense of "to get" in the references to "ch'iu tse te^b chih^g" (seek it and one will get it) in 6A:6 and 7A:3, and it is also used in other passages in the sense of getting what one seeks (2B:4, 3B:6, 5B:7, 7B:30).[48] Second, "te^b" has the sense of "to do well" in such contexts as "pu te^b yü^a chün" (not do well with regard to the ruler) in 5A:1 (cf. 4A:28, 7B:14), and "ch'iu" can mean "to seek" in the sense of "to make demands on," as in the use of "ch'iu" in 7B:32 in connection with the demands that one makes of others. The two characters are used together in these senses in 4A:4: "When one does not *teᵇ* [do well] in one's actions, one should turn back and *ch'iu* [seek in, make demands on] oneself."[49] Third, "*teᵇ*" has the sense of "to understand" when used with "ch'iu" in 1A:7; in connection with replacing the ox with a lamb, King Hsüan said that "having done it, I turn back and *ch'iu* [seek it], but do not *teᵇ* [understand] my own heart/mind." These three senses are related since the last two are themselves a matter of getting favorable responses or getting the proper understanding of things.

Although I am more inclined to the first interpretation of "*teᵇ*" and "ch'iu," because they are used more often in this sense in the *Meng-tzu*, there seems insufficient textual evidence to adjudicate between the three interpretations. However, once we agree that "yen" has to do with doctrines about yiᵃ, there might not be that much difference between the three interpretations. In these interpretations, the first half of the maxim says that one should not seek *yiᵃ* in the heart/mind or make demands on the heart/mind if one does not get *yiᵃ* from doctrines or does not understand or do well in relation to doctrines about *yiᵃ*. In any of these interpretations, Kao Tzu's view is that *yiᵃ* cannot be obtained from the heart/mind if one does not obtain it from doctrines.[50] Since Mencius rejected the first half of the maxim, it follows that he regarded *yiᵃ* as something that one derives from the heart/mind.

As for the second half of the maxim, Kao Tzu's observation in 6A:4 that *jenᵃ* is internal and *yiᵃ* external might suggest that whereas the first half of the maxim concerns *yiᵃ*, the second half concerns *jenᵃ*.[51] In this proposal, the two halves of the maxim together make the point that *jenᵃ* is internal and *yiᵃ* external to the heart/mind. However, the fact that Mencius went on to talk about *yiᵃ* in explaining the second half of the maxim suggests that the second half may also be about *yiᵃ*. That the same thing is under consideration in the two halves of the maxim also gains some support from a passage in the *Chuang-tzu*, which I consider in the next section and which refers to listening neither with the ear nor with the heart/mind, but with *ch'iᵃ* (CT 4/26–28). The continuity running through the references to the ear, the heart/mind, and *ch'iᵃ* suggests that it is the same thing that is at issue, and the parallel with Kao Tzu's maxim in turn suggests that it is the same thing that is at stake in both halves of the maxim. Hence, it is likely that the second half of the maxim is saying that one should not seek *yiᵃ* from or make demands on *ch'iᵃ* if one does not obtain *yiᵃ* from the heart/mind.[52] However, the main claim of my discussion—that Mencius regarded *yiª* as something derived from the heart/mind—is based only on the proposed interpretation of Mencius's disagreement with the first half of the maxim and does not depend on this interpretation of the second half.

Something close to this interpretation of Mencius's understanding of Kao Tzu's maxim has been proposed by Huang Tsung-hsi (1/ 14b.7–15b.1; cf. 2/55a.1–5), David S. Nivison, and T'ang Chün-i and suggested by an unknown individual to Chu Hsi (MTHW 3/2a.9– 3a.10), who dismisses the suggestion.[53] The proposed interpretation has four advantages. First, it presents Kao Tzu's maxim as expressing a substantive position about the ethical life—the first half concerns how one comes to know *yiª*, and the second half concerns shaping one's motivations in accordance with *yiª*. This does justice to the observation that Kao Tzu was a serious thinker and explains why Mencius believed that his disagreement with Kao Tzu resulted in differences in their methods of self-cultivation.

Second, the proposed interpretation fits with the way Mencius viewed his disagreement with Kao Tzu concerning the internality/externality of *yiª*. From Mencius's perspective, Kao Tzu's view that *yiª* is external is a rejection of the idea that *yiª* can be derived from the heart/mind, and this explains why, in the first half of the maxim, Kao Tzu opposed seeking *yiª* from the heart/mind. Mencius's rejection of the first half of the maxim shows that he believed that *yiª* can be derived from the heart/mind, a position that he expressed by saying that *yiª* is internal.

Third, the proposed interpretation explains how the second half of the maxim is related to Mencius's subsequent discussion of the relation between the directions of the heart/mind and the vital energies. In this interpretation, Kao Tzu believed that having come to know *yiª* through ethical doctrines, one's knowledge of *yiª* helps set the directions of the heart/mind. These directions then guide the vital energies to shape them in an ethical direction; this, as we have seen, is the way Mencius elaborated on the relation between the directions of the heart/mind and the vital energies. But if the heart/mind does not know *yiª*, there is no point in seeking *yiª* in the vital energies because the vital energies do not themselves have an ethical direction; rather, they are only a source of motivational strength requiring guidance from the heart/mind.

Finally, the proposed interpretation enables us to make sense of Mencius's observation in 2A:2 that Kao Tzu did not know *yiᵃ* despite having attained an unmoved heart/mind. What Kao Tzu did was to obtain *yiᵃ* from ethical doctrines, impose it on the heart/mind, and then let it guide *ch'iᵃ*. By firmly holding to certain doctrines and shaping his motivations accordingly, Kao Tzu attained an unmoved heart/mind in the sense that he was firmly committed to the doctrines he endorsed.[54] Mencius, in saying that his strong points (presumably by comparison to Kao Tzu's) were that he knew *yen* and was good at nourishing *ch'iᵃ*, was saying by implication that Kao Tzu did not know *yiᵃ* (which *yen* is about) and that Kao Tzu was not good at nourishing *ch'iᵃ*. Kao Tzu did not know *yiᵃ* because he regarded it as external and was therefore mistaken about its source, and he was not good at nourishing *ch'iᵃ* because he was helping *ch'iᵃ* grow by imposing a mistaken conception of *yiᵃ* from the outside. The observation that *ch'iᵃ* will collapse if it does not unite with *tao* (the Way) and *yiᵃ* suggests that Mencius probably thought that Kao Tzu's unmoved heart/mind would not last, since it was not rooted in a correct conception of *yiᵃ*.

So far, my discussion has concerned how Mencius understood Kao Tzu's maxim as seen from his comments on it; I have defended the proposed interpretation on the grounds that, by comparison to other interpretations, it makes better sense of things said by Mencius in relation to the maxim. However, if we bracket Mencius's comments and confine attention just to the maxim itself, there is not much in it that allows us to adjudicate between the different interpretations. Hence, my objections to the other interpretations are objections to them only as interpretations of Mencius's understanding of Kao Tzu's maxim, and this leaves open the possibility that one of these interpretations may well describe Kao Tzu's own understanding of the maxim.

Having discussed the passages in the *Meng-tzu* that refer to Kao Tzu, I turn now to the issue of Kao Tzu's affiliation. I begin by trying to locate Kao Tzu's thinking in the intellectual scene of the fourth to early third centuries B.C. by considering the "Chieh" and "Nei yeh" (along with "Hsin shu hsia") chapters of the *Kuan-tzu*, as well as parts of the *Chuang-tzu*.

4.4.4 *Kao Tzu and His Affiliation*

Following A. C. Graham and W. Allyn Rickett, I take the "Chieh" chapter to date probably to the fourth or early third century B.C.[55] The chapter has a generally Confucian tone. Its main theme is that proper government depends on the appointment of officials with good character and ability, an idea expressed in both this chapter (*KT* 2/16.9) and the *Lun-yü* (*LY* 12.22) in terms of the notion *chihᵃ jenᵇ* (know and appreciate a person). Appointment of the right kind of officials results in the ruler's not having to take active part in government, an idea expressed in terms of the ruler's not having to move (*pu tung*) in the "Chieh" chapter (*KT* 2/16.6–8) and in terms of not acting (*wu weiᵃ*) in the *Lun-yü* (*LY* 15.5). The "Chieh" chapter also contains the idea that goodness (*shan*) leads to submission of the people only if one uses it to nourish the people but not to vanquish them (*KT* 2/18.13–14); a similar idea can be found in the *Meng-tzu* (*M* 4B:16).[56] Furthermore, *jenᵃ* is explicated in terms of filial piety, obedience to elder brothers, conscientiousness (*chungᵃ*), and trustworthiness (*hsinᵇ*), all of which are Confucian ideas (*KT* 2/16.11–12).

In addition to these Confucian ideas, the chapter describes *shengᵃ* (life) in terms of the senses and movements and in terms of the six emotions, which are related to the six *ch'iᵃ*, showing that it probably has a biological conception of *shengᵃ* (*KT* 2/15.14–16.1). As Graham has observed, it is possible that the reference to *shengᵃ* in the "Chieh" chapter is also a reference to *hsingᵃ*, although the chapter uses "*shengᵃ*" instead of "*hsingᵃ*" because "*hsingᵃ*" is conceived of in biological terms and hence viewed as constituted by *shengᵃ*.[57] This observation gains support from the parallel between the characterization of *shengᵃ* in this chapter and Kao Tzu's characterization of *hsingᵃ*. The "Chieh" chapter describes *shengᵃ* as having resources but no direction (*KT* 2/15.10); this is similar to Kao Tzu's comparison of *hsingᵃ* to whirling water, which has energy but no direction (*M* 6A:2).

There are other parallels between the two. For example, the "Chieh" chapter advocates a state in which the heart/·mind does not move (*KT* 2/16.8–9), and Kao Tzu was said to have achieved an unmoved heart/mind (*M* 2A:2). It states that *jenᵃ* comes out from (or following) the inside, and *yiᵃ* is done/made from (or following) the outside (*KT* 2/16.2), which appears similar to Kao Tzu's view that *jenᵃ* is internal and *yiᵃ* external (6A:4). Probably, by the fourth or early third century B.C., a trend of thought existed that regarded *hsingᵃ*/*shengᵃ* as having resources but no direction, onto which *yiᵃ* is to be imposed. This conception of *hsingᵃ*/*shengᵃ* is like the Yangists' in that *hsingᵃ*/*shengᵃ* is explicated in terms of biological tendencies or life forces, but, unlike the Yangist conception, it advocated imposing *yiᵃ* on *hsingᵃ/shengᵃ*.

Next, let us consider the "Nei yeh" chapter of the *Kuan-tzu*, supplemented by the "Hsin shu hsia" chapter, which has some similarity in content to the "Nei yeh." Again, following Graham and Rickett, I take this chapter to date to the fourth or early third century B.C.[58] The chapter discusses the way emotions can distort the heart/mind and advocates quieting the heart/mind to nourish and give order to *ch'iᵃ* (*KT* 2/99.8–14, 2/100.6), as well as not letting things disturb the senses and thereby the heart/mind (*KT* 2/101.7–8). This is to be achieved by such Confucian practices as poetry, music, *liᵃ* (rites), and *ching* (reverence, seriousness; *KT* 2/103.12–13), and the goal is the *jenᵃ* of Heaven and *yiᵃ* of Earth (*KT* 2/101.6). Similar ideas, such as not letting things disturb the senses and thereby the heart/mind (*KT* 2/66.9) and using Confucian practices to quiet the heart/mind (*KT* 2/68.5–6), are found in the "Hsin shu hsia" chapter. In light of the parallels between the two chapters, I take them to express a similar trend of thought.[59] The "Hsin shu hsia" chapter contains a reference to the idea that *ch'iᵃ* is what fills the body and, unless what fills the body is good, the heart/mind will not *teᵇ* (get, do well, understand; *KT* 2/66.10–11). Thus, part of this trend of thought regards *teᵇ* of the heart/mind as dependent on the condition of *ch'iᵃ*. Furthermore, this trend is opposed to *yen*: the Way is opposed to sounds and is something that cannot be spoken about (*yen*), seen, or listened to (*KT* 2/100.8–9). This reflects a position different from both Kao Tzu's and Mencius's; there is an opposition to *yen* (like Mencius, but for a different reason), and one is supposed to seek in *ch'iᵃ* if one does not *teᵇ* in the heart/mind (unlike both Kao Tzu and Mencius).

Finally, let us turn to the *Chuang-tzu*. The text de-emphasizes *yen*, as seen from the reference to the teaching that cannot be put in words (*yen*; *CT* 5/2), the observation that one who knows does not speak (*yen*) whereas one who speaks does not know (*CT* 22/7), or the notion that speaking (*yen*) is for the purpose of conveying the meaning, and once the meaning is conveyed, one can forget about words (*yen*; *CT* 26/48–49). Ideally, one should not be guided by teachings describable in words, and the heart/mind should be vacuous (*hsü*) in the sense of not giving directions, so that one can respond spontaneously to situations. The idea is conveyed in the comparison of the heart/mind to a mirror (*CT* 7/31–33) or still water (*CT* 5/9–10), as well as through the

metaphor of archery. As we saw in §3.3, aiming in archery is sometimes taken as an analogy for *chih^c* (directions of the heart/mind) in
early texts. In the *Chuang-tzu*, the idea that ideally one should be free
from guidance by *chih^c* is expressed in passages referring to the
shooting that involves not shooting (CT 21/57–59; cf. *LiT* 2/3a.11–
3b.1) or to the idea that someone good at archery is someone who hits
the mark without aiming (CT 24/39).

One passage important for our purpose occurs in the "Jen chien
shih" chapter; in it we find Confucius discussing with Yen Hui the
idea of fasting the heart/mind. The following is given as an elaboration on this idea: "Make *chih^c* [directions of the heart/mind] one. Do
not listen with the ear, listen with the heart/mind; do not listen with
the heart/mind, listen with *ch'i^a*. . . . *Ch'i^a* is what is vacuous (*hsü*) and
awaits things" (CT 4/26–28). The passage is opposed to guiding *ch'i^a*;
one should not obtain guidance from outside the heart/mind (not listen with the ear), nor should one seek guidance from the heart/mind;
rather, one should let *ch'i^a* respond on its own, free from guidance by
chih^c. This looks like an inversion of Kao Tzu's maxim: seek neither in
doctrines nor in the heart/mind, but in *ch'i^a*.[60]

In light of this discussion, we may reconstruct part of the intellectual scene around the fourth to the early third centuries B.C. as follows. After the Yangists had made prominent the conception of
hsing^a/sheng^a as constituted primarily by biological life and as the
proper course of development of human beings, a number of movements of thought emerged. One is found in the "Chieh" chapter of the
Kuan-tzu. It retained a conception of *sheng^a* as constituted by life forces
but saw it as without direction. Accordingly, it is to be given a direction by *yi^a* learned from outside the heart/mind, a direction probably
understood in Confucian terms. Another is found in the "Nei yeh"
and the "Hsin shu hsia" chapters of the *Kuan-tzu*. It regarded the vital
energies, *ch'i^a*, as already having an ethical direction, probably understood in Confucian terms. All that is needed to realize that direction is
to quiet the heart/mind via Confucian practices and to allow *ch'i^a* to
respond freely. Furthermore, there is an opposition to *yen* (words),
since *tao* (the Way) cannot be captured in words. As commentators
have noted, this trend of thought involves a blending of ideas characteristic of Confucian and Taoist thought.[61] There is a similarity between the trend of thought represented in the "Nei yeh" and "Hsin
shu hsia" chapters and that represented in the *Chuang-tzu*; the latter

work further advocates letting *ch'iᵃ* respond freely via quieting the heart/mind and regards *tao* as not expressible in *yen*. However, unlike the "Nei yeh" and "Hsin shu hsia" chapters, the *Chuang-tzu* does not regard *ch'iᵃ* as having a Confucian direction when allowed to respond freely.

To return to Kao Tzu, there are at least five different views concerning his affiliation. First, some interpret him as a Confucian. Benjamin I. Schwartz, for example, defends this interpretation on the grounds that Kao Tzu and Mencius did not disagree on the content of proper behavior.[62] Ch'en Ta-ch'i argues that Confucius's view that "people are close to one another in *hsingᵃ* but diverge as a result of practice" (*LY* 17.2) shows that Kao Tzu's view that there is neither good nor bad in *hsingᵃ* is close to Confucius's position.[63] Robert Eno argues that Kao Tzu's concern with *jenᵃ* and *yiᵃ* shows that he was either a Confucian or a Mohist, and that his statement in 6A:4 about loving one's brother but not the brother of someone from Ch'in shows that he rejected the Mohist doctrine of indiscriminate concern for each and hence was a Confucian.[64]

Second, some interpret Kao Tzu as a Taoist. For example, Wang Fu-chih (529–31, 540–41; cf. 544) interprets Kao Tzu's maxim in 2A:2 to advocate emptying the heart/mind in the way that the Taoists did, and interprets the externality of *yiᵃ* as a claim that we should not impose *yiᵃ* on the heart/mind to avoid disturbing it. Hsü Fu-kuan likewise treats Kao Tzu as a Taoist. He takes Kao Tzu's explication of *hsingᵃ* in 6A:3 to be close to the Yangist conception and interprets the externality of *yiᵃ* to mean that one should have no concern for *yiᵃ*, taking the willow analogy in 6A:1 to show that Kao Tzu regarded *yiᵃ* as doing violence to *hsingᵃ*.[65] Third, some interpret Kao Tzu as a Mohist. For example, David S. Nivison considers the possibility that the Kao Tzu referred to in the *Meng-tzu* is the same as the one referred to in the *Mo-tzu*, and that Kao Tzu was a renegade disciple of Mo Tzu and an older contemporary of Mencius.[66] Fourth, some interpret Kao Tzu as both a Confucian and a Mohist. For example, Chao Ch'i (C 6A) takes him to have studied both Mohist and Confucian teachings and to have studied under Mencius. Fifth, some interpret Kao Tzu as a Mohist with a Taoist twist. For example, T'ang Chün-i notes that Kao Tzu was like the Mohists in regarding *yiᵃ* as external, and like the Taoists in his explication of *hsingᵃ*, although he was not exactly a Taoist because he was concerned about *yiᵃ*.[67]

As far as I know, there is no evidence for Chao Ch'i's suggestion that Kao Tzu studied under Mencius, and the suggestion seems unlikely since the dialogues in 6A:1–4 proceed with Kao Tzu's stating and defending his position against Mencius's criticism rather than with his posing questions for Mencius, as one would expect of a disciple.[68] It is possible that the Kao Tzu referred to in the *Meng-tzu* was the same as the one in the *Mo-tzu*.[69] Of the three references to Kao Tzu in the *Mo-tzu* (*MT* 48/81–87), the first reports Kao Tzu's criticism of Mo Tzu for not practicing Mo Tzu's doctrines (*yen*) about *yiᵃ*. The second contains Mo Tzu's criticism of Kao Tzu for practicing *jenᵃ* in a way that will not last, like one who stands on his toes to extend his height or who broadens his chest to extend his breadth. The third contains Mo Tzu's criticism of Kao Tzu for not practicing what Kao Tzu himself preached. All three passages refer to the difficulty of practicing one's doctrines, and the second criticizes Kao Tzu in a way similar to Mencius's criticism of Kao Tzu in terms of helping things grow.[70] Still, even if both texts are referring to the same Kao Tzu, it remains unclear that Kao Tzu was a disciple of Mo Tzu's rather than a philosophical adversary.

Let us consider in turn the possibility of Kao Tzu's being a Confucian, a Mohist, or a Taoist. The similarity between his views on *hsingᵃ* and parallel ideas in the "Chieh" chapter, which has a generally Confucian tone, might seem to show that Kao Tzu was a Confucian. But this conclusion does not follow. For example, although the *Chuang-tzu* exhibits certain similarities to the "Nei yeh" and "Hsin shu hsia" chapters, which have a Confucian tone, the *Chuang-tzu* itself advocates an ideal unlike the Confucian ideal. For similar reasons, even if we grant Ch'en Ta-ch'i's claim (which some might dispute) that Confucius believed in the neutrality of *hsingᵃ*, by itself this point of similarity does not show that Kao Tzu was a Confucian, since Kao Tzu may not have endorsed the Confucian ideal.

From Mencius's perspective, Kao Tzu probably advocated imposing *yiᵃ* on *hsingᵃ*, where *hsingᵃ* is understood primarily in biological terms. This represents a position opposed to the trend of thought represented in the "Nei yeh" and "Hsin shu hsia" chapters. Against this trend of thought, Kao Tzu as understood by Mencius held that if one does not get proper directions from the heart/mind, there is no point in seeking help from *ch'iᵃ* since *ch'iᵃ* has no direction. Furthermore, contrary to the opposition to *yen* in the "Hsin shu hsia" chapter, Kao

Tzu held that it is from *yen* that one gets proper direction. However, if we bracket Mencius's comments on Kao Tzu's position, there is only one passage that suggests that Kao Tzu might have a concern for *yiᵃ*. Kao Tzu's own statements of his position as reported in 6A:1–3 and 2A:2 are compatible with his having no such concern; the only evidence for such concern comes from the parts of 6A:4 in which Kao Tzu seemed to endorse *yiᵃ* behavior.

Suppose we grant on the basis of 6A:4 that Kao Tzu did have a concern for *yiᵃ*; even so, it is still not clear that he was a Confucian. Schwartz defends this suggestion on the grounds that Kao Tzu and Mencius did not disagree about the content of *yiᵃ*. However, that the two did not debate the content of *yiᵃ* does not show that they are in agreement; it might well be due to their greater concern about other issues, such as the content of *hsingᵃ* and the source of *yiᵃ*. Eno argues that Kao Tzu's remark about love for brothers was directed against the Mohist ideal of indiscriminate concern for each and shows Kao Tzu to have been a Confucian. But some may suggest that Kao Tzu's remark is about actual human dispositions and is not opposed to indiscriminate concern, which has to do with ideal human dispositions. It is possible that Kao Tzu was a Mohist who believed that since people are not predisposed to practice indiscriminate concern, they need to learn from the outside that it is *yiᵃ* to do so and to reshape their motivations accordingly. Alternatively, some may grant that Kao Tzu's remark was directed against the doctrine of indiscriminate concern, much like Wu-ma Tzu's similar remark (*MT* 46/52–60). Even so, this does not show that Kao Tzu was a Confucian, just as Wu-ma Tzu's remark does not show that he was a Confucian. Kao Tzu's remark about not loving the brother of someone from Ch'in is not one that a Confucian would make, and it remains unclear what kind of ideal he espoused. There is therefore no clear evidence that Kao Tzu was a Confucian.

As for the suggestion the Kao Tzu was a Mohist, there appears to be no evidence that Kao Tzu advocated a way of life similar to the Mohist ideal. Suppose we grant him a concern for *yiᵃ* and view him, in the way that Mencius probably did, as someone who advocated getting *yiᵃ* from *yen* and imposing it on the heart/mind. His position would then exhibit a similarity to the Mohist position concerning the source of *yiᵃ*, which we considered in §2.2.2. Even so, it does not follow that he viewed the content of *yiᵃ* the way the Mohists did. The idea of imposing *yi^a* from the outside can also be found in the "Chieh" chapter, but, as we have seen, that chapter has a generally Confucian tone. Also, there was another trend of thought during that period, represented in the "Nei yeh" and "Hsin shu hsia" chapters, which was opposed to *yen*. This makes it likely that the question whether one gets *yi^a* from *yen* was a common one during that period and that the idea of deriving *yi^a* from *yen* was not specific to the Mohist school. Furthermore, Kao Tzu's view that *jen^a* is internal and *yi^a* external and his conception of *hsing^a* are not explicitly Mohist doctrines and may have come from other sources. There is therefore no clear evidence that Kao Tzu was a Mohist.

Finally, let us consider whether Kao Tzu was a Taoist. Wang Fu-chih and Hsü Fu-kuan make the suggestion on the grounds that Kao Tzu's maxim and his claim that *yi^a* is external show that he lacked concern for *yi^a*. Although this is a possible interpretation of Kao Tzu if we bracket Mencius's comments, there is no clear evidence that Kao Tzu's position should be so interpreted — the Mencian interpretation of him as someone with a concern for *yi^a* is also compatible with Kao Tzu's statement of his position. Kao Tzu's conception of *hsing^a* as having no ethical direction is probably the aspect of his thinking closest to the Taoist, but it is possible that he also favored imposing *yi^a* on *hsing^a*. And, as mentioned earlier, his contribution to the debate in 6A:4 might provide some evidence for ascribing to him a favorable attitude toward *yi^a*. Furthermore, his maxim as reported in 2A:2 seems opposed to two ideas in the "Nei yeh" chapter both of which are characteristic of the Taoist movement; the first half seems to show a favorable attitude toward *yen*, unlike the opposition to *yen* in the "Nei yeh" chapter, and the second half seems opposed to the idea in the "Nei yeh" chapter that *te^b* (getting, doing well, understanding) of the heart/mind depends on the condition of *ch'i^a*. There is thus no clear evidence that Kao Tzu was a Taoist.

Based on the available evidence, I do not think it is possible to determine Kao Tzu's affiliation, whether as Confucian, Mohist, or Taoist. We know little of his biography, and, as I have tried to show, the content of his thinking does not point clearly in any one direction. Indeed, since this distinction between philosophical schools is drawn retrospectively, it is quite possible that they were not distinguished clearly during that period, and that Kao Tzu's thinking drew upon ideas from different philosophical movements. If so, this might well explain why his thinking is resistant to classification into our standard categories.

4.5   Mencius's Criticism of the Mohist Yi Chih in 3A:5

4.5.1   *The Text*

To further our understanding of Mencius's thinking, let us turn to Mencius's debate with the Mohist Yi Chih in 3A:5. The debate was conducted through an intermediary, and it began with Mencius criticizing Yi Chih for his lavish burial of his parents, contrary to Mohist teachings. Yi Chih defended himself by saying:

> "The Confucians talk about how the ancients treated others 'as if caring for an infant.' What does this saying mean? In my opinion, it means that one should have concern for all without discrimination, though the practice of it starts with one's parents."

To this, Mencius responded:

> "Does Yi Chih really believe that one's affection for one's elder brother's child is just like one's affection for one's neighbor's child? He is drawing upon cases like the following: when an infant crawling about is on the verge of falling into a well, this is not its fault. Moreover, *t'ien* has produced things in such a way that they have one root [*pen*]. And yet Yi Chih treats them as having two roots, and this is the cause [*ku*] of his confusion. Presumably, in ancient times, there were people who did not bury their parents. When their parents died, they carried their bodies and threw them in the gullies. Later, when passing them by, they saw foxes devouring the bodies and flies biting at them. A sweat broke out on their brows, and they could not bear to look. The sweating was not put on for others to see. It was an outward expression of their innermost heart/mind. They went home, came back with baskets and spades, and buried the bodies. If this was really right, then filial sons and *jen^a* [benevolent, humane] people, in burying their parents, must have *tao* [the Way]."

Yi Chih's response was directed at Mencius's initial criticism of his lavish burial of his parents, and Mencius's rejoinder was directed at the supposed error of Yi Chih as revealed in his response. Mencius's rejoinder has two parts: that Yi Chih had drawn upon cases like that of an infant about to fall into a well, and that he treated things as having two roots when they in fact have one. The reference to Yi Chih's regarding things as having two roots is supposed to explain Yi Chih's error, as seen from the use of "ku" (cause, reason) immediately after the reference to two roots, and the idea of one root is presumably illustrated by the account of how ancient people came to bury their parents. Accordingly, an adequate interpretation of the passage has to explain how Yi Chih's response addresses Mencius's initial criticism and how the two halves of Mencius's rejoinder supplement each other as a diagnosis of Yi Chih's supposed error.

4.5.2   *Traditional Commentaries*

Let us begin by surveying what some traditional commentaries have to say about the passage. None of those I have consulted explains how Yi Chih's response addresses Mencius's initial criticism. For example, Chao Ch'i (C), whose interpretation is followed by Sun Shih, takes Yi Chih to be emphasizing that his lavish burial of his parents is compatible with the Mohist doctrine of indiscriminate concern; it is just that he began with his parents in practicing this doctrine. But, in this interpretation, Yi Chih's response does not explain why he departed from the Mohist teaching of frugality in funerals in the first place, something he needed to do to address Mencius's criticism. Huang Tsung-hsi (1/40b.2–6) and Chang Shih explicitly acknowledge that Yi Chih had failed to address the criticism. According to Huang Tsung-hsi, Yi Chih had no response to that criticism, and he simply tried to mitigate its force by saying that his lavish burial of his parents was only a slight modification of Mohist teachings, one compatible with the doctrine of indiscriminate concern. According to Chang Shih, because Yi Chih had no response to the criticism, he turned to criticizing Confucian teachings, saying that the Mohist doctrine of indiscriminate concern is implicit in the Confucian saying about treating others "as if caring for an infant."

As for the first half of Mencius's rejoinder, commentators generally agree that Mencius's reference to cases like an infant about to fall into a well was directed at Yi Chih's belief that the Mohist doctrine of indiscriminate concern is already implicit in Confucian teachings. According to Chao Ch'i (C), Chang Shih, and Sun Shih, Mencius thought that Yi Chih came to have this belief because he thought that the Mohist doctrine is illustrated by the fact—which Mencius himself emphasized—that one would have compassion on such an infant whether it is one's elder brother's child or that of a neighbor.

Finally, concerning the second half of Mencius's rejoinder, commentators generally agree that Mencius intended the account of how ancient people came to bury their parents as a criticism of Yi Chih. The usual suggestion, made by Chao Ch'i (C), Chu Hsi (MTCC), and Chang Shih, is that the account was supposed to illustrate the observation that funeral practices in some sense originate in certain reactions of the heart/mind and, somehow, this observation was supposed to be a criticism of Yi Chih. There are two common interpretations of the idea of one root. Chao Ch'i (C) takes "pen," which I have translated as "root," to refer to one's biological origin; we have one root in the sense of one biological origin, namely, our parents. This interpretation is adopted by Sun Shih and sometimes by Chu Hsi (MTCC 3A:5; MTHW 5/4b.11–12), and is also found in Dobson's translation. But Chu Hsi (YL 1313) sometimes seems to have in mind a different interpretation, one also defended by Chang Shih, which regards "pen" as referring to the basis for cultivating the proper form of affection for people. According to Mencius, we should start with our love for parents and then extend this feeling to other people and living things; in doing so, there will be a gradation in our affection for others. There is one root to the process in that it has a single starting point, namely, love for parents.

Although I find the traditional commentaries helpful, I believe there are a number of ways in which we can add to and improve on their treatment of the passage. First, concerning Yi Chih's response, since that response is directed at Mencius's initial criticism and since Mencius's rejoinder is directed at that response, we need a way of interpreting it so that it addresses Mencius's criticism, reveals certain assumptions subsequently challenged by Mencius's rejoinder, and fits with Yi Chih's overall Mohist position. I believe there is such a way of interpreting the response, unlike the traditional commentaries, which have given up on trying to make sense of it as really addressing Mencius's initial criticism.

Second, concerning the first half of Mencius's rejoinder, without disagreeing with its treatment in traditional commentaries, I believe more can be said about how it fits with the rest of the passage. The example of the infant also occurs in 2A:6, where Mencius described as a starting point for self-cultivation one's compassion toward such an infant. His description in 2A:6 of one's reaction to the sight of an infant about to fall into a well is similar to the description, in the second half of his rejoinder in 3A:5, of the reaction of ancient people who saw wild animals devouring their parents' bodies. This suggests a close link between the two halves of his rejoinder.

Third, concerning the second half of Mencius's rejoinder, neither Chao Ch'i's nor Chu Hsi's interpretation is entirely satisfactory. In Chao Ch'i's interpretation, Mencius regarded a root as a biological origin and thought that to advocate indiscriminate concern as Yi Chih did is to treat other people as if they were one's parents and hence to treat oneself as having two roots. It is unclear, however, how the idea of one root is illustrated by the account of the origin of burial practices, and it seems that to say that Yi Chih failed to treat things as having one root is not to diagnose Yi Chih's supposed error, but merely to express in rhetorical terms one's disagreement with indiscriminate concern. Furthermore, it is unclear in what sense Yi Chih treated things as having two roots. If the number of roots has to do with the number of biological origins, it would appear that indiscriminate concern involves treating everyone as one's parent and hence treating oneself as having millions of roots (cf. Chu Hsi, YL 1313–14). Or, to put it the other way around, indiscriminate concern involves treating one's parents as if they were no different from other people and hence treating oneself as having no root. Either way, it is difficult to make sense of the reference to the *twoness* of roots. Indeed, in light of Mencius's observation in 3B:9 that the Mohists treated people as having no father, we would expect him to describe Yi Chih as having treated things as having no root, if a root is just a biological origin.

Chu Hsi's alternative interpretation regards a root as a basis for cultivating the proper form of affection for people. It takes Mencius to be saying that in order to know the proper form of concern for others, we should begin with love for parents and, in doing so, somehow come to see that there should be a gradation in our concern for others. This interpretation is in certain ways similar to the one I defend, but, as it stands, it leaves certain questions unanswered. It remains unclear how the idea of one root as so interpreted is illustrated by the account of the origin of burial practices. Also, in this interpretation, Mencius's criticism of Yi Chih is that he did not regard love for parents as playing a role in determining the proper form of affection for people. It remains unclear how this criticism is expressed by describing Yi Chih as treating things as having two roots.

Other interpretations of the idea of one root are found in the literature. For example, some take "a root" to mean a principle of conduct.[71] In both advocating indiscriminate concern and treating his parents in a special manner, Yi Chih employed two incompatible principles of conduct and so treated things as having two roots. However, this interpretation does not explain how the speculative account of the origin of burial practices is supposed to illustrate the idea of one root, and the observation that Yi Chih treated things as having two roots does not provide a diagnosis of Yi Chih's error but serves only to express in rhetorical terms one's disagreement with him. Also, the reference to *t'ien* producing things in a way that they have one root seems rather heavy machinery to make the point that one should have consistent principles of conduct.[72] However, instead of attempting an exhaustive discussion of the interpretations of the passage found in the literature, I will defend an alternative interpretation, drawing upon the work of David S. Nivison.[73]

4.5.3 *An Alternative Interpretation Defended*

Yi Chih's response can be made intelligible in light of a difficulty for Mo Tzu's thinking described earlier. In §2.2.2, we saw evidence that Mo Tzu did not believe that human beings share inclinations that are realized in the practice of indiscriminate concern. In the absence of such inclinations, the practice of indiscriminate concern poses a difficulty, and Mo Tzu did not seem to have a satisfactory response to the objection raised by his opponents about the impracticality of the Mohist ideal. Although it might be possible to manage one's emotions and motivations to put the Mohist ideal into practice, it would probably require a lengthy process of cultivation, a subject Mo Tzu did not address.

Yi Chih's response to Mencius's criticism can be made intelligible as a way of addressing this difficulty. To practice the Mohist ideal, one has to begin by cultivating affection for the people with whom one has frequent interactions, especially immediate family members. After doing so, one can then extend, under the guidance of the Mohist doctrine, one's affection from family members to other people, including those with whom one had no previous interaction. To cultivate affection for immediate family members, one can act in ways that someone with such affection would act; so acting will have a feedback effect on one's emotions and feelings, thereby promoting the development of such affection. Lavish burial of parents is one such way of acting, since it can foster one's sense of attachment to other family members who are still alive as well as one's remembrance of deceased parents. Thus, lavish burial of parents is itself justified in terms of its role in facilitating the practice of indiscriminate concern.

This, I suggest, is the nature of Yi Chih's response to Mencius's initial criticism. Although his defense of lavish burial of parents departs from Mo Tzu's teaching about frugality in funerals, it does not depart from the spirit of Mo Tzu's thinking. Mo Tzu's criticism of lavish burials is based on the observation that the practice is detrimental to the public good. Yi Chih's defense of lavish burials is compatible with one's regarding the public good as the criterion for assessing such a practice; although the practice might not directly benefit the public, it will do so indirectly by facilitating the practice of indiscriminate concern, which will directly benefit the public.

Besides defending himself against Mencius's charge that his lavish burial of his parents conflicted with Mohist teachings, Yi Chih also launched a counterattack on Mencius. Referring to the Confucian saying that the ancients treated others "as if caring for an infant," he claimed that the saying illustrates the Mohist doctrine of indiscriminate concern. If we are to care for everyone as if we were caring for an infant, it seems that we should have equal affection for all. Hence, it seems that the Confucian idea of love with distinction is in conflict with this Confucian saying.

As for Mencius's rejoinder, unlike Mo Tzu, Mencius believed that human beings share predispositions that determine the proper form of affective concern for others. These predispositions are of two kinds. Some, such as reactions of compassion as exemplified in the example of the infant, are directed toward beings that need not stand in any special relation to oneself. Accordingly, no difference in the degree and nature of one's affection is involved when one extends such reactions to other beings. Others, such as love for parents, are directed toward people standing in a special relation to oneself, and a difference in the degree and nature of one's affection is involved as one extends such love to other people. Consequently, *jenᵃ*, which results from our extending these two kinds of predispositions, differs from the Mohist ideal of indiscriminate concern.

In this view, one may come to advocate indiscriminate concern only if one has made one or both of two mistakes: one has confined attention to the first kind of predispositions to the exclusion of the second, or one does not regard the proper form of affection for others as determined by such shared predispositions. These two criticisms are highlighted in the two halves of Mencius's rejoinder. In the first half, he addressed Yi Chih's claim that the doctrine of indiscriminate concern is implicit in the Confucian saying about treating others "as if caring for an infant." According to Mencius, it is indeed the case that Confucians regarded one's compassion toward an infant crawling toward a well as having a bearing on the proper form of affection for people, and that extending such reactions does not involve a gradation in affection. What Yi Chih had done is to draw upon this aspect of Confucian teachings to criticize the Confucian idea of love with distinctions.

But, according to Mencius, this criticism fails because Confucians also regarded another kind of predispositions, those directed specifically toward immediate family members, as having a bearing on the proper form of affection for others. An example is one's affection for one's elder brother's child, which differs from one's affection for a neighbor's child. Another example is the reaction, described in the second half of Mencius's rejoinder, of ancient people who saw wild animals devouring their parents' bodies. The description of this reaction is in various ways similar to the description in 2A:6 of one's compassion toward the infant: both are described as reactions of the heart/mind, as spontaneous and not guided by such ulterior motives as gaining the approval of others, as involving a kind of unbearable feeling, and as inclining one to act in certain ways. But there is one important difference between them. The example of the infant highlights a kind of affective reaction that one has independently of any special relation one stands to the object of the reaction. On the other hand, the example of wild animals devouring one's parents' bodies highlights a kind of reaction that one has only toward immediate family members. As noted by Chu Hsi (MTCC), one would not have reacted in the same way if the bodies were those of strangers. One might, for example, react with disgust and be moved to stay away from the bodies, instead of blaming oneself for what happened to the bodies and being moved to bury them.

The observation that Yi Chih had not considered those shared predispositions directed specifically toward immediate family members is a response to his attempt to read Mohist ideas into Confucian teachings, but it is not a criticism of Yi Chih's own position. In his response, Yi Chih revealed his Mohist assumption that one can arrive at a conception of the proper form of affection for others without reference to any affective predispositions of the heart/mind. Given this assumption, Yi Chih could admit the existence of shared special affection for immediate family members and still insist that this has no bearing on the form of affection that one should cultivate. Mencius challenged the Mohist assumption in the second half of his rejoinder. In giving the account of how ancient people came to bury their parents, he was not engaged in mere speculation about the origin of burial practices. He went on to claim that it illustrates why there is *tao* in burying parents. Hence, it appears that he also intended the account to illustrate his alternative position that what is proper is itself revealed in certain affective predispositions of the heart/mind, contrary to Yi Chih's Mohist assumption.

That the speculative account about the origin of burial practices is probably intended to show that burying parents is proper gains support from two other texts. First, in the *Mo-tzu*, there is a reference to different ways of dealing with the dead bodies of parents, in the context of criticizing confusion of what is customary with what is proper (*yi^a*; MT 25/75–81). Since Mencius gave the speculative account in the context of a debate with a Mohist, it is likely that it served as a response to the Mohists by making the point that burying parents is not mere custom but is proper because it has a basis in the kind of reaction described. Second, there is a similar account of the origin of burial practices in the *Lü-shih ch'un-ch'iu* (LSCC 10/5a.1–5), and the account there is followed by the observation that in light of the account there is therefore (*ku*) *yi^a* in burying the dead. This shows that it was not unknown in early Chinese thought to defend the propriety of burial practices on the basis of the kind of reaction described. Also, the account in the *Lü-shih ch'un-ch'iu* emphasizes that the kind of reaction described is directed toward people one loves and values, confirming the observation that one might not have reacted in this way if the dead body were that of a stranger.

This account of the second half of Mencius's rejoinder suggests an alternative interpretation of the idea of one root, one due to David S. Nivison.[74] In the Mohist position to which Yi Chih subscribed, living a proper life involves two things. One first arrives at a conception of the proper way of life, and one does this without the need to attend to any affective predispositions of the heart/mind. One then puts that conception into practice by cultivating the emotional dispositions required for living that way of life; to do so, one draws upon and manages the emotional resources of the heart/mind. Hence, the proper way of life has two roots — the propriety of that way of life originates in something independent of the emotional resources of the heart/

mind, and the emotional resources required for living that way of life come from the heart/mind. Mencius, on the other hand, regarded the content of the proper way of life as itself revealed in certain affective predispositions of the heart/mind. And, to live a proper life, all one needs to do is to manage and develop these predispositions in the direction indicated by the predispositions themselves. Thus, for Mencius, both the validity of the proper way of life and the emotional resources required for living it have one root in the relevant predispositions.

This interpretation of 3A:5 has a number of advantages over traditional interpretations. First, it explains how Yi Chih's response addresses Mencius's initial criticism, and it does so in such a way that the response fits Yi Chih's overall Mohist position and reveals certain assumptions that are subsequently challenged by Mencius's rejoinder. In this interpretation, Yi Chih defended the lavish burial of parents in terms of the role it plays in putting into practice the Mohist doctrine of indiscriminate concern. Second, this interpretation tells us how the two halves of Mencius's rejoinder fit together. The first half points out that Yi Chih, in regarding the Mohist doctrine of indiscriminate concern as implicit in Confucian teachings, had confined attention exclusively to one of the two kinds of predispositions that Confucians regarded as the basis for cultivating the proper form of affection for people. The second half gives an example of the other kind of predispositions and, to further supplement the criticism of Yi Chih in the first half, challenges his assumption that the proper form of affection for people can be determined independently of the predispositions of the heart/mind. Third, this interpretation enables us to make sense of the description of Mencius and Yi Chih as having treated things as having one root and two roots, respectively, and to see how the idea of one root is illustrated by the example about burial practices. Their difference revolves around the issue of whether the validity of the proper way of life and the emotional resources required for living that life have one or two sources. Mencius held that they have a common source in certain affective predispositions of the heart/mind and used the example about burial practices to illustrate this idea. In this interpretation, 3A:5 provides further evidence, in addition to the earlier discussion of 6A:1–5 and 2A:2, for thinking that Mencius regarded propriety as something derived from the heart/mind.

5 Self-Cultivation

5.1 Ethical Predispositions of the Heart/Mind

5.1.1 Ethical Predispositions

The discussion in the previous chapter shows that Mencius believed the human heart/mind has certain predispositions already directed toward the ethical ideal. This idea is reflected in other parts of the *Meng-tzu*. For example, 6A:6 describes the ethical attributes of *jen*[a], *yi*[a], *li*[a], and *chih*[b] as already in human beings and not welded onto human beings from the outside, and 6A:17 observes that each person already has what is truly honorable within him- or herself (here what is truly honorable probably refers to the ethical attributes; cf. 6A:16). Also, he described being ethical or unethical as a matter of preserving or losing something in one's heart/mind. For example, 6A:10 describes the worthy person as one who is able not to lose the heart/mind that everyone shares, and 6A:8 and 6A:11 describe being unethical as a matter of losing one's heart/mind and learning as a matter of seeking the lost heart/mind.[1] Passage 4B:19 describes the superior person as preserving and the ordinary person as losing the slight element that distinguishes human beings from other animals, and 4B:28 says that what makes the superior person different from others is that he preserves the heart/mind.[2] Passage 4B:12 describes the great person as not losing the heart/mind of the newborn; one possible interpretation of this observation is that the ethical ideal is a realization of predispositions already in the heart/mind.[3]

In addition, the notion that the ethical ideal is a realization of certain directions built into the predispositions of the heart/mind is reflected in two analogies in the *Meng-tzu*. The first is the taste analogy already considered in connection with 6A:4–5. Passage 6A:7 likewise uses the taste analogy to make the point that just as people's palates share a common taste for food, their hearts/minds share something in common. The phrase *hsin^a chih^g so t'ung jan che* can be taken to mean "that which is common to all hearts/minds" (cf. Lau). Alternatively, if we take *jan* to be used verbally to mean "approve," as suggested by the parallel between *t'ung jan, t'ung ch'i, t'ung t'ing,* and *t'ung mei* in the passage, the phrase can be read as "what all hearts/minds agree in approving of" (cf. Legge; Chao Ch'i [C]; Chu Hsi [MTCC, YL 1390–91]; Tai Chen, no. 4). Either way, the subsequent remark that *li^c yi^a* (pattern and propriety) delights the heart/mind in the way that certain kinds of meat delight the palate shows that Mencius regarded *yi^a* as something that the heart/mind takes delight in.[4] Also, 2A:2 says both that the flood-like *ch'i^a* shrivels up unless united with *yi^a* and that it shrivels up when one's actions are dissatisfying to the heart/mind; this shows that what is contrary to *yi^a* is dissatisfying to the heart/mind.

These passages show that Mencius believed that everyone takes pleasure in *yi^a* and finds dissatisfying what is contrary to *yi^a*. Minimally, this means that one takes pleasure in one's own behavior if it accords with *yi^a* and finds it dissatisfying if it is contrary to *yi^a*. Chu Hsi (YL 1391) thinks Mencius also believed that everyone agrees in approving conduct in human beings that accords with *yi^a* and in disapproving conduct that does not. Tai Chen (no. 4) likewise takes the sensitivity to *yi^a* to concern not just one's own behavior but human behavior as such. This reading is compatible with 6A:7 and fits the reference to the heart/mind of *hsiu wu^b* as one of the four beginnings — *hsiu* (regard as below oneself) is directed at things that bear a special relation to oneself, whereas *wu^b* (aversion) may be directed at the behavior of oneself or of others.

Another analogy used by Mencius is a vegetative one in which he compares ethical development to the growth of a plant. For example, 2A:2 observes that not attending to one's ethical development is like not cultivating the sprouts, and forcing one's ethical development is like helping a plant to grow. Passages 6A:7 and 6A:8 compare ethical development to the growth of barley and of trees on Ox Mountain, 6A:9 draws an analogy between lack of persistence in one's ethical development and inadequate nourishment of plants, and 6A:19 describes the maturing of *jen^a* in terms of the ripening of the five grains. The vegetative analogy suggests the idea that the ethical development of human beings is like the growth of sprouts into mature plants. The idea also fits the references in 2A:6 to the four germs (*tuan*) as the starting point for ethical development (part of the character *tuan* is a picture of a sprouting plant with roots). Since the direction in which a sprout develops if uninjured is built into the constitution of the sprout, the analogy suggests that a certain direction of development is built into certain predispositions of the heart/mind.

Mencius's appeal to such ethical predispositions played two roles in his thinking. He often referred to these predispositions to show that human beings have the ability (*neng*) to be ethical. People have the four germs and so should not regard themselves as being unable (*pu neng*) to be ethical (2A:6), King Hsüan's compassion for the ox shows that his indifference to his people is a matter of not acting rather than being unable to act (1A:7), and the love for parents and respect for elder brothers that people share show that they have certain abilities (7A:15).

As we saw in §2.2.2, one common challenge to Mo Tzu came from those who doubt that people are able to practice indiscriminate concern. Wu-ma Tzu challenged this doctrine on the grounds that he lacked the appropriate emotional dispositions to practice it (*MT* 46/52–60). Mencius's appeal to the predispositions of the heart/mind to demonstrate the human ability to be ethical suggests that he was probably aware of this challenge to the Mohists, a suggestion that gains support from his citing as an example of genuine inability one's holding a mountain and jumping over a river (1A:7), an example also found in the *Mo-tzu* (15/29–31, 16/46–48).[5] In emphasizing that the human heart/mind has predispositions in the direction of the Confucian ideal, Mencius was in part trying to show that human beings have the ability to practice the Confucian ideal, and hence that the Confucian proposal is not open to the same kind of objections as the Mohist one.

In addition, it is likely that Mencius also emphasized the ethical predispositions of the heart/mind as part of an attempt to defend the Confucian ideal. The main Mohist challenge to which he was responding did not concern one's ability to practice the ethical ideal, since this was as much a problem for the Mohists as for the Confucians. Instead, the Mohists attacked the kind of practices that the Confucians defended and appealed to *li*[b] (benefit, profit) as a basis for *yi*[a] (propriety). As we saw in the previous chapter, Mencius responded to this challenge by arguing that our recognition of *yi*[a] derives from certain features of the heart/mind, more specifically, from shared pre-dispositions that already point in the direction of the ethical ideal.

The two roles played by the ethical predispositions are related – if the ethical ideal is a realization of a direction built into these predispo-sitions, then the predispositions are also what make people able to live up to the ideal. Since the practical need to motivate people to practice the ideal may in certain circumstances require invoking considera-tions that have a more immediate appeal, we may expect Mencius to invoke such considerations on occasion, while pointing to the ethical predispositions to convince his audience that they are able to practice the ideal. This is probably what is going on in some of Mencius's dia-logues with rulers of states in which he attempted to motivate the rul-ers to practice *jen^a* on the grounds that doing so will have certain po-litical advantages and also appealed to the predispositions of the heart/mind to show the rulers that they had the ability to practice *jen^a* government. His appeal to political advantage probably resulted from practical need and does not show that he regarded the ethical predis-positions of the heart/mind as having no role in defending the ideal. Since the appeal to political advantage would have an effect only on those in certain political positions and with certain ambitions, and since Mencius was attempting to combat the Mohists and other oppo-nents before a wider audience, political advantage is unlikely to be the only consideration he regarded as bearing on a defense of the Confu-cian ideal. More likely, the appeal to the shared ethical predisposi-tions of the heart/mind also played this role, in addition to showing that people have the ability to be ethical.[6]

5.1.2   *Ethical Predispositions and Ethical Direction*

How do these ethical predispositions indicate an ethical direction? Consider first the spontaneous reactions that Mencius highlighted, such as King Hsüan's compassion for the ox (1A:7), one's alarm at seeing an infant about to fall into a well (2A:6), one's response to the sight of the bodies of deceased parents being devoured by wild ani-mals (3A:5), and one's indignation upon being given food with abuse (6A:10). These reactions occur when one suddenly encounters certain unexpected situations; the suddenness is made explicit in 2A:6, and in each of the other three cases, the subject encounters something ex-pected.[7] Unlike ongoing activities shaped by pre-existing goals, such as King Hsüan's oppressing the people (1A:7) or someone accepting ten thousand bushels of grain contrary to propriety (6A:10), such reactions reveal something deep in the heart/mind and show one the kind of person one really is.[8] Since one is caught unprepared, the reactions are not guided by ulterior motives but come directly from the heart/mind. That no ulterior motive is involved is made explicit in 2A:6 and 3A:5, and presumably is implicit in 6A:10 (one gives up life, which is the most important thing among ordinary goals) and 1A:7 (the king's sparing of the ox led others to regard him as miserly and so presumably did not serve any of his purposes). Moreover, the reactions are supposed to be shared by all, and one comes to realize this not through empirical generalizations about human beings but through reflections on one's own heart/mind. The reactions described in 2A:6, 3A:5, and 6A:10 involve hypothetical situations, showing that Mencius was inviting us to imagine how we would react if placed in such situations. Although 1A:7 involves an actual occurrence, what Mencius did in that passage was to lead the king to examine his own heart/mind.

What, then, do these reactions reveal? The answer depends on the kind of reactions involved. As commentators have noted (Chu Hsi, MTCC; Chang Shih), the example in 6A:10, which is also found in the *Li-chi* (*LC* 3/18a.5–b.2), illustrates one of the four germs, that of *hsiu* (regarding as below oneself) and *wu*[b] (aversion). *Wu*[b] is explicitly mentioned in the passage, and the attitude of *hsiu* is suggested by the description of the beggar as disdaining (*pu hsieh*) acceptance of the food given with abuse. Such reactions move one to reject the food and presumably also to see the impropriety of accepting it. In this regard, the reaction described in 3A:5 is similar: it moves one to bury the dead bodies of parents and see the propriety of so acting. Indeed, although the reaction in 3A:5 is similar to the compassionate reaction described in 2A:6 in certain respects (each comes directly from the heart/mind and involves being unable to bear certain things), the former is also like a reaction of *hsiu wu*[b] in that it leads one to remedy a situation to which the reaction is directed.

The reactions under consideration not only lead one to see what is proper in an immediate context of action but also can guide one's future behavior or behavior in other contexts. For example, the reaction in 3A:5 can lead one to realize the propriety of burying family members in the future. And the reaction in 6A:10 seems intended to lead one to a certain view of one's behavior in the political context. The comparison to accepting food given with abuse shows that the reference to accepting ten thousand bushels of grain is probably a reference to accepting an offer from someone in power who has failed to treat one in accordance with *li*[a].[9] The passage, it seems, is geared to lead the audience to see that accepting the offer is improper in the same way that accepting food given with abuse is, and thereby to motivate the audience not to so act in the political context. Accepting food given with abuse will lead to life, which is more important than the external possessions made possible by accepting the ten thousand bushels of grain. Since one would give up life in deference to propriety in the one case, it would be a loss of one's sense of what is important to accept the ten thousand bushels of grain contrary to propriety in the other case.

Further evidence that spontaneous reactions of the heart/mind can guide behavior can be found in 1A:7. The passage begins with King Hsüan asking Mencius about Dukes Huan and Wen and Mencius leading the king into a discussion of what it takes to be a true king (*wang*[a]). According to Mencius, the king could become a true king by caring for and protecting the common people. To show the king that he had the ability to do this, Mencius reminded him of a past occasion on which he was moved by compassion and spared an ox about to be killed for the purpose of consecrating a bell. This was supposed to show that the king had the ability to care for and protect the people, thereby becoming a true king. Mencius then asked why the king's bounty did not extend to the people and urged the king to measure his own heart/mind. The king responded by referring to his supreme ambition, which Mencius identified as territorial expansion. Mencius then argued that the way to achieve this ambition is to care for and protect the people and to practice *jen*[a] government.

The interpretation of the passage is a matter of controversy. Mencius was in part trying to show the king that he had the ability to care for his people; this much seems clear, given Mencius's repeated reference to the king's ability. But what is less clear is whether Mencius was at the same time trying to motivate the king to care for his people and, if so, how this is supposed to come about. One possible suggestion is that the king initially wanted to care for the people but believed that he was unable to do so and that Mencius's sole purpose was to show that the king had this ability. However, the way the dialogue proceeded suggests that probably something more was going on. Although the king did ask early on whether he was capable of caring for the people, he did not at that point display an interest in caring for the people as such, other than hoping thereby to attain the political status of a true king. But later in the passage, Mencius seemed to expect a change in the king's attitude toward his people. Mencius asked the king why he did not extend his bounty to the people in a way that suggests the king himself should find it puzzling that he had not done so and hence that there is something that moved the king to be more caring. Furthermore, since the king appealed to his political ambitions to explain why he had not been more caring, what moved the king was independent of political considerations. So, at least from Mencius's perspective, something happened in the course of the dialogue that contributed to the king's motivation to look after the people.

It is, however, difficult to determine how the change came about. One issue of disagreement is whether the added motivation the king acquired was a mere causal outcome of his dialogue with Mencius, or whether it depended on his coming to see things in a certain way, such as acquiring what from Mencius's perspective constituted a better understanding of himself. Another issue of disagreement concerns what, from Mencius's perspective, the king's attitude toward his people was at the beginning of the dialogue, and what Mencius was drawing upon in the process of trying to add to the king's motivation. To facilitate presentation of the different possibilities, I will describe a range of proposals on the second issue and then, for each of these proposals, distinguish between two ways of elaborating on it that correspond to two different positions on the first issue of disagreement.

At one extreme is the suggestion that the king had no concern for his people to start with. In trying to motivate the king to be more caring toward his people, Mencius pointed to a similarity between the situation of his people and that of the ox. Since the king's reaction to the ox was a response to its suffering despite its innocence, and since he also knew about the suffering of the people despite their innocence, the king would be motivated to have compassion on his people and spare them. This suggestion can be developed in two ways. One is to take the awareness of the similarity to play a mere causal role in generating the new motivation, without depending on the king's viewing the similarity as a ground for having compassion on the people. Another is to say that the king regarded the similarity as a ground for having compassion on the people, and that it is this view of things that generated the new motivation.[10]

At another extreme is the suggestion that, even before the dialogue with Mencius, the king had compassion for the people in a full-fledged form, although it did not manifest itself because of the distortive influence of certain political ambitions. By reminding the king of his compassion for the ox, Mencius helped to facilitate the manifestation of the king's compassion for the people. Again, one variant of this suggestion regards the change in motivation as a mere causal process that did not depend on the king's becoming aware that he already had compassion on the people to start with. Another variant regards the king as being led to this awareness by reflecting on the ox accident, such awareness in turn generating the new motivation.[11]

The two suggestions represent two extremes in that the latter assumes the prior presence of full-fledged concern for the people and the former allows that the king might have no concern for the people to start with. Between these two extremes are other suggestions that assume the king had some degree of concern for the people. For example, one suggestion is that by leading the king to see that the plight of his subjects is like that of the ox, Mencius helped to crystallize the king's incipient concern for the people, thereby motivating him to spare the people.[12] By guiding the king to become more mindful of the plight of his subjects and acquiring a more vivid awareness of their suffering, Mencius helped to activate the king's concern for the people and to develop his awareness of their suffering beyond an impersonal level.[13]

The passage does not contain enough details to provide decisive evidence for any of these interpretations. Parts of the passage speak against the interpretation at the first extreme. For example, the king's compassion for the ox is described as involving his viewing the ox as if it were an innocent person being led to the place of execution. This suggests that the king had some concern for the people to start with and that Mencius was attempting to help this concern materialize in action. As Wang Fu-chih (513–14, 516) has noted, Mencius was primarily urging the king to extend (*t'ui*) his actions, rather than to come to have the same concern for the people that he had for the ox. Indeed, that the king's compassion for the ox involved viewing the ox as if it were an innocent person suggests that he probably had more concern for human beings than for other animals.

This observation gains further support from the analogies Mencius used to describe the king's relation to the ox and his relation to his people: the former is like lifting a heavy weight and seeing the tip of a fine hair, whereas the latter is like lifting a feather and seeing a cartload of firewood. The analogies show that Mencius thought it would be easier for the king to be compassionate toward his people than toward the ox. Presumably, this comparative judgment is not based on the king's physical abilities; it would have been physically as easy for the king to issue an order to spare the ox as it is to issue an order to spare the people. Rather, in light of the observation in §2.2.2 that ability (*neng*) in the ethical context was often viewed as dependent on the appropriate emotional dispositions, the comparative judgment was probably based on the assumption that the king in some sense had more concern for the people than for animals.

However, although it is likely that the king had some prior concern for the people, it is not clear that it was initially present in a full-fledged form. It is possible that it needed to be crystallized or activated by the king's viewing the people in an appropriate way, and reminding the king of his compassion for the ox served such a purpose. As far as I can tell, there is insufficient evidence in the passage to defend any particular proposal about the form in which the concern was initially present and how exactly Mencius expected the dialogue to contribute to motivating the king to action.

The discussion of 6A:10 and 1A:7 helps make sense of 7A:17.[14] The passage presents being ethical as a matter of *wu wei*[a] *ch'i*[b] *so pu wei*[a], *wu yü*[b] *ch'i*[b] *so pu yü*[b] (do not do what oneself/others do not do, and do not desire what oneself/others do not desire). Chao Ch'i (C; CC) interprets the passage to concern different individuals, others as well as oneself: do not make others do or desire what one oneself does not do or desire. Accordingly, he takes the passage to be about not imposing on others what one does not desire for oneself, and relates it to the way *shu*[a] (reciprocity) is explained in the *Lun-yü* (*LY* 15.24).[15] Ware probably follows this interpretation in translating 7A:17 as "do not have done (desired) what you yourself would not do (desire)." Some translators take the passage to be about oneself and others instead; for example, Lau has "do not do (desire) what others do not choose to do (desire)," and Lyall has "do (wish) nothing they do not do (wish)." But comparison with 7B:31, which says that *jen*[a] and *yi*[a] result from one's extending what one oneself cannot bear and would not do to what one can bear and would do, makes it unlikely that 7A:17 concerns different individuals. That 7A:17 concerns the same individual is reflected in the translations by Ch'ai and Ch'ai, Dobson, and Legge; it has to do with one's not doing or desiring what one oneself would not do or desire. Chai and Chai and Dobson take *so pu wei*[a] and *so pu yü*[b] to concern what one ought or should not do or desire. Legge takes them to concern what one's "sense of righteousness" tells one not to do or desire, thereby capturing the view that there are certain things in oneself that tell one what not to do or desire.

Since Mencius held the view that the heart/mind has ethical predispositions indicating certain ethical directions, it is likely that 7A:17 refers to the directions revealed by these predispositions.[16] That 7B:31 refers to the heart/mind of not desiring to harm others suggests that what one does not desire is harming others, and 6A:10 and 1A:7 provide examples, respectively, of one's not doing certain things and one's not desiring to harm others. Hence, the point of 7A:17 is probably that although there are things that human beings as a matter of fact do or desire, such as accepting ten thousand bushels of grain contrary to propriety (6A:10) or desiring to exploit one's subjects for one's own political ambitions (1A:7), something in the ethical predispositions of the heart/mind shows that one really would not do or desire such things. This in turn provides an interpretation of *ch'ung* (fill, develop) in 7B:31 and *k'uo ch'ung* (expand and fill) in 2A:6 — they refer to the process of developing oneself in the directions indicated by the ethical predispositions of the heart/mind.

To complete this discussion of how the ethical predispositions can indicate ethical direction, we need to consider how Mencius would defend the idea of love with distinction against the Mohist challenge. Mencius regarded as a starting point for ethical development certain reactions and attitudes directed specifically at family members. The reaction described in 3A:5 is directed at the dead bodies of one's parents, and the passage implies that one has more love for one's brother's child than for a stranger's child. Passage 7A:15 describes love for parents and respect for elder brothers as the starting point for cultivating *jen*[a] and *yi*[a]. Passage 4A:27 describes serving parents and following elder brothers as the *shih*[b] of *jen*[a] and *yi*[a], respectively, where "shih[b]" has been interpreted to mean the real substance (as opposed to *ming*[b], or name), the concrete aspect (as opposed to *hsü*, or what is abstract), or the fruit (as opposed to *hua*, or flowering) of *jen*[a] and *yi*[a].[17] The reference to reactions and attitudes directed specifically at family members probably plays a role in Mencius's defense of love with distinction.

In 7A:15, Mencius described *jen*[a] and *yi*[a] as resulting from one's extending (*ta*) to everyone one's love (*ai*) for or attachment (*ch'in*) to parents as well as one's respect (*ching*) for elder brothers. Hu Pingwen's elaboration on Chu Hsi's (MTCC) interpretation takes this idea to mean that one should not restrict such love and respect to oneself but should also make everyone know that they should have such love and respect. In this interpretation, what is extended is the subjects of love and respect: the process begins with one's having such love and respect and ends with others' also having love and respect for their own parents and elders. Chao Ch'i (CC) relates 7A:15 to *shu*ᵃ (reciprocity), and this suggests a similar interpretation: one helps others acquire what one oneself has, namely, love for parents and respect for elders. But, elsewhere, Chao Ch'i (C) describes extending as a matter of one's exercising one's love and respect in relation to others. This suggests an interpretation that takes what is extended to be the objects of love and respect: the process begins with one's having love and respect for one's parents and elders and ends with one's having love and respect for everyone.

There are three reasons why the second interpretation is more plausible. First, the idea of extending the objects of certain attitudes from family members to others is found in other passages; for example, 1A:7 refers to letting the attitude of treating an elder as elderly, which is initially directed to elders of one's own family, reach the elders of others. Second, *ta* (extend), which occurs in 7A:15, is used in other passages to refer to extending the objects of one's attitudes. For example, 7B:31 speaks of extending what one would not bear or do to what one bears or does; as we saw earlier, this has to do with extending to other objects the attitudes one initially has toward certain objects.[18] Third, 7A:15 makes the claim that everyone has love for parents as a child and respect for elders as one grows up. This makes it unlikely that the point of 7A:15 is to urge one to bring it about that other people also have such love and respect.

Although one is supposed to extend the objects of one's love and respect, one is still supposed to retain a special attitude toward members of one's own family. Passage 7A:45 refers to treating as parents one's own parents (*ch'in ch'in*), which is an attitude not directed at other people, and 3A:5 has the implication that there should be a gradation in extending one's love outward from the family.[19] Passage 6A:5 implies that one should have more respect for one's eldest brother than for an older villager even if the villager is older by a year. How, then, would Mencius defend this gradation in one's attitude? As far as I can tell, the *Meng-tzu* does not contain sufficient details for reconstructing Mencius's position on this issue. All I can do is to describe, without actually ascribing to Mencius, one possible way of defending the gradation that draws on the work of David B. Wong and that is consistent with Mencius's appeal to shared predispositions of the heart/mind in defending the Confucian ideal.[20]

Consider first the affective concern for others that *jen^a* emphasizes. Given the existence of the institution, it is within the family that one first develops such concern. Furthermore, it is a fact about human beings that as they are brought up within the family, they come to have attachment to those who care and provide for them, these individuals typically being their parents. The attachment can become more conceptualized over time; the child comes to see the objects of attachment as parents, and starting with a desire to be close to them, the child comes to acquire conceptions of what constitutes the well-being of parents and is moved to act for their well-being. With time, one can also become more reflective about one's relation to parents; one comes to learn about how parents have provided for one materially, and how they also shaped the kind of person one is.[21] As a result, one may come to regard one's attachment to and concern for parents as warranted by what they have done for one. In addition, one may regard the attachment and concern as also warranted in part by the fact that one owes one's life to parents; that is, the biological link can be seen as a relevant consideration in itself. At this point, one's attachment and concern are not just mere causal facts but things that one regards as warranted by certain features of the objects of attachment and concern.

Suppose next that one reflects on the relation one should ideally have to parents. Two kinds of considerations provide grounds for retaining the special attachment and concern just described. First, one recognizes it is a fact about human psychology that, having been raised by parents, one has such special attachment and concern. There is nothing disrespectable about such attachment and concern, which are deeply rooted in human motivations, and the ethical life should make accommodation for this fact about human motivations. Second, one also regards such attachment and concern as justified by what the parents have done for one in the past, such as material provisions, the way they shaped one's character, and perhaps also their being the source of one's life. Although one did not come to have this attachment and concern on such grounds, one can, given the existence of the attachment and concern, still regard them as justified on such grounds.[22] These considerations provide grounds for regarding special attachment to and concern for parents as legitimate parts of the ethical life.

A similar account can be given for other people, such as friends and spouse, with whom one develops a like relationship later in life. These individuals have cared for one and contributed to one's life in various ways, and although one's attachment to and concern for them evolved as a matter of fact and not on the basis of grounds, one can come to see this attachment and concern as justified both because of what these individuals have contributed to one's life and because such attachment and concern reflect something respectable and deep-rooted in human motivations. One's concern for friends is not comparable to one's concern for parents given the difference in the histories of interaction, but this gradation can itself be justified in terms of the greater contribution the parents have made to one's life and the fact that having a special concern for parents to whom one stands in a unique relation is a respectable fact about human motivations. In this way, a gradation in one's concern for others can be seen as a legitimate part of the ethical life.

A similar account can also be given for respect for elders, a starting point for cultivating the attribute yi^a. Yi^a involves a commitment to what is proper, as defined by certain ethical standards to which one should defer. Again, given the existence of the family institution, one typically first develops such an attitude of deference within the family. Initially one learns how to behave simply by following the guidance of older members of the family; one's attitude involves following or obeying (*ts'ung*) the elders as well as *ching* (reverence, seriousness), which is a matter of devoting attention to and lowering oneself before the elders. As one grows older, one comes to see that such an attitude is indeed appropriate, since the elders are wiser and more experienced than oneself and since, having had a history of interaction with oneself, they know more than anyone else about one's needs and interests. One's reverence for them becomes more conceptualized, and one sees that it is an appropriate response to what one has learned from the elders and to their greater experience and wisdom. Further reflection leads one to see that this special attitude toward elders of one's family is a legitimate part of the ethical life for reasons similar to those described for concern for parents. Having such a special attitude is a fact about human motivations that is respectable and deep-rooted, and it is also warranted by what one has learned from the elders as well as by their ability to continue to provide appropriate guidance.

As the circle of one's interactions expands, one comes to have a similar attitude toward others, such as teachers and superiors. One still retains a special respect for elders in the family, with whom one has had a more extended history of interaction. This is a respectable fact about human motivations that the ethical life should accommodate, and it is also warranted by the fact that these are people from whom one has learned more in the past and who know more about one's special circumstances and so are in a better position to continue to provide guidance. In this way, a gradation in one's reverence can be seen as a legitimate part of the ethical life.

5.2 Self-Reflection and Self-Cultivation

5.2.1 *Self-Reflection and ssu^b (Reflect, Think)*

In the previous section, we considered the variety of ways in which the ethical predispositions of the heart/mind may indicate an ethical direction. Sometimes, as in the example described in 3A:5, one comes to see what is proper in certain situations on the basis of one's spontaneous response to them. Sometimes, as in the examples described in 1A:7 and 6A:10, one comes to see what is proper in certain contexts by reflecting on how one reacts in other contexts. Although the process by which one derives ethical direction takes different forms, for convenience I refer to this process as *self-reflection*, with the qualification that self-reflection may or may not involve actually reflecting on one's own ethical predispositions. Although Mencius related the ethical attributes to cultivating oneself in the direction indicated by the ethical predispositions of the heart/mind, this does not mean that these attributes are end points whose content is spelled out in detail and which guide one in the process of self-cultivation.[23] Rather, they serve more to describe different aspects of the direction revealed through self-reflection; for example, *jen^a* emphasizes the aspect having to do with affective concern, and *yi^a* the aspect relating to a commitment to propriety.

With this discussion of self-reflection as background, let us consider the notion of *ssu^b* (reflect, think). Mencius often explained ethical failure in terms of a lack of *ssu^b* (6A:6, 6A:13, 6A:17). In 6A:15, he observed that one gets it if one (or the heart/mind) *ssu^b* but not if one (or the heart/mind) does not *ssu^b*. What one is supposed to get is not clear from the passage. Giles and Lyall leave unspecified the object of the getting, Chai and Chai have "obtains what is good," Dobson has "receives what is transmitted to it," Lau has "will find the answer," and Legge has "gets the right view of things."[24] Comparison with 6A:6, which observes that "one gets it if one seeks but not if one lets go" (cf. 7A:3) and whose context is the ethical attributes *jen^a*, *yi^a*, *li^a*, and *chih^b*, shows that what one is supposed to get through *ssu^b* has something to do with the ethical ideal. Commentators generally agree on this point; for example, Chu Hsi (MTCC) thinks what is attained via *ssu^b* is *li^c* (pattern, principle), Chang Shih takes it to be *t'ien li^c* (pattern/principle of Heaven), which resides in the heart/mind, and Wang Fu-chih (696–97) takes it to be *yi^a* (propriety). It is less clear, however, what *ssu^b* involves and what its object is.

"Ssu^b" occurs frequently in the *Shih-ching*, often as a transitive verb meaning reflecting on something or turning an object over in one's mind, where the object is in many instances something toward which one has a favorable attitude. For example, one may think about or turn over in one's mind a person to whom one is attached (*SC* 27/3–4, 28/4, 38/3, 87/1–2), and worry or be concerned about such a person (*SC* 44/1–2, 62/3–4, 66/1). *Ssu^b* can also involve recalling or remembering something, as opposed to forgetting (*wang^b*) (*SC* 201/3), and it can also involve pondering on or thinking about something to which one need not be favorably disposed (*SC* 26/4–5, 109/2, 114/1–3). Given these uses of "ssu^b," Arthur Waley is probably correct in taking it to have the primary meaning of focusing attention on something, a process more akin to concrete observation than to an elaborate process of deliberation.[25] The *Meng-tzu* uses "ssu^b" in the sense of thinking of something (2A:2, 2A:9, 4B:24, 4B:29, 5A:7, 5B:1), where what is thought of can be something toward which one is favorably disposed (7B:37) or something one is thinking of doing (3A:5, 4B:20, 6A:9). Also, *ssu^b* is described as something pertaining to the heart/mind that can be exhausted (4A:1).

Since *ssu^b* is supposed to be necessary to attaining the ethical ideal, the object of *ssu^b* is presumably related to the ideal. Some commentators have interpreted the object of *ssu^b* in this way; for example, Chao Ch'i (C) takes its object to be goodness (*shan*). We just saw that to *ssu^b* something involves directing attention to and reflecting on the thing, and this is often something toward which one is favorably disposed. As noted by David S. Nivison, the observation in 6A:7 that the heart/mind takes pleasure in *li^c yi^a* (pattern and propriety) just as the senses take pleasure in their ideal objects suggests that the object of *ssu^b* is probably *li^c yi^a*.[26] This suggestion gains further support from the fact that "ssu^b" and "ch'iu" (seek) are used in parallel structures

(6A:15, 6A:6, 7A:3) and that, as we saw in §4.4.3, the object of *ch'iu* in Kao Tzu's maxim is probably *yi*[a]. Furthermore, as Nivison has also noted, the use of "ssu[b]" and "ch'iu" in parallel structures suggests that *ssu*[b] also involved a kind of seeking.[27] So, for Mencius, *ssu*[b] probably involved directing attention to and seeking the ideal object of the heart/mind, namely *yi*[a].

Ssu[b] also takes *yi*[a] as an object in other early texts (e.g., *LY* 14.12, 16.10, 19.1; *TC* 627/14, 736/9), and the point that *ssu*[b] directed toward goodness or *yi*[a] is crucial to one's becoming good is made in the following passage from the *Kuo-yü*:

> When the people are worked hard, they will *ssu*[b]; if they *ssu*[b], the heart/mind of goodness [*shan*] will grow. If they are allowed to be lax, they will be indulgent; being indulgent, they will forget [*wang*[b]] goodness, and if they forget goodness, the heart/mind of evil will grow. . . . Where the soil is poor, all the people direct themselves toward *yi*[a]; this is due to their having been worked hard. (*KY* 5/8a.11–8b.2)

The contrast in this passage between *ssu*[b] and forgetting goodness shows that *ssu*[b] is a matter of directing attention to goodness and keeping it in mind. Furthermore, since working the people hard is supposed to lead to *ssu*[b] and also to people's directing themselves to *yi*[a], *ssu*[b] is also a matter of directing oneself to *yi*[a]. Thus, the passage makes the similar point that *ssu*[b] directed toward goodness or *yi*[a] is crucial to one's becoming good.

To return to 6A:15, that passage contrasts the heart/mind with the senses by saying that the former *ssu*[b] whereas the latter do not. The senses are described as *pu ssu*[b] *erh pi yü*[a] *wu*[a], *wu*[a] *chiao wu*[a], *tse yin chih*[g] *erh yi yi* (not *ssu*[b] and are exhausted/obscured by things; when things come into contact with things, they draw them along and that is it). Commentators generally agree in taking *pi yü*[a] *wu*[a] to mean the senses are *pi* with regard to their ideal objects, *wu*[a] *chiao wu*[a] to mean such ideal objects come into contact with the senses, and *yin chih*[g] to mean the former pull the latter along.[28] The interpretation of *pi* is controversial. Chu Hsi (*YL* 1415) takes it to mean "being obscured" or "blinded," and Wang Fu-chih (705–6) "in its entirety" (cf. *LY* 2.2) in the sense that the operation of the senses lies entirely in their relation to sense objects.

The question we need to address is the difference between the heart/mind and the senses, which 6A:15 describes in terms of the difference between *ssu*[b] and not *ssu*[b]. One proposal is to take the contrast as one between the different ways the heart/mind and the senses move one to act. The operation of the senses is spontaneous in that when confronted by their ideal objects, they are moved to pursue these objects without deliberation. This spontaneity may be shared by the operation of the heart/mind, since the responses of the heart/mind described in such passages as 2A:6 and 3A:5 are also spontaneous in this sense. However, the operation of the senses is also automatic in that having been so moved, they lead the person to pursue the ideal objects unless the heart/mind intervenes. This is unlike the operation of the heart/mind. Even if the heart/mind reacts spontaneously with compassion, this does not automatically lead to action. Instead, the person has to deliberate and, having decided to act on the reaction, put that decision into practice. Thus, the senses will lead to one's doing certain things without one's having to do anything to make this possible, whereas the heart/mind will lead to one's doing certain things only after one has actively done something, namely, having deliberated and decided.[29]

This proposal has some plausibility, although it needs to be qualified. Consider, for example, the reaction of compassion described in 1A:7, which pertains to the heart/mind. Having reacted with compassion for the ox, King Hsüan did not have to engage in deliberation before actually sparing the ox. On the contrary, his sparing the ox immediately followed the reaction of compassion; the thought about the need to consecrate the bell only came into play later, leading him to substitute a lamb. Likewise, in the example of rejecting food described in 6A:10, one gets the impression that rejection of the food is supposed to follow immediately upon one's regarding it as below oneself to accept the food, without deliberating about whether to act on the reaction. Thus, it seems that the operation of the heart/mind can be as automatic as that of the senses, and hence that the contrast between the two has to be located elsewhere.

The difference between them is perhaps that when the senses come into contact with their ideal objects, they are pulled along by the objects and have neither the capacity to reflect on the propriety of the course of action nor the capacity to refrain from being pulled along, even when the pursuit is improper. Being pulled along by the ideal objects that they come into contact with is the only way the senses operate, and this provides an interpretation of *wu^a chiao wu^a tse yin chih^g erh yi yi* (when things come into contact with things, they draw them along and that is it). Thus, the senses do not *ssu*[b] in that they lack the capacity to reflect on what is proper, and they are obscured by external things or have their operation lying entirely in their relation to external things (*pi yü*[a] *wu*[a]) in that when confronted by their ideal objects, they are just pulled along by such objects without further reflection.

By contrast, although the heart/mind can have spontaneous reactions that automatically lead to action without further deliberation, it also has the capacity to intervene. It can reflect on what is proper, and when it regards a course of action issuing from its own reaction as improper, it has the capacity to halt that course of action. Hence, one main difference between the heart/mind and the senses is that only the former has the capacity to reflect on what is proper and to regulate one's action accordingly. Another difference has to do with the relation of the heart/mind and the senses to their respective ideal objects. Unlike the senses, which attain their ideal objects by being pulled along when they come into contact with them, the heart/mind attains its ideal object, *yi*[a], only through *ssu*[b], which involves actually directing attention to and seeking *yi*[a].

This interpretation of the difference between the heart/mind and the senses fits the earlier proposal that *ssu*[b] is the activity of directing attention to and seeking *yi*[a]; the capacity to engage in this activity is distinctive of the heart/mind and absent from the senses. In what way, then, does one go about directing attention to and seeking *yi*[a]? We have seen that *ssu*[b] is linked to *ch'iu* (seek), and in §4.4.3 we also saw that Mencius's disagreement with the first half of Kao Tzu's maxim in 2A:2 implies *yi*[a] is to be sought (*ch'iu*) in the heart/mind. This makes it likely that *ssu*[b] also involves directing attention to and seeking *yi*[a] in the heart/mind. If this is correct, then *ssu*[b] probably has to do with the process of self-reflection described earlier, which is a process guided by the ethical predispositions of the heart/mind. However, given the relatively few references to *ssu*[b] in the text, it is not possible to provide more compelling evidence for this interpretation of *ssu*[b], although it fits with the rest of Mencius's thinking.

5.2.2   *The Process of Self-Cultivation*

Having discovered a direction of change through self-reflection, one still has to act to change oneself in that direction. There is little description in the *Meng-tzu* of this self-cultivation process, but there are at least two relevant passages. One is the part of 2A:2 describing the way to nurture the flood-like *ch'i^a*, and the other is 4A:27, which concerns the role of joy in the development of *jen^a* and *yi^a*.

In 2A:2, the flood-like *ch'i^a* is said to shrivel up if not properly related to *yi^a* and if one's conduct is dissatisfying to the heart/mind or if it does not measure up to its standards. Hence, self-cultivation involves acting in accordance with *yi^a*, which, given Mencius's view that the heart/mind takes pleasure in *yi^a*, is also to act in a way that is satisfying to the heart/mind.[30] Mencius also described the flood-like *ch'i^a* as being born of *chi yi^a* (accumulating *yi^a*) rather than being appropriated by *yi^a hsi* (*yi^a* attacking).

There are at least three common interpretations of the contrast between *chi yi^a* and *yi^a hsi*. The first takes it to be a contrast between deriving *yi^a* from the heart/mind and acquiring *yi^a* from sources independent of the heart/mind. The second takes it to be a contrast between acting in accordance with *yi^a* while being fully inclined to so act and forcing oneself to act in accordance with *yi^a* against one's inclinations. The third takes it to be a contrast between regularly and persistently acting in accordance with *yi^a* and sporadically acting in accordance with *yi^a*. Many commentators, including Chao Ch'i (C), Chang Shih, Huang Tsung-hsi (1/16a.6–b.7, 1/18a), Sun Shih, and Wang Fu-chih (540), relate the contrast to the distinction between treating *yi^a* as internal and treating it as external, but it is often not clear from their explanations of the contrast whether they endorse the first interpretation or the second. Chu Hsi (MTCC, YL 1259–63), on the other hand, proposes the third interpretation, one endorsed by Hsü Fu-kuan and several translators, including Chai and Chai, Dobson, Giles, Lau, Legge, and Lyall.[31] There are also less common interpretations; for example, Yü Yüeh (MTTI) takes the contrast to be one between *ch'i^a* being guided by *yi^a* and *yi^a* being made subordinate to *ch'i^a*. As far as I can tell, there is insufficient textual evidence to adjudicate the issue.

Mencius continued in the passage under discussion to describe the self-cultivation process by saying *pi yu shih^a yen erh wu cheng^b hsin^a wu wang^b wu chu chang yeh*. This is followed by the story about the farmer from Sung who tried to help his grain seedlings grow by pulling on them and then by a criticism of those who abandon self-cultivation and those who force or help it grow. *Pi yu shih^a yen* is taken by most commentators, including Chu Hsi (MTCC), Chang Shih, and Hsü Ch'ien, to mean that one should regularly devote oneself to practicing *yi^a*.[32] *Wu cheng^b* or *wu cheng^b hsin^a*, depending on punctuation, has been interpreted by some, such as Ch'eng Ming-tao as reported by Huang

Tsung-hsi (1/17a.8–b.3), to mean not consciously aiming at the desired result, presumably because doing so might undermine one's efforts. Others, such as Chu Hsi (MTCC; MTHW 3/5a.6–12), take it to mean not expecting the result to come quickly; otherwise, one either does not devote effort because one expects the result to come of its own accord, or one devotes some effort and then gives up or forces the process when the result does not come immediately.[33]

It is likely that *cheng*[b] concerns some kind of overeagerness that undermines one's efforts. In the line under consideration, *pi yu shih*[a] appears to be paired with (*hsin*[a]) *wu wang*[b], and *wu cheng*[b] (*hsin*[a]) with *wu chu chang*. Since *chu chang* (help grow) is illustrated by the story about the farmer from Sung, which concerns overeagerness that undermines one's efforts, it is likely that *cheng*[b] also concerns such overeagerness. *Hsin*[a] *wu wang*[b] or *wu wang*[b], depending on punctuation, is generally taken to mean keeping in mind and not letting one's efforts lapse (e.g., Chu Hsi, MTCC), and *wu chu chang* to mean not forcing the process out of overeagerness about the desired result (e.g., Huang Tsung-hsi, 1/17a.3).

The emphasis in 2A:2 on the need to keep in mind the goal of ethical development and to be persistent in one's efforts is found in other passages. For example, 6A:9 criticizes a ruler for lack of devotion and persistence, and 7B:21 observes that lack of persistence can retard one's progress. As for the dangers of overeagerness, it is not entirely clear from 2A:2 how overeagerness can undermine one's efforts. In suggesting that one who is overeager may give up efforts when the desired result does not come immediately, Chu Hsi is probably drawing upon an implication of 6A:18, which says that *jen*[a] winning out over the lack of *jen*[a] is like water winning out over fire. Those who practiced *jen*[a] in Mencius's time were criticized for insufficient efforts: having failed to extinguish a cartload of burning firewood with a cupful of water, they said that water cannot overcome fire. What it means for *jen*[a] to win out over the lack of *jen*[a] is subject to different interpretations; it can be a matter of one's practicing *jen*[a] to overcome one's own lack of *jen*[a] or, as Huang Tsung-hsi (2/69a.3–7) reads it, a matter of a ruler's practicing *jen*[a] to win over other rulers who lack *jen*[a]. Whichever interpretation we adopt, the passage emphasizes that practicing *jen*[a] requires persistence, and that overeagerness about the result can lead to one's abandoning the effort when the desired result does not come immediately.

However, although it fits with 6A:18, Chu Hsi's proposal does not quite fit the point of the story in 2A:2 about the farmer from Sung; in that story, the detrimental effect is due to overdoing things rather than lack of persistence. Another way of understanding the detrimental effect of overeagerness is that it is consciously aiming at the result that undermines one's efforts. For example, an aspiring concert pianist has to keep that overall goal in mind, but consciously aiming at this goal while practicing could divert one's attention in a way that hinders progress. Similarly, one engaged in self-cultivation has to keep in mind the overall goal of ethical improvement, but consciously aiming at this goal in dealings with people may prevent one from acquiring the genuine concern for others that is part of the goal. Still another way of understanding the detrimental effect of overeagerness is suggested by the story about the farmer from Sung, in which the plants suffer from his forcing their growth. This suggests the possibility that even in self-cultivation, one has to edge into the desired way of life gradually, and that proceeding too fast can have a detrimental effect.[34] Although these two proposals are compatible with Mencius's overall thinking, there is insufficient textual evidence for adjudicating between them.

Passage 4A:27 describes serving parents and obeying elder brothers as the *shih*[b] of *jen*[a] and *yi*[a]. Some interpret *shih*[b] to mean "fruit," as when it is combined with *hua* (flowering) in *hua shih*[b] (Chu Hsi, MTHW; YL 1333; Sun Shih). Others interpret it to mean the "real substance," in contrast to *ming*[b] (name, reputation; Chiao Hsün), or what is concrete, in contrast to *hsü* (abstract; Huang Tsung-hsi, 2/20a.7–21a.1). The *shih*[b] of *chih*[b] (wisdom) and of *li*[a] (rites) are explained in terms of knowing without discarding and adorning "these two things." The two things referred to can be *jen*[a] and *yi*[a], or serving parents and obeying elder brothers. The latter interpretation is adopted by most commentators, including Chao Ch'i (C), Chiao Hsün, Chu Hsi (MTCC), and Wang Fu-chih (616), and it is more likely in light of the parallel between the reference in 4A:27 to knowing "these two things" and the reference in 7A:15 to knowing to love one's parents and to respect one's elder brothers.

This passage goes on to explain the *shih*[b] of joy/music (*le/yüeh*) in terms of taking joy in "these two things," and it is said that *le tse sheng*[a] *yi, sheng*[a] *tse wu*[b] *k'o yi yeh, wu*[b] *k'o yi tse* . . . . "*Le tse sheng*[a] *yi*" has been taken by some translators (e.g., Lau, Yang Po-chün) and commentators (e.g., Wang Fu-chih, 616) to mean "joy arises"; they presumably take "le" to be the subject of "*sheng*[a]." But the occurrences of "tse" in the next two clauses have the meaning of "if/when . . . , then . . . ," as these translators also acknowledge, and this favors reading the "tse" between "le" and "sheng^a" similarly. Furthermore, "sheng^a" in "sheng^a tse wu^b k'o yi yeh" probably refers back to "sheng^a" in "le tse sheng^a yi," the latter being used verbally. This favors taking "le" in "le tse sheng^a yi" verbally, referring back to one's taking joy in "these two things" ("le ssu erh che"). For this reason, I am inclined to interpret "le tse sheng^a yi" as saying that when one takes joy in "these two things," they will grow (cf. Chu Hsi, MTCC); furthermore, when they grow, they become irrepressible.

Earlier, I gave reasons for taking "these two things" to refer to serving parents and obeying elder brothers. That serving parents and obeying elder brothers are the two things that are supposed to grow gains support from the fact that these are the *shih^b* of *jen^a* and *yi^a*, and 7B:31 refers to *shih^b* as something to be expanded or to be developed (*ch'ung*). However, whatever the referents of "these two things" may be, the passage implies that as one takes joy in the self-cultivation process, dispositions toward *jen^a* and *yi^a* will grow and become irrepressible.[35] That one will come to take joy in the self-cultivation process fits with Mencius's belief that human beings share a disposition to take pleasure in *yi^a*, and one's taking joy will presumably involve at least being appropriately inclined and no longer having to force oneself to do such things.[36]

It is sometimes suggested that Mencius also believed that when one acts without the proper feelings and has to force oneself to act in accordance with *yi^a*, this can be harmful to self-cultivation. A number of considerations might be cited in this connection. First, Mencius said in 2A:2 that the flood-like *ch'i^a* shrivels up when one's actions are dissatisfying to one's heart/mind, and this may be interpreted to mean that acting against one's inclinations is harmful to self-cultivation.[37] Second, 4A:27 may be interpreted as saying that only action in which one takes pleasure contributes to self-cultivation. Third, Mencius's objection to forcing self-cultivation or helping it grow may be interpreted as making the point that doing what is proper against one's inclinations can have a detrimental effect on the process.[38] Fourth, Mencius's objection to treating *yi^a* as external may be interpreted as an objection to doing what is proper contrary to one's inclinations.[39] Finally, the distinction in 4B:19 between acting out of *jen^a yi^a* (*yu jen^a yi^a hsing*) and putting *jen^a yi^a* into practice (*hsing jen^a yi^a*) may be interpreted as a distinction between doing what is proper while being so inclined and forcing oneself to do what is proper, with Mencius opposing the latter.[40]

This is an interesting suggestion, although I suspect the textual evidence is inconclusive. Concerning the first consideration, the remark in 2A:2 that acting in a way dissatisfying to the heart/mind causes $ch'i^a$ to shrivel up can be interpreted as saying that improper action, rather than proper action against one's inclinations, is harmful to self-cultivation.[41] This alternative interpretation gains support from Mencius's comment in the same passage that $ch'i^a$ will shrivel up if not properly related to yi^a. As for the second consideration, it is not clear that 4A:27 carries the implication it is thought to have. The passage can be interpreted as saying that although one initially has to force oneself to do what is proper, one can, through regularly so acting, come to take joy in such behavior; when this happens, one's disposition to so act will grow and become irrepressible.[42] As for the third consideration, we have seen that 2A:2 does not contain enough details to adjudicate the different interpretations of the observation that overeagerness in self-cultivation can be detrimental to the process. The fourth consideration assumes an interpretation of the internality/externality of yi^a that I gave reasons for rejecting in §4.3.3. The fifth consideration concerns 4B:19, which I will discuss further below. At this point, in light of the fact that the context of the passage concerns the sage-king Shun, we can at least say that Mencius's advocacy of acting out of jen^a yi^a as opposed to putting jen^a yi^a into practice probably has to do with his conception of how a person should ideally act, rather than with how a person should act in the process of self-cultivation. Given the inconclusiveness of the textual evidence, I will refrain from ascribing to Mencius the view that acting in accordance with yi^a without the proper feelings can be harmful, while leaving it open that Mencius might have held such a view.

5.2.3   *Ch'iᵃ (Vital Energies) and the Body in Self-Cultivation*

In discussing the idea of nourishing $ch'i^a$ in 2A:2, we saw that Mencius regarded self-cultivation as affecting not just the heart/mind but also $ch'i^a$. There is evidence that he also regarded self-cultivation as affecting the body.[43] Passage 4A:15 concerns how the way one is cannot be hidden (*shou*) from those who observe one's words and eyes. Commentators (e.g., Chao Ch'i, C; Chu Hsi, MTCC) agree in taking "shou" to mean "hide" (cf. *LY* 2.10) and take the passage to say that the condition of one's heart/mind cannot be hidden when others listen to one's words and observe the pupils of one's eyes. Chu Hsi (MTCC) and Chang Shih make the additional point that although one can put on a pretense in speech, one cannot do so with the pupils of one's eyes.

Passage 7A:21 concerns how the ethical attributes are manifested in one's physical form — jen^a, yi^a, li^a, and $chih^b$ are rooted in one's heart/mind and manifest themselves in one's face, back, and the four limbs; of the four limbs, it is said that there is "understanding without speaking." Commentators agree that the mention of the four limbs refers to one's outward conduct, but they disagree about the interpretation of the reference to "understanding without speaking." Chao Ch'i (C) takes it to mean that even if one does not speak, others will understand one's four limbs in the sense of understanding the way one conducts oneself. Chu Hsi (MTCC; YL 1444) takes it to mean that one's four limbs can understand one's intentions, even though one does not speak and issue orders to the four limbs. Yü Yüeh (MTPI) objects to Chu Hsi's interpretation on the grounds that what Chu Hsi takes to be the meaning of "understanding without speaking" is true of everyone and has nothing specifically to do with the ethical attributes. He also rejects the alternative proposal that others can understand one's four limbs without the four limbs speaking, on the ground that the four limbs cannot speak. His own proposal is to emend the text to eliminate the reference to the four limbs. Yü Yüeh's objection against Chu Hsi's interpretation might not have force, since Chu Hsi's point might well concern the effortlessness of the ethical conduct of someone with the ethical attributes (the four limbs move properly without one's having to make an effort), which is the way Chang Shih interprets the passage. But Chao Ch'i's interpretation is also possible, and there seems insufficient textual evidence to adjudicate between these interpretations. Still, whichever interpretation we adopt, the passage implies that the ethical attributes are manifested in one's body.

Mencius's view of self-cultivation as affecting the body as well as $ch'i^a$ can also be seen from 7A:36, where he said that one's dwelling can affect one's $ch'i^a$, whereas nourishment can affect one's body ($t'i$). The same is said to be true of the loftiest dwelling in the empire, where "the loftiest dwelling" probably refers to jen^a — 3B:2 refers to "the loftiest dwelling" in an ethical context, and 4A:10 and 7A:33 (cf. 2A:7) refer to one's dwelling in jen^a. Here, again, the passage concerns how one's ethical qualities affect not just the heart/mind but also $ch'i^a$ and the body.[44] Since 2A:2 describes $ch'i^a$ as what fills the body and as something guided by and supporting *chih^c*, the directions of the heart/mind, *ch'i^a* probably serves as the aspect of the person that mediates between the heart/mind and the body.[45]

In what way, then, does self-cultivation make a difference to *ch'i^a* and the body? In recent writings, Yang Rur-bin has made the interesting proposal that just as self-cultivation involves one's realizing a direction of development implicit in the heart/mind, it also involves realizing a direction of development implicit in *ch'i^a* and in the body.[46] In support of this proposal, Yang points to the parallel in 6A:8 between Mencius's view of *ch'i^a* and his view of the heart/mind, as well as the comment in 7A:38 that only the sage can *chien^b* (tread on, enact) *hsing^b* (shape, physical form). To assess this proposal, I consider the two passages in turn.

Passage 6A:8 observes in connection with one's *ch'i^a* in the early morning that there is a "slight element" in its likes and dislikes that is common to human beings and that failing to preserve one's *ch'i^a* in the night leaves one not far removed from lower animals. The reference to *ch'i^a* in the early morning and in the night probably serves to emphasize the condition of *ch'i^a* when free from the influence of ordinary human endeavors, just as the reference in 2A:6 to the suddenness of one's seeing a child on the verge of falling into a well emphasizes the condition of the heart/mind when free from such influences. Also, the reference to the "slight element" common to the *ch'i^a* of human beings, whose loss leaves one close to lower animals, parallels the reference in 4B:19 to the "slight element" that distinguishes human beings from lower animals and that the superior person preserves. These parallels show that, for Mencius, just as the human heart/mind has certain ethical predispositions that are most conspicuous when one is free from the influence of ordinary human endeavors and that should be preserved and nourished, the *ch'i^a* of human beings also has a shared element that is most conspicuous when one is free from such influences and that should be preserved and nourished.[47] So, there is evidence for Yang's observation that self-cultivation involves developing *ch'i^a* in a direction already implicit in it, an observation that also gains support from Mencius's use of the vegetative analogy in 2A:2 and 6A:8 in talking about the growth of *ch'i^a*.

To turn to 7A:38, Chao Ch'i (C) takes "*chien^b*" to mean "reside in" and "*chien^b hsing^b*" to refer to the ethical attributes residing in one's physical form. On the other hand, Chu Hsi (MTCC; MTHW; YL 1451–52) rejects Chao's reading and takes "*chien^b*" to mean "fulfill," as in "chien[b] yen" (to fulfill one's words); citing Ch'eng I with approval, he takes "chien[b] hsing[b]" to refer to one's filling up (*ch'ung*) one's physical form (*hsing[b]*) by exhausting its pattern (*li[c]*). Chang Shih's interpretation is similar to Chu's; he understands "chien[b] hsing[b]" as following and exhausting the pattern (*li[c]*) of one's physical form. Yang correctly points out that Chao Ch'i's interpretation is compatible with regarding one's physical form as ethically neutral and as something that the ethical attributes just happen to reside in, unlike Chu Hsi's interpretation, which regards one's physical form as having an ethical dimension whose fulfillment depends on the ethical attributes. Without committing himself to Chu Hsi's views about pattern (*li[c]*), Yang favors an interpretation that regards one's physical form as having an ethical dimension whose fulfillment depends on the ethical attributes.

These two interpretations can also be found among other commentators and translators. Some interpret "chien[b] hsing[b]" to involve giving completion or fulfillment to one's physical form. For example, Tai Chen (no. 29) takes "chien[b]" in "chien[b] hsing[b]" to mean "fulfill" (as in "chien[b] yen"). Lau translates "chien[b] hsing[b]" as "give his body complete fulfillment," and Lyall as "attain his full shape." Some interpret "chien[b] hsing[b]" to involve living up to or satisfying the design of the physical form. For example, Chai and Chai translate "chien[b] hsing[b]" as "conform to the design of his stature," Legge renders it as "satisfy the design of his bodily organization," and Ware has "live up to the stature." Since these commentators and translators take the ethical attributes to be necessary to completing one's physical form or living up to its design, presumably they regard the physical form as having an ethical dimension. By contrast, other commentators and translators regard the physical form as by itself neutral, although use is made of it in self-cultivation. For example, Wang En-yang takes "chien[b] hsing[b]" to refer to residing in or making use of one's physical form to put the Way into practice, and Chan translates it as "put his physical form into full use," and Dobson as "properly manipulate (the functions of the body)."

An examination of the use of "chien[b]" by itself does not suffice to adjudicate the issue. The *Shuo-wen* explains "chien[b]" as "li[d]" (tread), and "li[d]" as where the foot treads. Since there may or may not be a direction or design that the foot follows in treading a path, this explanation of "chien[b]" leaves open the question whether *chien[b] hsing[b]* involves following a direction of development or fitting a design that one's physical form already has. "Chien[b]" is used in both ways in early texts. Sometimes, what one *chien^b* need not have a direction that one follows or a design that one fits, as in references to treading (*chien^b*) a certain place (*KY* 19/10b.2) or to the fact that the hooves of horses can tread (*chien^b*) snow (*CT* 9/1). Sometimes, to *chien^b* something involves following certain directions or fitting certain designs; examples include acting on (*chien^b*) one's words (*LC* 1/2a.4–5), enacting (*chien^b*) *te^a* (virtue, power) (*KY* 3/2a.1), and following (*chien^b*) certain given paths (*LY* 11.20). And sometimes, although what one *chien^b* may have a certain direction or design, to *chien^b* the thing need not imply that one follows that direction or fits that design. For example, to *chien^b* an official position involves one's occupying a position with given responsibilities, without necessarily implying that one fulfills such responsibilities (e.g., *TC* 159/14; *KY* 17/2b.1). This is the way *chien^b* is used in 5A:5 of the *Meng-tzu*, which refers to Shun's occupying (*chien^b*) the position of ruler. Thus, as far as the use of *chien^b* by itself is concerned, it does not favor any of the interpretations of 7A:38 over the others.

Interestingly, however, a parallel in 5A:5 throws light on 7A:38. Passage 5A:5 says that it was only after the people had responded to Shun in certain ways following Yao's death that Shun came to occupy the position of ruler. The context implies that certain conditions have to be met before it is appropriate for someone to occupy (*chien^b*) the position of ruler, even if it does not imply that the person will actually fulfill the responsibilities associated with that position. Now, 7A:38 says that it is only after one has become a sage that one can *chien^b* one's physical form. Again, the context implies that only by meeting certain conditions associated with one's physical form, which the reference to sageness shows to be ethical conditions, is it appropriate for one to *chien^b* one's physical form. As I will show in §6.3.2, the use of "k'o yi" (capable, possible) in connection with *chien^b* *hsing^b* also carries the implication that certain conditions have to be met for it to be possible or appropriate for one to *chien^b* one's physical form.

These observations show that Mencius probably regarded the physical form as having some kind of ethical dimension, although the passage by itself leaves it open how we spell out this ethical dimension — whether the physical form has a certain design that the sage fits or a direction of development that the sage realizes. In §2.1.2, we discussed two ideas in connection with the political thought of the *Lun-yü*. One is the idea of *chih^a jen^b*, understood in the sense of appreciating the qualities of a person and employing the person on such a basis.[48] The other is the idea that a cultivated person has the power to attract and transform others, and ideally this power should provide the basis for government. Both ideas are related to the idea that one's ethical qualities are inevitably manifested in one's physical form — it is because they are so manifested that they can be discerned by others and can have a transformative effect. And since a cultivated person has such a transformative effect, it follows that the effect of self-cultivation extends beyond one's own person.

This idea can be found in some passages in the *Meng-tzu*. For example, the comment in 2A:2 that the flood-like *ch'i*[a] one cultivates is vast and unyielding and fills the space between Heaven and Earth suggests that the effect of self-cultivation extends beyond the person to the cosmic order.[49] Probably, as Chao Ch'i (C) and Hsü Ch'ien have noted, the reference to "filling the space between Heaven and Earth" has to do in part with the extension of the effect of self-cultivation beyond oneself, including the way a cultivated person deals with everything. In addition, we saw in §3.3 that *ch'i*[a] is viewed in early texts as something whose proper balance is linked to order in both the human and the natural realm, and this view of *ch'i*[a] is probably also at work in this passage. Passages 7A:13 and 7B:25 also describe the transformative power of a cultivated person, and 7A:13 observes that the superior person is "in the same stream as Heaven above and Earth below." In addition, 4A:12 says that self-cultivation is the basis for the political order, and that *ch'eng* (wholeness, being real) has a transformative power; *ch'eng* is described as the way of *t'ien*, and reflecting on *ch'eng* as the way of human beings (cf. 7A:4). Probably, the transformative power of a cultivated person is compared to the work of *t'ien* in that, just like *t'ien*, its manner of operation is subtle and indiscernible (cf. 7A:13), and its effect reaches everything, enabling everything to be nourished and transformed (cf. Chao Ch'i, C; Chu Hsi, MTCC; and Chang Shih, on 7A:13). To better understand this aspect of Mencius's thinking, I turn to a discussion of his political thought.

5.3 Self-Cultivation and the Political Order

Like Confucius, Mencius regarded the transformative power of a cultivated person as the ideal basis for government. If the ruler is *cheng*[b] (correct, rectified), then everyone will be *cheng*[b] and there will be order in human society (4A:20; cf. 7A:19, 4A:4). And, as in the *Lun-yü*, the *Meng-tzu* discusses various details of government despite the emphasis on transformative power.[50] Examples include the importance of appointing worthy and able officials (1B:7, 2A:4–5), the need for agriculture so as to provide for the needs of the people (1A:3, 1A:7), the importance of education (1A:3, 1A:7, 3A:3, 7A:14; cf. 7A:20, 40), the proper way to impose taxation (1A:5, 2A:5, 3B:8) and the regulation of land use (1B:5, 3A:3). The policies of a *jen^a* (benevolent, humane) government or of a government unable to bear (*pu jen*) the suffering of the people are manifestations of the *jen^a* heart/mind or of the heart/mind unable to bear the suffering of the people (2A:6, 4A:1). It is important to have not just a *jen^a* heart/mind but also guidance from the *jen^a* policies transmitted from the past; on the other hand, properly appropriating such policies requires a *jen^a* heart/mind and skill (4A:1; cf. 7B:5).

In addition to these ideas, which we have considered in §2.1.2 in connection with the *Lun-yü*, Mencius highlighted three other ideas. First, he spelled out more explicitly the idea that order in society depends on proper attitudes within the family, which in turn depend on cultivating oneself. Passage 7B:32 links self-cultivation to peace in the empire, and 4A:11 and 4A:28 link proper attitudes within the family to peace and order (cf. *LY* 1.2, 8.2). Passage 4A:5 describes the person as the basis of the family, the family as the basis of the state, and the state as the basis of the empire; a parallel though somewhat different progression is found in 4A:12.

Second, Mencius stressed that gaining the heart/mind of the people is the basis for legitimate government. Passage 4B:16 makes the point that becoming a true king depends on gaining the genuine allegiance of the people, which in turn depends on nourishing the people with goodness; 4A:9 emphasizes that it is by gaining the heart/mind of the people through practicing *jen^a* government that one succeeds in becoming a true king (cf. 7A:14, 7B:14). Accordingly, it is the response of the people that reveals who has the authority from *t'ien* to take up the position of ruler (5A:5–6).

Third, Mencius made the point that since people will be drawn to the *jen^a* ruler, the *jen^a* ruler will be able to unify the empire, bring peace and order to society, and be without enemies or be invincible. The reference to the *jen^a* ruler's being *wu ti* (without enemies, invincible) occurs several times (2A:5, 3B:5, 4A:7, 7B:3–4); as Ch'en Ta-ch'i has noted, *wu ti* can mean either that such a ruler has no enemies or that such a ruler has no enemies who can stand against him.[51] Mencius sometimes observed that by gaining the allegiance of the people, the *jen^a* ruler will be *wu ti* in the sense of not confronting any hostility (e.g., 1A:5). Yet at times he also spoke of how the *jen^a* ruler, if forced to fight, will inevitably win (e.g., 2B:1); according to him, no one can resist a ruler with the allegiance of the people (1A:6–7, 2A:1), and victory will require little effort when the *jen^a* ruler wages war against a ruler who is not *jen^a* (7B:3). Probably, Mencius regarded the *jen^a* ruler as *wu ti* in both senses. On the one hand, the *jen^a* ruler enjoys the allegiance of the people and, ideally, is *wu ti* in the sense of not confronting any hostility. On the other hand, a few corrupt rulers may try to oppose the *jen^a* ruler; since the *jen^a* ruler has the allegiance of the people, he will easily defeat such opposition and be *wu ti*.

In his attempt to motivate rulers to practice *jen^a* government, Mencius often appealed to the idea that practicing *jen^a* will enable one to be without enemies or to be invincible and as a result become a true king. This is understandable given the political realities of his time—the consequences that he ascribed to *jen^a* are exactly those that rulers aspired to. He also related *jen^a* to honor (*jung*) and lack of *jen^a* to disgrace (*ju^b*) or disdain (*ch'ih*) (e.g., 2A:4, 2A:7, 4A:7, 4A:9), presumably because *jen^a* leads to commanding others' allegiance, which is a position of honor, whereas the lack of *jen^a* results in subordination to others, which is a disgraceful or disdained position. In addition, to motivate rulers to practice *jen^a* government, he also pointed out that people will reciprocate the ruler's treatment of them. People will respond with love and reverence to being treated with love and reverence and will take joy in the ruler's joys if the ruler takes joy in their joys (1B:4, 4B:28). Conversely, if the ruler treats his subordinates and the people harshly, they will regard him as an enemy (4B:3, 7B:7).[52]

References to the political advantage of *jen^a* government also occur in 1A:1 and 6B:4, which contrast *jen^a yi^a* with *li^b* (profit, benefit). In these two passages, Mencius said to King Hui and Sung K'eng that a concern with *li^b* in government can lead to disastrous consequences for a state, whereas a concern with *jen^a yi^a* has desirable consequences. Certain aspects of the passages may suggest that Mencius was advocating the use of *jen^a yi^a* rather than *li^b* as a slogan in politics—in 1A:1, he urged King Hui to talk about *jen^a yi^a* rather than *li^b*, and in 6B:4, he again urged Sung K'eng not to talk to the kings of Ch'in and Ch'u about *li^b*. This has led some commentators, such as Chao Ch'i (C 1A:1;

CC 1A:1, 6B:4), Chiao Hsün (1A:1), and Sun Shih (1A:1), to take Mencius as concerned primarily with what slogans to use in politics.

However, although in 1A:1 Mencius started by describing a situation in which everyone from the ruler down talks about li^b, he went on to discuss what happens when everyone from the ruler down actually seeks li^b. Likewise, in 6B:4, he discussed the consequences of everyone taking pleasure in or being moved by ($yüeh^b$) jen^a yi^a as opposed to li^b.[53] His concern was probably not just with slogans but also with practices in government. His urging King Hui and Sung K'eng not to talk about li^b probably stemmed from his views on the serious consequences of what one talks about—3B:9 and 6A:1 refer to the disastrous consequences of the teachings of Yang Chu, Mo Tzu, and Kao Tzu, and 2A:2 and 3B:9 discuss the disastrous consequences of faulty teachings. In the two passages under consideration, he probably thought that King Hui's stress on li^b would lead those in lower positions to become obsessed with li^b, and Sung K'eng's discussion of li^b would lead the kings of Ch'in and Ch'u to become preoccupied with it.

It may seem puzzling that given Mencius's ascription of political advantage to jen^a government, he should oppose a concern with li^b, especially since both the *Tso-chuan* and the *Kuo-yü*, which often refer to Confucian ideas, describe yi^a as the basis for producing li^b (e.g., TC 200/12, 339/10, 391/1, 437/6, 627/14; KY 2/1b.9–11, 7/5b.9–10, 8/7b.9–11, 10/8b.5; cf. KY 3/3a.1–2, 3/3b.2). The explanation cannot be that the Confucians always used li^b pejoratively, since it is sometimes used in a positive sense in both the *Lun-yü* (LY 20.2) and the *Meng-tzu* (M 7A:13) in connection with benefiting the people.[54]

There are a number of possible answers to this question. One suggestion is that although Mencius could have advocated li^b in the respectable sense of benefiting the people, he tended to use the term in a pejorative sense (e.g., M 7A:25), because Confucius himself often spoke in a way opposed to li^b (e.g., LY 4.16, 14.12) and because he needed to distance himself from the Mohists, who advocated li^b. A second suggestion is that although Mencius was not opposed to li^b that conforms to yi^a, any li^b that follows upon yi^a will come of its own accord as long as one concerns oneself with yi^a, and hence there is no need for one to be concerned with li^b.[55]

A third suggestion is that in the political context, li^b usually refers to such things as military strength or acquiring territories and wealth; according to Chao Ch'i (C 1A:1) and Chu Hsi (MTCC 1A:1), this was how Mencius understood King Hui's reference to li^b. Since Mencius did not think rulers should be preoccupied with accomplishments of this kind, he avoided the use of li^b in the political context. Wang Ch'ung (100/1–5) criticizes Mencius for unjustifiably construing King Hui's reference to li^b in such terms rather than in terms of the security of the people. But, in light of passages like 6B:9, it seems likely that what constituted li^b for rulers of that time was indeed this kind of political accomplishments (cf. Yü Yün-wen, TMHP 1/1a.3–2a.2; Hu Yü-huan, 1A:1).

Finally, another suggestion, related to the previous one, is that advocating li^b in the political context could easily lead rulers and those in office to seek li^b in the partial sense of benefiting one's state, family, or self.[56] This can be seen from 1A:1 in which King Hui of Liang explicitly talked about profiting *his* state and in which Mencius described the king's concern as leading those below him to be concerned with profiting their own families or themselves. This aspect of 1A:1 might even be an implicit criticism of the Mohist advocacy of li^b; that is, talk of li^b in the political context inevitably leads to a partial concern with li^b of the kind that Mo Tzu regarded as the source of disorder.

These are likely explanations of Mencius's opposition to a concern with li^b, despite the political advantage of jen^a government. However, there is another explanation, which can be highlighted by considering a tension between two ways of viewing the relation between yi^a and li^b sometimes found in early texts. For example, in the *Lü-shih ch'un-ch'iu*, although li^b is sometimes presented as resulting from yi^a (e.g., LSCC 4/10b.7, 19/11b.4–5, 22/4b.1–2; cf. 13/10b.5–7), it is also seen as something that can come into conflict with yi^a (e.g., LSCC 11/9b.9–10). One possible resolution of this apparent tension is to say that the li^b that may conflict with yi^a concerns one's partial interest, whereas the li^b that results from yi^a concerns what benefits the public.[57] But another possibility is suggested by an observation in the *Lü-shih ch'un-ch'iu* that the petty person aims at li^b and as a result fails to get li^b, and that it is by not aiming at li^b that one can attain li^b (LSCC 22/1a.8–1b.1). This observation suggests that even with regard to li^b in the sense of profiting oneself, aiming at li^b can itself undermine the attainment of li^b. Thus, an opposition to a concern with li^b may stem not from anything undesirable about li^b as such but from the view that such a concern can undermine the attainment of its object. This kind of idea is familiar from Taoist texts; it pervades the *Lao-tzu* and is also explicitly found in texts like the *Huai-nan-tzu* (e.g., *HNT* 14/8a.2) and the *Lieh-tzu* (e.g., *LiT* 8/7a.6–8).

To return to Mencius, although he opposed a preoccupation with the kind of political advantage that obsessed the rulers of his time, he did not seem to regard the objects of such concern as undesirable per se. In his conversations with rulers, he pointed out that such objects could be attained if the ruler would practice *jen*ᵃ government (1A:7) and that attaining such things as wealth is not problematic as long as the ruler shares his enjoyment of such things with the people (1B:5). Thus, in urging rulers not to be concerned with *li*ᵇ, Mencius was not saying that there was something problematic with *li*ᵇ as such but was making the point that *li*ᵇ could be attained only by practicing *jen*ᵃ *yi*ᵃ without aiming at *li*ᵇ. As various commentators, including Chu Hsi (MTCC; MTHW 1/2a.5–2b.5; YL 1218–19), Chang Shih, Hsü Ch'ien, and Su Che, have noted in commenting on 1A:1, Mencius's point was that the object of a ruler's concern can be attained only if he practices *jen*ᵃ without aiming at such objects.

What the practice of *jen*ᵃ accomplishes may turn out to be something akin to, but not exactly the same as, what the ruler initially wanted. For example, the ruler might initially desire to be *wu ti* in the sense of having superior military strength, but what *jen*ᵃ government accomplishes is *wu ti* in the sense of confronting no or minimal hostility. Still, what *jen*ᵃ government accomplishes is something that a ruler wants and, furthermore, probably something more satisfying to the ruler than the initial objects of his concern.[58] The belief that such consequences follow from the practice of *jen*ᵃ only if one practices *jen*ᵃ without aiming at such consequences provides an additional explanation of why Mencius opposed a concern with *li*ᵇ.

There are other passages implying that the consequences of *jen*ᵃ follow without one's aiming at such consequences; such as 4A:9, which observes that a ruler who is fond of *jen*ᵃ cannot fail to become a *wang*ᵃ even if he does not wish to. Other passages make the stronger claim that attaining the consequences of *jen*ᵃ depends on not aiming at such consequences, such as 3B:5, which describes people as looking up to T'ang upon realizing that he did not engage in expeditions out of a desire to possess the empire. In addition, 4B:16 and 6A:16 contain statements of such ideas, and 2A:3 and 4B:19 can also be interpreted in terms of these ideas.

Passage 6A:16 concerns not just a ruler seeking to be *wang*ᵃ but also people seeking official ranks in government. Although the ranks of human beings (official ranks) will come to one if one cultivates the ranks of *t'ien* (the ethical attributes), those who cultivate the ranks of *t'ien* in order to achieve the ranks of human beings will inevitably fail. As various commentators, such as Chu Hsi (MTHW 11/10a.1–5; cf. MTCC), Chang Shih, and Hsü Ch'ien, have noted, Mencius's point is that the ranks of human beings follow upon one's cultivating the ranks of *t'ien*, but only if one is not cultivating the latter as a means to getting the former.

Passage 4B:16 observes that those who rely on goodness to gain others' allegiance (*yi shan fu jen^b*) cannot succeed in gaining others' allegiance, whereas those who rely on goodness to nourish others (*yi shan yang jen^b*) will gain the allegiance of the empire and thereby become a true king (*wang^a*). Here, the contrast is probably between those who make use of goodness in order to gain others' allegiance and those who are truly good and nourish others without aiming at others' allegiance; only the latter can succeed in gaining others' allegiance (cf. Chang Shih). The point is again that goodness has certain political consequences only when it is not practiced for the purpose of bringing about such consequences.[59]

The contrast between truly practicing *jen^a yi^a* and practicing *jen^a yi^a* for political advantage provides a possible interpretation of 2A:3, which describes overlords (*pa*) as relying on force and making use of or pretending to practice *jen^a* (*yi li chia jen^a*), unlike true kings (*wang^a*), who rely on *te^a* and truly practice *jen^a* (*yi te^a hsing jen^a*). The former may try to practice *jen^a* or even pretend to practice *jen^a* to achieve political advantage, but they cannot truly gain the allegiance of others. The latter has *te^a* and practices *jen^a* without aiming at political advantage and, as a result, can truly gain the allegiance of others. The contrast also provides a possible interpretation of the observation in 4B:19 that Shun acted out of *jen^a yi^a* (*yu jen^a yi^a hsing*) rather than just putting *jen^a yi^a* into practice (*hsing jen^a yi^a*). Chu Hsi (MTHW 1/5a.4–9) interprets the observation in this manner, taking it to emphasize that Shun was truly *jen^a yi^a* and acted out of it, unlike the overlords who made use of *jen^a yi^a* to achieve political advantage. However, there are other equally viable interpretations. For example, it is possible to interpret this observation in terms of the contrast between those who are truly *jen^a yi^a* and those who have to force themselves to practice *jen^a yi^a* to cultivate themselves (e.g., Chu Hsi, MTCC; YL 1349), the contrast between those who practice *jen^a yi^a* without thinking in such terms and those who have a conception of *jen^a yi^a* and seek to put it into practice (e.g., Huang Tsung-hsi, 2/32b.1–3), or the contrast between those who fully develop their ethical predispositions to become *jen^a yi^a* and those who impose *jen^a yi^a* from the outside (e.g., Chiao Hsün; cf. Sun Shih).

It seems clear that Mencius was opposed to practicing *jen^a yi^a* for political advantage. There is, however, one passage that seems to conflict with this interpretation. In 7A:30, taking "chih^g" (it) to refer to *jen^a* in light of the parallel between "chia chih^g" in 7A:30 and "chia jen^a" in 2A:3, we again find a description of the five overlords as making use of or pretending (*chia*) to practice *jen^a*. However, the passage goes on to say that if one makes use of or pretends to practice *jen^a* for long, it cannot be known that one does not have *jen^a*. Chao Ch'i (C), followed by Chang Shih, Chiao Hsün, Sun Shih, and Yü Yün-wen (TMP 1/15b.8–16b.1; TMHP 2/1b.8–2a.3), takes this last remark to say that one will come to truly have *jen^a* if one makes use of or pretends to practice *jen^a* for long; this reading is adopted by a number of translators, including Lau, Ware, Yang, and possibly Lyall. Chang Shih, Chiao Hsün, and Yü Yün-wen add the qualification that the five overlords were unable to make use of or pretend to practice *jen^a* for long and so failed to become truly *jen^a*; Yü Yün-wen adds that Mencius was making the remark in order to encourage rulers to persist in practicing *jen^a*. But, even with these qualifications, the point that one who makes use of or pretends to practice *jen^a* for political advantage can come to have *jen^a* seems to conflict with the point made in other passages that one cannot achieve the political advantage of *jen^a* if one practices *jen^a* for such purposes.

It is not clear, however, that the remark in 7A:30 should be interpreted in this manner. Chu Hsi (MTCC; cf. YL 1449) opposes this interpretation and takes the remark to say that if one makes use of or pretends to practice *jen^a* for long, one or perhaps other people will not realize that one does not really have *jen^a*. This interpretation is adopted by a number of commentators, including Hsü Ch'ien and Huang Tsung-hsi (2/83b.8–84a.5). As far as I can tell, the passage by itself does not favor one interpretation over the other, although Mencius's opposition in other passages to practicing *jen^a* for political goals provides some support for Chu Hsi's interpretation.

To complete this discussion of Mencius's political thought, let us turn to his response to a criticism of his conduct in the political context. The *Meng-tzu* contains several examples of his refusing to see a ruler or someone in power because he had not been treated in accordance with *li^a*. This led to the criticism that if he had only been willing to have audience with those in power despite a breach of *li^a*, he might have been able to effect desirable political changes and thereby help the people. As we saw in §§3.1.2 and 3.3, Mencius himself acknowledged that *li^a* can sometimes be overridden by other considerations, and he was also opposed to rigidity in political behavior when criticizing Yi Yin, Liu Hsia Hui, and Po Yi in 5B:1. And yet it seems that he was himself overly rigid in his insistence on an adherence to *li^a* in the political realm and put *li^a* above the well-being of the people. This line of criticism is found in 3B:1, in which Ch'en Tai asked why Mencius was unwilling to bend a little to achieve desirable political changes, and in 4A:17, in which Ch'un-yü K'un used the example of a drowning sister-in-law to make the point that Mencius could have saved the empire if only he had overlooked a breach of *li^a*.

Mencius's response in 3B:1 is that Ch'en Tai was concerned with *li^b* (profit, benefit) in proposing that one should "bend the foot in order to straighten the yard" in the political realm; if *li^b* is the main consideration, one may as well "bend the yard to straighten the foot." That Mencius should speak of bringing about *li^b* by "bending the yard to straighten the foot" may seem puzzling, since it would be odd to speak of *li^b* if one should give up something of greater significance for something of lesser significance. Some have suggested that this was a slip on Mencius's part.[60] Another possibility, however, is that Mencius was referring to gains of a specific kind, and that what is supposed to have been given up, although of a greater significance, does not constitute a gain of this kind.

We saw that when Mencius opposed a concern with *li^b* in 1A:1 and 6B:4, *li^b* was understood in terms of such political advantage as acquiring territories, wealth, and military strength. Given the political context of 3B:1, Mencius probably took Ch'en Tai to be talking about political advantage of a similar kind in speaking of "bending the foot to straighten the yard." If so, Mencius's reference to *li^b* was a reference to such political advantage. This proposal gains support from the example of the charioteer in the same passage, which concerns one's bending oneself to enable another to achieve such material gains as catching birds. In this proposal, "bending the yard" refers to subjecting oneself to a humiliating treatment that is comparatively more significant than the political advantage to which "straightening the foot" refers. Since li^b concerns political advantage and since subjecting oneself to humiliating treatment would not have detracted from political advantage if indeed it comes about, it is no longer puzzling to speak of li^b resulting from "bending the yard to straighten the foot."

Still, the question remains why Mencius did not bend himself a little, if his opponents were correct in suggesting that he could have brought about significant political accomplishments by doing so. The answer is that, for Mencius, the only way to benefit the people is to guide rulers to jen^a government rather than to help them acquire territories, wealth, and military strength. But, at the end of 3B:1, Mencius pointed out that it is not possible to bend oneself and yet straighten ($chih^f$) others; a similar claim is made in 5A:7 in terms of rectifying ($cheng^b$) others. Similar ideas are found in the *Lun-yü* and expressed in terms of rectifying ($cheng^b$) oneself to rectify others (*LY* 13.13; cf. 12.17, 13.6) as well as using what is straight ($chih^f$) to straighten what is bent (*LY* 2.19, 12.22); the notions of rectifying (*LY* 1.14) and straightening (*LY* 18.2) are both linked to the Way. Mencius took as his task rectifying ($cheng^b$) the heart/mind of people (e.g., 3B:9), and his reference to rectifying or straightening others shows that in the political realm his goal was rectifying the ruler rather than bringing about political accomplishments of the kind that concerned rulers. According to Mencius, one cannot rectify those in power if one bends oneself, presumably because one would be setting a bad example and also because bending oneself would lead to a lack of the kind of transformative power needed to transform others.

A similar point is made in 4A:17. In §3.1.2 we considered the use of $ch'üan^b$ in connection with the example of the drowning sister-in-law. In mentioning this example, Ch'un-yü K'un was criticizing Mencius's insistence on the observance of li^a in the political context, on the grounds that if Mencius had been willing to overlook violations of li^a and have an audience with those in power, he might have been able to gain their trust and as a result save the empire. According to Mencius, $ch'üan^b$ in the sister-in-law example would tell a man to overlook li^a and extend his hand to save the sister-in-law; in this case, the means of saving the sister-in-law is the hand, and a breach of li^a does not affect this means. In the political context, however, one saves the empire with the Way, and to overlook a violation of li^a would undermine this means; this explains the passage's ending with the query whether one is supposed to save the empire with the hand (in lieu of the Way). Presumably, the underlying assumption is that in the political context overlooking violations of *li*ᵃ in the way one is treated would not be in accordance with the Way, a point that can also be seen from the end of 3B:1, where Mencius linked bending oneself to bending the Way. Since one who bends himself or the Way will not be able to straighten others, such a person would also fail to convert those in power and as a result fail to save the empire.[61]

5.4 Ethical Failure

Having considered the nature of self-cultivation and its relation to the political order, let us turn to ways in which one may fail to be ethical. The *Meng-tzu* contains several general descriptions of ethical failure. For example, it is described as a case of one's letting go of or losing one's heart/mind (6A:8, 6A:10, 6A:11), or losing one's sense of balance, letting what is less important do harm to what is more important, namely, the heart/mind (6A:15; cf. 6A:14).[62] Such general descriptions, while emphasizing that ethical failure is a failure to preserve or nurture the heart/mind, do not tell us much about the source of the failure.

There are other more specific descriptions of ethical failure, which fall into three groups. First, there are people who are not drawn to the ethical ideal at all. Passage 4A:10 describes people who do violence to themselves in that their *yen* is opposed to *li*ᵃ *yi*ᵃ (rites and propriety); presumably, these are people who already have a conception of *li*ᵃ *yi*ᵃ but who consciously oppose it. It is not clear from the passage who the target of criticism is, but it may include philosophical opponents who consciously opposed the Confucian ideal as well as those who opposed *li*ᵃ *yi*ᵃ because they were preoccupied with other pursuits apparently in conflict with *li*ᵃ *yi*ᵃ. Such was the situation of King Hui of Liang, who was preoccupied with profit (1A:1) – probably things such as strengthening one's state (1A:5) and increasing its population (1A:3) – and who was condemned in severe terms by Mencius as not *jen*ᵃ (7B:1) and as killing his people with his government (1A:4).

Second, there are people who are drawn to the ethical ideal to some extent but exert little or no effort in that direction. One may exert no effort because of preoccupation with other pursuits, but this will presumably be accompanied by a rationalization justifying one's lack of effort. This probably is the situation of those who claim a lack of ability (*neng*) to be ethical, a phenomenon that Mencius referred to on several occasions. For example, 2A:2 describes people who do not cultivate themselves because they think it will have no effect; 2A:6 and 4A:10 characterize those who regard themselves as lacking the ability to be ethical as people who rob themselves or give themselves up. One actual example is King Hsüan of Ch'i, who asked whether he was capable (*k'o yi*) of caring for his people and who attributed his failures in that respect to certain political ambitions (1A:7) or disorderly desires (*chi*[b]; 1B:3, 1B:5). In addition, there are those who exert some but not enough effort because they lack devotion or because they expect immediate results and give up when the results do not come quickly; the former is the situation of the king described in 6A:9, and the latter is a phenomenon discussed in §5.2.2.[63]

Third, there are those who are drawn to the ethical ideal and actively devote themselves to it, but who nevertheless fail. This can be due to forcing the process out of overeagerness or being drawn to the ideal for the wrong kind of reasons. The former phenomenon is discussed in §5.2.2, and the latter in §5.3 in connection with those who aspire to *jen*[a] in order to attain certain political advantages.

The preceding discussion shows that ethical failure can have different sources, such as erroneous teachings, preoccupation with other pursuits, insufficient devotion and persistence, or overeagerness. Among them, Mencius particularly emphasized erroneous teachings and distortive desires. Passages 2A:2 and 3B:9 describe how erroneous *yen* (teachings) can lead to bad policies and have disastrous consequences, and 3B:9 and 6A:1 refer to the disastrous consequences of the *yen* of Mo Tzu, Yang Chu, and Kao Tzu. The *yen* Mencius opposed include the teachings of philosophical opponents, but they probably also include the advice one gives to rulers. For example, 6B:4 describes how Sung K'eng's emphasis on *li*[b] (profit, benefit) in· talking to the kings of Ch'in and Ch'u will have disastrous consequences for the states, and 3B:6 and 6A:9 observe that a king's improvement requires the company of those who are good and offer proper advice.[64]

The reference to distortive desires occurs in 1A:7, in which King Hsüan referred to his great desire to expand his territories and rule over the empire, and in 1B:3 and 1B:5, in which he referred to his *chi*[b] of being fond of valor, wealth, and women. *Chi*[b] can mean sickness (*LY* 2.6), an aversion to something (*LY* 8.10, 14.32, 15.20), being quick (*M* 6B:2), or being eagerly devoted to something (*MT* 13/56, 25/57, 35/37, 36/23). It can also refer to a kind of internal disorder; for example, both the *Mo-tzu* (14/2) and the *Kuo-yü* (14/10a.11–10b.1) compare *chi*[b] in a person to disorder in government. In the context of 1B:3 and 1B:5, *chi*[b] probably refers to an intense and extreme form of desire running wild in oneself. It is presented by King Hsüan as an obstacle to his practicing *jen*[a] government, probably because when the king had finished talking to Mencius and gone back to the practical affairs of government, his *chi*[b] led him to act against Mencius's advice or even to stop seeing merit in it. It is probably the dangers of the distortive effect of desires that Mencius had in mind when he advocated reducing desires in 7B:35.[65] Also, his emphasis that the "constant heart/mind" of the common people depends on a "constant means of support" can be explained by the fact that if their basic needs are not met, people become preoccupied with their sustenance in a way that obstructs their ethical development (1A:7, 3A:3). An overly luxurious life can have its dangers too, however, since one can become overindulgent and not attend to ethical pursuits (6A:7).

Mencius's acknowledgment of these sources of ethical failure poses a problem for the picture of ethical failure found in 6A:15. In that passage, ethical failure is explained in terms of following the less important part of oneself (the senses) rather than the more important part (the heart/mind); furthermore, the ethical ideal will be attained as long as the heart/mind *ssu*[b] (reflect, thinks). The passage seems to locate the source of ethical failure entirely in the senses, and it is difficult to reconcile this idea with the account of the sources of ethical failure just described.

The problem is not that the senses cannot operate on their own without involving the heart/mind, since even if this is correct, one can still regard the senses as the primary source of ethical failure in that the operation of the heart/mind alone will not lead to ethical failure whereas the operation of the senses along with that of the heart/mind can.[66] Also, the problem is not that Mencius elsewhere described ethical failure as a matter of "losing" one's heart/mind and hence as something involving the heart/mind; even if ethical failure involves the loss of the heart/mind, the loss may be due primarily to the operation of the senses. And the problem is not the one raised by Wang Fu-chih (695), who thinks that since Mencius described ethical failure as a matter of following the less important part of the person (6A:15) or harming the more important part for the sake of the less important part (6A:14), there must be a subject that follows the less important part and harms the more important part for its sake. Since that subject, according to Wang Fu-chih, is the heart/mind, ethical failure is still traceable to the heart/mind. The observation that the subject must be the heart/mind is not entirely clear; it may well be the person as a whole. And even if the observation is correct, one can still regard the senses as the primary source of ethical failure in that it is always the inclinations of the senses that lead the heart/mind to follow the less important part.

Rather, the problem is that, given the different ways in which ethical failure may come about, it seems that it may sometimes have its source primarily in the heart/mind, contrary to what is suggested in 6A:15. For example, subscription to erroneous doctrines may well be traceable primarily to errors in the functioning of the heart/mind, rather than to the operation of the senses. Also, it is not clear that all distortive desires leading to ethical failure are traceable to the operation of the senses. For example, although a ruler's preoccupation with territorial expansion may arise from his desire for sensory satisfaction, it may also arise from a desire for power not necessarily related to sensory satisfaction. Wang Fu-chih formulates a related problem in terms of ssu^b; 6A:15 observes that one attains the ethical ideal if one ssu^b, but if ssu^b can be a reflection of any kind, it seems that ssu^b can also be in error. One response Wang Fu-chih (701) gives to the problem is that the kind of ssu^b that Mencius referred to in 6A:15 is not just reflection of any kind, but ssu^b directed toward yi^a. This proposal fits the interpretation of ssu^b described in §5.2.1, which takes ssu^b to involve reflecting on and seeking yi^a. However, the point remains that unethical behavior can result from certain operations of the heart/mind, even if such operations are not instances of the kind of ssu^b referred to in 6A:15.

As for remedying the two main sources of ethical failure, one cure for erroneous teachings is to expose their errors, and this Mencius presented as his reason for engaging in disputation (3B:9). As for distortive desires, they can lead one to reject the ethical ideal, or even if one is drawn toward it to some extent, they can still lead one to lose sight of ethical considerations when the moment of action comes or to rationalize one's lack of effort in terms of a lack of ability. One remedy is to convince someone under the influence of such desires that being ethical will bring about what one desires rather than conflict with it, and Mencius often used such a strategy. He said to King Hui, for example, that the practice of jen^a yi^a will have desirable political consequences (1A:1), and to King Hsüan that jen^a government and sharing one's enjoyment of things with the people was compatible with, and may even help the king achieve, what he greatly desired (1A:7, 1B:1, 1B:5).

The use of such a strategy may lead to the impression that Mencius was advocating *jen^a yi^a* on the grounds that they bring personal advantage, and Herrlee G. Creel has even suggested on the basis of these passages that Mencius was advocating a kind of "enlightened selfishness."[67] Although this may describe part of what is happening in Mencius's dialogues with King Hui and King Hsüan, it does not fully capture Mencius's views. Although he did appeal to political advantage in talking to rulers, we have seen that he also defended the Confucian ideal in terms of realizing a direction of development implicit in the ethical predispositions of the heart/mind. The appeal to political advantage probably did not capture Mencius's basic views about the grounds for practicing *jen^a yi^a*, although it helped to motivate rulers preoccupied with such advantage.[68]

To complete this discussion of ethical failure, let us consider Mencius's views about certain semblances of goodness. According to him, although practicing *jen^a yi^a* can gain others' approval and a good reputation, one who practices *jen^a yi^a* for such purposes is not truly ethical but will only attain certain semblances. In 6A:17, he described a good reputation as a consequence of having *jen^a yi^a* in oneself, and yet, in describing the spontaneous reactions of the heart/mind in 2A:6 and 3A:5, he emphasized that the reactions are not directed toward gaining the approval of others. Passage 7B:11 can be interpreted as describing how someone out to make a name can act in certain ways, such as giving away a state of a thousand chariots, but reveals his true self when caught unaware, as seen from a reluctance to give away even a basketful of rice and a bowlful of soup. However, this is not the only possible interpretation; 7B:11 has been interpreted by Chao Ch'i (C), Chang Shih, and Sun Shih to describe two different kinds of individuals, those who are out to make a name for themselves and those who are not.

The most elaborate account of someone who aims at others' approval and has only a semblance of goodness is the description of the honest villager in 7B:37. In that passage, which refers back to ideas in the *Lun-yü* (*LY* 13.21, 17.13, 17.18; cf. 13.24), Mencius elaborated on Confucius's comment that failing to find those who accord with the Way as associates, he would fall back on the wild and squeamish.[69] The wild is characterized as one who rushes forward, aspiring to be like the ancients; the squeamish as one who would not do certain things. The idea of not doing certain things (*pu wei[a]*) is highlighted in 4B:8 and 7A:17 and associated with *yi[a]* in 7B:31; 7B:31 gives the examples of not boring through or climbing over a wall to get a wife (cf. 3B:3) and not accepting abusive forms of address (cf. 6A:10). It is also linked in 7B:37 to disdain (*pu hsieh*) for the unclean and probably has to do with *ch'ih*, a sense of what is below oneself, which Mencius regarded as crucial to self-improvement (7A:7, cf. 7A:6).[70] The honest villager is characterized as one whose way of life is entirely geared to social opinion. His goal is others' good opinion, and since he adjusts his way of life accordingly, it is difficult to find anything in him that is obviously criticizable. His way of life appears good, everyone approves of him, and he regards himself as living properly. Yet he does not truly have *te[a]*, although he resembles someone with *te[a]* in a way that makes it easy for people to mistake him as having *te[a]* and hence to give him the name of *te[a]*; in this sense, he is a thief of *te[a]*.

What is common to both the wild and the squeamish is that they are motivated to improve themselves, by an aspiration to be like the ancients in one case and by a sense of what is below oneself in the other. This is one main respect in which the honest villager differs from these two: he has no serious commitment to improving himself beyond gaining others' approval, and he is content and regards himself as living properly as long as he gains that approval. His is a typical case of improving oneself for others (*wei[a] jen[b]*) rather than for the self (*wei[a] chi[a]*), and his practicing goodness for others' approval makes what he practices a semblance rather than genuine goodness.[71]

Given Mencius's criticism of those who gear their way of life to others' opinion, it might seem puzzling that he himself sometimes spoke as if self-cultivation should be guided by others' response. For example, 4A:4 observes that one should examine oneself for *jen[a]* (benevolence, humaneness), *chih[b]* (wisdom), and *ching* (reverence, seriousness) if others do not respond to one's love, government, and courtesy with affection, order, and courtesy; it also observes in general that one should always examine oneself if one does not fare well in dealing with others. Passage 4B:28 likewise describes how the superior person engages in self-examination whenever he does not fare well in dealing with others, and 2A:7 (cf. *LC* 20/12a.5–7) compares the practice of *jen[a]* to archery—when one misses the mark, one turns to oneself to see if one has properly straightened oneself. These observations are probably explained by Mencius's views about the transformative effect of a cultivated character. Since a cultivated character leads to certain responses from others, lack of the appropriate response reveals a deficiency in one's character. In altering oneself in light of others' responses, one is not making others' responses one's goal in self-cultivation but merely using them as a way of assessing one's progress.

6 Hsing^a (Nature, Characteristic Tendencies)

6.1   Jen^b (Human) hsing^a

6.1.1   The Use of "hsing^a"

Having considered Mencius's views on self-cultivation, let us turn to his views on *jen^b hsing^a*. Roger T. Ames has recently challenged the common translation of "jen^b hsing^a" as "human nature" and proposed that although Mencius might have believed that certain things pertaining to human beings are unlearned and shared by all human beings, he viewed *jen^b hsing^a* more as a cultural achievement that is accomplished against the background of what is unlearned and shared.[1] The proposal has led to further debate, and the issues involved include not just the issue of translation but also substantive questions of how the term "hsing^a" is used in the *Meng-tzu* and how Mencius viewed *jen^b hsing^a*.[2] These are distinct though related questions. For example, although perhaps the term "hsing^a" by itself does not carry the connotation of something unlearned and shared, Mencius may nevertheless have regarded what constitutes *jen^b hsing^a* as something unlearned and shared. I will consider these two questions in turn.

We saw in §2.3.1 that the term "hsing^a" was used in early texts to refer to a thing's direction of growth over its lifetime, to its needs and desires by virtue of being alive, or to its characteristic tendencies or inclinations. The *Meng-tzu* uses "hsing^a," at least on some occasions, to refer to a thing's characteristic tendencies. This can be seen from the verbal uses of "hsing^a" in passages 7A:21, 7A:30, and 7B:33, and the parallel uses of "hsing^a" and "ch'ing^a" (fact, what is genuine) in 6A:6 and 6A:8.

"Hsing^a" is used verbally in 7A:21, 7A:30, and 7B:33: 7A:21 has "chün tzu so hsing^a" (that which the superior person *hsing^a*); 7A:30, "Yao Shun hsing^a chih^g yeh" (Yao and Shun *hsing^a* it); 7B:33, "Yao Shun hsing^a che yeh" (Yao and Shun are those who *hsing^a*). In each passage, *hsing^a* probably concerns *jen^a* or *jen^a yi^a li^a chih^b*. Passage 7A:21 contrasts what one desires, what one takes joy in, and what one *hsing^a*, where the object of *hsing^a* is *jen^a yi^a li^a chih^b*. In 7A:30, the contrast is between Yao and Shun, who *hsing^a* it, T'ang and Wu, who embodied (*shen^a*) it, and the five overlords, who made use of or made a pretense of (*chia*) it. Since an overlord is described in 2A:3 as someone who made use of or made a pretense of *jen^a*, the object of "*hsing^a*" in 7A:30 is probably *jen^a*. In 7B:33, the contrast is between Yao and Shun, who *hsing^a*, and T'ang and Wu, who returned to it (*fan chih^g*); comparison with 7A:30 shows that the contrast is likely to concern these individuals' relation to *jen^a*.

Let us first consider 7A:21. Commentators propose at least three interpretations of what it means for the superior person to *hsing^a* the ethical attributes *jen^a yi^a li^a chih^b*. The first is that the superior person has the ethical attributes by birth. For example, Chu Hsi (MTCC; YL 1443–44) takes "chün tzu so hsing^a" to refer to what the superior person receives from *t'ien*, and Chang Shih to what the superior person receives at birth. In this interpretation, which is also implicit in Legge's translation, to say that circumstances do not add to or detract from what the superior person *hsing^a* is to say that the ethical attributes pertain to the superior person by birth and do not vary with circumstances.

In the second interpretation, to *hsing^a* something is to cultivate oneself so that the thing truly becomes part of oneself. Roger T. Ames probably interprets "chün tzu so hsing^a" in this way, given his translation of the passage as "what the (superior) person cultivates as (*hsing^a*)."[3] Here, the reference to not being affected by circumstances amounts to the claim that one has cultivated the ethical attributes in oneself with such firmness that one cannot be swayed by circumstances, whether favorable or unfavorable.

Wang Fu-chih's (738–40) comment on the passage suggests a third interpretation: namely, for the superior person to *hsing^a* something is for the person to regard the thing as *hsing^a* and hence to follow and nourish it. This interpretation is proposed by A. C. Graham and Mou Tsung-san and reflected in Lau's and Ware's translations.[4] It relates 7A:21 to 7B:24, in which Mencius's concern also seems to be with what may properly be regarded as *hsing^a*. In this interpretation, the comment about not being affected by circumstances can be interpreted as the claim that the superior person regards the ethical attributes as *hsing^a* because they are within one's control. One can attain the ethical attributes regardless of circumstances, but controlling extensive territories and a vast population or standing in the center of the empire and bringing peace to the people is dependent on circumstances. Yen Hui, for example, attained the former but not the latter.

All three interpretations can be applied to 7A:30 and 7B:33. The first interpretation would say that Yao and Shun had *jen^a* by birth without the need for learning and cultivation, unlike T'ang and Wu, who had to learn and cultivate themselves to attain *jen^a*.[5] The second interpretation would say that Yao and Shun *hsing^a jen^a* in that they truly embodied *jen^a* and were able to practice it without effort.[6] And the third interpretation would say that Yao and Shun *hsing^a jen^a* in that they regarded *jen^a* as their *hsing^a* and nourished and followed it.[7]

The first interpretation takes the ethical attributes to pertain to the superior person (7A:21) and to Yao and Shun (7A:30, 7B:33) by birth; this presumably distinguishes them from those with whom they are contrasted. This interpretation is unlikely since there is no evidence in the *Meng-tzu* that Mencius regarded people as differing in their ethical qualities by birth. On the contrary, in 6A:7, he claimed that the ancient sages were of the same kind as other human beings, and that what distinguished the sages was that they first discovered and attained what is common to the heart/mind of everyone. In 4B:32, he emphasized that Yao and Shun were basically the same as other human beings, and in 4B:28, he said that Shun was a human being just like everyone else. In 4B:19, he observed that only a slight element distinguishes human beings from other animals, and that what distinguishes the superior person from others is that the former alone preserves this element; a similar point is implied in 4B:28. Also, in 4B:28 Mencius described the superior person as someone who aspires to such attributes, making it unlikely that he regarded the superior person as having such attributes by birth. Passage 4B:14 can be read as having a similar implication: that which the superior person desires to attain and in which the superior person resides with ease is probably *jen^a*, since *jen^a* is described in 4A:10 (cf. 7A:33) as that in which one resides with ease.[8]

As for the other two interpretations, there is one main objection to the third interpretation. It takes the verbal use of "*hsing^a*" to mean "regard as one's *hsing^a*"; if we adopt this interpretation, we should give a parallel reading to the verbal use of "yü^b" and "le" in 7A:21 and of "shen^a" and "chia" in 7A:30. However, such a parallel reading is unlikely for some of these characters. Wang Fu-shih (739), for example, makes this move with 7A:21, taking the verbal use of "yü^b" and "le" to mean regarding something as what one desires (*yü^b*) or takes joy in (*le*); it seems, however, more straightforward to read "yü^b chih^g" and "le chih^g" as "desiring it" and "taking joy in it." And, in 7A:30, "chia" seems to concern making use of or pretending to practice something rather than regarding something as *chia*, since the overlords are also described in terms of *chia jen^a* in 2A:3, where *chia jen^a* is contrasted with *hsing jen^a* (putting *jen^a* into practice) and so presumably has to do with making use of or pretending to practice *jen^a*.

This leaves us with the second interpretation, which takes the verbal use of "hsing^a" to mean embodying something or making it part of oneself. In §2.3.1, we saw that "hsing^a" can be used as a nominal to refer to tendencies characteristic of a thing, and this nominal use of "hsing^a" fits with the verbal use just described. Hence, the arguments for the second interpretation of the verbal use of "hsing^a" give some reason for interpreting its nominal use in this manner.

More direct evidence comes from the way "hsing^a" is related to "ch'ing^a" (fact, what is genuine) in the *Meng-tzu*. In 6A:6, when asked about his position on *hsing^a*, Mencius responded by talking about *ch'ing^a*. In 6A:8, when using the vegetative analogy to make the point that even a corrupt person has certain ethical endowments, Mencius shifted from speaking of the *hsing^a* of a mountain to speaking of the *ch'ing^a* of human beings. These observations suggest that *hsing^a* and *ch'ing^a* were, for Mencius, closely related. *Hsing^a* and *ch'ing^a* are also related in other early texts. For example, the *Shang-chün-shu* characterizes the *hsing^a* of the common people in terms of their seeking food, rest, enjoyment, and honor when hungry, exhausted, in misery, and in disgrace, respectively, and then refers to these as the *ch'ing^a* of the common people (*SCS* 13/5–6). Also, both "hsing^a" and "ch'ing^a" are used in early texts to characterize the relation between the senses and their ideal objects. On the one hand, the *Meng-tzu* characterizes the relation of the senses to their ideal objects as *hsing^a* (6A:7, 7B:24), and the Tzu-hua Tzu passage in the Yangist chapters of the *Lü-shih ch'un-ch'iu* characterizes "sheng^a," a term used interchangeably with "hsing^a" in the Yangist chapters, in terms of sensory desires (*LSCC* 2/7a.4–8a.6). On the other hand, the relation of the senses to their ideal objects are characterized in terms of *ch'ing^a* in both the Yangist chapters (*LSCC* 2/8a.8–10) and other chapters (*LSCC* 5/9b.6–10) of the *Lü-shih ch'un-ch'iu*.

To better understand the relation between these two terms, let us first consider the use of "ch'ing^a." "Ch'ing^a" is often used in early texts to refer to the facts about a situation. For example, in sentencing someone, one should be guided by the *ch'ing^a* of the situation (*TC* 85/5; *KY* 4/1b.3), and in government it is important to understand the *ch'ing^a* of those below one (*MT* 13/2–7). *Ch'ing^a* is something that one can inform others about (e.g., *KY* 19/11b.8; *TC* 643/2), conceal (e.g., *TC* 476/8, 552/3), or hear about (e.g., *TC* 394/1). It is often linked to *shih^b*, the way things really are (e.g., *KT* 3/37.4, 3/40.13; *LSCC* 17/20a.1), and contrasted with one's reputation (e.g., *TC* 815/3) and with false appearances (*wei^c*) (e.g., *TC* 204/5; *KT* 1/78.8–9; *LSCC* 3/16b.1; *MT* 36/2). When used in the context "X chih^g ch'ing^a" to talk about the *ch'ing^a* of X, "ch'ing^a" generally refers to certain characteristic features of X. For example, it is the *ch'ing^a* of the senses to desire their ideal objects (*LSCC* 5/9b.6–10a.1) and the *ch'ing^a* of human beings to desire life and honor and to have an aversion to death and disgrace (*LSCC* 5/10a.7–8, 8/4b.2–5). Sometimes the *ch'ing^a* of X can be certain characteristic features of X's as a class, without such features obtaining of each individual X. For example, that the common people have different abilities is described as the *ch'ing^a* of the common people (*ST*, p. 250, no. 33), and the distinction between genders is described as the *ch'ing^a* of human beings (*MT* 6/35). But often, the *ch'ing^a* of X includes characteristic features that obtain of X's as a class by virtue of their obtaining of each individual X, as when "ch'ing^a" is used to refer to the tendency of the senses to seek their ideal objects or to the desires and aversions that human beings have.

When used of characteristic features of things of a kind, "ch'ing^a" often refers to certain deep features that reveal what things of this kind are really like. For example, in the *Kuo-yü*, the *ch'ing^a* of a person is described as the person's *shih^b*, or what lies behind the person's appearances and reveals what the person is really like (*KY* 11/1b.4–2a.3). In the *Lü-shih ch'un-ch'iu*, the *ch'ing^a* of teaching (*LSCC* 4/12b.9–13a.1), of what is treasurable (*LSCC* 5/7b.1–9), of music (*LSCC* 5/7b.9–8b.4), and of burial (*LSCC* 10/5a.1–6a.1) are presented as what these things are really like, contrary to current practices or opinions. And, in the *Mo-tzu*, *ch'ing^a* is presented as something that cannot be altered even by the sages (*MT* 6/33–40).

For this reason, I am inclined to agree with A. C. Graham's interpretation of "ch'ing^a" in terms of what a thing is genuinely like. I would hesitate, however, to follow Graham in translating "ch'ing^a" as "essence" and interpreting *ch'ing^a* in terms of Aristotelian essence, partly because I hesitate to ascribe an Aristotelian framework to early Chinese thinkers and partly because it is unclear that early Chinese thinkers drew a distinction between essential and accidental properties.[9] Graham defends the interpretation of "ch'ing^a" as "essence" by citing Hui Shih's query in the *Chuang-tzu* whether a human being without *ch'ing^a* can be called a human being (CT 5/54–60). Suppose we confine our attention to Hui Shih's query and put aside the fact that Hui Shih and Chuang Tzu are presented here as disagreeing about the use of "ch'ing^a"; and let us also put aside the possibility that "ch'ing^a" in Hui Shih's query might refer to emotions. Even so, "ch'ing^a" might still refer just to certain characteristic features of human beings that are particularly conspicuous, pervasive, and difficult to alter, without necessarily having the connotation of what is essential as opposed to accidental.[10]

The preceding discussion shows that "ch'ing^a" could be used in early texts to refer to characteristic features of things of a kind that reveal what such things are really like. Earlier, we saw that the use of "hsing^a" is linked to "ch'ing^a" in both the *Meng-tzu* and other early texts. Also, in §2.3.1, we saw that "hsing^a" could be used in early texts to refer to characteristic tendencies of an object. These observations suggest that the use of "hsing^a" and the use of "ch'ing^a" are probably related in the following manner. The *ch'ing^a* of X's has to do with certain characteristic features of X's, features revealing the way X's are really like. Now, sometimes the *ch'ing^a* of X's can be features that obtain of X's as a class but not of each member of the class, as when the difference in the abilities of the common people is described as the *ch'ing^a* of the common people. But often, the *ch'ing^a* of X's has to do with features that obtain of X's individually, especially tendencies that each individual X has; examples include the reference to the desire for life and aversion to death as the *ch'ing^a* of human beings, or the reference to the senses being drawn toward their ideal objects as the *ch'ing^a* of the senses. When "ch'ing^a" refers to such tendencies, the tendencies can also be referred to as the *hsing^a* of X's, and this explains the parallel uses of "hsing^a" and "ch'ing^a."

However, there is still a difference in emphasis between the two. Whereas "ch'ing^a" emphasizes the fact that X's have certain characteristic tendencies, "hsing^a" emphasizes the presence of such tendencies as part of the constitution of X's. Also, whereas "ch'ing^a" emphasizes that the presence of the tendencies is something difficult to alter and reveals what X's are really like, "hsing^a" emphasizes that the tendencies are subject to all kinds of influences and can be nourished or harmed.[11] In addition, "hsing^a" also differs from "ch'ing^a" in that whereas "X chih^g ch'ing^a" can refer to characteristic features of X's as a class that are not also features of each individual X, "X chih^g hsing^a" cannot be so used. Take, for example, *Meng-tzu* 3A:4, which refers to the difference between things as the *ch'ing^a* of things. The point cannot be made by saying that such difference is the *hsing^a* of things; instead, if we are to use "hsing^a" to make a comparable observation, we would have to say that the *hsing^a* of things differ. Thus, whereas "hsing^a" and "ch'ing^a" are closely related in a way that sometimes makes it possible to shift from one character to the other, it is not the case that the two characters are synonymous or always interchangeable.[12]

Given the way "hsing^a" and "ch'ing^a" are related in the *Meng-tzu*, it is likely that the nominal use of "hsing^a" in the *Meng-tzu* refers to characteristic tendencies of things. This fits with the earlier observation that the verbal use of "hsing^a" in the *Meng-tzu* has to do with making certain things part of oneself. Returning to the question whether the use of "hsing^a" has the connotation of something unlearned, I am inclined to answer in the negative but with a qualification. There is no obvious reason why tendencies characteristic of a thing have to be unlearned, and to the extent that "hsing^a" refers to such tendencies, it need not carry such a connotation. It may appear that if X *chih^g hsing^a* comprises tendencies characteristic of X's, a thing must already have such tendencies in being an X and thus could not have acquired such tendencies. That this conclusion does not follow can be seen by considering the reference to the *hsing^a* of the petty person in the *Tso-chuan*. Even if one already has the aggressive tendencies under consideration in being a petty person, the tendencies may have been acquired in the process of becoming a petty person. That is, a human being (*jen^b*) might have learned such tendencies in the process of becoming a petty person (*shao jen^b*).[13] Still, the line of thought under consideration does reveal something interesting about the term "jen^b hsing^a"; assuming that no learning is involved in the process of becoming a *jen^b*, it seems to follow from this line of thought that the *hsing^a* of *jen^b* comprises tendencies that are unlearned. However, even if this is correct, it does not affect the point that "hsing^a" by itself need not carry the connotation of something unlearned.

As for the question whether "hsing^a" has the connotation of something shared, nothing in the use of the term precludes the possibility that the *hsing^a* of things of a kind differ. In *Meng-tzu* 6A:6, Kung-tu Tzu reported a position that regards the *hsing^a* of human beings as different.[14] In 6A:7, Mencius himself contemplated the possibility of *hsing^a* being different from person to person with regard to the disposition of palates toward tastes. It is not entirely clear whether it is the *hsing^a* of human beings or of palates that is referred to in 6A:7.[15] But, either way, the fact that Mencius contemplated (though eventually rejected) the possibility of its being different for things of the same kind shows that the use of "hsing^a" itself does not carry the connotation that *hsing^a* must be the same for all things of the same kind. This observation also provides reason for not taking "hsing^a" to refer to the essence of things of a kind, if what constitutes the essence is supposed to be the same for all things of the same kind.

6.1.2 *Mencius's Views on jen^b hsing^a*

For the reasons given in the preceding section, I am inclined to the view that the use of "hsing^a" by itself does not carry the connotation of something unlearned and shared, with the qualification that there is a line of thought that may lead to the conclusion that *jen^b hsing^a* is something unlearned. The next question is whether Mencius, in thinking about *jen^b hsing^a*, viewed it as something unlearned and shared by all human beings. To address this question, we need to look at what Mencius actually said about *jen^b hsing^a*.

In §5.1.2, we saw that Mencius believed that the heart/mind has certain ethical predispositions with a direction of development realized in the ethical ideal. His characterization of this development is in various ways like the way the Yangists characterized *hsing^a/sheng^a*. Just as the Yangists advocated subordinating sensory satisfaction and external possessions to *hsing^a/sheng^a* and described letting the former harm the latter as a loss of balance, Mencius similarly regarded sensory satisfaction (e.g., 6A:15) and external possessions (e.g., 6A:10) as subordinate to the development of the heart/mind and described the harming of this development as a loss of balance (6A:14–15). And just as the Yangists spoke of nourishing *hsing^a/sheng^a* and thought of *hsing^a/sheng^a* as due to *t'ien*, Mencius spoke of nourishing *hsing^a* to serve *t'ien*, this being a matter of preserving the heart/mind (7A:1). These parallels, along with the linking of *hsing^a* to the heart/mind in

7A:1 and the linking of *hsing^a* to the ethical attributes in 7B:24, show that Mencius regarded *hsing^a* as constituted by, or at least as having as its central component, the direction of development implicit in the ethical predispositions of the heart/mind.[16]

The question is whether he regarded these ethical predispositions as something unlearned and shared. One consideration that some might cite to show that Mencius regarded the ethical predispositions as unlearned is his use of the character "liang" to characterize the knowledge (*liang chih^a*) and ability (*liang neng*) involved in loving parents and respecting elder brothers (7A:15), the heart/mind (6A:8), and the true honors of *jen^a* and *yi^a* (6A:17). Chu Hsi (MTCC 6A:8, 6A:17, 7A:15) takes "liang" to refer to original goodness (*pen jan chih^8 shan*), and Chang Shih (7A:15) to have both the meaning of "original" (*pen jan*) and "good" (*shan*). However, the interpretation of "liang" as "original" is controversial. Chao Ch'i (C 7A:15) takes the character to mean "shen$^{c''}$ (very, excel), Wang Fu-chih (735) to mean "shan" (good), and P'ei Hsüeh-hai (7A:15) to mean "what is truly so." Chiao Hsün (6A:8, 6A:17, 7A:15) thinks it has the meanings of "shan" (good), "mei" (beautiful), and "shen$^{c''}$ (very, excel). The interpretation of "liang" as "good" allows us to make sense of many occurrences of "liang" in both the *Meng-tzu* (e.g., 3B:1, 6B:9) and other early texts that describe as *liang* things like horses, physicians, ministers, craftsmen, farmers, and merchants. On some occasions, "liang" probably takes on the meaning of what is truly so, as when *yi^a* is described as what is truly treasurable (*MT* 46/27–30). But, as far as I can tell, none of the occurrences of "liang" in early texts requires our taking "liang" to mean "what is original." For this reason, the use of "liang" in the *Meng-tzu* in connection with the heart/mind and its ethical predispositions does not by itself provide evidence that Mencius regarded such predispositions as unlearned.

Still, there is evidence that Mencius did regard the ethical predispositions as at least involving something unlearned. Despite the uncertainty about the interpretation of "liang" in 7A:15, Mencius did in that passage describe love for parents and respect for elder brothers as something one knows and is able to do without learning. Another consideration is the linking of such predispositions to *t'ien*. *Hsing^a* is linked to *t'ien* in 7A:1, and in 3A:5, if the interpretation of the passage described in §4.5.3 is correct, Mencius described one's reaction to the sight of the dead bodies of parents as coming from *t'ien* and as that by virtue of which burying parents is proper. Since in 5A:6 Mencius also ascribed to *t'ien* what is not due to human beings, the ascription of such reactions to *t'ien* implies that such reactions are not acquired through learning.

Even though Mencius believed that the ethical predispositions of the heart/mind involve something not acquired through learning, it is possible that what is unlearned has to be refined and nurtured by upbringing for them to develop into the form presented in some passages. For example, although there may be certain instinctual compassionate responses not acquired through learning, these have to be refined and nurtured via upbringing for them to develop into the kind of compassionate response described in 1A:7. In that passage, King Hsüan is described as viewing the ox as if it were an innocent person being led to the place of execution; such a reaction presupposes a conception of innocence that has to be learned.[17] Similarly, the response to abusive treatment described in 6A:10 presupposes a grasp of what constitutes proper treatment of people, again something that has to be learned.

Or consider again 7A:15, which describes love for parents and respect for elders as a starting point for cultivating *jen^a* and *yi^a*. Although love for parents may initially take the form of an attachment to individuals from whom one has received care and nourishment, love in a more refined form involves acquiring a conception of the objects of such attachment as parents as well as a conception of what constitutes their well-being. Similarly, respect for elders may initially take the form of deference to certain individuals whom one does not conceptualize as elders, but a subsequent grasp of the distinction between senior and junior members of the family and subscription to norms governing conduct between them requires learning. Thus, although Mencius probably believed that there are certain unlearned responses bearing an affinity to the ethical ideal, the kind of ethical predispositions that provide the basis for self-reflection probably involve refinement of such responses through appropriate upbringing.[18]

Did Mencius regard such ethical predispositions, or at least the unlearned responses of which they are refinements, as something generally shared? In 2A:6 and 6A:6, he said that the four germs are shared by all *jen^b*, and in 2A:6, he remarked that one who lacks the four germs would not be a *jen^b*. In 6A:6 he distanced himself from the view that *hsing^a* differs in different individuals, and in 6A:7 he emphasized that the sages and the ordinary people belong to the same kind and that a disposition to take pleasure in propriety is shared by the heart/mind of everyone. In 6A:10 he claimed that every *jen*ᵇ desires propriety (*yi*ᵃ) more than life, and in 7A:15 he described all children as knowing to love their parents and, later in life, to respect elder brothers. These observations provide evidence that he regarded the ethical predispositions, or at least certain unlearned responses of which they are refinements, as shared by all *jen*ᵇ. However, although I have up to this point translated "jen*ᵇ*" as "human beings," the questions what the scope of *jen*ᵇ is and what sort of claim Mencius was making in saying that all *jen*ᵇ share such responses remain.

Roger T. Ames has suggested the interesting possibility that "jen*ᵇ*" may refer not to biological human beings as such, but to people who are already to some extent cultured.[19] This possibility gains support from certain occurrences of "jen*ᵇ*" in early texts. For example, in *Lun-yü* 14.9, in response to a question about what Kuan Chung is like, Confucius said that Kuan Chung was a *jen*ᵇ; here, "jen*ᵇ*" seems to refer to someone with certain accomplishments.[20] In addition, the frequent use of "ch'eng jen*ᵇ*" (complete *jen*ᵇ) to refer to someone of accomplishment (e.g., *TC* 704/17) seems to imply that certain accomplishments are needed for one to be fully a *jen*ᵇ.

However, some early texts, such as the *Mo-tzu* (e.g., *MT* 6/35, 32/30), also use "jen*ᵇ*" to refer to human beings as a species distinct from other animals, and this seems to show that one can be a *jen*ᵇ independently of one's accomplishments. It is likely that these two usages are related; although "jen*ᵇ*" is often used to refer to human beings as a species, early thinkers viewed what distinguishes human beings as a species in social terms. For example, although the *Mo-tzu* uses "jen*ᵇ*" to refer to human beings as a species distinct from other animals, it also comments that human beings can become like other animals in the absence of social distinctions and norms governing such distinctions (*MT* 12/4–5). Likewise, the *Hsün-tzu* describes what makes a *jen*ᵇ a *jen*ᵇ (*jen*ᵇ *chih*ˢ *so yi wei*ᵃ *jen*ᵇ) in terms of social differentiations (*pien*) and distinctions (*fen*; *HT* 5/23–28; cf. 9/69–73). Thus, what distinguishes *jen*ᵇ from other animals is not their biological constitution, but their capacity for certain cultural accomplishments. But if "jen*ᵇ*" refers to a species characterized by the capacity for cultural accomplishments, it is a natural extension to use "jen*ᵇ*" in such a way that certain accomplishments are needed for one to be (truly) a *jen*ᵇ or to be a complete *jen*ᵇ.

To return to the *Meng-tzu*, "jen*ᵇ*" is also used to refer to human beings as a species distinct from other animals, as seen from the reference to "jen^b" as a kind (6A:7) and from the contrast between "jen^b" and other animals (4B:19). Moreover, "jen^b" can be used to refer to members of the species who are not yet cultured, as when "jen^b" is used to refer to both the common person and the superior person (4B:19) or to young children—one's compassion for a young child is described as the heart/mind of being unable to bear the suffering of *jen^b* (2A:6), and a young child's love for parents is cited to illustrate what a *jen^b* knows and is capable of without having to learn (7A:15). Still, what distinguishes *jen^b* as a species is not their biological constitution, but their capacity for certain cultural accomplishments; for example, the text describes one who denies social distinctions (3B:9) or fails to make use of his capabilities (6A:8) as one who is, or has become close to, lower animals.

Thus, in the *Meng-tzu* as in other early texts, *jen^b* is viewed as a species distinguished from lower animals by its social capability. We just saw that Mencius believed that certain ethical predispositions, or at least certain unlearned responses of which such predispositions are refinements, are shared by all *jen^b*. In §5.1.1, we also saw that he regarded such predispositions or responses as that by virtue of which one is able to live up to the ethical ideal. Probably, his view is that the capacity for cultural accomplishment that defines the species of *jen^b* is something that *jen^b* possess by virtue of their sharing such predispositions or responses. To the extent that one lacks such predispositions or responses, one lacks the capacity for such cultural accomplishments. Since human beings as a species are characterized in terms of the capacity for such cultural accomplishments, it also follows that one who lacks such predispositions or responses is not a *jen^b*.

Thus, this last observation by Mencius is not a mere terminological claim about the use of "jen^b." Instead, it is a substantive comment involving two claims—that members of the species of *jen^b* share certain ethical predispositions or responses, and that the capacity for cultural accomplishments that makes one a *jen^b* depends on the presence of such predispositions or responses. On the other hand, his observation is not just a straightforward empirical generalization that is falsifiable by a single instance of someone without such predispositions or responses. Instead, an admission that *jen^b* can lack such predispositions or responses would lead to a reconsideration of what it is that makes a *jen^b* capable of cultural accomplishments. As we will see in §6.4, Hsün Tzu denied Mencius's observation and proposed that the capacity for cultural accomplishments that makes one a *jen^b* is a matter of *k'o yi* (capability), which, unlike *neng* (ability), does not depend on the presence of ethical predispositions.

6.1.3   *Passage 4B:26*

The view that *hsing^a* is constituted by the direction of development implicit in certain ethical predispositions of the heart/mind was probably one among many responses to the Yangist conception, which construed *hsing^a/sheng^a* in biological terms and regarded *hsing^a/sheng^a* as the proper direction of development for human beings. The trend of thought represented by the "Chieh" chapter of the *Kuan-tzu* (and also by Kao Tzu in one interpretation of his position) retained the first feature but rejected the second; it construed *hsing^a/sheng^a* in terms of the life forces but advocated imposing *yi^a* on *hsing^a/sheng^a*. In a way, the trend of thought represented by the "Nei yeh" chapter of the *Kuan-tzu* retained both features but with a modification. It construed *hsing^a/sheng^a* in terms of *ch'i^a*, the vital energies, and advocated nourishing *ch'i^a* by quieting the *heart/mind*; however, when *ch'i^a* responds free of interference by the heart/mind, it is supposed to lead one in a Confucian direction. Mencius's response, on the other hand, retains the second feature but rejects the first. For Mencius, *hsing^a* is still the proper direction of development for human beings, but it is no longer seen as identical with *sheng^a*, where *sheng^a* is understood in biological terms (cf. M 6A:3). Instead, *hsing^a* is constituted by the direction of development of the ethical predispositions of the heart/mind, and ideally the heart/mind should guide *ch'i^a*, the vital energies (cf. M 2A:2).

Mencius's conception of *hsing^a* thus differs from those of others in that he no longer construed *hsing^a* in biological terms. That Mencius was probably aware of his differences from others can be seen from 4B:26, in which he commented on prevalent views on *hsing^a*. There is disagreement whether the passage is focused more on *hsing^a* or on wisdom (*chih^b*). Although the passage begins with a reference to the way people in Mencius's time discoursed on *hsing^a*, it continues with a discussion of wisdom, and some have observed that the passage is primarily about wisdom rather than *hsing^a* (e.g., Chu Hsi, MTCC, citing Ch'eng I with approval; Hu Ping-wen). However, others have questioned why the passage should begin by referring to *hsing^a* if it is primarily about wisdom and argued that the passage's focus is more on *hsing^a* (e.g., Wang Fu-chih, 637). It is not important for my purpose to decide whether wisdom or *hsing^a* is the primary focus, since my concern is only to see what the passage reveals about Mencius's attitude to contemporary views of *hsing^a*.

The passage may be divided into three parts. Part (a) characterizes as *ku* the prevalent views of *hsing^a* and claims that *ku* takes *li^b* (smooth, profit) as the basis (*pen*). Part (b) opposes the kind of wisdom that involves boring through or chiseling, and observes that ideal wisdom should involve *wu shih^a* (not causing things to happen) and resemble the way Yü channeled water. Part (c) observes that if one seeks *ku* with regard to Heaven's height and the stars' distance, one can arrive at the solstices of a thousand years. The interpretation of (b) is relatively uncontroversial; commentators generally agree that it advocates following *hsing^a* rather than imposing things on it, although the character "hsing^a" does not occur in part (b) (e.g., Chu Hsi, MTCC; Chang Shih; Sun Shih). The interpretation of "ku" in part (c) is unclear and is an issue of disagreement among commentators, but it seems clear that part (c) is speaking favorably of *ku*. The main issue of disagreement concerns the interpretation of the occurrences of "ku" and "li^b" in part (a). "Li^b" has been interpreted to mean "profit," used pejoratively by Mencius, or to mean "smooth" or "following the course of things," as in the combination "li^b k'ou" (smooth talk) in 7B:37. In part (a), *ku* has been interpreted in at least four different ways: the path (*chi^c*) or the original condition (*pen*) of *hsing^a*; the bringing about of things, as in "shih^a ku"; what is former or in the past (*chiu*); or what is customary or usual. Corresponding to these four readings of "ku" are four different interpretations of part (a).[21]

The first interpretation, proposed by Chu Hsi (MTCC; YL 1351–54), takes "ku" to mean the "path" (*chi^c*) of *hsing^a* and "li^b" to mean "following the natural course of things." According to Chu Hsi, *hsing^a* is not directly visible, but its manifestation has a path that is easily seen and that follows the natural course of things; thus, in discoursing on *hsing^a*, one should seek *hsing^a* in the path (*ku*) of its manifestation, which follows the natural course (*li^b*) of things. Similarly, Yü Yüeh (MTPI) takes "ku" to mean the "original condition" (*pen*) of *hsing^a*, and "li^b" to mean "following the original condition." Chang Shih and Huang Tsung-hsi (2/38a.8–40b.1) have a similar interpretation, which is also implicit in the translations by Legge and Yang. The interpretation can be taken in two directions: as saying that the current views of *hsing^a* did succeed in seeking the *ku* of *hsing^a*, or as saying that those views, although seeking the *ku* of *hsing^a*, failed to do so and hence misunderstood *hsing^a*. If we adopt the proposed reading of "ku" and "li^b," the second direction would be more plausible, since, in light of the views of *hsing^a* reported in 6A:6 that differ from Mencius's, and in light of Mencius's debate with Kao Tzu about *hsing^a* in 6A:1–3 and his references to the influence of Yangist thought in 3B:9 and 7A:26, we would expect him to express disagreement with the prevalent views of *hsing^a*.[22]

The second interpretation takes "ku" to mean "bringing about," as in the use of "ku" in "shih^a ku," and "li^b" to mean "profit." In this interpretation, *ku* involves *yu shih^a* (causing things to happen), which is contrasted with *wu shih^a* (not causing things to happen) in part (b) of the passage; in devoting oneself to bringing things about, one aims at profit, and in this sense *ku* takes *li^b* (profit) as a basis. In this interpretation, the prevalent views of *hsing^a* understood it in terms of bringing things about, and hence failed to understand *hsing^a*, which has to do with what is spontaneous or does not involve causing things to happen (*wu shih^a*). This interpretation is proposed by Sun Shih and defended at length by Huang Chang-chien.[23]

The third interpretation takes "ku" to mean "former" ("chiu"), an interpretation defended by A. C. Graham on the basis of the occurrences of the character in other early texts, especially the pairing of "ku" and "chih^b" (wisdom) in the *Kuan-tzu* and the *Chuang-tzu*.[24] According to Graham, those texts oppose *chih^b* in the sense of clever invocation and *ku* in the sense of skill in adducing precedents that binds one to the past. However, in the context of part (a) of 4B:26, Graham takes *ku* to concern the physical appetites with which one is born; that is, the prevalent views of *hsing^a* regarded *hsing^a* as no more than the physical appetites with which one is born; the link to *li^b* (profit) is presumably that satisfaction of such appetites profits one.[25] A variation of this reading can be found in Lau's translation, which takes *ku* to refer to former theories; Lau probably takes "li^b" to mean smooth, since he takes part (a) to be saying that people in the world followed theories of the past because these could be explained with ease.

The fourth interpretation takes "ku" to mean "customary or habitual" and "li^b" to mean "profit." On the basis of the occurrence of "ku" in a passage in the *Chuang-tzu* (19/51–54) that explains *ku* in terms of one's settling at the place where one is born, Hsü Fu-kuan argues that it means "customary" and that part (a) of the passage says that the prevalent views of *hsing^a* concern what people customarily do, namely, work for profit (*li^b*).²⁶ A similar interpretation of part (a) is implicit in Lyall's translation.

I find the first of these four interpretations less plausible than the others. It presents the prevalent views of *hsing^a* as being in the right direction in seeking the path or the original condition of *hsing^a*, even if they do not succeed in doing so. However, we have seen that Mencius disagreed with prevalent views, and since part (b) goes on to criticize certain kinds of so-called wisdom, the criticism is probably directed against the prevalent views of *hsing^a* mentioned in part (a). Since the criticism in part (b) is that an account of *hsing^a* should not involve chiseling or boring through things but should follow the natural course of things, it is unlikely that Mencius could have conceded in part (a) that the prevalent views were in the right direction in seeking the path or the original condition of *hsing^a*. That "li^b" is often understood in a pejorative sense in the *Meng-tzu* might also seem to speak against the first interpretation, which takes "li^b" to be used in a positive sense. But this consideration is not compelling, since, as we saw in §5.3, "li^b" is sometimes used in a positive sense in the *Meng-tzu*.²⁷ A more compelling consideration is Graham's observation that the pairing of "ku" and "chih^b" in 4B:26 suggests that the use of "ku" in the passage is probably similar to the use of "ku" in the pairing of "ku" and "chih^b" in the *Kuan-tzu* and the *Chuang-tzu*. Given the negative way "ku" is viewed in these texts, it is unlikely that the character as it occurs in part (a) of 4B:26 can have the positive connotation that the first interpretation ascribes to it.

An examination of the occurrences of "ku" in conjunction with "chih^b" in the *Kuan-tzu*, however, suggests that "ku" probably carries the meaning of "bringing things about," the meaning ascribed to it by the second interpretation, rather than the meaning of "former" that Graham ascribes to it. The two references to discarding *chih^b* and *ku* in the *Kuan-tzu* (*KT* 2/63.4–9, 2/65.8–66.2) advocate non-action (*wu wei^a*), which involves responding (*ying*) without preconception (*she*) and moving (*tung*) without choosing (*ch'ü*), as opposed to "using of the self" (*tzu yung*). This makes it likely that the *ku* that is opposed is a matter of devoting oneself to bringing about certain goals, and the reference to responding (*ying*) and moving (*tung*) immediately after talking about discarding *chih^b* and *ku* suggests that the reference to moving without choosing is what is involved in discarding *ku*.

Support for this last observation comes from the fact that the section that contains the second reference to discarding *chih^b* and *ku* (*KT* 2/65.8–66.2) opposes moving (*tung*) on the basis of *ku* and advocates moving in a way that follows pattern or principle (*li^c*) without choosing (*ch'ü*). This shows that moving on the basis of *ku* involves choosing goals and being guided by such goals rather than following the natural course of things. Since the reference to discarding *chih^b* and *ku* in the *Chuang-tzu* (*CT* 15/11–12) also occurs in a context that refers to the way to respond and move and to following the pattern or principle of *t'ien*, it is likely that "ku" here carries a similar meaning. Thus, if we follow Graham in taking *ku* in part (a) of 4B:26 to be used in a way similar to its occurrence in the references to discarding *chih^b* and *ku* in the *Kuan-tzu* and the *Chuang-tzu*, it seems that the second interpretation is correct in taking "ku" to mean bringing things about in contrast to following the natural course of things.

Several other considerations support this interpretation of "ku."[28] First, interpreting "ku" in terms of "shih^a" allows us to make sense of the link between part (a) and part (b) of 4B:26. In contrasting the ideal form of *chih^b* with other forms of *chih^b*, part (b) characterizes the former in terms of *wu shih^a*, illustrating the idea by referring to how Yü channeled water by following its natural course, an idea similar to the reference in the *Kuan-tzu* and the *Chuang-tzu* to following pattern or principle. This suggests that the forms of wisdom being opposed are those involving *yu shih^a*, and if we interpret "ku" in terms of "shih^a ku," parts (a) and (b) are linked in that the kind of wisdom opposed in part (b) is precisely the kind illustrated by the prevalent views of *hsing^a* referred to in part (a).

Second, the proposed interpretation gains support from another part of the *Chuang-tzu* that speaks of not letting human beings bring destruction to *t'ien* and not letting *ku* bring destruction to *ming^a*; preceding this observation, what is due to *t'ien* is illustrated by the example of oxen and horses having four feet, and what is due to human beings by putting a halter on the horse's head and piercing the ox's nose (*CT* 17/51–52). Given the close link between *t'ien* and *ming^a*, "ku" in this context probably concerns activities due to human beings that go against the natural course of things.

Third, occurrences of "ku" in other texts are close in meaning to the proposed interpretation. For example, the *Huai-nan-tzu* links *ku* to deceit—when those above exercise *ku*, those below will exercise deceit (*HNT* 9/2b.6, 10/2b.11). This suggests that "ku" as it occurs here refers to plotting or scheming, and this is close to the interpretation of "ku" as devoting oneself to bringing about things.

Fourth, both "ku" and "shih^a" are related to "li^b" in the sense of profit in Yangist and Mohist teachings. For example, the Yangist chapters of the *Lü-shih ch'un-ch'iu* speak of taking as *ku* one's completing (what one gets from) *t'ien* (LSCC 1/6a.10–6b.2) or facilitating *sheng^a* (life; LSCC 2/11b.6), where "ku" is likely to refer to that to which one devotes oneself. They also speak of what *li^b* one's *hsing^a/sheng^a* as a guiding consideration (e.g., LSCC 1/8a.3–4). The *Mo-tzu* regards promoting the *li^b* (benefit) of people in the world as what the *jen^a* (benevolent, humane) person devotes himself to (*shih^a*; MT 15/1, 16/1) and also speaks of devoting oneself to (*shih^a*) benefiting (*li^b*) others' parents (MT 16/66–69). In light of Mencius's reference to Yangist and Mohist teachings as two dominant influences of his time, and his characterization of the prevalent views of *hsing^a* in terms of *ku* and *li^b*, it is likely that part (a) of 4B:26 contains a criticism of prevalent views that talked about *hsing^a* in connection with devoting oneself to bringing about *li^b* (profit, benefit).

For these reasons, I am inclined to accept the second interpretation of part (a) of 4B:26. In this interpretation, the prevalent views of *hsing^a* are not really about *hsing^a* but about devoting oneself to things that bring about *li^b* (profit, benefit). Such views exemplify the objectionable form of *chih^b* referred to in part (b). In part (b), the reference to boring through or chiseling probably concerns how such prevalent views advocate devoting oneself to things that go against *hsing^a*; presumably, the targets of criticism include the views of the Yangists and Kao Tzu. Instead, true wisdom should involve following the course of one's *hsing^a*, in the way that Yü followed the natural course of water in guiding it.

Graham mentions other considerations in support of his reading of "ku." He takes the reference to discarding *ch'iao ku* in the *Lü-shih ch'un-ch'iu* (LSCC 3/13a.9–10) to refer to skillful *ku*, with "ku" interpreted to mean "former"; probably what he has in mind is skill in adducing precedents binding one to the past. However, the context in which "ch'iao ku" occurs does not point unambiguously to any specific interpretation of "ku"; for example, "ku" could well refer to the kind of plotting and scheming that the *Huai-nan-tzu* passages describe as leading to deceit. Graham also cites the reference in the *Han-fei-tzu* to discarding *chiu* (what is former) and *chih^b* (wisdom), taking the pairing of "chiu" and "chih^b" here to show that "ku," when paired with "chih^b," should mean "chiu" (former; *HFT* 5.1.26). Although this is a significant observation, its force as evidence for the third interpretation is counterbalanced by the opposition to *shih^a* and *chih^a* (knowing) in the *Chuang-tzu* (*CT* 7/31). Since the *Chuang-tzu* also speaks of discarding *chih^b* and *ku*, and since *chih^a* (knowing) and *chih^b* (wisdom) are closely related, this also provides support for interpreting "ku," when paired with "chih^b," to mean "shih^a."

Although I am inclined more to the second interpretation, two considerations might favor the third or fourth interpretation over the second. One is that part of the *Chuang-tzu* explains "ku" in terms of being contented with living where one is born (*CT* 19/51–54); here, "ku" is likely to mean what is former (Graham) or customary (Hsü Fukuan). Another consideration is that the second interpretation understands the "ku" in part (a) differently from the "ku" in part (c), whereas the third or the fourth interpretation reads both occurrences of "ku" alike — one can arrive at the solstices of a thousand years on the basis of the past or customary behavior of the stars. For these two reasons, although I am inclined to accept the second interpretation on the basis of the balance of evidence, I do not regard the evidence cited in its support as decisive.

6.2   *Hsin^a* (Heart/Mind), *hsing^a*, and *t'ien* (Heaven)

6.2.1   *Hsing^a* and the Heart/Mind

The discussion of 4B:26 in the preceding section shows that Mencius was consciously opposing certain prevalent views on *hsing^a* and proposing his own alternative. Probably, he was directing attention away from a construal of *hsing^a* in biological terms, as exemplified in the views of the Yangists and of Kao Tzu. He was not opposed to biological tendencies as such. For example, he stressed the importance of food (e.g., 1A:3, 1A:7) and of the relation between men and women (e.g., 5A:2; cf. 1B:5), where eating and having sex are two tendencies Kao Tzu included in *hsing^a*. But he also stressed that such biological tendencies should be subject to normative constraints (e.g., 6B:1). What was novel about his views on *hsing^a* is that he regarded *hsing^a* as constituted primarily by the development of the ethical predispositions of the heart/mind. Since there are other tendencies in human beings, such as eating and having sex or the tendencies of the senses to take pleasure in ideal sensory objects, the question arises why Mencius emphasized the ethical predispositions of the heart/mind in his characterization of *hsing^a*.

Part of the answer probably has to do with pragmatic considerations. Since *hsing^a* comprises tendencies characteristic of a thing, going against one's *hsing^a* suggests the thought of radically altering oneself, and hence people might feel disinclined to engage in activities contrary to their *hsing^a*. Accordingly, viewing *hsing^a* as comprising tendencies that can conflict with ethical pursuits might lead people to be less motivated to be ethical (cf. 6A:1). Still, even taking into account such pragmatic considerations, the question of what is distinctive about the ethical predispositions of the heart/mind that sets them apart from other tendencies remains. There are at least three possible answers to this question, all of which have been proposed by commentators and have some textual basis.

The first proposal is that Mencius emphasized the ethical predispositions of the heart/mind because they distinguish human beings from other animals, unlike biological tendencies, which are shared by other animals. The concern with what is distinctive of human beings is seen in 4B:19, which observes that the slight element that distinguishes human beings is what the superior person preserves. Since Mencius elsewhere spoke of being ethical as a matter of preserving the heart/mind, the "slight element" in 4B:19 probably has to do with the ethical predispositions of the heart/mind. That Mencius regarded *hsing^a* as what distinguishes human beings from other animals can be seen from his debate with Kao Tzu in 6A:3, which ends with a query by him implying that the *hsing^a* of human beings differs from that of hounds and that of oxen. This proposal has been made by Ch'en Ta-ch'i, Fung Yu-lan, Lao Ssu-kuang, and D. C. Lau; was considered by T'ang Chün-i at an earlier stage of his work; and is mentioned by A. C. Graham and Hsü Fu-kuan along with other proposals.[29]

The second proposal is that Mencius emphasized the ethical predispositions of the heart/mind because their development is fully within human control, unlike other human tendencies. According to Mencius, one attains the ethical attributes if one seeks (*ch'iu*) them (6A:6) and reflects or thinks (*ssu^b*) (6A:15); not attaining them is due to letting them go (6A:6, 8) or not reflecting or thinking (6A:6, 13, 15, 17). Also, not attaining them is not a matter of not being able to, but of not acting (e.g., 6B:2). By contrast, other pursuits are not fully within one's control. For example, having distinguished between the ranks of *t'ien* and the ranks of human beings in 6A:16, in 6A:17 Mencius contrasted that which is truly exalted and is in everyone with that which is exalted by human beings but is not truly exalted. Comparison with 6A:16 suggests that the contrast in 6A:17 is between the ranks of *t'ien* and the ranks of human beings, namely, a contrast between the ethical attributes and official ranks. Of official ranks, it is said that "those that Chao Meng exalts, Chao Meng can also humble"; the implication is that attaining such ranks depends on others in a way that being ethical does not.[30] The contrast between ethical development, which is within one's control, and other pursuits, which are not, is also implicit in 7A:3 (see §3.5.2). The proposal that Mencius emphasized what is fully within human control in his characterization of *hsing^a* was considered by T'ang Chün-i at an earlier stage of his work and by Hsü Fu-kuan along with the first proposal.[31]

The third proposal is that Mencius emphasized the ethical predispositions of the heart/mind because their development has priority over other pursuits such as life (6A:10) and the satisfaction of sensory desires (6A:15). It is likely that Mencius would oppose Kao Tzu's explication of *hsing^a* on such grounds. We find in 6A:10 the idea that *yi^a* (propriety) is more important than getting food, and in 3B:3 the idea that *yi^a* is more important than getting a wife. The same point is implicit in 7B:31, and 6B:1 makes the similar claim that *li^a* (rites) is generally more important than eating and having sex except in certain exigencies. These observations were probably directed in part against Kao Tzu's position, which regards *hsing^a* as comprising eating and having sex.

The proposal that Mencius emphasized the ethical predispositions of the heart/mind in his characterization of *hsing^a* because their development has priority over other pursuits has been put forward by T'ang Chün-i. T'ang considered the first two proposals at an earlier stage of his work but saw a problem with both. Even if the ethical predispositions are distinctive of human beings and their development is fully within human control, it does not follow that one should pursue or subordinate other pursuits to their development. On the other hand, Mencius viewed *hsing^a* as something to be developed and to which other pursuits should be subordinated. According to T'ang, the really crucial difference between ethical pursuits and other pursuits such as satisfying sensory desires is that the latter are subject to normative constraints, but the former are not because they are pursuits to which other pursuits should be subordinated.[32]

Something like this proposal can also be found in A. C. Graham's writings. Having noted that Mencius believed that the human heart/mind has certain ethical predispositions, Graham poses the question of why, given that human beings also share other tendencies, Mencius should regard *hsing^a* as good simply because of the presence of the ethical predispositions. Citing such passages as 6A:10 and 6A:15, Graham proposes that this is because Mencius believed human beings give priority to developing the ethical predispositions over other kinds of pursuits.[33] There is, however, one important difference between T'ang's and Graham's positions. Graham observes that the *hsing^a* of a thing is treated in early Chinese thought as an observable fact about it and that we can establish the *hsing^a* of human beings in the way we establish the *hsing^a* of water, by discovering how human beings develop when free of interference.[34] T'ang, on the other hand, observes that early Chinese thinkers regarded the *hsing^a* of human beings not as a fact that can be established by external observation, but as something that each person discovers by self-reflection.[35] Put in such general terms, it is not clear that T'ang's observation is correct; for example, it is not apparent that either the Yangists (putting aside the Tzu-hua Tzu passage) or Kao Tzu regarded *hsing^a* as something discovered by self-reflection. But, as an observation about Mencius, the observation is plausible and fits the discussions in §§5.1.2 and 5.2.1 that one discovers the direction of development of the heart/mind for oneself via self-reflection.[36]

The three proposals are not the same, since it is possible for certain tendencies to have the characteristics of *hsing^a* highlighted in one proposal without having the characteristics highlighted in another. For example, certain tendencies may be distinctive of human beings and not shared by other animals, such as the tendency to enjoy music of certain kinds, but fulfilling such tendencies is not fully within human control. To the extent that we have to choose between the three proposals, T'ang is probably correct in thinking that the third allows us to make better sense of Mencius's conception of *hsing^a* as something that should be developed and to which other pursuits should be subordinated. However, each of the three proposals has a textual basis, and this suggests that they are to some extent related.

Starting with the third proposal, which T'ang regards as more basic, there is a line of thought that links the three characteristics these proposals regard as crucial to *hsing^a*. In the third proposal, one crucial characteristic of *hsing^a* is that it is a direction of development proper to human beings to which other pursuits should be subordinated. To discover what has priority and what is of less importance, it would not suffice to observe the development of human beings from the outside. Instead, each person has to reflect carefully on what is of greater or lesser importance. In this process of self-reflection, one discovers certain directions of development, which are also something that one believes one can realize, since otherwise it would be difficult to see how one could conclude that one should develop in that direction.

For example, imagine that, out of a concern for order in society, one starts by regarding oneself as having a responsibility to undertake certain political endeavors to put the Way into practice. Persistent failure of such attempts, however, may lead one to the realization that it is not within one's power to bring about such changes, and that there is nothing more one can do at this point to further such a goal. Upon such realization, reflection would yield further guidance concerning what one should do: that one should not complain against *t'ien* or blame human beings, that one should not attempt to achieve the goal by improper means, or that one should live in withdrawal the way Yen Hui did. The guidance one discovers through such reflections concerns things that are in one's power, since one has already taken into account what is not within one's power in one's reflections. Normative directions are, so to speak, discovered against a background of what one takes to be the causal constraints.[37] Hence, the direction of change that one discovers through self-reflection is something that is within one's power to realize, and this is the characteristic of *hsing^a* highlighted in the second proposal.

Also, in the process of self-reflection, one discovers in oneself things that one does not see in other animals.[38] For example, in responding in the way described in 6A:10 to food given with abuse, one sees that this kind of response is not found in other animals, which, if starving, have no hesitation in accepting food, however provided. The response is not idiosyncratic, for one also sees that other human beings react similarly. In this way, one comes to realize that the direction of development that constitutes *hsing^a* also distinguishes human beings from other animals, and this is the characteristic of *hsing^a* highlighted in the first proposal.

In sketching this line of thought, I am not suggesting that the three proposals are equivalent or that Mencius consciously engaged in the line of thought just described. Rather, the point is only to show that the three characteristics highlighted in the three proposals are not un-related, thereby explaining how they can come together in the way Mencius viewed *hsing^a*. It is possible that Mencius did not draw a clear distinction among these three characteristics in thinking about *hsing^a*, and perhaps for this reason some commentators, such as A. C. Gra-ham, Hsü Fu-kuan, and T'ang Chün-i, have considered more than one of these three characteristics in their discussions.

6.2.2 Passage 7B:24

With the discussion in the preceding section as background, we can now consider 7B:24, a passage in which Mencius contrasted the ethical attributes with the senses. This passage says of the relations of the mouth, eye, ear, nose, and the four limbs to tastes, colors, sounds, smells, and rest, respectively, that "these are *hsing^a*, but therein also lies *ming^a*, and the superior person does not describe them as [*pu wei^b*] *hsing^a*." By contrast, it says of the relation of *jen^a*, *yi^a*, *li^a*, *chih^b*, and the sages to the father-son relation, ruler-minister relation, host-guest re-lation, worthy people, and the Way of Heaven (*t'ien tao*) that "these are *ming^a*, yet therein also lies *hsing^a*, and the superior person does not describe them as [*pu wei^b*] *ming^a*."

There is some uncertainty about the interpretation of "yü^a," which links the references to the senses and four limbs to the references to sensory objects and rest, and correspondingly the interpretation of "yü^a" in the second half of the passage.[39] "Yü^a" can be interpreted to mean "pertaining to" or "being drawn to." The second interpretation would easily fit the way the four limbs relate to rest and the sages re-late to the Way of Heaven, but it requires taking the references to sen-sory objects in the first half as references to ideal sensory objects, and the references to *jen^a*, *yi^a*, *li^a*, *chih^b* in the second half as references to people who are *jen^a*, *yi^a*, *li^a*, *chih^b*.[40] I will make reference to the different interpretations of "yü^a" as it becomes relevant.

Another issue of controversy concerns whether "sheng^b jen^b" (sages) should be emended to "sheng^b" (sageness). Chu Hsi (MTCC) cites someone who proposes the emendation, but elsewhere (MTHW 14/4a.9-10) he deals with the passage without adopting the emenda-tion. Yü Yüeh (MTPI) argues for the emendation on the ground that "sheng^b" (sageness) is paired with "chih^b" (wisdom) in 5B:1 and in other early texts such as the *Lao-tzu*, and P'ang P'u argues for the emendation on the grounds that *sheng^b* is grouped along with *jen^a*, *yi^a*, *li^a*, and *chih^b* in the "Essay on the Five Processes" in the Ma-wang-tui silk manuscripts.[41] I take both possibilities into account in the following discussion.

There are two main questions concerning the interpretation of the passage. The first concerns what Mencius was doing in contrasting the senses with the ethical attributes. There are at least three possible and not incompatible answers to this question. First, in its reference to the superior person, the passage may be describing the superior person. It may be reporting that the superior person describes the relation of the senses to their objects not as *hsing^a* but as *ming^a*, and the relation of ethical attributes to human relations not as *ming^a* but as *hsing^a*. A related proposal by Tai Chen (no. 28) and apparently endorsed by Chiao Hsün is that "pu wei^b" does not literally mean "not describe as" but means "not use as an excuse." In this proposal, the passage is still describing the superior person – the superior person does not indulge in sensory pursuits on the excuse that such pursuits are matters of *hsing^a* and does not refrain from ethical pursuits on the excuse that such pursuits are matters of *ming^a*. Other commentators, such as Chao Ch'i (C) and Juan Yüan, also take the passage to be at least in part a description of the superior person, in contrast to the ordinary person.

Second, one may take the passage to be an exhortation to people to view sensory pursuits as *ming^a* and ethical pursuits as *hsing^a* and, as a result, to devote themselves to the latter rather than the former. The interpretation has been proposed by A. C. Graham and David S. Nivison.[42] A similar interpretation is cited by Chu Hsi (MTCC) as his teacher's (Li Yen-ping's) interpretation and endorsed by Wang Fu-chih (748). This proposal is compatible with the first since Mencius might well be describing the superior person as a way of exhorting people to devote themselves to ethical pursuits. Indeed, the first proposal leads naturally to the second since a reference to what the superior person is like is often a way of guiding people in certain directions.

Third, one may take the passage to be about what *hsing^a* really amounts to, or how one should view *hsing^a*, in opposition to other views of *hsing^a*. For example, T'ang Chün-i takes Mencius to be giving grounds in 7B:24 for viewing *hsing^a* primarily in terms of the ethical predispositions of the heart/mind.[43] In this proposal, 7B:24 fits with other passages such as 4B:26, 6A:1-3, and 6A:6 as part of an attempt by Mencius to oppose competing views of *hsing^a* and to advocate an alternative view. This proposal is compatible with the first two since the passage can at the same time be doing all three things described in these proposals. Also, in advocating his alternative view of *hsing^a*, Mencius need not be denying that other things like sensory desires can also be described as *hsing^a* in some ordinary sense.[44] Indeed, it seems that Mencius would admit that sensory desires may in a sense be described as *hsing^a* — he himself used "hsing^a" in connection with the relation of the palate to tastes in 6A:7. Even in 7B:24, he began by using "hsing^a" in connection with sensory desires before going on to describe the view of the superior person. Still, he did tend to view *hsing^a* primarily in terms of the ethical predispositions, and this distinguishes his account from other current views.

A second question concerning the interpretation of 7B:24 has to do with the nature of the contrast between *hsing^a* and *ming^a*, and this question arises whether we take 7B:24 to be exhorting people to ethical pursuits or to be advocating a novel account of *hsing^a*. The answer to this question depends on which dimension of "ming^a" is emphasized.

Suppose we take "ming^a" to be primarily descriptive, emphasizing what is not within one's control. The first half of the passage can then be interpreted as saying that although the relation of the senses to sensory objects, or the way they are disposed to their ideal objects, can be characterized as *hsing^a* in some ordinary sense, the satisfaction of sensory desires is not entirely within human control and is in that sense a matter of *ming^a*. The superior person does not regard the sensory desires as *hsing^a* and indulge in them, or does not indulge in them on the excuse that they pertain to *hsing^a*.[45] This observation about the superior person can then be taken as an exhortation to engage in ethical pursuits, or as describing it as a good habit of mind for one to regard sensory pursuits as *ming^a* rather than *hsing^a*.[46] In addition, while admitting that Mencius would acknowledge that sensory desires pertain to *hsing^a* in some ordinary sense of the term, we can interpret the first half of 7B:24 as advocating a more restrictive understanding of *hsing^a*, such that only what is fully within human control really pertains to *hsing^a*.[47]

By contrast, ethical pursuits are matters of *ming^a* in that the realization of *jen^a*, *yi^a*, and *li^a* in human relations and of *chih^b* in the employment of worthies, and the ability of the sages (or of sageness) to make the Way of Heaven prevail depend on external circumstances, such as the actual existence of such human relations, the opportunity to encounter people of worth, or the political opportunity to put the

Way into practice.[48] However, there is *hsingᵃ* in ethical pursuits in that people already have predispositions in that direction that are within their power to realize. Although their actualization in human relations and in the political realm may depend on external circumstances not within one's control, the cultivation of such attributes is fully within one's control—for example, although Yen Yüan lived in withdrawal because of political circumstances, he was described as sharing the Way with Yü and Chi, who had the opportunity to put the Way into practice (cf. 4B:29). Thus, the superior person does not regard ethical pursuits as *mingᵃ* and thereby give up trying, or does not use *mingᵃ* as an excuse for not engaging in ethical pursuits. This observation about the superior person can then be taken as an opposition to a common tendency to view ethical pursuits as *mingᵃ* and thereby give up trying, or as urging people to form the good habit of mind of viewing ethical pursuits as *hsingᵃ* rather than as *mingᵃ*. In addition, one can also see Mencius as advocating a more restrictive understanding of *hsingᵃ* so that only ethical inclinations, whose realization is fully within human control, can be described as *hsingᵃ*.

Suppose, on the other hand, that we take "*mingᵃ*" to be primarily normative. The first half of the passage can then be interpreted as saying that although sensory desires can be described as *hsingᵃ* in some ordinary sense, there is *mingᵃ* in that there are normative constraints on the satisfaction of such desires: there is a distinction between proper and improper ways of seeking the satisfaction of such desires.[49] The observation that the superior person does not view sensory pursuits as *hsingᵃ* can be interpreted in the different ways described earlier—as urging one not to act unethically under the pretext that it is *hsingᵃ* to pursue sensory satisfaction, or as advocating a more restrictive understanding of *hsingᵃ* that takes *hsingᵃ* to include only inclinations whose realization is not subject to further normative constraints.[50] As for ethical pursuits, there is *mingᵃ* in that the ethical attributes impose certain normative constraints on human life, and yet there is *hsingᵃ* in that there are predispositions in us already pointing in that direction, making it possible or even enjoyable for us to cultivate such attributes. Accordingly, the superior person does not describe them as *mingᵃ*, either because one does not view the ethical attributes as normative constraints coming from outside the heart/ mind, or because the development of the shared ethical predispositions is not itself subject to further normative constraints. Again, this observation about the superior person can be taken as an exhortation to ethical pursuits or as advocating a more restrictive understanding of *hsing^a* in which only ethical inclinations, whose development is not subject to further normative constraints, fall within the scope of *hsing^a*.

These two ways of interpreting the occurrences of "ming^a" differ in that one takes "ming^a" to be primarily descriptive, referring to causal constraints on human endeavors, whereas the other takes its use to be primarily normative, referring to normative constraints. It is difficult to adjudicate between the two interpretations, since each highlights ideas in Mencius's thinking that can be found in other passages. Some commentators, such as Chu Hsi (MTCC), actually shift from one interpretation to the other — Chu initially understod "ming^a" as referring to constraints due to external circumstances and later to the constraints of *yi^a li^c* (propriety and pattern).[51] As mentioned in §2.1.1, it is quite possible that Mencius himself did not draw a clear distinction between the two dimensions of "ming^a," and hence did not clearly distinguish between the two lines of thought sketched in these two interpretations.

6.2.3 *Hsing^a and t'ien*

We saw in §6.1.2 that Mencius regarded the ethical predispositions of the heart/mind as due to *t'ien*. Since he also characterized *hsing^a* primarily in terms of the development of such predispositions, *hsing^a* is also related to *t'ien* (7A:1). There has been scholarly disagreement about his view of *t'ien*, disagreement that also arises for the way *t'ien* is viewed in the *Lun-yü*. The disagreement revolves around at least two issues: whether *t'ien* is understood as a kind of personal deity (*jen^b ko shen*) and whether it has a transcendent (*ch'ao yüeh*) dimension.

A number of authors have proposed that *t'ien* in these texts is a kind of personal deity. For example, both Hou Wai-lu and Jen Chi-yü believe Confucius viewed *t'ien* as a personal deity with a will, and both take *Lun-yü* 17.19, which describes how the four seasons proceed and the hundred things grow without *t'ien* speaking, to be evidence that *t'ien* can speak but chooses not to.[52] Fung Yu-lan and Fu P'ei-jung have observed that *t'ien* in Confucius's and Mencius's thinking retained part of the personal characteristics that are traditionally ascribed to *t'ien*.[53]

Other authors have focused less on the personal characteristics of *t'ien* and more on its transcendent (*ch'ao yüeh*) dimension. Mou Tsung-san acknowledges that *t'ien* in the *Lun-yü* still carries the traditional connotations of a personal deity, but thinks that the transcendent dimension is dominant and that this dimension becomes even more conspicuous in the *Meng-tzu*.[54] The transcendent dimension is explained as a kind of creativity; a dimension of immanence (*nei tsai*) is said to be present as well. Several other authors have emphasized the idea that *t'ien* in the *Lun-yü* and the *Meng-tzu* carries both a transcendent and an immanent dimension.[55]

In contrast, another interpretation denies that *t'ien* has connotations of a personal deity or a transcendent dimension. Both Hsü Fukuan and Lao Ssu-kuang have argued that neither Confucius nor Mencius regarded *t'ien* as having a "metaphysical" (*hsing^b shang*) dimension; Hsü thinks that in the *Meng-tzu t'ien* has to do largely with the heart/mind and the *hsing^a* of human beings, and Lao that it has to do largely with the natural order.[56] Others have also explicitly opposed the idea that *t'ien* has a transcendent dimension and have queried whether the ideas of transcendence and immanence can be combined without incoherence.[57] This has led to further debates, particularly concerning the notion of transcendence.[58]

To sidestep the terminological issues, I will avoid the use of the terms "transcendence" and "personal deity" and instead attend to some of the substantive claims about *t'ien* made with the use of these notions.[59] A survey of the use of "t'ien" in the two texts shows that *t'ien* is sometimes spoken of as if it has personal characteristics, and that this way of speaking about *t'ien* is more pervasive in the *Lun-yü* than in the *Meng-tzu*. The *Lun-yü* contains references to offending *t'ien* (*LY* 3.13), *t'ien* using Confucius in a certain way (*LY* 3.24), *t'ien*'s curse on someone (*LY* 6.28), *t'ien* intending culture to be destroyed (*LY* 9.5), and *t'ien* having left someone bereft (*LY* 11.9), as well as complaints about *t'ien* (*LY* 14.35); the *Meng-tzu* contains a reference to *t'ien* not wishing to bring peace to the empire (*M* 2B:13). In addition, *t'ien* is sometimes presented as the source of what is not within human control, such as wealth and honor (*LY* 12.5), success in one's political endeavors (*M* 1B:14, 1B:16), and more generally things that are done without human action (*M* 5A:6).

T'ien also has an ethical dimension in the *Meng-tzu*. For example, the ethical way of life is referred to as *t'ien tao* (7B:24), *jen^a* and *yi^a* are described as the ranks of *t'ien* (2A:7, 6A:16), and *t'ien* is described as the source of the heart/mind (6A:15) and its ethical predispositions (3A:5). The ethical dimension of *t'ien* is less clear in the *Lun-yü*, although two occurrences of "t'ien" (*LY* 5.13, 7.23) can be interpreted as having ethical connotations. Finally, in both texts, self-cultivation is presented as involving some relation to *t'ien*, such as knowing or standing in awe of *t'ien ming^a* (*LY* 2.4, 16.8) or knowing and serving *t'ien* (*M* 7A:1).

This survey of the use of the character shows that personal characteristics continue to be ascribed to *t'ien* (especially in the *Lun-yü*), that *t'ien* is viewed as having an ethical dimension (especially in the *Meng-tzu*), and that *t'ien* is seen as something that one should venerate or serve. For this reason, it is unlikely that "t'ien" refers merely to an impersonal natural order. On the other hand, *t'ien* is not viewed as a being that exists separately from human beings; for Mencius, the ethical predispositions of the heart/mind have their source in *t'ien* and provide human beings with an access to *t'ien*. I will confine my comments to these observations about the use of "t'ien" in the two texts and not try to decide whether we should describe *t'ien* as a personal deity, since this depends largely on what connotations we build into the term.

As for the question whether *t'ien* carries a transcendent or immanent dimension, the notion of transcendence is sometimes used to highlight that the ethical ideal in the *Lun-yü* and the *Meng-tzu* has a dimension beyond merely presenting human beings with a guide to life, and the notion of immanence to emphasize the intimate link between the ethical ideal and human beings. The reference to *t'ien* draws attention to at least two features of our ethical experiences. In judging certain things as proper, one feels that their propriety is independent of what one may happen to want and that one's life should be oriented toward them, even if doing so involves sacrificing one's life. There is, so to speak, a sense of demands that come from beyond oneself. At the same time, one is aware of external conditions of life not within one's control, conditions that are to be accepted in the process of cultivating oneself to live up to the ideal.

These two aspects of our ethical experiences are highlighted by ascribing both the ethical ideal and the external limitations to *t'ien*, with *t'ien* being viewed as an object of reverence and awe as well as something that one should serve through self-cultivation. On the other hand, living up to the ideal to serve *t'ien* does not involve a renunciation of the social world; instead, it requires the fulfillment of human relations and full social engagement. Furthermore, in the *Meng-tzu*, one's heart/mind is supposed to serve as a link to *t'ien* in that the ethical ideal is revealed in certain ethical predispositions of the heart/mind that originate with *t'ien*.

These aspects of the ethical ideal in the *Lun-yü* and the *Meng-tzu* illustrate the ways in which the ethical ideal and its source, *t'ien*, have both a dimension going beyond mere guidance and a dimension emphasizing the intimate link to the human realm. To the extent that *hsing^a*, for Mencius, has its source in *t'ien* and has an ethical direction, *hsing^a* also has these two dimensions. Again, I will confine my comments to noting these two dimensions of *t'ien* and *hsing^a* and will not try to decide whether we should characterize them in terms of transcendence or immanence, since this also depends largely on the connotations of the terms.

6.3   *Hsing^a* Is Good

6.3.1   *Interpretation of the Claim*

Mencius's claim that *hsing^a* is good is reported in 3A:1 and 6A:6, and explained and defended by Mencius in 6A:2 and 6A:6. If we accept that Mencius regarded *hsing^a* as constituted by the direction of development implicit in certain ethical predispositions of the heart/mind, the claim amounts to the assertion that this direction of development is directed toward goodness. However, a number of commentators have proposed other interpretations, and I will consider some of these proposals.

According to Herrlee G. Creel, the claim that *hsing^a* is good is tautological because "shan" (good) means whatever is congruent with *hsing^a*.[60] Creel does not explain why he thinks "shan" has this meaning, but perhaps the thought is that "hsing^a" was used by Mencius and perhaps by certain other early thinkers to refer to the direction of development proper to human beings, and hence that *shan* is whatever conforms to the direction of *hsing^a*. In this view, "shan" is a formal term in that it can have any content, depending on the content of *hsing^a*.

It is unlikely that "shan" was used in this way in early Chinese thought, given the extensive disagreements reported in 6A:6 about whether *hsing^a* is *shan*. One could counter that although "shan" was not generally used as a formal term in early texts, it was so used by Mencius; that is, Mencius used "shan" in such a way that the statement *hsing^a* is *shan* is tautological. But if this proposal were correct, we would expect Mencius's disagreement with opposing views about *hsing^a* to be largely about the use of words, and that Mencius's explanation of his own position would focus on his use of "shan." This, however, is not the way he explained his position in 6A:6; instead, his explanation stresses that the ethical attributes *jen^a*, *yi^a*, *li^a*, and *chih^b* are in some sense already in human beings.

More likely, he understood *shan* in terms of the attributes *jen^a*, *yi^a*, *li^a*, and *chih^b*, and his view that *hsing^a* is *shan* amounts to a claim that the heart/mind has predispositions toward these attributes. If one believed that *hsing^a* is opposed to these attributes, it would follow, not that one should revise one's conception of what *shan* is, but that such a view of *hsing^a* might pose problems by leading people to regard the ethical life as involving a radical change in oneself. This, as we saw in §4.2.1, is Mencius's response in 6A:1 to Kao Tzu's *ch'i* willow analogy for *hsing^a*.

Another interpretation of Mencius's view that *hsing^a* is good is suggested by some remarks by D. C. Lau, although these remarks may not be fully representative of Lau's position.[61] According to this interpretation, Mencius's claim that *hsing^a* is good amounts to the assertion that human beings are moral agents. To hold that *hsing^a* is good is to hold that human beings have the ability to distinguish right and wrong, to approve of doing right, and to feel shame if they do wrong. To hold that *hsing^a* is bad is to hold that human beings approve of doing wrong and feel shame if they do right, and this is an inconsistent position. Thus, according to Lau, the contrary of the view that *hsing^a* is good is not that *hsing^a* is bad, but that *hsing^a* is amoral in the sense that human beings cannot draw a distinction between right and wrong.

It is difficult to see how this interpretation could make sense of the debate between Mencius and Kao Tzu about *hsing^a*. It has difficulty explaining why Mencius opposed Kao Tzu's explication of *hsing^a* in terms of *sheng^a* in 6A:3 and how we might make sense of their disagreement about analogies in 6A:1-2.[62] Also, in this interpretation, it is difficult to make sense of the disagreement between different views of *hsing^a* reported in 6A:6, as well as the way some of these views are explained in terms of what allegedly happened in history. In this interpretation, the term "shan" is again treated as a formal term; to hold that *hsing^a* is *shan* is to hold that human beings can draw a distinction between right and wrong and be moved accordingly, however that distinction is to be drawn. It is unlikely that "shan" was used in this manner in early Chinese thought; on the contrary, "shan" seems to have had substantive connotations, involving specific judgments as to what behavior counts as *shan*.

Although the claim that human beings share the capacity to distinguish right and wrong does not fully capture Mencius's view that *hsing^a* is good, it is a substantive claim about human beings that may be disputed and probably captures part of Mencius's view. And, in fairness to Lau, the interpretation just described is probably not fully representative of his position, since he sometimes takes Mencius's view that *hsing^a* is good to include the further claim that human beings are already inclined toward goodness.[63] This additional component of Mencius's view allows us to make sense of Mencius's disagreement with Kao Tzu's analogies in 6A:1-2 and with the views of *hsing^a* reported in 6A:6.[64]

To further understand Mencius's claim that *hsing^a* is good, let us briefly consider a recent controversy concerning its interpretation. Fu P'ei-jung recently proposed that the claim amounts to the assertion that the *hsing^a* of human beings is directed toward goodness (*hsiang shan*), but not that *hsing^a* is originally good (*pen shan*).[65] In response, a number of scholars have argued that Mencius's view does include a claim that *hsing^a* is originally good.[66] Resolution of the issue depends on deciding what the claim of original goodness amounts to. Mencius does not seem to be proposing that human beings are already fully good, since Mencius ascribed to human beings only the beginnings of goodness, which still need to be nourished.[67] On the other hand, if the claim is that the heart/mind of human beings already contains an ethical direction, so that human beings do not need to seek ethical guidance from outside the heart/mind, the claim does seem to be part of Mencius's view.[68] As I have argued in the last two chapters, Mencius regarded the heart/mind as having an ethical direction, and this allows one to obtain ethical guidance through self-reflection. Having made these observations, I will not try to decide whether we should describe Mencius as believing in the original goodness of *hsing^a*, since what remains is a largely terminological issue.

6.3.2 *Passages 6A:6-8*

My interpretation of Mencius's claim that *hsing^a* is good takes him to hold the view that *hsing^a* points in an ethical direction. Part of 6A:6 seems to pose a problem for this interpretation, and I now turn to 6A:6

along with the related passages 6A:7–8. In 6A:6, Kung-tu Tzu reported three views on *hsingᵃ*:

(a) (Kao Tzu) *hsingᵃ wu shan wu pu shan* (there is neither good nor bad in *hsingᵃ*);
(b) *hsingᵃ k'o yi weiᵃ shan k'o yi weiᵃ pu shan* (*hsingᵃ* is capable of becoming good and capable of becoming bad);
(c) *yu hsingᵃ shan yu hsingᵃ pu shan* (there are those with good *hsingᵃ* and those with bad *hsingᵃ*).

He then asked, in reference to Mencius's view that *hsingᵃ* is good, whether Mencius regarded the other views as all mistaken. Mencius responded that:

"nai jo ch'iᵇ ch'ingᵃ tse k'o yi weiᵃ shan yi, nai so weiᵇ shan yeh. Jo fu weiᵃ pu shan, fei ts'ai chihᵍ tsui yeh."

(Lau: "As far as what is genuinely in him is concerned, a man is capable of becoming good. That is what I mean by good. As for his becoming bad, that is not the fault of his native endowment.")

The problem posed by the passage is that Mencius explained his views in terms of one's being capable of (*k'o yi*) becoming good. Being capable of becoming good, however, does not seem to require one's being in any significant sense directed toward goodness, and this seems to conflict with my proposed interpretation, which takes Mencius's view to include a claim that the heart/mind has predispositions toward goodness. In fact, the problem is not specific to my proposed interpretation but is internal to the text itself. Since human beings are apparently equally capable of becoming bad as they are of becoming good, the capability of becoming good does not seem to indicate in what way *hsingᵃ* is good rather than bad. That is, as far as capability is concerned, there seems to be no asymmetry between goodness and badness. But other passages show that Mencius did believe in some asymmetry; for example, the way he spelled out the water analogy in 6A:2 shows that he regarded *hsingᵃ* as related to goodness in a way that it is not related to badness. To put the problem differently, if the view that *hsingᵃ* is good amounts to the claim that human beings are capable of becoming good, this view seems quite compatible with Kao Tzu's view, which holds that although there is neither good nor bad in *hsingᵃ*, human beings can be made to become good. Accordingly, it becomes unclear why Mencius should oppose Kao Tzu's position.

To address this problem, we need to examine the use of the expressions "nai jo . . . jo fu . . . ," "ch'i^b," "ch'ing^a," "k'o yi," and "ts'ai." Chao Ch'i (C), followed by Sun Shih, Chang Shih, and P'ei Hsüeh-hai, takes "jo" in "nai jo" to mean "shun" (to follow). "Jo" can have this meaning, and reading "jo" in this way and taking "ch'ing^a" to be used interchangeably with "hsing^a" provides a way to address the problem.[69] The move allows us to interpret Mencius's explanation of *hsing^a shan* as saying that one is capable of becoming good if one follows *hsing^a*, and this explanation implies that *hsing^a* is already directed toward goodness.[70] However, "nai jo" can also be used to introduce a subject matter, meaning "as far as . . . is concerned" (e.g., *MT* 15/16,26,29). Chu Hsi (MTCC), followed by Chao Shun-sun, interprets "nai jo" in this way, as do some translators including Lau and Yang Po-chün. This interpretation is more likely because the structure "nai jo . . . jo fu . . ." also occurs in 4B:28, where it has the meaning of "as far as . . . is concerned . . . , as for . . . ."

"Ch'i^b" (its) may refer to human beings (*jen^b*) or to *hsing^a*. The latter interpretation is more likely if the subject of "k'o yi wei^a shan" is "ch'i^b," since comparison with the statement of position (b) shows that the subject of "k'o yi wei^a shan" is likely to be "hsing^a." However, as I will show, it is likely that "ch'ing^a," which follows "ch'i^b," is used in a way closely related to "hsing^a," and hence that the subject of "k'o yi wei^a shan" is "ch'i^b ch'ing^a" rather than "ch'i^b." This favors taking "ch'i^b" to refer to human beings; this interpretation gains further support from the fact that "jen^b chih^g ch'ing^a" is an idiomatic expression that occurs in 6A:8 and in other early texts.[71]

"Ch'ing^a" has been interpreted in at least three different ways. First, Chu Hsi (MTCC; YL 1380–81; MTHW), Chang Shih, and Hu Ping-wen understand it to refer to the activation of *hsing^a*, which takes the form of emotions and from which *hsing^a* can be known. Uchino takes "ch'ing^a" to refer to the activation of *hsing^a*, and Giles, Legge, Lyall, and Ware translate it as "feelings." Second, Tai Chen (no. 30) takes "ch'ing^a" to mean "shih^b," what a thing is really like. This interpretation is defended by Ch'en Ta-ch'i and Mou Tsung-san and is reflected in Lau's translation of "ch'ing^a" as "what is genuine" (6A:6, 6A:8).[72] Third, Yü Yüeh (MTPI) takes "ch'ing^a" to be used interchangeably with "hsing^a." This interpretation is also found in P'ei Hsüeh-hai and Hu Yü-huan; Ts'en I-ch'eng argues that it is more plausible to take "ch'ing^a" to mean "hsing^a" than to mean "shih^b" (what a thing is really like).[73]

Of the few occurrences of "ch'ing^a" in the *Meng-tzu* other than those in 6A:6 and 6A:8, none can plausibly be interpreted as referring to the emotions. Commentators, including Chu Hsi (MTCC) and Chao Ch'i (CC), generally agree that its occurrence in 4B:18, which is contrasted with "sheng^c" (reputation), concerns what one is really like (*shih^b*). Passage 3A:4 refers to the inequality of things as their *ch'ing^a*; this occurrence of the character is again unlikely to refer to emotions. In the absence of any clear example of such usage of the character in the *Meng-tzu*, I am disinclined to read the occurrence of "ch'ing^a" in 6A:6 in terms of the emotions.

The use of "ch'ing^a" seems closely related to "hsing^a" in 6A:6 and 6A:8, and some commentators and translators even interpret the occurrence of "ch'ing^a" in 3A:4 as hsing^a. For example, Chao Ch'i (C 3A:4) links the two, and Lau translates "ch'ing^a" in 3A:4 as "nature," which is also his translation of "hsing^a."[74] However, as mentioned in §6.1.1, "hsing^a" probably differs from "ch'ing^a" in that it is not used in early texts to refer to a feature of a class of things (such as their inequality) that is not itself a feature of each individual member of that class. If this is correct, "ch'ing^a" cannot be used interchangeably with "hsing^a" in 3A:4. However, since the occurrences of "ch'ing^a" in 6A:6 and 6A:8 differ from the occurrence in 3A:4 in that the former concern features of a class of things that are also features of individual members of that class, this still leaves open the possibility that "ch'ing^a" is interchangeable with "hsing^a" in 6A:6 and 6A:8. The third interpretation just described therefore remains a possibility.

However, the second and third interpretations are not that far apart. In §6.1.1, I gave evidence that "ch'ing^a" is often used in the sense of "shih^b," the way things really are. Furthermore, "ch'ing^a" often refers to certain characteristic tendencies of a class of things that obtain of each individual member of that class and reveal what things of that class are really like. When "ch'ing^a" is used in this way, the tendencies involved can also be referred to as the *hsing^a* of those things, since "hsing^a" can also refer to the characteristic tendencies a thing has. The two characters still have different emphases. "Ch'ing^a" stresses that certain tendencies are characteristic features of certain things, a fact that is difficult to alter and reveals what these things are like. "Hsing^a" emphasizes the presence of such tendencies as part of the constitution of such things, tendencies that are subject to influences and can be nourished or harmed. For this reason, I tend to agree with Mou Tsung-san who, although explicating "ch'ing^a" in terms of "shih^b," also thinks that "ch'ing^a" and "hsing^a" are interchangeable in the context of 6A:6.[75] Probably Mencius shifted from speaking of *hsing^a* to speaking of *ch'ing^a* in 6A:6 to emphasize that although *hsing^a* may be subject to the different influences that Kung-tu Tzu described in putting his question to Mencius, all human beings have something in common that is directed toward goodness and reveals what they are really like, even if only some develop it.[76]

As for "k'o yi," it is Mencius's explanation of *hsing^a shan* in terms of *k'o yi wei^a shan* that poses a problem.[77] A survey of the use of "k'o yi" in early texts, such as the *Lun-yü* and the *Meng-tzu*, shows that often only when certain conditions are met is one said to *k'o yi* do certain things. For example, in the *Lun-yü*, it is said that one's *k'o yi* endure adversity for long depends on *jen^a* (benevolence, humaneness; LY 4.2), *k'o yi* talk to a person about great things depends on the person's being above average (LY 6.21), *k'o yi* be without great fault depends on having time to learn the *Yi-ching* (LY 7.17), and *k'o yi* be a complete person depends on one's having certain qualities (LY 14.12). In the *Meng-tzu*, one's *k'o yi* become a true king is said to depend on having territories of a certain size (1A:5) and having *te^a* (virtue, power) of a certain kind (1A:7). It is only when one has a certain position that one *k'o yi* wage war against or even kill a corrupt ruler (2B:8). It is only after having put Yi Chih down the day before that Mencius *k'o yi* have a dialogue with him through an intermediary (3A:5). The conditions may be ones that have to be met for something literally to be possible (as in the case of qualities needed for one to *k'o yi* be a complete person or a true king), or that have to be met for something to be appropriately done (as in the case of Mencius putting Yi Chih down before he *k'o yi* have a dialogue with him through an intermediary).[78] This observation about the use of "k'o yi," however, does not by itself address the problem, since the condition required for *k'o yi wei^a shan* may well just be a mere capacity that does not by itself point in the direction of goodness.

The key to addressing the problem, I think, lies in the relation between *k'o yi* (capability) and *neng* (ability). In a dialogue between Mo Tzu and Wu-ma Tzu in the *Mo-tzu*, Wu-ma Tzu said that he lacked the *neng* to practice indiscriminate concern for each because he had more concern for himself than for his parents, and more concern for those closer to him than for those more distant from him (*MT* 46/52–53). This observation shows that doubts about one's *neng* to practice a proposed ethical ideal may be raised on the grounds that one lacks emotional dispositions in the direction of the proposed ideal. Similarly, those who held to discrimination doubted that they had the *neng* to treat the body or parents of a friend as their own bodies or parents (*MT* 16/24), and rulers who held to discrimination doubted that they had the *neng* to treat the bodies of their people as their own bodies (*MT* 16/36). Such doubts were also presented in terms of *k'o*; opponents raised doubts whether people *k'o* practice (*MT* 16/46, 16/72) or *k'o* use (*MT* 16/22) indiscrimination; sometimes there is a shift from speaking of *k'o* to speaking of *neng* (*MT* 16/22–24).

Thus, in the *Mo-tzu*, one main objection to the doctrine of indiscriminate concern is its impracticability, expressed in terms of both *neng* and *k'o*, and one's *neng* to practice indiscriminate concern is supposed to depend on one's having emotional dispositions in the appropriate direction. In response, Mo Tzu took pains to emphasize the practicability of indiscriminate concern, on one occasion using the analogy of carrying Mount T'ai and crossing a river to illustrate what is genuinely not practicable (*MT* 15/29–31, 16/46–48). Probably his attempt to show that the practice of indiscriminate concern profits oneself or those to whom one stands in a special relation was in part a response to this objection; it shows that although human beings may not yet have emotional dispositions that correspond to indiscriminate concern, indiscriminate concern is linked to certain motivations that they already have.

Mencius was similarly concerned with the practicability of the Confucian ideal and defended it on the grounds that people already have the appropriate emotional dispositions. In 1A:7, having reminded King Hsüan of his compassion for the ox, he pointed out that the king had the *neng* to practice *jen^a* (benevolent, humane) government and that his not doing so was a matter of not acting rather than lack of *neng*; he then used the example of carrying Mount T'ai and crossing the North Sea to illustrate what is genuinely not practicable.[79] In 2A:6, he cited the presence of the four germs to show that everyone *neng* practice the Confucian Way, and in 7A:15 he cited love for parents and respect for elder brothers as instances of what one *neng* without learning. This concern with *neng* recurs in other passages such as 4A:1 and 4A:10, where he said that to regard one's ruler or oneself as lacking the *neng* to practice the Confucian Way is to rob one's ruler or to abandon oneself.

What is interesting, however, is that Mencius at times shifted from talking about *k'o yi* to talking about *neng* in the ethical context. One example is the conversation with King Hsüan in 1A:7, which begins with the king's asking whether he *k'o yi* become a true king or *k'o yi* care for and protect the people, and continues with Mencius talking about the king's not caring for and protecting the people as a case of not acting rather than a lack of *neng*. Another example is 6B:2, which begins with Mencius endorsing the view that everyone *k'o yi* become a Yao or Shun and continues with his observing that it is not that people lack *neng*. Thus, it seems that Mencius did not distinguish between *neng* and *k'o yi* in the ethical context, and to the extent that *neng* depends on having the appropriate emotional dispositions, *k'o yi* would similarly be so dependent.

Later, we will see that Hsün Tzu highlighted the distinction between *k'o yi* and *neng* in the ethical context in the "Hsing o" chapter and opposed a conflation of the distinction between *k'o yi* and not *k'o yi* with the distinction between *neng* and not *neng* (HT 23/61–75). Since Mencius is clearly the target of criticism in that chapter, this provides further evidence for the observation that Mencius did not draw a distinction between *neng* and *k'o yi*. This observation helps address the problem concerning Mencius's explanation of his view that *hsing^a* is good in terms of *k'o yi wei^a shan*. Since Mencius used "k'o i" interchangeably with "neng" in the ethical context and since *neng* in the ethical context requires possession of emotional dispositions already directed toward goodness, what Mencius's explanation of his view amounts to is the claim that human beings already have emotional dispositions structured in a way that is directed toward goodness. That he was indeed using "k'o yi" interchangeably with "neng" in 6A:6 and that "k'o yi" requires the presence of appropriately structured emotional dispositions gains further support from the fact that the explanation of his view in terms of "k'o yi wei^a shan" in 6A:6 is immediately followed by a reference to the four germs, which are emotional dispositions already directed toward goodness and cited in 2A:6 to show that everyone *neng* practice the Confucian Way.

Finally, let us turn to the character "ts'ai." Chu Hsi (MTCC), Chang Shih, and Hu Ping-wen explain "ts'ai" in terms of "neng."[80] Mou Tsung-san and T'ang Chün-i both take "ts'ai" to have the meaning of "neng" and to refer specifically to the *neng* that is rooted in the emotional predispositions of the heart/mind as seen from the four germs.[81] That "ts'ai" is closely related to "neng" can be seen from the parallels between the use of the two characters in the *Meng-tzu* and in other early texts. For example, just as there are references to employing those who are worthy and have *ts'ai* in government (LY 13.2; M 6B:7), there are references to employing those who are worthy and have *neng* in government (*M* 2A:5). Also, both "ts'ai" and "neng" can be exhausted (*chin; M* 6A:6; HFT 28.2.27), and although badness is described in 6A:6 as not the fault of *ts'ai*, it is also said in 1A:7 not to be due to a lack of *neng*. These parallels show that "ts'ai" and "neng" are closely related, probably in that one's *ts'ai* is that by virtue of which one has *neng*. That is, *ts'ai* is an endowment that enables one to attain certain accomplishments.

There is also evidence for Mou's and T'ang's observation that in the context of 6A:6, *ts'ai* concerns the emotional predisposition of the heart/mind as exemplified in the four germs, by virtue of which one has the *neng* to attain the ethical ideal. The observation in 6A:6 that badness is not the fault of *ts'ai* is followed immediately by a reference to the four germs, and the passage refers to exhausting (*chin*) one's *ts'ai* just as 7A:1 refers to exhausting one's heart/mind. Passage 6A:7 observes that variation in people's character is not due to differences in people's *ts'ai* and goes on to talk about what is common to all heart/minds. Passage 6A:8 observes by implication that everyone has the heart/mind of *jen^a yi^a* and that it is a mistake to think that one who is ethically uncultivated does not have *ts'ai*. And, in both 6A:7 and 6A:8, *ts'ai* is compared to the seeds of plants, an analogy that Mencius also used for the emotional predispositions of the heart/mind. These observations together show that *ts'ai* has to do with the emotional predispositions of the heart/mind.

Having considered the key terms, let us return to Mencius's explanation of *hsing^a shan* as a whole. For reasons mentioned earlier, I will take "nai jo" to mean "as far as . . . is concerned," "ch'i^b" to refer to human beings (*jen^b*), and "ch'ing^a" to mean "shih^b," or what a thing is really like.[82] For Mencius, *k'o yi* in the ethical context involves not just a mere capacity but emotional dispositions in the appropriate direction. "Ts'ai" in the ethical context refers to the emotional predispositions of the heart/mind. Ch'ing^a and *ts'ai* are related since what human beings are really like (*ch'ing^a*) is that they have *ts'ai* of a certain sort; for example, in 6A:8, Mencius observed that the *ch'ing^a* of human beings is such that it is not that they do not have *ts'ai*. And *ts'ai* and *k'o yi* are related in that it is by virtue of the presence of the emotional predispositions that constitute the *ts'ai* of human beings that human beings *k'o yi* become good.

Thus, in saying that human beings *k'o yi* become good, Mencius was saying that human beings have a constitution comprising certain emotional predispositions that already point in the direction of goodness and by virtue of which people are capable of becoming good; this, according to Mencius, is what he meant by *hsingᵃ shan*. One's becoming bad is not the fault of one's constitution, but a matter of one's injuring or not fully developing the constitution in the appropriate direction. The way this constitution has an asymmetrical relation to goodness and badness can be illustrated with an analogy of A. C. Graham's: human beings have a biological constitution such that they *k'o yi* live to 70 under normal circumstances; if one dies at 20, this is not the fault of one's biological constitution but due to one's growth having been injured in some way.[83] Another analogy is Mencius's own vegetative analogy: a sprout has a constitution such that it would, in normal circumstances and with adequate nourishment, develop into a mature plant; if it does not do so, this is due not to a fault in its constitution but to its growth having been injured.

To complete the discussion of 6A:6, let us consider the three other views of *hsingᵃ* reported in the passage and how the passage relates to 6A:7 and 6A:8. Position (a) is Kao Tzu's view that there is neither goodness nor badness in *hsingᵃ*, and position (c) holds that people differ with regard to *hsingᵃ*. Now, 6A:6 claims that human beings have a constitution involving emotional predispositions directed toward goodness, and this distinguishes Mencius's position from position (a). To distinguish his position from position (c), Mencius denied that *hsingᵃ* differs from person to person. The denial is found in 6A:7, where Mencius observed that even if people differ depending on environment, this is not due to a difference in their endowment (*ts'ai*); the rest of 6A:7 then discusses the element common to all hearts/minds. A similar observation is made in 6A:8 in which Mencius emphasized that even if a person ends up being bad, this is not due to the lack of a constitution directed toward goodness. Since position (c) is illustrated with examples of how some may be bad in a favorable environment and some good in an unfavorable environment, some commentators have taken (c) to imply that some human beings are unchangeable.[84] To the extent that position (c) has this implication, Mencius responded in 6A:6 by emphasizing that everyone can become good as long as they seek it.

As for position (b), which is illustrated with examples of how people's character may vary with the environment, it has been interpreted in at least three different ways. First, D. C. Lau takes it to hold that *hsingᵃ* is such that a person can become good or bad, a view compatible with Kao Tzu's or Mencius's position, and in fact any position on *hsing^a* that does not deny the fact that some people do become good and some do become bad.[85] Second, Chao Ch'i (C) compares it to Kao Tzu's position, presumably taking it to hold that *hsing^a* is neutral and that a person can become good or bad. The second interpretation is unlike the first since it explicitly states that *hsing^a* is neutral.[86] Third, Huang Tsung-hsi (2/60a.5–b.3) takes it to hold that *hsing^a* has a component that is *k'o yi wei^a shan* and a component that is *k'o yi wei^a pu shan*. Furthermore, "k'o i" is supposed to describe not just a mere capacity but a direction; that is, there is a component pointing in the direction of goodness and a component pointing in the direction of badness. Accordingly, Huang takes it to be like Yang Hsiung's position that there is both good and bad in *hsing^a*. Yang Po-chün (citing K'ung Kuang-shen) and A. C. Graham likewise take it to be like Shih Shih's position, as reported by Wang Ch'ung (28/11–12), that there is both good and bad in *hsing^a*.[87] All of these interpretations are compatible with the emphasis on the changeability of people's character, implicit in the examples given to illustrate (b).

Of these interpretations, the second is unlikely since it identifies position (b) with position (a), thereby making the reference to (b) redundant. The first interpretation is possible, although it is unlikely since it makes (b) compatible with the other positions including position (c), when the examples cited by Kung-tu Tzu seem to be highlighting a contrast between (b) and (c). Still, these considerations are not decisive, and it is difficult to tell what the exact content of (b) is in the absence of further elaboration.[88]

However, as far as Mencius is concerned, he probably understood position (b) in the manner described in the third interpretation. One consideration is that he regarded *k'o yi* in the ethical context as the same as *neng* and as dependent on appropriate emotional predispositions. If *k'o yi* is understood in this manner, the statement of position (b) implies that there are in *hsing^a* both emotional predispositions directed toward goodness and emotional predispositions directed toward badness, which is the third interpretation of (b).

Another consideration is that he would not have objected to (b) if the first interpretation is correct, and since the second interpretation takes (b) to be the same as (a), he did not have to do anything more to distance his position from (b) if the second interpretation is correct. If the third interpretation is correct, however, he would need to show that there is no component in *hsing^a* directed toward badness in order to distance his position from (b). That he did make this point in 6A:6

suggests that he probably understood (b) in the manner described in the third interpretation. In 6A:6, while agreeing with the first half of (b) about *k'o yi wei^a shan*, he opposed the second half by claiming that badness is due to the fault not of one's *ts'ai* but of one's not exhausting *ts'ai*. Without disagreeing with the point, illustrated by the examples cited in connection with (b), that people's character varies with the environment, 6A:7 goes on to explain this variation in terms of developing or failing to develop a common constitution directed toward goodness, rather than in terms of a constitution with mixed qualities. This serves to supplement 6A:6 to distance Mencius's position from position (b) in the third interpretation.

6.4   Mencius and Hsün Tzu on *hsing^a*

6.4.1   *Hsün Tzu on hsing^a*

It is well known that Mencius regarded *hsing^a* as good (*shan*) and that Hsün Tzu regarded *hsing^a* as evil (*o*), and it would further our understanding of Mencius to consider in what ways, if any, their views differ. Mencius's view is mentioned in three passages of the *Meng-tzu*: by Mencius himself in 6A:2 when debating with Kao Tzu about *hsing^a*, by Kung-tu Tzu in 6A:6 when contrasting Mencius's position on *hsing^a* with those of Kao Tzu and others, and by the editor in 3A:1 as a report of the teachings that Mencius sought to convey to a prince. Hsün Tzu's view is not mentioned outside the "Hsing o" chapter of the *Hsün-tzu*; in that chapter, Mencius is clearly the primary target of criticism.[89] These observations suggest that the apparently opposing claims about *hsing^a* were often made in a slogan-like fashion, as a way of contrasting one's position to those of others. The claims are just convenient ways of referring to more elaborate pictures of the ethical life and its relation to human beings, and an understanding of the differences between the apparently opposing claims about *hsing^a* requires an understanding of the substantive differences between the underlying pictures.

Hsün Tzu characterized *hsing^a* as that which is as it is from birth (*HT* 22/2), which is due to *t'ien* (*HT* 22/63, 23/11), which cannot be learned or acquired by effort (*HT* 23/11–12), and whose operations are spontaneous and do not require effort (*HT* 23/25–27). By contrast, *wei^c* is characterized as that which requires the heart/mind's deliberation (*HT* 22/3–4), which is acquired by learning and brought to completion by effort (*HT* 23/11–13), and which does not operate spontaneously but awaits the effort of human beings (*HT* 23/27). Hsün Tzu regarded as unacquired and due to *t'ien* sensory capacities, the capacities of the heart/mind, and desires and emotions (*HT* 17/10–12), and regarded the superior person and the petty person as sharing by birth various desires and capacities such as sensory capacities (*HT* 4/32–47). However, when specifying the content of *hsing^a*, although sometimes relating *hsing^a* to capacities such as sensory capacities (*HT* 23/13–14), he tended more often to emphasize desires and emotions (*HT* 22/63), including various self-regarding desires such as the desire for profit and sensory desires (*HT* 23/1–3, 23/25–26). This is probably because "hsing^a" still carried dynamic connotations, and thus is more appropriately used of emotions and desires, which incline one in certain directions. And, according to Hsün Tzu, *hsing^a* is the same in all human beings, whether Yao and Shun or Chieh and Chih, or whether a superior person or a petty person (*HT* 23/53–54).

To understand the differences between Mencius and Hsün Tzu, we need to know what Hsün Tzu regarded as pertaining to human beings by birth. As far as desires are concerned, parts of the text suggest that he believed that human beings share by birth only self-regarding desires but not other-regarding concerns. In one place, he said that human beings are born petty individuals concerned only with profit and not knowing *li^a yi^a* (rites and propriety) or *tz'u^a jang* (declining and yielding to others; *HT* 4/49–51). Elsewhere, he similarly observed that human beings are fond of profit and, in the natural state, will fight even against their own brothers (*HT* 23/29–32). In addition, he characterized *hsing^a* in terms of the desire for food, warmth, and rest and described yielding to or taking up burdens in place of fathers and elder brothers as going against one's *hsing^a* (*HT* 23/17–21).

However, there is some evidence in the "Li lun" chapter that Hsün Tzu also believed that human beings share certain emotions that are not entirely self-regarding.[90] In explaining the basis of the three-year period of mourning, he pointed out that, just like other animals with consciousness, human beings have a love for those of their own kind (*HT* 19/96–103). And, in explaining the basis of the sacrificial rites, he referred to one's remembrance of and longing for the deceased (*HT* 19/117). Although he did not explicitly state that these emotions pertain to human beings by birth, that he invoked them in an account of the basis of certain *li^a* practices shows that he regarded them as emotions that human beings share before they are shaped by li^a. If so, it seems that Hsün Tzu did acknowledge that human beings share in the natural state certain emotions that have to do with one's attachment to other human beings, especially those with whom one has had a history of close interaction.

This aspect of Hsün Tzu's thinking may seem to conflict with the parts of the text cited earlier that observe that human beings would not yield to even fathers and elder brothers and that brothers will fight each other in the natural state. There are at least two possibilities, and there seems insufficient textual evidence for adjudicating between them. One is that there is indeed a tension in Hsün Tzu's thinking, one possibly explained by the observation that the apparently conflicting parts of the text, especially the "Hsing o" and "Li lun" chapters, represent different stages in the development of Hsün Tzu's thinking and address different concerns. Whereas the "Hsing o" chapter is directed against Mencius, the "Li lun" chapter might have been an attempt to defend li^a practices against the Mohist challenge.[91] Another possibility is that there is no genuine tension between the different parts of the text, although there is a difference in emphasis. Hsün Tzu's view may well be that even though human beings share some concern for family members, they nevertheless put their own interests above those of family members in the natural state. That is, even if some concern for others may be present in the natural state along with self-regarding desires, the concerns might not be present in the right degree and structured in the right way, and without regulation by the heart/mind, there will still be strife and disorder even within the family.[92] This suggestion fits with the fact that although Hsün Tzu described certain li^a practices as having their basis in other-regarding emotions, he also believed that li^a serves to regulate such emotions, restraining them when they are excessive and extending them when they are deficient (*HT* 19/63–64, 19/96–103). Although some other-regarding concerns may be present, they serve only as raw materials to be shaped by li^a yi^a.[93]

Going beyond desires and emotions, let us consider other psychological elements that Hsün Tzu might have regarded as pertaining to human beings by birth. On one occasion, he mentioned various self-regarding desires and a fondness for profit and then went on to say that people's $k'o$ yi become a Yao or Yü and their $k'o$ yi become a Chieh or Chih is also something they are born with (*HT* 4/42–47). Elsewhere, he also observed how every human being $k'o$ yi become a Yü, and then went on to draw a distinction between *k'o yi* and *neng*, claiming that the distinction between *k'o yi* and not *k'o yi* is not the same as the distinction between *neng* and not *neng* (*HT* 23/60–75). Whereas everyone *k'o yi* become a sage, not everyone *neng* become a sage, although they *k'o yi chih^a* and *k'o yi neng*; this is supposed to be analogous to the fact that although everyone *k'o yi* become a carpenter, not everyone *neng* become a carpenter.

In light of the point made in §6.3.2 about Mencius's tendency to use "k'o i" and "neng" interchangeably, along with the fact that Mencius is clearly the target of criticism in this chapter, Hsün Tzu was probably here criticizing what he regarded as Mencius's failure to distinguish between *k'o yi* and *neng*. *Neng* in the ethical context, as we have seen, requires possession of emotional dispositions structured in a way congenial to the ethical ideal, and in saying that not everyone *neng* become a sage, Hsün Tzu was probably making the point that not everyone possesses the appropriate emotional dispositions. The claim that everyone *k'o yi* become a Yao or Yü and *k'o yi* become a Chieh or Chih suggests, on the other hand, that *k'o yi* is understood as a mere capacity — everyone *k'o yi* become a sage in that everyone has the capacity to acquire the appropriately structured emotional dispositions by virtue of which one *neng* become a sage. This reading fits the analogy of the carpenter — whereas everyone has the capacity (*k'o yi*) to learn the skills by virtue of which one *neng* become a carpenter, not everyone in fact has such skills.

If this interpretation is correct, then Hsün Tzu's view is that the appropriately structured emotional dispositions required for one to *neng* become a sage are something that human beings do not already have but need to be learned. This fits with the earlier observation that even if Hsün Tzu might have held the view that human beings already have love for other members of their own kind, such love does not yet have the appropriate structure.[94] To acquire the appropriately structured emotional dispositions, the heart/mind has to exercise two of its capacities: *k'o yi chih^a* and *k'o yi neng*. Since Hsün Tzu also sometimes spoke of *chih^a* (knowing) as coming before *neng* (*HT* 22/5–6), his view is probably one in which the heart/mind exercises first its capacity to know what is proper and then its capacity to cultivate the appropriately structured emotional dispositions that make possible attaining the ethical ideal.

In another passage, when discussing what distinguishes human beings from animals, plants, fire, and water, Hsün Tzu observed that human beings alone have *yi^a* (HT 9/69–73). Although this may seem close to Mencius's position, the context of the passage shows that "yi^a" here refers to a certain capacity, rather than the kind of inclinations that Mencius regarded as a starting point for cultivating the attribute *yi^a*. Hsün Tzu characterized *yi^a* in terms of the capacity to draw social distinctions (*fen*) and form organizations (*ch'ün*). Elsewhere, the feature that makes a *jen^b* a *jen^b* (*jen^b chih̆s so yi wei^a jen^b*) is again described in terms of social differentiations (*pien*) and distinctions (*fen*; HT 5/23–28). Thus, *yi^a* in the present context is probably a capacity to draw social distinctions and to abide by and be transformed by the norms governing such distinctions; it does not involve prior inclinations of the kind that Mencius highlighted.[95] Such a capacity distinguishes human beings from other animals: although the latter can have *chih^a* (knowing), probably including not just consciousness but also intelligent action (such as storing food for the winter), they cannot create, abide by, and let themselves be transformed by normative practices in the way that human beings can.

The notion of what is distinctive of *jen^b*, or what makes a *jen^b* a *jen^b*, is different from the notion of *jen^b hsing^a*, which Hsün Tzu characterized in terms of what pertains to *jen^b* by birth. This is not just because what makes an X an X (X *chih̆s so yi wei^a* X) need not be something that pertains to X by birth — for example, what makes a Yü a Yü (HT 23/61) is what distinguishes Yü from other human beings and is not the same as that which pertains to Yü by birth and is shared by all human beings (HT 5/24–25). In addition, even if what makes a *jen^b* a *jen^b* is also something that pertains to *jen^b* by birth, not everything that pertains to *jen^b* by birth is what makes a *jen^b* a *jen^b* — what pertains to *jen^b* by birth can include things shared by other animals. That Hsün Tzu viewed the capacity to draw, abide by, and be transformed by social distinctions as what is distinctive of *jen^b* supports the observation in §6.1.2 that *jen^b* is viewed as a species defined in social rather than biological terms.

6.4.2   Mencius and Hsün Tzu on hsing^a

Having considered Hsün Tzu's position, we can now turn to a comparison of Mencius and Hsün Tzu. We noted earlier that the claims that *hsing^a* is good and that *hsing^a* is evil are often presented in a slogan-like fashion, and that an understanding of the differences between them requires an understanding of the substantive differences between the underlying views. For this reason, it can be misleading to approach such claims by putting too much weight on the question how a thinker construed the scope of *hsing^a*. This approach can lead to the conclusion that a thinker's claims about *hsing^a* are largely a function of a certain way of construing the scope of *hsing^a* and that the difference between different claims about *hsing^a* is largely a terminological disagreement. Such conclusions can obscure the fact that a thinker's claims about *hsing^a* may reflect a substantive view of the ethical life and its relation to human beings, and that the difference between different claims about *hsing^a* may reflect substantive differences between such views.

Consider, for example, Hsü Fu-kuan's observation that although Hsün Tzu's characterization of *hsing^a* in terms of what pertains to human beings by birth should allow *hsing^a* to include sensory and other capacities in addition to desires, Hsün Tzu confined the scope of *hsing^a* to desires and excluded various capacities. According to Hsü, Hsün Tzu's claim that *hsing^a* is evil depends on this move, and this move is inconsistent with Hsün Tzu's official definition of "hsing^a."[96] Similarly, a number of authors have objected that even Hsün Tzu acknowledged that human beings have the capacity to become good and that if he had allowed this capacity to count as part of *hsing^a* (as his official definition of "hsing^a" suggests he should), he would not have been in a position to claim that *hsing^a* is evil. For example, Fu Ssu-nien thinks that the fact that human beings share the capacity of *wei^c* contradicts the claim that *hsing^a* is evil, and Lao Ssu-kuang thinks that Hsün Tzu's belief that sages can create *li^a yi^a* and that human beings can transform themselves through *li^a yi^a* contradicts his claim that *hsing^a* is evil.[97]

It appears true that Hsün Tzu tended to restrict the scope of *hsing^a* to emotions and especially desires, even though his characterization of *hsing^a* allows for the inclusion of other capacities. It is unclear, however, that if he had allowed *hsing^a* to include these other capacities, he would not have been in a position to claim that *hsing^a* is evil. The objections just described assume that this claim amounts to the assertion that there is something that constitutes *hsing^a* and is evil, and hence that the claim depends on a certain way of construing the scope of *hsing^a*. But this approach does not seem to do justice to the substance of Hsün Tzu's views. Even though he tended to restrict the scope of *hsing^a* to emotions and desires, he was not, in claiming that *hsing^a* is evil, saying that such emotions and desires are evil. The emotions and desires are not bad in themselves; the goal of self-cultivation is not to get rid of or reduce the desires one has by birth, but to have the heart/mind regulate and redirect the desires (*HT* 22/55–62). Rather, the claim has to do with the strife and disorder that results if the heart/mind does not regulate the pursuit of satisfaction of desires and the expression of emotions (*HT* 23/1–13), and this observation does not depend on restricting the scope of *hsing^a* to emotions and desires. Even if he had allowed *hsing^a* to include the capacities of the heart/mind, *hsing^a* would still be evil in exactly the same sense — unless the heart/mind exercises control over the emotions and desires, strife and disorder will result.

We saw earlier that Hsün Tzu might have believed that human beings also share by birth certain other-regarding concerns such as love for members of one's own kind. Even so, such concerns are not structured in the right way, and strife and disorder will still result in the absence of regulation by the heart/mind. He emphasized that there is nothing in human beings that points in the ethical direction by comparing the sages to craftsmen (*HT* 23/22–29, 23/50–53).[98] Thus, behind Hsün Tzu's claim that *hsing^a* is evil is this picture of human psychology, and his claim is not dependent on a certain way of construing the scope of *hsing^a*.

As another example of how an overemphasis on the way a thinker construed the scope of *hsing^a* can be misleading, consider Ch'en Ta-ch'i's argument that there is no substantive difference between Mencius and Hsün Tzu because they included different things in *hsing^a*. Ch'en proposes that the way to approach these claims about *hsing^a* is to first determine the scope of *hsing^a* and then assess whether what falls within its scope is good or evil.[99] According to him, Hsün Tzu took *hsing^a* to include desires and emotions but not other capacities and inclinations that may be described as good. Thus, what Hsün Tzu did was to make the statement that *hsing^a* is evil true by excluding from the scope of *hsing^a* anything that might threaten this idea.[100] Mencius, on the other hand, took *hsing^a* to include ethical inclinations but not sensory desires, thereby making the statement that *hsing^a* is good true.[101] What Mencius regarded as good, Hsün Tzu also regarded as good, and what Hsün Tzu regarded as evil, Mencius also regarded as evil; it is just that Mencius included in *hsing^a* what Hsün Tzu excluded, and Hsün Tzu included what Mencius excluded. Hence, according to Ch'en, there is actually no substantive difference between them despite their apparently opposing claims about *hsing^a*.[102]

This way of viewing the disagreement between Mencius and Hsün Tzu is not uncommon. For example, Hsü Fu-kuan also proposes that there is no substantive difference between Mencius and Hsün Tzu with regard to *hsing^a*; each simply restricted the scope of *hsing^a* in different ways.[103] And, indeed, Mencius and Hsün Tzu did seem to have different emphases in talking about *hsing^a*, and Hsün Tzu was probably opposing Mencius's understanding of *hsing^a* when he insisted that the real difference between *hsing^a* and *wei^c* lies in the contrast between what is unlearned and what is learned (*HT* 23/10–13). As we saw in §6.1.1, Mencius used "*hsing^a*" in a way closely related to "*ch'ing^a*." "*Ch'ing^a*" is contrasted with "*wei^c*" in early texts, where the contrast is between what genuinely pertains to a thing and what is superficial appearance. Correspondingly, Mencius used "*hsing^a*" to emphasize tendencies characteristic of a thing that reveal what the thing is really like, and his focus in talking about the *hsing^a* of human beings is on what is distinctive of human beings. Hsün Tzu, on the other hand, characterized *hsing^a* as what pertains to a thing by birth and is not learned or acquired, this being contrasted with *wei^c* understood as what is due to human effort. The emphasis is on what is unlearned, rather than on what is distinctive of human beings; for the latter purpose, Hsün Tzu would speak instead of what makes a human being a human being (*jen^b chih^g so yi wei^a jen^b*).[104] Thus, there is indeed a difference in emphasis in Mencius's and Hsün Tzu's understanding of *hsing^a*.

Even so, as various authors have noted, it does not follow that their opposing claims about *hsing^a* do not reflect substantive differences.[105] Even though some of Hsün Tzu's arguments against Mencius might not be directed against the actual views of Mencius, such as those directed against the view that everyone is already fully ethical (e.g., *HT* 23/29–36, 23/36–50), Hsün Tzu did say things opposed to Mencius's position. For example, his claim at the beginning of the "Hsing o" chapter (*HT* 23/1–3) that following *hsing^a* leads to wrangling and strife, violence and crime, and license and wantonness, was probably directed against Mencius's observation (*M* 2A:6) that human beings share the germs of yielding to others (*tz'u^a jang*), of commiseration (*ts'e yin*), and of aversion and regarding as below oneself (*hsiu wu^b*).[106] His subsequent account (*HT* 23/17–22) of how sons will not yield to fathers, or younger brothers to elder brothers, was probably directed against Mencius's claim (7A:15) that love for parents and respect for elder brothers are some things human beings share in having without learning.

In addition, as we have seen, Hsün Tzu's emphasis on the distinction between *k'o yi* and *neng* (*HT* 23/74–75) was probably directed against Mencius's tendency to use "k'o yi" and "neng" interchangeably (*M* 1A:7, 6B:2). Also, his claim that all that human beings have by birth are *k'o yi chih^a* and *k'o yi neng* (*HT* 23/60–68) was probably directed against Mencius's claim that there are certain things that human beings *chih^a* and *neng* without having to learn (*M* 7A:15). His observation that everyone *k'o yi* become a Yü but not *neng* become a Yü (*HT* 23/72–73) was probably directed against Mencius's shift from the observation that everyone *k'o yi* become a Yao and Shun to the observation that one's not practicing the way of Yao and Shun is not a matter of a lack of *neng* (*M* 6B:2). Finally, his observation that the petty person *k'o yi* become a superior person and the superior person *k'o yi* become a petty person (*HT* 23/70–71), which parallels his observation that everyone *k'o yi* become a Yao or Yü and *k'o yi* become a Chieh or Chih (*HT* 4/45–47), probably served to highlight the point that nothing in one's constitution points toward goodness and away from badness. This point is opposed to Mencius's characterization of the human constitution in 6A:6 in terms of *k'o yi wei^a shan*, which for Mencius was not a mere capacity to become good but involved emotional predispositions directed toward goodness and away from badness.

Probably, a main difference between Mencius and Hsün Tzu concerns the extent to which ethical inclinations are already shared by human beings.[107] Although Hsün Tzu might have held the view that human beings share some concern for others, he did not regard such concern as structured in the appropriate way. As a result, human beings in the natural state would still put their own interests above those of family members, leading to the kind of strife within the family described in the "Hsing o" chapter. Accordingly, in the natural state, human beings lack the *neng* to attain the ethical ideal, such *neng* being dependent on appropriately structured emotional dispositions. What human beings have in the natural state is only *k'o yi neng*—that is, the capacity to have their emotions and desires appropriately reshaped so that they acquire the *neng* to practice the Confucian Way. This process involves a radical transformation of such emotions and desires, and this radical transformation Hsün Tzu compared to straightening a crooked piece of wood (*HT* 23/5, 23/48–49). In this view, what human beings already share, including any concern for others that they may have in the natural state, serve only as raw materials to be reshaped by learning.

By contrast, Mencius probably regarded human beings as sharing emotional dispositions already structured in the appropriate way, so that even in the natural state one defers to parents and elders of the family. Because of the presence of such emotional dispositions, human beings already have the *neng* to attain the ethical ideal. Such emotional dispositions would still need to be refined through appropriate upbringing, but they are not just raw materials to be reshaped by learning. Instead, an ethical direction is built into such predispositions, and self-cultivation is a more continuous process involving the nurturing and development of such predispositions.

Reference Matter

Notes

For full author names, titles, and publication data for works cited here in short form, see the Bibliography, pp. 269–80. See pp. xiii for a list of abbreviations used here.

Chapter 1

1. To the best of my knowledge, no serious doubts have been raised about the authenticity of the text—see, e.g., Lau, *Mencius*, app. 3. I have therefore used the text as a whole in reconstructing Mencius's thinking, with the exception of 4A:12 and 7A:4, which refer to *ch'eng* (wholeness, being real). Despite the significance of the subject, I have deferred discussing the notion of *ch'eng* to a later occasion because there is insufficient textual basis in the *Meng-tzu* for reconstructing Mencius's views on *ch'eng* and because of the parallel between 4A:12 and part of the *Chung-yung*.

2. In stating this qualification, I have deliberately left open the question whether what can be reconstructed from the relevant text(s) fully represents the thinker's views or whether it might include elements introduced by the compilers and/or editors. Addressing this question requires a study of the history of transmission of texts, which I have not taken up in the present study. I am indebted to Chad Hansen for alerting me to the need to make explicit the open-endedness of this qualification.

3. Although this claim about the underlying practical concerns may seem uncontroversial to some, I have stated it as an assumption since it needs to be justified by historical evidence. I am indebted to Thomas Metzger for alerting me to the need to make this point explicit.

4. Since the way I introduce the notion of the ethical leaves its content open—it need not be linked, for example, to other-regarding concerns or to a concern with social obligations—it is possible to speak of these thinkers as sharing an ethical concern.

5. Eno (app. B) raises doubts whether the group was referred to as "ju[a]" at that time; Hu Shih (pp. 6–44) and Fung Yu-lan (*Pu-p'ien*, pp. 4–30) disagree about the origin of the group. Despite such disagreements, it is generally

agreed that such a group existed in early China—see Eno, app. B; Fung Yu-lan, *Pu-p'ien*; Lao Ssu-kuang, pp. 30–32.

6. See Fung Yu-lan, *Chung-kuo che-hsüeh-shih*, pp. 70–78, 89–92; idem, *Pu-p'ien*, pp. 5, 30, 41; Lao Ssu-kuang, pp. 31–32, 37.

7. E.g., Eno, pp. 6–7; Knoblock, *Xunzi*, p. 52.

8. The picture has recently been challenged by Eno, whose position I discuss in my "Review of Eno." Despite disagreeing with its depiction of early Confucian thought, I think the book has made an important contribution both in highlighting certain important methodological issues and in its discussion of specific topics not dealt with in my review.

9. This depiction of early Confucian thought can be found in various writings, sometimes in the context of contrasting Chinese thought with Western philosophical traditions. See, e.g., Mou Tsung-san, *T'e-chih*, chaps. 1, 2, 12 (esp. pp. 4–6, 9–11); idem, *Shih-chiu-chiang*, chap. 3 (esp. pp. 46–49); idem, *Shih-ssu-chiang*, chaps. 1, 2 (esp. pp. 9, 18, 21). Cf. Fung Yu-lan, *Chung-kuo che-hsüeh shih*, pp. 8–9; T'ang Chün-i, *Chung-hsi che-hsüeh*, pp. 52–56; Wei Cheng-t'ung, "Chi-tien jen-shih," pp. 213–15.

10. See Wu K'un-ju, pp. 55–60, for some qualifications to this general characterization.

11. For example, Fung Yu-lan (*Chung-kuo che-hsüeh shih*, pp. 4–6, 8–14, 25–26) observes that ideas ascribable to early Chinese thinkers exhibit interesting interconnections and different degrees of centrality. Likewise, Hsü Fu-kuan (*Jen-hsing-lun shih*, "Preface to Second Edition," pp. 3–4) observes that these thinkers were reflective individuals with a body of coherent and connected ideas, and that one main task of the study of early Chinese thought is to extract these ideas from the texts and display their interconnections (cf. idem, *Lun-chi*, pp. 2–3, 114, 133–34; idem, *Lun-chi hsü-p'ien*, pp. 441–42). See also Lao Ssu-kuang, pp. 7–8; Liu Shu-hsien, "Fang-fa yü t'ai-tu," p. 223; Mou Tsung-san, *T'e-chih*, p. 3.

12. Something like this line of thought can be found in Eno, who claims that the Confucians (or, as he refers to them, the Ru) denied "the ultimate value of logic and reason in the search for knowledge" (p. 7), disregarded the "goal of systematic coherence" (pp. 10–11), and were "doctrinally hostile toward analytic rigor in argument" (p. 172).

13. Even Eno himself points out that the relevant texts do contain attempts to resolve apparent inconsistencies and arguments to defend certain positions. For example, he mentions that texts such as the *Meng-tzu* and *Hsün-tzu* contain "sophisticated argumentation" "to defend Confucian doctrine" (pp. 3, 10), and that the *Meng-tzu* contains "arguments over . . . logical consistency" (p. 115) and attempts to "rationalize apparent contradictions in [Mencius's] doctrines or actions" (p. 109).

14. Something like this line of thought can be found in Eno; see my "Review of Eno."

15. Cf. Lao Ssu-kuang, pp. 360–61; Liu Shu-hsien, "Fang-fa yü t'ai-tu," p. 226; Schwartz, pp. 4–7.

16. Cf. Isenberg, pp. 235–41; Liu Shu-hsien, "Fang-fa yü t'ai-tu," p. 222.

17. Fung Yiu-ming ("Che-hsüeh") traces something like this line of thought in the literature.

18. Cf. Liu Shu-hsien, "Fang-fa yü t'ai-tu," pp. 224–27; Mou Tsung-san, *T'e-chih*, p. 6; T'ang Chün-i, "Hsin-fang-hsiang," pp. 134–35; Wei Cheng-t'ung, "Chi-tien jen-shih," p. 206.

19. E.g., Hsü Fu-kuan, *Lun-chi*, p. 3; Lao Ssu-kuang, pp. 19–21, 360–62.

20. See Richards, pp. 9–10. Richards (pp. 86–93) himself suggests some strategies for dealing with this difficulty, such as the use of multiple definitions and alertness to a range of possible meanings when studying key terms in early Chinese texts and to the possibility of other purposes and different structures of thought that serve other purposes.

21. Cf. Hansen, pp. 2–7.

22. I am indebted to David Nivison for help on this point; cf. Nivison, "On Translating Mencius," pp. 111–12.

23. Cf. T'ang Chün-i, "Hsin-fang-hsiang," pp. 132–33.

Chapter 2

1. Cf., e.g., Fu Ssu-nien's view (pp. 204–5) with Harwood's (pp. 137, 184) summary of Creel's and Dobson's research in this area.

2. For a discussion of the four texts, see Lin Yü-sheng, pp. 201–3; and Schwartz, pp. 40–41.

3. See Eno, pp. 80–81; and Lau, *Analects*, app. 3.

4. E.g., Graham, *Disputers*, p. 10; and Schwartz, p. 62.

5. See Munro, p. 185.

6. See Nivison, "Investigations," lecture 1.

7. See, e.g., Dobson's view as reported in Harwood, p. 143; and Hsü Fu-kuan, *Jen-hsing-lun shih*, pp. 37–39.

8. Note, however, that some of these odes might well be using "t'ien" as an indirect way of referring to the king.

9. See Li Tu, pp. 37–39.

10. For examples, see Li Tu, pp. 37–42.

11. E.g., Hsü Fu-kuan, *Jen-hsing-lun shih*, p. 52. But Hsü (p. 56) also acknowledges that "ming^a" is sometimes used in connection with obligations, as in the example just cited from *TC* 263/1–7.

12. The interpretation of the occurrences of "ming^a" in *SC* 21/1–2 is ambiguous, but both Fu Ssu-nien (p. 227) and Lao Ssu-kuang (p. 26) take these occurrences to refer to happenings not within human control.

13. In light of the explanation in *LY* 12.22, I take "chih^a" in *LY* 14.35 to mean appreciating a person's character and ability and employing the person on that basis. The issue is discussed in §2.1.2.

14. See Eno, chap. 4.

15. E.g., Fu Ssu-nien, pp. 236–37, 331–32; Lao Ssu-kuang, pp. 67–72; Ts'ai Shang-ssu, pp. 84–86, 94–95; possibly also Graham, *Disputers*, pp. 17–18.

16. E.g., Ts'ai Shang-ssu, pp. 84–86.

17. E.g., Hsü Fu-kuan, *Jen-hsing-lun shih*, pp. 83–90; D. C. Lau, *Analects*, pp. 27–29. However, in his *Lun-chi hsü-p'ien*, p. 385, Hsü presents the different view that although some occurrences of "ming[a]" in the *Lun-yü* concern what is not fully within human control, most occurrences have to do with one's obligations.

18. E.g., T'ang Chün-i, *Tao-lun p'ien*, pp. 512–18. In taking "ming[a]" to refer to *yi[a]*, T'ang finds his cue in the conjunction of "ming[a]" and "yi[a]" in *Meng-tzu* 5A:8.

19. See T'ang Chün-i, *Yüan-tao p'ien*, pp. 110–19. Hsü Fu-kuan (*Lun-chi hsü-p'ien*, p. 385) also describes how the use of "ming[a]" captures the sense that one's obligations originate independently of oneself.

20. Fu Ssu-nien notes that Confucius did not hold a general fatalistic view (pp. 331–32), but still thinks that Confucius was a fatalist with regard to certain areas of life and that this fatalistic attitude is what the Mohists later opposed (p. 237).

21. Cf. Hsü Fu-kuan, *Lun-chi hsü-p'ien*, pp. 384–85; in this account, the descriptive use of "ming[a]" need not embody the kind of fatalistic belief opposed in the *Mo-tzu*.

22. This is the way T'ang Chün-i (*Tao-lun p'ien*, pp. 512–18) interprets *LY* 14.36, which observes that it is *ming[a]* whether the Way prevails. A similar transition from the descriptive to the normative dimension can be seen, for example, in Cheng Li-wei, pp. 126–36. Hall and Ames (pp. 214–15) note that the use of "ming[a]" in the *Lun-yü* concerns how one relates to the determining conditions of one's existence, although they are making the different point that what counts as determining conditions is a function of the extent to which one has approximated sagehood.

23. A related difference is that "tzu," but not "chi[a]," can be used as a reflexive pronoun to refer to families and states (e.g., *M* 4A:8).

24. In "Problem of the Self," Fingarette argues against the use of the notions of self and self-cultivation in discussing Confucius's teachings. His elaboration on his position in "Response to Roger T. Ames," however, shows that what he is opposing is a notion of self associated with the idea of some "mysterious interior self" that is a kind of "inner entity" or "private ego and will." My use of the notion of self is free from such associations, and in §5.2.3, I show how, for Mencius, cultivating the self involves cultivating the whole person, including the physical body.

25. Ted Slingerland drew my attention to this link between one's acceptance of adverse outcomes and one's not worrying about them in a paper he wrote for a graduate seminar I taught in 1993.

26. See Boodberg, p. 328.

27. Proponents of this view include Dobson, p. xv; Graham, *Disputers*, p. 19; Hsü Fu-kuan, *Lun-chi hsü-p'ien*, pp. 358–65; Lin Yü-sheng, pp. 172–83; Waley, *Analects*, p. 27. Hsü and Lin cite as support the two occurrences of "jen[a]" in the *Shih-ching*.

28. Proponents of this view include Wing-tsit Chan, "Evolution," p. 2; T'ang Chün-i, *Yüan-tao p'ien*, p. 71; Tu Wei-ming, *Confucian Thought*, pp. 84–85, citing Fang Ying-hsien on p. 92n23. Chan takes the early use of "jen^a" to refer primarily to the kindness of a ruler toward his subjects.

29. T'ang Chün-i (*Yüan-tao p'ien*, chaps. 1–2) describes how "jen^a," originally referring to love, could have come to refer to an all-encompassing ideal for human beings. Hsü Fu-kuan (*Lun-chi hsü-p'ien*, pp. 365–77; cf. *Jen-hsing-lun shih*, pp. 90–100), describes how the character, originally referring to attributes of distinctive members of certain aristocratic clans, could have come to refer to love.

30. See Lau, *Analects*, pp. 16–19.

31. See Roetz, pp. 124–25.

32. Some scholars, such as Fingarette (*Confucius*) and Eno, have claimed that the content of *jen^a* is constituted primarily by *li^a*. I know of no convincing argument for this claim; on this issue, I tend to agree with Schwartz, pp. 80–81.

33. E.g., Lao Ssu-kuang, p. 40; Schwartz, pp. 67–68; Ts'ai Shang-ssu, pp. 238, 240. An exception is Graham (*Disputers*, p. 11), who thinks "li^a" as used in the *Lun-yü* concerns good manners.

34. Chad Hansen alerted me to this point.

35. E.g., Chao Chi-pin, 2: 288–325; Ts'ai Shang-ssu, pp. 106–7, 238–40, 282–85.

36. E.g., Lin Yü-sheng, pp. 193–96; see Hsü Fu-kuan, *Jen-hsing-lun shih*, pp. 69, 90. *LY* 9.3 contrasts with *LY* 3.17 in which Confucius opposed dispensing with a sacrificial sheep required by *li^a*—Donald Munro alerted me to this point in conversation.

37. See Boodberg, p. 330.

38. E.g., Lau, *Analects*, pp. 26–27; T'ang Chün-i, *Yüan-tao p'ien*, pp. 158–59.

39. E.g., Chung-ying Cheng, chap. 8; Cua, "Confucian Vision," p. 230; Hall and Ames, pp. 84, 100, 108–10; Lao Ssu-kuang, pp. 45–47; Lau, *Analects*, pp. 37–39, 47–50; Schwartz, p. 80.

40. In my "*Jen* and *Li* in the *Analects*," I discuss the attitude toward *li^a* and the relation between *li^a* and *yi^a* in the *Lun-yü*.

41. Boodberg (p. 323) notes the two possibilities, and Schwartz (pp. 103–4) takes the use of legitimate force to be the earlier meaning of "cheng^a" (government).

42. This implication of *LY* 2.21 is noted in Ch'en Ta-ch'i, *K'ung-tzu hsüeh-shuo*, p. 301.

43. For discussions of this issue, see Ch'en Ta-ch'i, *K'ung-tzu hsüeh-shuo*, pp. 301–23; Liu Shu-hsien, *Ju-chia ssu-hsiang*, pp. 1–16; Schwartz, pp. 103–9; Ts'ai Shih-chi.

44. Creel, *What is Taoism?*, pp. 58–60.

45. Metzger ("Some Ancient Roots," p. 74) makes the interesting observation that the idea of appreciating others is the counterpart to the idea of

self-examination in that the two concern evaluation of others and of oneself, respectively.

46. Chan (*Source Book*, chap. 1) describes this development as the "growth of humanism," and Hsü Fu-kuan (*Jen-hsing-lun shih*, chaps. 2–3) refers to it as the emergence of the humanistic spirit.

47. A point emphasized by Fingarette (*Confucius*) in connection with *li*ᵃ. Chan (*Source Book*, p. 3) observes that the humanism that emerged does not slight the idea of a supreme power. Hsü Fu-kuan (*Jen-hsing-lun shih*, pp. 51–56) speaks of a humanization of a religious kind.

48. See Graham, *Disputers*, pp. 35–36, 51–53, for a discussion of the differences between factions of the Mohist school and the classification of chaps. 8–37 by factions.

49. For a discussion of the earlier meaning of the character, see Graham, *Later Mohist Logic*, p. 188.

50. Graham, *Disputers*, p. 41.

51. The exact difference between Mohist indiscriminate concern and Confucian love with distinction is not entirely clear. The form of discrimination that Mo Tzu criticized at the beginning of the "Chien ai" chapters does not seem something Confucians would advocate, since they did not advocate harming others to benefit oneself or those to whom one stands in special relations. As to whether and how the indiscriminate concern that the Mohist advocated is opposed to the Confucian ideal, I find insufficient textual basis in the *Mo-tzu* for addressing this question. I am indebted to Craig Ihara for alerting me to a need to discuss this issue. For different treatments of the subject, see Metzger, "Some Ancient Roots," p. 80; and Wong, "Universalism Versus Love with Distinction." Metzger thinks that Mohist indiscriminate concern is not opposed to Confucian graded obligations; Wong focuses on the differences between the Mohists and the Confucians.

52. Examples of similar uses of "yi"ᵃ and "yen" can be found in other texts, such as the *Lü-shih ch'un-ch'iu*, which refers to Mo Tzu's view as a *yi*ᵃ and subsequently as a *yen* (*LSCC* 19/5b.7–6a.2).

53. See Graham, *Disputers*, pp. 37–39.

54. See T'ang Chün-i, *Yüan-tao p'ien*, pp. 171–72.

55. Here, I follow the emendation reported in Sun Yi-jang's commentary on the relevant line in *MT* 46/54–55.

56. As we will see in §4.4.3, Mencius also regarded doctrines as having serious consequences.

57. E.g., Schwartz, pp. 142, 262.

58. Nivison, "Philosophical Voluntarism," p. 19, citing the "So jan," "Chien ai," and "Shang t'ung" chapters, as well as Mo Tzu's comparison of cultivating oneself to building a wall (*MT* 47/29–30). My discussion in the remainder of this section owes much to Nivison's paper.

59. As noted by T'ang Chün-i, *Yüan-tao p'ien*, p. 222; idem, *Tao-lun p'ien*, pp. 90–93.

60. Nivison, "Philosophical Voluntarism," pp. 19–21; and idem, "Weak-

ness of Will," pp. 6–8. Nivison suggests that Mo Tzu probably believed that human beings have the ability to initiate emotional changes at will.

61. E.g., Schwartz, pp. 259–60.

62. Fung Yu-lan, *Chung-kuo che-hsüeh shih*, pp. 173–79; Graham, "Dialogue," p. 294; idem, "Right to Selfishness," p. 74; idem, *Disputers*, p. 55.

63. Concerning the first observation, see Graham, "Background," pp. 7–8; Hsü Fu-kuan, *Jen-hsing-lun shih*, pp. 5–6; Schwartz, p. 175; T'ang Chün-i, *Yüan-hsing p'ien*, pp. 9–10. Concerning the second observation, see Graham, "Background," pp. 9–10; Hsü Fu-kuan, *Jen-hsing-lun shih*, pp. 4–11.

64. E.g., Graham "Background," pp. 7–11; Schwartz, p. 175; T'ang Chün-i, *Yüan-hsing p'ien*, pp. 9–10.

65. E.g., Hsü Fu-kuan, *Jen-hsing-lun shih*, pp. 9–10, 30–31; Mou Tsung-san, *Hsin-t'i yü hsing-t'i*, 1: 197–99.

66. Graham, "Background," p. 9.

67. Here, I follow the Wei commentary in adopting the translations "weapons" and "agricultural tools."

68. Graham, "Background," p. 11; Hsü Fu-kuan, *Jen-hsing-lun shih*, pp. 56–61; Mou Tsung-san, *Hsin-t'i yü hsing-t'i*, 1: 205–7; T'ang Chün-i, *Yüan-hsing p'ien*, pp. 11–13.

69. This point need not conflict with Graham's observation that the use of "hsing^a" is normative ("Background," pp. 14–15), partly because Graham's observation is made more in connection with the Yangist movement, which viewed *hsing^a* as the proper course of development for human beings, and partly because there is a sense of "normative" in which the normativity of *hsing^a* is compatible with the undesirability of *hsing^a*. Namely, *hsing^a* may be normative in the sense that one who views certain tendencies as *hsing^a* may regard going against such tendencies as doing violence to oneself and as a result be disinclined to so act, even though someone viewing the tendencies from the outside may regard them as undesirable. I am indebted to Irene Bloom and Bryan Van Norden for help in clarifying my thoughts on this point.

70. Schwartz, p. 176.

71. Graham, "Background," pp. 11–12.

72. Ibid., p. 13.

73. Schwartz, pp. 175–79.

74. Graham, "Dialogue."

75. Graham, *Disputers*, pp. 54–55; idem, "Right to Selfishness," p. 74.

76. Hou Wai-lu et al., pp. 337–48; the authors think the latter trend is closer to Taoism.

77. E.g., Graham, "Right to Selfishness," p. 75; idem, "Background," p. 10; idem, *Disputers*, p. 56; Hsü Fu-kuan, *Jen-hsing-lun shih*, pp. 8, 441–44.

78. The same point can be seen in the chapters of the *Chuang-tzu* Graham identifies as Yangist. Although there is emphasis on longevity (*CT* 28/58) and nourishing the body (*CT* 28/13–14), there are also references to the contentedness of the mind and bodily comfort (*CT* 29/77–82) as well as to sen-

sory satisfaction (CT 29/48–49). That the Yangist conception of *hsing*ᵃ also includes sensory satisfaction is acknowledged by Graham, "Background," p. 13.

79. Graham, *Disputers*, pp. 63–64.

80. Graham himself takes "tsun" to be verbal, translating "tsun shengᵃ" as "honor life."

81. See, e.g., Fung Yu-lan, *Chung-kuo che-hsüeh shih*, p. 170; Graham, "Dialogue," p. 295, idem, "Right to Selfishness," p. 76; Lau, "Introduction," in *Mencius*, p. 30.

82. An alternative reading of the statement of Yangist teaching in the *Han-fei-tzu* (*HFT* 50.4.4) is that the Yangist would not exchange a hair for the greatest profit in the empire.

83. Lau, "Introduction," in *Mencius*, p. 30.

84. Graham, "Right to Selfishness," pp. 76–77; idem, "Dialogue," p. 296; idem, *Disputers*, p. 61.

85. Graham, "Dialogue," p. 299.

86. Graham, *Disputers*, pp. 53–54, 56.

87. Graham, *Disputers*, pp. 57–58, also acknowledges in connection with the Tan-fu passage that the Yangists probably were concerned for the *hsing*ᵃ/*sheng*ᵃ of others.

88. Even the Confucians idealized those not concerned for political power (e.g., *LY* 8.1), and the idea can also be found in Taoist texts (e.g., *LT* 13).

89. I tried out the ideas in this section in a graduate seminar I taught in 1991 and benefited from discussions with Michael Millner, who subsequently wrote a paper on the subject for the seminar.

Chapter 3

1. A point noted by Ch'en Ta-ch'i, *Ch'ien-chien chi*, pp. 161–63.

2. These two aspects of *jen*ᵃ were noted by Wang Fu-chih (549).

3. My position differs from that of Roetz (p. 211), who claims that the Confucian attitude toward the treatment of animals is basically one of moderation in the use of natural resources, and that the Confucians devalued nonhuman nature. I am indebted to Liu Shu-hsien for help on this issue. The issue of the scope of "wuᵃ" in the *Meng-tzu* has bearing on the issue of the extent to which the later Confucian conception of *jen*ᵃ as forming one body with all things can be traced to Mencius. Another relevant passage is 7A:4, in which Mencius spoke of the ten thousand things being already in one.

4. My approach to this issue differs from that of Ch'en Ta-ch'i, *Ch'ien chien chi*, pp. 167–73. Ch'en distinguishes between a general and a specific use of "ch'in," "jenᵃ," "ai," suggesting that, in the specific use, *ch'in* involves *jen*ᵃ and *tsun* (to honor), whereas *jen*ᵃ involves *ai* and *ching* (reverence, seriousness). This, according to Ch'en, explains why *jen*ᵃ is not directed toward animals (for which one has no reverence) and *ch'in* is not directed toward the

common people (whom one does not honor). Ch'en's proposal, however, does not explain why "jen[a]" is not used verbally in connection with parents, although "ai" is so used.

5. I am indebted to Craig Ihara for alerting me to this aspect of *li[a]*; that mastery of *li[a]* is like mastery of a skill is also emphasized in Eno.

6. Cf. Hsü Fu-kuan, *Jen-hsing-lun shih*, pp. 20–24.

7. Ch'en Ta-ch'i, *Tai-chieh-lu*, pp. 119–21.

8. I am not fully confident about this account of *kung* since I am not sure how it fits in with the way *kung* and *ching* are contrasted in *M* 4A:1.

9. Ch'en Ta-ch'i, *Tai-chieh-lu*, pp. 141–43. An interesting contrast to the point Ch'en makes is a case in which *kung* involves *tz'u[a]*—Liu Hsia Hui's failure to decline (*tz'u[a]*) low official positions (6B:6) is described in another context as not disdaining such positions and hence as not respectful (*kung*; 2A:9).

10. I have been helped by Derek Hertforth on this point.

11. On this issue, I differ from Eno who observes that the two notions are "in many instances . . . functionally equivalent" (p. 112); cf. my "Review of Eno."

12. I owe this point to Roetz (p. 177), who mentions both examples.

13. The contrast is noted by Chu Hsi (YL 1333–34). An interesting question is why Mencius regarded as a starting point for cultivating the ethical attribute *yi[a]* reverence for and obedience to elder brothers. One possible answer is that these involve one's treating the elder brothers seriously and with caution and being strict with oneself in following them, and so provide a starting point for cultivating a similar attitude toward the ethical standards governing one's conduct and character.

14. This is probably why, in *M* 6A:11, after having characterized *jen[a]* in terms of the heart/mind and *yi[a]* in terms of the path of human beings, Mencius said that all that is involved in learning is to seek the heart/mind, as if *yi[a]* is already involved in *jen[a]* (cf. Chu Hsi, MTCC 6A:11).

15. Cf. Hall and Ames, pp. 83–110.

16. The analogy fails to hold in one regard: a skilled archer can aim at any target, unlike the person with *chih[b]* whose aims are always proper aims. But the point of analogy is that a skilled archer can successfully aim at any target, just as the person with *chih[b]* can successfully aim at proper conduct in any situation. I am indebted to Craig Ihara for help on this point.

17. Chu Hsi (MTCC 5B:1; YL 1366) takes sageness to include the ability to act with ease to accomplish one's aims. Chao Ch'i (C 5B:1; cf. CC 5B:1) makes the further point that Mencius regarded sageness as like strength in that it has a limit and cannot be further increased, unlike *chih[b]*, which resembles skill in that it can be increased by learning.

18. Graham, "Relating Categories to Question Forms," pp. 406–7.

19. See Huang Chün-chieh, *Meng-tzu*, pp. 48–55; and idem, *Ssu-hsiang-shih lun*, pp. 32–40, for a more elaborate discussion.

20. *LY* 9.26 likewise compares one's *chih[c]* to the commander of an army,

but makes the further point that whereas an army can be deprived of its commander, even a commoner cannot be deprived of chih[c].

21. Cf. Hsü Fu-kuan, *Lun-ch'i*, p. 143. Most translations I have consulted adopt the first interpretation, although Lau and Uchino give the second interpretation.

22. This fits in with the characterization in the *Lun-yü* of chih[a] (knowing, understanding) in terms of the absence of perplexity (*LY* 9.29, 14.28); perplexity is also linked in the *Lun-yü* to the directions of the heart/mind (*LY* 14.36).

23. A similar contrast between Confucius and others is also expressed through Confucius's own mouth in *LY* 18.8.

24. There are different interpretations of "pu pi" in 4B:11. Chao Ch'i (C), Sun Shih, and Chiao Hsün take it to mean "need not," whereas Chang Shih takes it to mean "do not aim at."

25. Ch'en Ta-ch'i, *Ming-li ssu-hsiang*, pp. 30–39, gives a detailed discussion of different kinds of examples.

26. Munro, pp. 74–77.

27. I have deliberately referred to the scenario in vague terms because further problems of interpretation arise: does the scenario involve Mencius's being made a minister of Ch'i (which is the more common interpretation) or his occupying a position above the ministers of Ch'i, and was Kung-sun Ch'ou referring to Mencius's having been made a minister of Ch'i in the past (2B:6 refers to Mencius's actually occupying that position) or to a contemplated future possibility?

28. Riegel, pp. 434–36.

29. Examples of exceptions are Ware, "poise"; Lyall "not shrink"; and Riegel, p. 438 (cf. *n*18), "bound tight."

30. A point noted in Hsü Fu-kuan, *Lun-chi*, p. 143; and Lee Ming-huei, "'Chih-yen-yang-ch'i' chang."

31. Both Chu Hsi (MTCC) and Chang Shih note with regard to this passage that ideal courage is guided by yi[a].

32. The interpretation of "chih[f] yang" is relatively uncontroversial. Most commentators and translators take it to mean that ch'i[a] should be nourished with yi[a] (Chao Ch'i, C) or with rectitude (Legge; Dobson), integrity (Lau), or uprightness (Chan), or that ch'i[a] should be properly nourished (Giles) or cultivated (Chai and Chai). There are, however, different interpretations of "p'ei yi[a] yü tao"—unite yi[a] and tao (Lau), be mate and assistant of yi[a] and tao (Legge; cf. Chu Hsi, MTCC), be accompanied by yi[a] and tao (Chan), be fit recipient for yi[a] and tao (Dobson).

33. The character involved, "ch'ien," has the meaning of "satisfying" in a few occurrences in the *Lü-shih ch'un-ch'iu* (*LSCC* 1/7a.10–7b.4, 16/10a.7–8) and is so interpreted by most commentators and translators. Some commentators (e.g., Sun Shih) and translators (e.g., Lau) take it to mean measuring up to the standards of the heart/mind; Chu Hsi (MTCC) gives both readings.

34. Courage itself is often related to ch'i[a] in early texts (e.g., *LSCC* 8/

11a.2-4), and the combination "yung ch'iᵃ" sometimes appears (e.g., *TC* 85/8-9).

35. Most translators adopt some variation of Chu's interpretation, with the exception of Lau, who follows Chao; Legge, who takes "yiᵈ" to mean "be alone in being active"; and Dobson, who takes it to mean "be given primacy." See also Riegel, p. 454n29.

36. The immediately preceding reference to *chihᶜ* in the passage makes it likely that it is *chihᶜ* which is supposed to be not led into excesses, deflected, or bent.

37. See Ch'en Ta-ch'i, *Ch'ien-chien chi*, pp. 231-32.

38. Ch'en Ta-ch'i, *Tai-chieh-lu*, pp. 94-96.

39. Sun Shih's position is more ambiguous; he also speaks of what is done without being done *by human beings* in his commentary.

40. Dobson's translation takes "mingᵃ" to refer to *t'ien mingᵃ* as a source of political authority; this is a possible reading since the context concerns succession to the throne.

41. Chu Hsi (YL 1360), commenting on 5A:6, apparently distinguishes between these two dimensions of "mingᵃ."

42. Fu Ssu-nien takes "mingᵃ" to refer both to unalterable conditions of life and to *yiᵃ* (pp. 347, 355). Graham takes it to include all the unalterable conditions of human existence, including both how things are and the way they ought to be ("Background," p. 54).

43. Ch'en Ta-ch'i emphasizes the use of "mingᵃ" to refer to occurrences not within human control (*Tai-chieh-lu*, pp. 303-11), and Hsü Fu-kuan observes that the *Meng-tzu* does not use the combination "t'ien mingᵃ" and that "mingᵃ" in isolation means "destiny" (*Jen-hsing-lun shih*, p. 167). Lao Ssu-kuang thinks most occurrences of "mingᵃ" refer to destiny, but in some instances (such as 7A:1-2) the term refers to life (pp. 134-38).

44. T'ang Chün-i, *Tao-lun p'ien*, pp. 522-27. Cf. the discussion in §2.1.1 of T'ang's views on the use of "mingᵃ" in the *Lun-yü*.

45. There is a similar difficulty with the interpretation of "mingᵃ" in *Lun-yü* 14.36; here, again in a political context, Confucius remarked that *mingᵃ* resides in the prevailing or the disuse of the Way.

46. Cf. Fu Ssu-nien, p. 355; and T'ang Chün-i, *Tao-lun p'ien*, pp. 515-16.

47. Lyall has a reading similar to Huang's. Ware has a fourth interpretation that I find less plausible—he takes "not two" to mean that either premature death or longevity is something sure, presumably in the sense of being already determined.

48. Lao Ssu-kuang, p. 137, takes "mingᵃ" in this context to refer to life and death.

49. Fu Ssu-nien, p. 347; T'ang Chün-i, *Tao-lun p'ien*, pp. 522-27; idem, *Yüan-tao p'ien*, pp. 245-46.

50. Chiao Hsün has a different reading of the line "mo fei mingᵃ yeh." Taking "fei" to mean not correct, the opposite of *chengᵇ*, he interprets the line to be urging people to avoid *mingᵃ* that is not correct, presumably by avoid-

ing improper conduct and thereby avoiding what would have followed from improper conduct.

51. T'ang Chün-i, *Tao-lun p'ien*, pp. 522–27, esp. pp. 525–26.

52. Lau, "Introduction" in *Mencius*, p. 23, has a similar reading, taking Mencius to endorse a form of "limited fatalism."

53. And if we take the occurrence of "ming^a" in 7A:3 to be primarily descriptive, this gives reason for similarly interpreting the occurrence of "ming^a" in 5A:8, since both occurrences are related to attainment (*te^b*).

54. Although most commentators and translators take "yie^e" to mean "contribute to," Dobson takes it to mean "get value from." According to Dobson, the contrast concerns whether seeking gets its value from finding; in the latter case, whether one finds what is sought is preordained, and seeking does not derive its value from finding and therefore is of no value.

Chapter 4

1. I have been helped by Chad Hansen in thinking through these methodological issues.

2. Lau translates the first line of 6A:1b as "Can you make cups and bowls by following the nature of the willow?" The use of "by" suggests that Mencius demanded of Kao Tzu's analogy that it reflect the view that human beings will become good simply by following *hsing^a*. This demand, if made, would have been unfair to Kao Tzu since it requires his analogy to exclude possibility (d), when in fact Kao Tzu's view about *hsing^a* requires him to allow for that possibility. But grammatically the first line of 6A:1b concerns only one's following the *hsing^a* of the *ch'i* willow and at the same time making cups and bowls out of it, which is the way I translate that line.

3. In this way of viewing the debate, what Mencius said in 6A:2b does not constitute a genuine objection to Kao Tzu's analogy in 6A:2a. Graham ("Background," p. 44) suggests that Mencius attacked the analogy on the ground that water does tend downward and so has a direction. But this should not be a problem for Kao Tzu since the analogous claim in the case of human beings is just that human beings have certain tendencies, which Kao Tzu could accept as long as these tendencies allow for the·four possibilities described earlier with regard to goodness and badness. Ascribing tendencies to human beings would be a problem for Kao Tzu if we assume that any human tendency is either in the direction of goodness or opposed to it. Graham at times makes remarks that suggest this assumption: "The dynamic model [in 6A:2a] like the last [in 6A:1a] implies that human nature tends in a direction which, *if not good, will conflict with any good one tries to impose on it*. Kao Tzu has failed to produce a model for a conception of human nature as morally neutral" (*Disputers*, p. 121; italics added). But it is unclear why we should accept this assumption; for example, biological tendencies of human beings are in themselves neither directed to goodness nor opposed to it.

4. A point noted by Mou Tsung-san, *Yüan-shan lun*, p. 2.

5. See Ts'en I-ch'eng, "'Sheng-chih-wei-hsing' shih-lun," sections 2–3, esp. pp. 65–70. Ts'en points out that the "A chihs wei^b B" structure implies that A serves as a criterion for B, making it unlikely that "A" and "B" have the same meaning in such a structure. This is true even of the two occurrences of "pai" in "pai chihs wei^b pai," which Ts'en reads as saying that only what satisfies the criterion for *pai* is *pai*. Ts'en further distinguishes between A's being a necessary condition and its being a sufficient condition for B, suggesting that "A chihs wei^b B" can make one or both of these claims.

6. Examples of the structure ". . . chihs chihs wei^b . . ." occur in *M* 7B:25 and *CT* 12/7, 12/74.

7. Graham, "Background," pp. 45–46.

8. T'ang Chün-i, *Yüan-hsing p'ien*, pp. 17–18.

9. This interpretation is also found in Ch'en Ta-ch'i, *Tai-chieh-lu*, pp. 5–7; Hsü Fu-kuan, *Jen-hsing-lun shih*, p. 187; Lao Ssu-kuang, p. 99; and Ts'en I-ch'eng, "'Sheng-chih-wei-hsing'shih-lun," pp. 69–70. Chu Hsi (MTCC; YL 1376) probably reads the line similarly.

10. In §4.3.1 I will consider a complication—the more plausible interpretation of the parallel structure "chang N chihs chang" in 6A:4 regards the first "chang" as verbal, with "N chihs chang" as its object.

11. Dobson, who takes "sheng^a" to refer to the thing that gives life, and the first "pai" in "pai chihs wei^b pai" to refer to that which whitens, for some reason interprets "pai N chihs pai" as the whiteness of white N rather than as the whiteness that makes N white.

12. Lau ("Introduction," in *Mencius*, p. 36; "Method of Analogy," pp. 242–43), who takes "sheng^a" to refer to the inborn, makes this suggestion. According to Lau, the comparison is inappropriate because "hsing^a" is a formal term in that the content of N's *hsing^a* depends on what N is, unlike "pai," which is not a formal term in that the content of N's *pai* is not dependent on what N is. Mou Tsung-san (*Yüan-shan lun*, pp. 7–12) similarly observes that the comparison is inappropriate and that Mencius probably misunderstood Kao Tzu when he suggested the comparison; Kao Tzu should have rejected the comparison, thereby blocking the conclusion that Mencius drew from it. See also Yang Tsu-han, p. 24.

13. Mou Tsung-san (*Yüan-shan lun*, pp. 7–12) notes that "sheng^a chihs wei^b hsing^a" emphasizes biological tendencies.

14. Unlike Lau, both Graham ("Background," pp. 45–46) and Nivison ("Problems: Part I," p. 8) take Mencius as opposing Kao Tzu's statement "sheng^a chihs wei^b hsing^a" in 6A:3 and see him as stressing that the *hsing^a* of human beings is what is distinctive of them. In another context, however, Lau ("Introduction," in *Mencius*, pp. 15–16) also observes that Mencius wanted to relate *hsing^a* to what is distinctive of human beings.

15. This reading is adopted by Chao Ch'i (C), Chiao Hsün, Sun Shih, and Ware. However, since Kao Tzu was talking about my treating an old object as old, there appears little point to the denial that there is elderliness in me. This explains why, while interpreting the structure "yu N yü^a N'" to mean there

being N in N^j, many translators avoid rendering "chang" as "elderliness." Chai and Chai translate it as "regard for age," Dobson as "paying deference," Giles and Lyall as "recognition of age," Legge as "a principle of reverence to age," and Yang Po-chün as "the heart/mind of respect." It is, however, difficult to see how "chang" can be read in these ways.

16. This reading is adopted by Lau and considered by Nivison ("Problems: Part I," pp. 10–11).

17. A reading adopted by Chao Ch'i (C), Chiao Hsün, and most translators including Chai and Chai, Dobson, Giles, Lau, Legge, and Ware. Lyall has "comes from a whiteness that is outside me," taking "ts'ung" to mean "come from."

18. A reading adopted by Nivison ("Problems: Part I," pp. 11–12).

19. Some of the proposals include: punctuate as in (A) and regard "jen[b]" as an implicit subject before the first "yü[a]" (K'ung Kuang-shen cited by Chiao Hsün); punctuate as in (B) and take "yi[c] yü[a]" to be the same as "yi[c] hu," meaning "how strange" (Hu Yü-huan, P'ei Hsüeh-hai, Sung Hsiang-feng); punctuate as in (C) and take the loss of the expected parallel in (C) as an accepted practice in classical Chinese (Chao Ch'i [C]; K'ung Kuang-shen cited by Chiao Hsün); punctuate as in (D) and assign different subjects to the two halves (Nivison, "Problems: Part I," p. 12); emend the line by dropping the first two characters "yi[c] yü[a]" (a certain Mr. Chang reported in Chu Hsi [MTCC], Legge, Yang Po-chün); regard it as an accepted practice in classical Chinese to read the first occurrence of "*pai*" twice (Yü Yüeh [MTPI], Lau).

20. The first occurrence of "pai" in "pai N chih[g] pai" and the first occurrence of "chang" in "chang N chih[g] chang" are both read as adjectival by Dobson, Ware, and Nivison ("Problems: Part I," pp. 12–13). Both are read as verbal by Ch'ai and Chai, Lau, Legge, Lyall, Hattori, Kanaya, and Uchino. Giles and Yang apparently read the first as adjectival and the second as verbal, but this reading is unlikely given the parallel between c1 and c2.

21. In fact, it favors translation (ii) since the second occurrence of "chang" in "chang Ch'u jen[b] chih[g] chang" is likely to refer to the elderly ones among the people of Ch'u.

22. This reading is adopted by Chao Ch'i (C), Sun Shih, Hattori, Lau, Ware, Yang.

23. This reading is adopted by Chu Hsi (MTCC), Chang Shih, Chai and Chai, Giles, Kanaya, Legge, Lyall, Uchino, and Nivison ("Problems: Part I," pp. 13–14).

24. This reading is adopted by Dobson.

25. This reading is considered by Nivison ("Problems: Part I," pp. 21–22); Nivison cites the parallel structure "yi an she chi wei[a] yüeh[b] che yeh" from M 7A:19.

26. Chai, Dobson, Legge, and Lyall translate "yüeh" as "pleasure" or "feeling"; the difficulty with this interpretation of "yüeh[b]" is considered in Legge's exegetical notes and Waley, "Notes on *Mencius*," p. 104.

27. I am indebted to David Nivison for pointing out this possibility in

conversation, citing as evidence the line "wen ch'i[b] feng erh yüeh[b] chih[g]" (heard about their views and were moved by them) from the *Chuang-tzu* (*CT* 33/35, 43, 55, 63–64). This interpretation of "yüeh[b]" fits with its occurrences in *Meng-tzu* 3A:2, 3A:4, and 6B:4. Also, there are several occurrences of "shuo," presumably emendable as "yüeh[b]," in the *Tso-chuan* that probably also mean being moved (e.g., *TC* 215/10, 269/10).

28. See Lau, "Method of Analogy," p. 250n2; and idem, "Some Notes," pp. 78–79. The emendation is endorsed by Graham, "Background," p. 48.

29. Chu Hsi, YL 1378; Nivison, "Two Roots or One?," p. 756.

30. Chang Shih, 6A:4; Chiao Hsün, 6A:4a1–2; Tai Chen, no. 21; Lau, "Method of Analogy," p. 252.

31. Chiao Hsün, 6A:4d; Huang Tsung-hsi, 2/57b.1–5; Wang Yang-ming, no. 133; Hsü Fu-kuan, *Jen-hsing-lun shih*, p. 192; idem, *Lun-chi*, p. 147; Mou Tsung-san, *Yüan-shan-lun*, pp. 12–19; T'ang Chün-i, *Yüan-tao p'ien*, pp. 222–25; idem, *Yüan-hsing p'ien*, pp. 15–20.

32. Cf. Huang Tsung-hsi, 2/55a.1–56a.4.

33. In this interpretation, the contrast between *jen*[a] being internal and *yi*[a] being external is like Mencius's contrasting of *jen*[a] and *yi*[a], as discussed in §3.2.3. Since Mencius would not oppose such a contrast, he presumably understood the claim in a different way when opposing the claim that *jen*[a] is internal and *yi*[a] external.

34. Cf. Li Hsi; and Graham, *Later Mohist Logic*, pp. 270–71.

35. E.g., Huang Tsung-hsi, 2/57a.7–b.3; Hsü Fu-kuan, *Jen-hsing-lun shih*, p. 188; Mou Tsung-san, *Yüan-shan lun*, p. 15; Roetz, p. 206; Wang Pang-hsiung et al., pp. 34–35; cf. Wang Fu-chih (668).

36. T'ang Chün-i, *Yüan-hsing p'ien*, p. 18, seems to read the contrast in this way; see also idem, *Yüan-tao p'ien*, pp. 158–59.

37. See, e.g., Mao Ch'i-ling as cited by Chiao Hsün; Mou Tsung-san, *Yüan-shan lun*, p. 19; Yang Tsu-han, p. 19.

38. The suggestion is made by a certain Mr. Lin as reported in Chu Hsi, MTCC 6A:4; see also Lau, "Method of Analogy," p. 255.

39. A point noted by T'ang Chün-i, *Yüan-tao p'ien*, pp. 224–25.

40. Huang Tsung-hsi, 2/57b.1–58b.6, seems to be opposing this interpretation by Chu Hsi.

41. E.g., Wang Li-ch'ing.

42. See, e.g., Ch'en Ta-ch'i, *Ch'ien-chien chi*, pp. 286–90.

43. Su Che's interpretation is probably close to Sun Shih's, although it is less detailed.

44. Wang Fu-chih, pp. 529–31; Hsü Fu-kuan, *Lun-chi*, pp. 143, 147–48; Lao Ssu-kuang, pp. 105–6.

45. See Nivison, "Philosophical Voluntarism," pp. 7–8.

46. See ibid., pp. 9–10.

47. Nivison, "On Translating *Mencius*," p. 106; idem, "Philosophical Voluntarism," pp. 13–15; T'ang Chün-i, *Yüan-tao p'ien*, pp. 249–52. See also Riegel, pp. 439–40; Ts'en I-ch'eng, "'Chih-yen' ch'u-t'an"; Lee Ming-huei,

"'Chih-yen-yang-ch'i' chang." Among traditional commentaries, something close to this interpretation of "*yen*" is found in Huang Tsung-hsi, 1/14b.8. For an interesting and different approach to what it is to know *yen*, see Yang Rur-bin, "Chih-yen, chien-hsing yü sheng-jen."

48. Nivison, "Philosophical Voluntarism," pp. 10–13, interprets "te[b]" and "ch'iu" in Kao Tzu's maxim in this manner.

49. Lee Ming-huei, "'Chih-yen-yang-ch'i' chang," interprets "te[b]" and "ch'iu" in Kao Tzu's maxim in this manner. I am indebted to Lee Ming-huei for drawing my attention to this possibility.

50. Lee Ming-huei (ibid., p. 8) makes the interesting observation that the structure "pu . . . , wu . . ." also has the connotation that after something has come about, one can go on to do something else. If this is correct, then the first half of the maxim also has the implication that after obtaining yi^a from doctrines, one can go on to seek it in or make demands on the heart/mind, presumably in the sense of implanting yi^a in the heart/mind. This would in turn show that Kao Tzu did have a concern for yi^a.

51. A possibility considered in Nivison, "Philosophical Voluntarism," pp. 10–12; and Eno, p. 260n56. Nivison is inclined to regard the second half as about yi^a on the grounds that Mencius continued to talk about yi^a in explaining the second half of the maxim.

52. And if Lee Ming-huei's observation about the "pu . . . , wu . . ." structure is correct, the additional implication is that after obtaining yi^a from the heart/mind, one can go on to seek it in $ch'i^a$, presumably in the sense of letting $ch'i^a$ be shaped by the directions of the heart/mind, which now conforms to yi^a.

53. Nivison, "Philosophical Voluntarism"; and T'ang Chün-i, *Yüan-tao p'ien*, pp. 249–52. The interpretation was first suggested to me by T'ang's writings, but I have relied more on Nivison's writings in working out the arguments for that interpretation.

54. Cf. T'ang Chün-i, *Yüan-tao p'ien*, p. 250.

55. Graham, "Background," pp. 22–26; Rickett, *Guanzi*, pp. 376–77.

56. Because "shan" is contrasted with "o" (evil) in this context (*KT* 2/18.11), I translate "shan" as "goodness" rather than "skill," unlike Rickett, *Guanzi*, p. 383.

57. Graham, "Background," pp. 25–26.

58. Graham, *Disputers*, p. 100; Rickett, *Kuan-tzu*, p. 155.

59. Cf. Rickett, *Kuan-tzu*, p. 154.

60. The relation between this passage and Kao Tzu's maxim was first drawn to my attention by Nivison, "Philosophical Voluntarism," pp. 16–19.

61. Graham, *Disputers*, p. 100; Hsü Fu-kuan, *Jen-hsing-lun shih*, pp. 450–51.

62. Schwartz, p. 263; cf. p. 275.

63. Ch'en Ta-ch'i, *Ch'ien-chien hsü-chi*, pp. 195–99; Ch'en has another argument, which I find less appealing, to the effect that Kao Tzu was like Con-

fucius in emphasizing that knowledge of yi^a is based on the intellect (pp. 199–204).

64. Eno, pp. 54, 114, and 259n54.

65. Hsü Fu-kuan, *Jen-hsing-lun shih*, pp. 187–88; cf. p. 196; and idem, *Lun-chi*, pp. 147–48.

66. Nivison, "Philosophical Voluntarism," pp. 7–8, 19.

67. T'ang Chün-i, *Yüan-hsing p'ien*, pp. 15–20.

68. A point noted by Ch'en Ta-ch'i, *Ming-li ssu-hsiang*, pp. 128–29; for further elaboration, see idem, *Ch'ien-chien chi*, pp. 275–85.

69. Unlike Nivison, Ch'en Ta-ch'i (*Ch'ien-chien chi*, pp. 273–75) argues that the two are different.

70. See Nivison, "Philosophical Voluntarism," pp. 22–23.

71. E.g., Ch'en Ta-ch'i, *Tai-chieh-lu*, pp. 136–40; Graham, *Disputers*, p. 43; Lau, *Mencius*, p. 105n3. See also Kanaya Osamu's translation and Wang En-yang's commentary.

72. Ch'en Ta-ch'i (*Tai-chieh-lu*, pp. 139–40) acknowledges the difficulty of reconciling the interpretation of a root as a principle of conduct with the linking of *t'ien* to the idea of one root.

73. Nivison, "Two Roots or One?"; and idem, "Philosophical Voluntarism."

74. Nivison, "Two Roots or One?," p. 742.

Chapter 5

1. Chu Hsi (YL 1406–7, 1409) takes "fang hsin^a" to mean being lax and not paying attention, but the occurrence of "fang ch'i^b liang hsin^a" in 6A:8 and the description of chickens and dogs as *fang* in 6A:11 show that "fang" means "to lose."

2. Chang Shih reads "ts'un hsin^a" in 4B:28 to mean preserving the heart/mind. However, Chao Ch'i (C), Chu Hsi (MTCC; YL 1355), and Sun Shih take "ts'un hsin^a" to mean "keep something (*jen^a* and *li^a*) in mind." Chao probably bases his reading on the rest of 4B:28, which argues that the superior person always keeps in mind *jen^a* and *li^a*. However, the use of "ts'un" in 4B:19 in connection with the slight element distinguishing human beings from other animals and the pairing of "ts'un hsin^a" with "chin hsin^a" in 7A:1, where "chin hsin^a" probably means "fully realizing the heart/mind," make it likely that "ts'un hsin^a" has to do with preserving the heart/mind.

3. There is another possible interpretation of 4B:12. Whereas Chu Hsi (MTCC), Huang Tsung-hsi (2/27b.4–28a.6), and Chang Shih take "the heart/mind of the newborn" to refer to the heart/mind one is born with, Chao Ch'i (C; CC) and Chiao Hsün understand it as referring to the heart/mind of protecting and caring for the common people as if they were newborns. Only on the basis of the first interpretation, which Chao Ch'i notes but does not endorse, does the passage imply that the heart/mind already has predispositions in the ethical direction.

4. Graham ("Background," p. 37) notes that this observation by Mencius is a response to an observation by Tzu-hua Tzu in *LSCC* 4/11b.7–12a.1.

5. The point is noted in Nivison, "Philosophical Voluntarism," p. 21.

6. I have benefited from discussions with Bryan Van Norden in connection with these issues.

7. Hsü Ch'ien stresses this point in connection with the example in 6A:10.

8. Chu Hsi takes 7B:11 to be making a similar point. According to him (MTCC; MTHW; YL 1458), 7B:11 makes the point that one can yield a state when one is the focus of attention of everyone and if one is out to make a name, but if one is not the kind of person who truly can yield things to others, one would begrudge a basketful of rice and bowlful of soup when one is caught unaware, thereby revealing the kind of person one really is. This interpretation differs from that of Chao Ch'i, Chang Shih, and Sun Shih, who take the second half of the passage to concern a different kind of people, those who are not out to make a name. As far as I can tell, there is insufficient textual evidence to adjudicate between the two interpretations.

9. The reference to ten thousand bushels of grain occurs in 2B:10, in connection with a possible offer to Mencius.

10. Something like this suggestion can be found in Nivison, "Two Roots or One?," pp. 746, 753–54; and idem, "Mencius and Motivation," pp. 421–22; I have myself elaborated on the second variant of this suggestion in earlier writings. Van Norden ("Mencian Philosophic Psychology," chap. 3) points out the distinction between the two variants of this suggestion.

11. Something like this suggestion can be found in commentaries on this passage by later Confucian thinkers, such as Chu Hsi (MTCC 1A:7; YL 1223–24) and Chang Shih.

12. Something like this suggestion is in Wong, "Reason and Emotion," esp. pp. 38–40. Nivison seems to be suggesting a similar picture in "Problems: Part II," pp. 9–10, and "Motivation and Moral Action," pp. 26–27.

13. I have benefited from correspondence with Joel Kupperman in connection with these ideas.

14. For an elaborate discussion of this passage, see Nivison, "Problems: Part II."

15. Chao Ch'i (CC) also takes 7A:15 to be about *shu*[a].

16. This leaves open the question of how the predispositions indicate a direction. Later Confucians such as Chu Hsi (MTCC 7A:17) and Chang Shih (7A:17; cf. 7B:31) would interpret the passage in terms of one's originally being disposed not to do or desire certain things, although obscuration by selfish desires leads one to do or desire such things.

17. See §5.2.2.

18. The point is noted by Nivison ("On Translating *Mencius*," p. 115), who considers different interpretations of 7A:15 found among commentators and translators.

19. Cf. Nivison, "On Translating *Mencius*," p. 116.

20. Wong, "Universalism Versus Love with Distinctions."

21. See ibid., pp. 258–60.

22. Wong (ibid.) cites *Lun-yü* 17.21 in developing this aspect of his account. That passage can be read in two ways, as making the point that human beings are as a matter of fact and without reflection attached to those who have cared for and nourished them, or that human beings feel obliged to reciprocate, given their awareness of how parents have cared for and nourished them. The passage probably highlights the first point more, and in ascribing affection for parents to a young child still held in the arms, *Meng-tzu* 7A:15 also highlights the unreflective kind of affection that one has for parents at a very early stage in life.

23. Although agreeing with Ames's observation that Mencius did not conceive of ethical development as a process guided by "definite and specified goals" ("Mencian Conception," p. 159), I am inclined to see less flexibility in the direction of such development.

24. In his "Introduction" to *Mencius* (p. 15), Lau takes *ssu*[b] to involve thinking about moral duties, priorities, etc., showing that he takes *ssu*[b] to involve finding the answer to questions about these issues.

25. Waley, *Analects*, pp. 44–46.

26. Nivison, "Philosophical Voluntarism," p. 13; cf. idem, "Motivation and Moral Action," pp. 47–48.

27. Nivison, "Weakness of Will," p. 14.

28. There are exceptions. For example, P'ei Hsüeh-hai takes both occurrences of "wu[a]" in "wu[a] chiao wu[a]" to refer to external objects (objects of the senses), and "chiao" to refer to how one external object after another acts on the senses.

29. Something like this proposal can be found in Nivison, "Two Roots or One?," pp. 744–45; and idem, "Weakness of Will," p. 11.

30. Passage 6B:2 also makes the point that one becomes a sage by behaving in the way the sages do.

31. Hsü Fu-kuan, *Lun-chi*, p. 143.

32. Most translators read "pi yu shih[a] yen" similarly; Giles and Lyall, however, take "shih[a]" to mean difficulties and the phrase to mean that difficulties will inevitably arise.

33. Most translators adopt one or the other of these intepretations. There are exceptions: Chai and Chai take "cheng[b]" to mean "stop" (probably emending it to "chih[h]"), Giles takes it to mean "straighten out," and Lau emends "cheng[b] hsin[a]" to "wang[b]" (forget).

34. This proposal can be found in Nivison's writings, and I will return to it later.

35. Nivison discusses this aspect of the self-cultivation process in "Mencius and Motivation," p. 427, and "Two Roots or One?," p. 745.

36. Chu Hsi (MTCC; YL 1333) and Huang Tsung-hsi (2/19b.1–3) take "le" to have this implication.

37. E.g., Nivison, "Motivation and Moral Action," p. 46; Graham, "Background," p. 31.

38. E.g., Nivison, "Mencius and Motivation," p. 427.

39. This is one of the interpretations of the internality/externality of *yi*[a] described in §4.3.2.

40. E.g., Nivison, "Mencius and Motivation," pp. 422–23, 427.

41. Cf. Chao Ch'i (C) and Chu Hsi (YL 1254).

42. Cf. Chu Hsi (YL 1335–36).

43. A point noted in Ch'en Ta-ch'i, *Ch'ien-chien chi*, pp. 226–34; Huang Chün-chieh, *Ssu-hsiang-shih lun*, pp. 22–23, 61–63; Yang Rur-bin, "Lun Meng-tzu ti chien-hsing kuan"; and Yüan Pao-hsin, pp. 74–79.

44. This point fits with the observation in §2.1.2 that the self that is the object of self-cultivation is not some "inner" or "private" entity but the person as a whole.

45. Cf. Yang Rur-bin, "Lun Meng-tzu ti chien-hsing kuan," pp. 96, 111; idem, "Chih-li yü chien-hsing," pp. 431–32.

46. Yang Rur-bin, "Lun Meng-tzu ti chien-hsing kuan"; cf. idem, "Chih-li yü chien-hsing."

47. Indeed, the parallels are so close that Huang Tsung-hsi (2/64b.2–3) even identifies *ch'i*[a] in the early morning with *liang hsin*[a], which is referred to in 6A:8.

48. In "Some Ancient Roots," Metzger discusses the early Confucian optimism about one's ability, or at least the ability of those who are cultivated, to *chih*[a] *jen*[b].

49. Ch'en Ta-ch'i (*Ch'ien-chien chi*, pp. 231–32) makes the interesting observation that the vastness of the flood-like *ch'i*[a] refers to its filling the space between Heaven and Earth, and its unyieldingness refers to its not being movable by poverty, wealth, or superior force.

50. Cf. Hsü Fu-kuan, *Lun-chi*, pp. 138–40; Yüan Pao-hsin, pp. 117–24.

51. Ch'en Ta-ch'i, *Tai-chieh-lu*, pp. 129–35; my discussion in this paragraph draws on Ch'en's discussion.

52. Ch'en Ta-ch'i (*Ch'ien-chien chi*, pp. 190–91) notes the interesting parallel between these observations by Mencius and Mo Tzu's defense of indiscriminate concern on the ground that having concern for and benefiting others will lead others to treat one similarly.

53. See §4.3.1 in connection with the possibility that "*yüeh*[b]" can mean "being moved by."

54. "*Li*[b]" is used in parallel to "*te*[a]" in M 7B:10, but here "*li*[b]" might not be used in a positive sense—both Chao Ch'i (C; CC) and Chiao Hsün take the reference to *li*[b] to describe those concerned with their own profit at the expense of propriety.

55. Cf. Ch'en Ta-ch'i, *Tai-chieh-lu*, pp. 64–68.

56. Cf. Schwartz, pp. 260–62; Wang En-yang, 1A:1.

57. Fung Yu-lan (*Hsin-yüan-tao*, pp. 17–18) proposes this way of dealing

with the apparent tension in connection with Confucius's and Mencius's thinking.

58. In 1B:1, Mencius made this point with regard to enjoyment of music — sharing his enjoyment of music with the people would be more satisfying to the ruler than enjoyment of music by himself.

59. Passage 4B:16 seems to conflict with 2A:3, which contrasts those who rely on force to gain others' allegiance (*yi li fu jen*[b]) and those who rely on *te*[a] to gain others' allegiance (*yi te*[a] *fu jen*[b]); only the latter is supposed to succeed. The problem is posed by the fact that *yi shan fu jen*[b] is said in 4B:16 to fail, whereas *yi te*[a] *fu jen*[b] is said in 2A:3 to succeed. A way of resolving the problem is to say that the emphasis in 2A:3 is more on the contrast between force and *te*[a], and that "yi te[a] fu jen[b]" does not carry the connotation of practicing *te*[a] with the goal of bringing about others' allegiance.

60. E.g., Ch'en Ta-ch'i, *Tai-chieh-lu*, p. 86.

61. Cf. Lau's discussion of 4A:17 in "Method of Analogy," p. 245. Lau makes the interesting point that saving the empire involves causing the empire to have the Way, and this cannot be done by compromising the Way.

62. The reference to the heart/mind is not explicit in 6A:14, although the passage is so interpreted by Chao Ch'i (C) and Chu Hsi (MTCC). Comparison with 6A:15 gives support to this interpretation.

63. The contrast in 6A:9 between one who devotes one's *chih*[c] to learning chess and one who is distracted by thoughts of shooting at swans is interesting — setting one's *chih*[c] is sometimes compared to aiming in archery in early Chinese texts (see §3.3), and the reference to thoughts of shooting at swans is probably a way of emphasizing the distraction of one's *chih*[c].

64. I follow Chao Ch'i (C) and Chang Shih in interpreting the reference in 6A:9 to those who expose the king to the cold as a reference to those who offer corrupting advice.

65. Comparison with the occurrence of "ts'un hsin[a]" (preserving the heart/mind) in other passages (e.g., 4B:28, 6A:8) favors interpreting "ts'un" in 7B:35 to refer to preserving the heart/mind. Chu Hsi (MTCC) gives this interpretation, but Chao Ch'i (C) takes "ts'un" to refer to preserving one's life.

66. The idea that the operation of the senses involves the heart/mind is found in certain early texts (e.g., *LSCC* 5/9b.6–10a.1) and is highlighted by later Confucians such as Wang Yang-ming (e.g., no. 201).

67. Creel, *Chinese Thought*, pp. 86–87. By contrast, Ts'ai Hsin-an ("Ts'ung tang-tai," pp. 406–8; *Tao-te chüeh-tse li-lun*, pp. 150–54) takes Mencius to be defending the practice of *jen*[a] *yi*[a] on the grounds that it benefits the public.

68. Cf. Lee Ming-huei, *Ju-chia yü K'ang-te*, pp. 148–52, 183–94; Yüan Pao-hsin, pp. 138–39, 146–50.

69. Here, I take "chung[b]" in "chung[b] tao" to be used verbally.

70. In 7A:6, the expression "wu ch'ih chih[g] ch'ih wu ch'ih yi" has been given different interpretations: "the move from being lacking in *ch'ih* to hav-

ing *ch'ih* enables one to be free from *ch'ih*" (Chiao Hsün), "to *ch'ih* one's lack of *ch'ih* enables one to be free from *ch'ih*" (Chao Ch'i, cited by Chu Hsi, MTCC, and endorsed by Chang Shih), "the *ch'ih* of not having *ch'ih* is truly without *ch'ih*" (Lau; Yang Po-chün). The first interpretation is unlikely, since "chih8," which links "wu ch'ih" and "ch'ih," although often used in the sense of moving from one place to another, is rarely used in early texts to refer to a move from one state of character to another (cf. Yang Po-chün). It is difficult to adjudicate between the other two interpretations, both of which read the two occurrences of "wu ch'ih" differently: the first occurrence refers to one's not having a sense of what is below oneself; the second to being free from things that are below oneself (second interpretation) or truly lacking a sense of what is below oneself (third interpretation). Whichever interpretation we adopt, 7A:6 is clearly emphasizing the importance of *ch'ih*.

71. Passage 4B:6 refers to the kind of *li*[a] and *yi*[a] that is not truly *li*[a] and *yi*[a]. This may be interpreted as describing a situation like that of the honest villager: one appears to but does not really conform with *li*[a] and *yi*[a]. However, the passage can also be interpreted as describing overdoing things: although being respectful is *li*[a], being overrespectful is not *li*[a], although it may look like *li*[a] (e.g., Chang Shih, citing Master Ch'eng).

Chapter 6

1. Ames, esp. pp. 143–45.
2. E.g., Bloom; Liu Shu-hsien, "Some Reflections."
3. Ames, p. 153.
4. Mou Tsung-san, *Yüan-shan lun*, p. 161; Graham, "Background," pp. 32, 38.
5. E.g., Chu Hsi (MTCC) and Hsü Ch'ien. Graham, "Background," p. 28, probably has a similar interpretation in mind when he takes "hsing[a]" in 7A:30 and 7B:33 to mean "had it by nature."
6. Ames (p. 160) interprets "hsing[a] chih8" in 7A:30 in this way.
7. Wang Fu-chih (738–40) interprets "hsing[a] chih8" in 7A:30 in this way.
8. Wang Fu-chih (738–39) also argues against this interpretation of 7A:21.
9. Graham, "Background," pp. 33, 59–65; cf. idem, *Disputers*, pp. 98–99.
10. I am indebted to Irene Bloom and Bryan Van Norden for helpful comments on my discussion of Graham. Graham also cites the claims in *Meng-tzu* 6A:6 (in which "ch'ing[a]" occurs) and 2A:6 that certain ethical predispositions are shared by human beings and those that lack such predispositions are not human beings. I will discuss the nature of this claim in §6.1.2.
11. I owe this last observation to Irene Bloom.
12. I am indebted to Thomas Metzger for pointing out the need to add this qualification.
13. Graham ("Background," pp. 20–21) takes the reference to the *hsing*[a] of the petty person to illustrate the second half of the third view on *hsing*[a] reported by Kung-tu Tzu in 6A:6—that there are human beings whose *hsing*[a] is bad. However, although the aggressive tendencies under consideration are

characteristic of a petty person *as a petty person,* they need not be characteristic of the person *as a human being* and so need not be describable as *jen*[b] *hsing*[a].

14. And the remark in *Lun-yü* 17.2 about people being close to each other in *hsing*[a] also illustrates the point that nothing in the use of "hsing[a]" as such requires that the *hsing*[a] of things of a kind must be the same.

15. Graham ("Background," p. 39) takes the subject of "hsing[a]" to be Yi Ya. It is also possible that the subject has to do with palates; as we saw, the uses of "hsing[a]" and of "ch'ing[a]" are closely related, and the disposition of the senses toward their ideal objects is sometimes described as the *ch'ing*[a] of the senses (e.g., *LSCC* 5/9b.6–10a.1).

16. A point emphasized by T'ang Chün-i (*Yüan-hsing p'ien,* pp. 28–31).

17. And although 2A:6 does not mention the innocence of the young child toward whom one's compassionate response is directed, 3A:5 does make the point in citing the example.

18. A point highlighted in Wong, "Reason and Emotion"; cf. idem, "Universalism Versus Love With Distinctions."

19. Ames, p. 163; Hall and Ames, pp. 138–46.

20. Lau (*Analects*), however, regards this occurrence of "jen[b]" as corrupt.

21. The discussion that follows covers interpretations proposed in the major commentaries but is not intended to be exhaustive. For example, Dobson and Ware take "ku" to mean "ifs/whys and therefores," which is one possible meaning of the character. But since it is not clear from their translations how they understand part (a) of the passage, I have not considered this reading of "ku."

22. Wang Pang-hsiung et al., pp. 57–61, takes this direction.

23. See Huang Chang-chien.

24. Graham, "Background," pp. 49–53.

25. Ibid., p. 52; I am not sure why Graham does not, like Lau, take "ku" to refer to former views of *hsing*[a], which, like the Yangist view, aimed at profit.

26. Hsü Fu-kuan, *Jen-hsing-lun shih,* pp. 168–70.

27. Kanaya emended "li[b]" to "chih[b]" (wisdom). Although this move may provide a smoother transition from part (a) to part (b), I see no basis for the emendation.

28. I have been helped by Huang Chang-chien's article in developing these arguments.

29. Ch'en Ta-ch'i, *Ming-li ssu-hsiang,* pp. 129–32; Fung Yu-lan, *Chung-kuo che-hsüeh shih,* pp. 155–59; Graham, "Background," p. 35; Hsü Fu-kuan, *Jen-hsing-lun shih,* pp. 165–68; Lao Ssu-kuang, pp. 97–100, 104, 279; Lau, "Introduction," in *Mencius,* pp. 15–16; T'ang Chün-i, *Che-hsüeh lun-chi,* p. 128.

30. This is the interpretation of 6A:17 given by most commentators, including Chu Hsi (MTCC), Chang Shih, and Hsü Ch'ien.

31. Hsü Fu-kuan, *Jen-hsing-lun shih,* pp. 165–68; T'ang Chün-i, *Che-hsüeh lun-chi,* pp. 7–9, 133–34.

32. T'ang Chün-i, *Yüan-hsing p'ien,* pp. 20–24.

33. Graham, *Disputers,* pp. 125–32; idem, "Background," pp. 35–36.

34. Graham, "Background," pp. 14–15.
35. T'ang Chün-i, *Yüan-hsing p'ien*, pp. 3–4.
36. Others besides T'ang have made similar observations, such as Ch'en T'e, pp. 41–42; and Hsü Fu-kuan, *Jen-hsing-lun shih*, p. 174.
37. Compare the discussion in §§2.1.1 and 3.5 of T'ang Chün-i's views on *ming*ᵃ.
38. Cf. T'ang Chün-i, *Yüan-tao p'ien*, pp. 217–20, 235.
39. "Yü*ᵃ*" also links the references to the senses and the references to their objects in 6A:7.
40. Jeffrey Riegel alerted me in conversation to this possible complication. In this reading, a person who is *chih*ᵇ (wise) is drawn to worthy people in that wisdom involves an ability to appreciate people who are worthy and to employ them on that basis.
41. P'ang P'u, pp. 19–21.
42. Graham takes Mencius to be saying that it is a good habit of mind to think of moral inclinations as *hsing*ᵃ ("Background," pp. 38–39). Nivison takes him to be saying that it is wise to take a certain attitude toward morality ("Two Roots or One?," p. 745).
43. T'ang Chün-i, *Yüan-hsing p'ien*, pp. 20–28.
44. Tai Chen (no. 28) puts the point by saying that 7B:24 is claiming only that the superior person does not use *hsing*ᵃ as an excuse to indulge in sensory pursuits, not that the superior person does not regard sensory desires as *hsing*ᵃ. Chu Hsi (MTCC), in citing his teacher's view, says that although both sensory and ethical pursuits can be characterized in terms of *hsing*ᵃ and *ming*ᵃ, Mencius wanted to combat the tendency to view the former as *hsing*ᵃ and the latter as *ming*ᵃ. Likewise, Graham ("Background," pp. 38–39) thinks that Mencius would himself view both sensory and ethical pursuits in terms of both *hsing*ᵃ and *ming*ᵃ, although he regarded it as a good habit of mind to think of the former as *ming*ᵃ and the latter as *hsing*ᵃ.
45. The former reading is in Chao Ch'i (C) and Juan Yüan, and the latter in Tai Chen (no. 28), who is cited by Chiao Hsün, and also in Mou Tsung-san, *Hsin-t'i yü hsing-t'i*, 3: 426–30.
46. The former reading is in Chu Hsi (MTCC) and Wang Fu-chih (748), and the latter in Graham, "Background," pp. 38–39, and Nivison, "Two Roots or One?," p. 745.
47. E.g., Hsü Fu-kuan, *Jen-hsing-lun shih*, pp. 165–68; Mou Tsung-san, *Hsin-t'i yü hsing-t'i*, 3: 426–30; T'ang Chün-i, *Che-hsüeh lun-chi*, pp. 8–9, 133–35; idem, *Yüan-hsing p'ien*, pp. 20–28.
48. This interpretation of "*ming*ᵃ" in the second half of 7B:24 can be found in Chao Ch'i (C); Juan Yüan; and Mou Tsung-san, *Hsin-t'i yü hsing-t'i*, 3: 426–30. Chu Hsi (MTCC) and Chang Shih interpret "*ming*ᵃ" in terms of differences in endowment of *ch'i*ᵃ, an idea that I take to be alien to Mencius's thinking. Also, in connection with the father-son relation, it may appear that this is a relation that all or most people partake in. Even so, according to Mou Tsung-san (*Yüan-shan lun*, p. 152), whether *jen*ᵃ gets manifested in the relation

still depends on how one's father or son treats one, which is something not within one's control.

49. The normative dimension of "ming[a]" in this context is highlighted in Fu Ssu-nien, pp. 355–56; Lau, "Introduction," in *Mencius*, pp. 28–29; T'ang Chün-i, *Yüan-hsing p'ien*, pp. 22–24.

50. The former reading can be found in Lau, "Introduction," in *Mencius*, pp. 28–29, and the latter in T'ang Chün-i, *Yüan-hsing p'ien*, pp. 22–24.

51. A point noted by Mou Tsung-san, *Hsin-t'i yü hsing-t'i*, 3: 428–29.

52. Hao Wai-lu et al., pp. 153–54; Jen Chi-yü, pp. 194–95.

53. Fung Yu-lan, *Chung-kuo che-hsüeh shih*, pp. 82–83, 163–64; Fu P'ei-jung, pp. 122–35.

54. Mou Tsung-san, *T'e-chih*, pp. 20–24, 32–39, 65–66; idem, *Hsin-t'i yü hsing-t'i*, 1: 21–22, 26–29.

55. Liu Shu-hsien, "Transcendence and Immanence"; idem, "Some Reflections"; T'ang Yi-chieh, pp. 2–6; Tu Wei-ming, *Ju-chia ch'uan-t'ung*, pp. 199–211; Yang Tsu-han, pp. 76–78; Yü Ying-shih, pp. 9–13, 22–23; Yüan Pao-hsin, pp. 86–92. T'ang Yi-chieh notes that although the transcencent dimension of *t'ien* can be detected in both the *Lun-yü* and the *Meng-tzu*, the immanent dimension is highlighted more in the *Meng-tzu*.

56. Hsü Fu-kuan, *Jen-hsing-lun shih*, pp. 86–89, 99, 181; Lao Ssu-kuang, pp. 131–33, 139–40.

57. E.g., Fung Yiu-ming, "Ch'ao-yüeh-nei-tsai"; Hall and Ames, pp. 204–8.

58. E.g., Lee Ming-huei, *Tang-tai ju-hsüeh*, pp. 129–48.

59. For related discussions of the issue, see Schwartz, pp. 122–23; and T'ang Chün-i, *Yüan-tao p'ien*, pp. 131–34, 242–45.

60. Creel, *Chinese Thought*, pp. 88–89.

61. Lau, "Theories of Human Nature," pp. 548–50.

62. As we saw in §4.2.2, Lau interprets 6A:3 in such a way that Mencius was not really opposed to Kao Tzu's explication of *hsing[a]* in terms of *sheng[a]*.

63. See Lau's discussion of the heart/mind of commiseration and of respect, as well as his discussion of 7A:15 in "Theories of Human Nature," pp. 548–49, 558–60.

64. I have been helped by Sin-yee Chan in discussing Lau's position.

65. Fu P'ei-jung, pp. 78–81, 101–3, 173–81, 186–94.

66. E.g., Liu Shu-hsien, "Some Reflections"; Yang Tsu-han, pp. 58–60, 67; Yüan Pao-hsin, pp. 32–37, 93.

67. Fu P'ei-jung, pp. 78–81, sometimes understands the claim of original goodness in this manner; if we assume this understanding, Fu is justified in rejecting the claim.

68. Fu sometimes seems to understand the claim of original goodness in this manner and to deny that Mencius subscribed to such a claim (pp. 173–81). If this is Fu's position, then Yüan Pao-hsin (p. 93) is correct in rejecting this interpretation of Mencius. Fu's position, however, is ambiguous, since he sometimes seems to acknowledge that Mencius did regard the heart/mind as

having an ethical direction obviating the need to seek ethical guidance from the outside (pp. 101–3, 189, 193–94).

69. See Ts'en I-ch'eng, " 'Ch'ing' yü 'ts'ai,' " pt. I, p. 5, for examples illustrating that "jo" can have this meaning; Ts'en does not himself endorse this reading.

70. P'ei Hsüeh-hai employs this strategy in dealing with the problem.

71. In *Hsin-t'i yü hsing-t'i* (3: 416–18), Mou Tsung-san takes "ch'i^b" to refer to hsing^a; however, in *Yüan-shan lun* (pp. 22–24), he takes it to refer to human beings.

72. Ch'en Ta-ch'i, *Tai-chieh-lu*, pp. 8–10; Mou Tsung-san, *Hsin-t'i yü hsing-t'i*, 3: 416–17; idem, *Yüan-shan lun*, pp. 22–24.

73. Ts'en I-ch'eng, " 'Ch'ing' yü 'ts'ai,' " pt. I, pp. 6–7.

74. Ibid., p. 6, also takes "ch'ing^a" in 3A:4 to have the same meaning as "hsing^a."

75. Mou Tsung-san, *Hsin-t'i yü hsing-t'i*, 3: 416–18.

76. I owe this last point to Irene Bloom.

77. Some translators, such as Chai and Chai, Giles, and Ware, take "k'o yi wei^a shan" to mean "can be considered good," presumably taking "wei^a" to mean "consider" or "regard as." This reading avoids the problem since Mencius would then be saying that ch'ing^a can be considered good, not just that it is capable of becoming good. However, this reading is unlikely since other similar occurrences of "k'o yi wei^a" in the *Meng-tzu* are more plausibly read as "be capable of becoming," such as the statement of position (b) in 6A:6 as "k'o yi wei^a shan k'o yi wei^a pu shan," or the statement in 6B:2 that everyone "k'o yi wei^a Yao Shun."

78. Sometimes, "k'o yi V" is uttered in contexts in which there is already a presumption in favor of V-ing and, on such occasions, uttering "k'o yi V" (thereby affirming that the appropriate condition has been met) may generate the expectation that one will V.

79. That a similar example is used in both the *Mo-tzu* and the *Meng-tzu* has been noted by Nivision ("Philosophical Voluntarism," p. 21).

80. Sun Shih's reading differs slightly from Chu's—Sun explains "ts'ai" in terms of the *neng* of ch'ing^a, whereas Chu explains it in terms of the *neng* of jen^b (human beings).

81. Mou Tsung-san, *Hsin-t'i yü hsing-t'i*, 3: 416–23, cf. idem, *Yüan-shan lun*, pp. 22–24; T'ang Chün-i, *Yüan-hsing p'ien*, pp. 29–30.

82. Ts'en I-ch'eng, " 'Ch'ing' yü 'ts'ai,' " pt. I, p. 7, argues that "ch'i^b" should refer to hsing^a if "ch'ing^a" means "shih^b," and "ch'i^b" should refer to jen^b (human beings) if "ch'ing^a" means "hsing^a." It seems to me that "ch'i^b" can still refer to jen^b if "ch'ing^a" means "shih^b"; in fact, "jen^b chih^g ch'ing^a" is often used in early texts to refer to the way human beings are really like.

83. Graham, "Background," pp. 34–35.

84. E.g., T'ang Chün-i, *Yüan-hsing p'ien*, pp. 16–17. Some, such as Sung Hsiang-feng and Yang Po-chün, have compared position (c) to the view in

Lun-yü 17.3 that people of the highest and the lowest grades cannot be changed.

85. Lau, "Method of Analogy," p. 239.

86. T'ang Chün-i, *Yüan-hsing p'ien*, pp. 16–17, also thinks that (b) is related to Kao Tzu's position, although T'ang does not actually identify the two.

87. Graham, "Background," pp. 20–22; cf. p. 33.

88. The parallel between the statement of (b) and Hsün Tzu's (*HT* 4/45–47) view that everyone *k'o yi* become a Yao or Yü and everyone *k'o yi* become a Chieh or Chih shows that a proponent of position (b) may well have a view of *hsing*ᵃ similar to Hsün Tzu's.

89. Some have raised doubts about the authenticity of the "Hsing o" chapter, such as Munro (pp. 77–78), who cites the textual study of Kanaya Osamu. Since, to the best of my knowledge, there is no decisive evidence for the inauthenticity of the chapter, and since the ideas in the chapter appear to fit with ideas from other chapters, I have used the chapter along with the other chapters in reconstructing the thinking of Hsün Tzu.

90. See Wong, "Hsün Tzu on Moral Motivation." I have been helped by Wong's article in the discussion in this and the next paragraphs.

91. I have benefited from a discussion with John Knoblock in connection with these issues.

92. Cua, "Quasi-Empirical Aspect," p. 9, observes that Hsün Tzu could allow that human beings share a certain concern for others, although he would view such concerns as partial tendencies centered on the self and as problematic unless guided by reflection.

93. This way of understanding Hsün Tzu makes his position close to an interpretation of Kao Tzu's claim that *jen*ᵃ is internal (see §4.3.2).

94. Compare Wu-ma Tzu's claim that although he had some concern for others, such concern was not structured in a way conducive to indiscriminate concern, so that he lacked the *neng* to practice indiscriminate concern.

95. Cf. Nivison, "Hsün Tzu on 'Human Nature' "; and idem, "Critique of David B. Wong."

96. Hsü Fu-kuan, *Jen-hsing-lun shih*, pp. 229–38, 255.

97. Fu Ssu-nien, p. 362; Lao Ssu-kuang, pp. 280–83.

98. Cf. T'ang Chün-i, *Yüan-hsing p'ien*, pp. 53–55; idem, *Tao-lun p'ien*, pp. 119–20.

99. Ch'en Ta-ch'i, *Ch'ien-chien hsü-chi*, pp. 138–40.

100. Ch'en Ta-ch'i, *Hsün-tzu hsüeh-shuo*, pp. 47–53; idem, *Ch'ien-chien chi*, pp. 244–50.

101. Ch'en Ta-ch'i, *Ch'ien-chien chi*, pp. 244–50.

102. Ibid., pp. 251–54.

103. Hsü Fu-kuan, *Jen-hsing-lun shih*, p. 238.

104. That Mencius emphasized what is distinctive of human beings in talking about *hsing*ᵃ whereas Hsün Tzu emphasized what is unlearned has been noted by various authors, such as Lao Ssu-kuang, pp. 279–83.

105. For example, Graham thinks they differ on whether moral education is more a matter of nourishing spontaneous tendencies to the good or of disciplining spontaneous tendencies to disorder (*Disputers*, pp. 246, 250). Lau thinks they differ over whether morality is artificial or natural and whether human beings share natural moral tendencies ("Theories of Human Nature," pp. 558-59; "Introduction," in *Mencius*, pp. 21-22). Cua thinks they highlighted different dimensions of the ethical life; Hsün Tzu the basic motivational structure of human beings, which would lead to disorder in circumstances of scarcity, and Mencius what it is to be a moral agent and the fact that human beings have moral ideals ("Quasi-Empirical Aspect," pp. 12-15; cf. "Morality and Human Nature").

106. A point noted by T'ang Chün-i, *Tao-lun p'ien*, p. 119.

107. That the two disagreed on this issue has been noted by various authors, including Fung Yu-lan, *Chung-kuo che-hsüeh shih*, pp. 358-59; Lau, "Theories of Human Nature," pp. 559-65; idem, "Introduction" in *Mencius*, pp. 20-22; Mou Tsung-san, *Ming-chia yü Hsün-tzu*, pp. 224-26; Schwartz, pp. 291-94, 299-30; and Tu Wei-ming, *Humanity and Self-Cultivation*, pp. 58-59.

Character List

The translations given here are intended only as rough guides to the meaning of recurring terms to help in identifying them; consult the Index for page references to fuller discussions of these terms in the text.

ai (love, concern, sparing) 愛
ai jen^b (love fellow human beings)
　　愛人

chang (old, elderliness) 長
chang che . . . chang chih^g che . . .
　　長者 . . . 長之者 . . .
chang Ch'u jen^b chih^g chang
　　長楚人之長
chang ma chih^g chang yeh wu yi yi^c
　　yü^a chang jen^b chih^g chang
　　長馬之長也無以異於長人之長
ch'ao yüeh (transcendent) 超越
cheng^a (government) 政
cheng^b (correct, rectify) 正
ch'eng (wholeness, being real) 誠
ch'eng jen^b (complete person) 成人
chi^a (oneself) 己
chi^b (sickness, disorderly desire) 疾
chi^c (path) 迹
chi yi^a 集義
ch'i^a (vital energies, vital power) 氣
ch'i^b (its) 其
chia (make use of, make a pretense
　　of) 假

chia chih^g 假之
chia jen^a 假仁
ch'iao (skill) 巧
ch'iao ku 巧故
chieh^a (regulate) 節
chieh^b (being on guard) 戒
chien^a (indiscriminate) 兼
chien^a ai (indiscriminate concern
　　for each) 兼愛
chien^b (tread on, enact) 踐
chien^b hsing^b 踐形
chien^b yen 踐言
ch'ien (satisfying, measure up to)
　　慊
chih^a (know, understand) 知
chih^a jen^b (know and appreciate a
　　person) 知人
chih^b (wisdom) 智
chih^c (aims, directions of the
　　heart/mind) 志
chih^d (record, bear in mind) 誌
chih^e (extreme, arrive) 至
chih^f (straight) 直
chih^f yang 直養
chih^g (it, of it, be directed to) 之

chih[h] (stop) 止
ch'ih (disdain, regard as below
　　oneself) 恥
chin (exhaust) 盡
chin hsin[a] 盡心
ch'in (parent) 親
ch'in ch'in, jen[a] min, ai wu[a]
　　親親、仁民、愛物
ching (respect, reverence,
　　seriousness) 敬
ch'ing[a] (fact, what is genuine) 情
ch'ing[b] (being clear, becoming clear)
　　清
chiu (former) 舊
ch'iu (seek, put demand on) 求
ch'iu tse te[b] chih[g] 求則得之
ch'ü (choose) 取
ch'üan[a] (complete) 全
ch'üan[a] hsing[a] pao chen 全性保眞
ch'üan[b] (weighing, discretion) 權
ch'üeh (refuse) 卻
ch'üeh chih[g] ch'üeh chih[g] 卻之卻之
chün tzu (superior person) 君子
chün tzu so hsing[a] 君子所性
ch'ün (form organizations) 群
chung[a] (conscientiousness) 忠
chung[b] (middle, hit the mark) 中
chung[b] li[a] 中禮
chung[b] tao 中道
chung[b] tao erh li 中道而立
ch'ung (fill up)充

erh (two) 貳

fa[a] (injure, do violence to) 伐
fa[b] (standard, model, law) 法
fan chih[g] 反之
fang ch'i[b] liang hsin[a] 放其良心
fang hsin[a] 放心
fei (it is not the case, disapprove) 非
fei yu chang chih[g] chih[g] hsin[a] yü[a] wo
　　非有長之之心於我

fei yu chang yü[a] wo 非有長於我
fei yu ching yü[a] wo 非有敬於我
fen (distinction) 分

hai (injure) 害
heng (horizontal) 衡
hou (enrich) 厚
hsiang shan (directed toward
　　goodness) 向善
hsiao (filial piety) 孝
hsin[a] (heart/mind) 心
hsin[a] chih[g] so t'ung jan che
　　心之所同然者
hsin[b] (trustworthiness) 信
hsing jen[a] 行仁
hsing jen[a] yi[a] 行仁義
hsing[a] (nature, characteristic
　　tendencies) 性
hsing[a] k'o yi wei[a] shan k'o yi
　　wei[a] pu shan 性可以爲善
　　可以爲不善
hsing[a] wu shan wu pu shan
　　性無善無不善
hsing[b] (shape, physical form) 形
hsing[b] shang (metaphysical)
　　形上
hsiu (disdain, regard as below
　　oneself) 羞
hsü (abstract, vacuous) 虛
hua (flowering) 華
huan (worry, concern) 患
hui (favor) 惠
huo[a] (perplexity) 惑
huo[b] (bring disaster upon, regard
　　as a disaster) 禍

jan (it is the case, approve) 然
jan tse ch'i chih yi wu nei yü
　　然則耆炙亦無內歟
jan tse ch'i chih yi yu wai yü
　　然則耆炙亦有外歟
jang (yield to others) 讓

jen^a (benevolence, humaneness) 仁

jen^a ts'ung chung^b ch'u, yi^a ts'ung
   wai tso 仁從中出、義從外作

jen^a yi^a li^a chih^b, fei yu wai shuo wo
   yeh 仁義禮智、非由外鑠我也

jen^b (human beings, others) 人

jen^b chih^g ch'ing^a 人之情

jen^b chih^g so yi wei^a jen^b 人之
   所以爲人

jen^b hsing^a 人性

jen^b ko shen (personal deity)
   人格神

ju^a (Confucian) 儒

ju^a chia (the Confucian school of
   thought) 儒家

ju^b (disgrace) 辱

jung (honor) 榮

k'o (capable, permissible) 可

k'o yi (capable, possible) 可以

k'o yi chih^a 可以知

k'o yi neng 可以能

k'o yi wei^a pu shan 可以爲不善

k'o yi wei^a shan 可以爲善

k'o yi wei^a Yao Shun 可以爲堯舜

ku (former, cause, reason, bring
   about things) 故

k'uei (deplete, diminish) 虧

kung (respectfulness) 恭

kuo tsai wai, fei yu nei 果在
   外、非由內

kuo yu wai, fei tsai nei 果由
   外、非在內

k'uo ch'ung (expand and fill) 擴充

le (joy, take joy in) 樂

le tse sheng^a yi, sheng^a tse wu^b k'o yi
   yeh, wu^b k'o yi tse . . . 樂則
   生矣、生則惡可已也、惡可
   已則 . . .

le ssu erh che 樂斯二者

li^a (rites, observance of the rites) 禮

. . . li^a yeh, . . . ch'üan^b yeh . . .
   禮也 . . . 權也

li^b (smooth, profit, benefit) 利

li^b k'ou (smooth talk) 利口

li^c (pattern, principle) 理

li^d (tread) 履

liang (good, truly so, utmost) 良

liang chih^a 良知

liang hsin^a 良心

liang neng 良能

mei (beautiful) 美

mi (fulfill) 彌

min (common people) 民

ming^a (decree, destiny) 命

ming^b (name, reputation) 名

mo fei ming^a yeh 莫非命也

nai jo . . . jo fu . . . 乃若 . . .
   若乎 . . .

nai jo ch'i^b ch'ing^a tse k'o yi wei^a
   shan yi nai so wei^b shan yeh
   jo fu wei^a pu shan fei ts'ai
   chih^g tsui yeh 乃若其情
   則可以爲善矣乃所謂善也若
   夫爲不善非才之罪也

nei (internal, inside) 內

nei tsai (immanent, inner) 內在

neng (ability) 能

o (evil) 惡

pa (overlord) 霸

pai (white, whiteness) 白

pai chih^g wei^b pai 白之謂白

pao (preserve, protect, care for)
   保

p'ei yi^a yü tao 配義與道

pen (basis, root, original) 本

pen jan (original) 本然

pen jan chih^g shan (original
   goodness) 本然之善

pen shan (originally good) 本善

pi yu shih^a yen erh wu cheng^b hsin^a wu wang^b wu chu chang yeh 必有事焉而勿正心勿忘勿助長也

pieh (discrimination) 別

pien (differentiation) 辨

p'o (oppress, force) 迫

pu hsieh (disdain) 不屑

pu jen (unable to bear) 不忍

pu jen jen^b chih^g cheng^a 不忍人之政

pu jen jen^b chih^g hsin^a 不忍人之心

pu neng 不能

pu pi 不必

pu shan (bad) 不善

pu ssu^b erh pi yü^a wu^a, wu^a chiao wu^a, tse yin chih^g erh yi yi 不思而蔽於物、物交物、則引之而已矣

pu te^b (not get, not do well, not understand) 不得

pu te^b yü^a chün 不得於君

pu te^b yü^a yen, wu ch'iu yü^a hsin^a, pu te^b yü^a hsin^a, wu ch'iu yü^a ch'i^a 不得於言、勿求於心、不得於心、勿求於氣

pu tung (not move) 不動

pu tung hsin^a (unmoved heart/mind) 不動心

pu wei^a (not do) 不爲

pu wei^b (not describe as, not regard as) 不謂

pu yi^a chih^g sheng^a p'o sheng^a yeh 不義之生迫生也

pu yi^a p'o sheng^a 不義迫生

pu yü^b (not desire) 不欲

shan (good) 善

shang (injure) 傷

shao jen^b (petty person) 小人

shao jen^b chih^g hsing^a 小人之性

she (preconception) 設

shen^a (body, person, embody) 身

shen^b (caution, attention) 慎

shen^c (very, excel) 甚

sheng^a (life, growth, give birth to) 生

sheng^a chih^g chih^g wei^b hsing^a 生之之謂性

sheng^a chih^g wei^b hsing^a 生之謂性

sheng^b (sageness) 聖

sheng^b jen^b (sage) 聖人

sheng^c (sound, reputation) 聲

shih min (employing the common people) 使民

shih^a (affairs, responsibilities, devote oneself to) 事

shih^a ku (causing things to happen) 事故

shih^b (consolidates, real, concrete, fruit) 實

shih^c (it is the case, approve) 是

shih^c yi chang wei^a yüeh^b che yeh 是以長爲悅者也

shih^c yi wo wei^a yüeh^b che yeh 是以我爲悅者也

shou (hide) 瘦

shu^a (reciprocity) 恕

shu^b (way, method) 術

shun (to follow) 順

shuo (explanation) 說

so (straight, upright) 縮

ssu^a (await) 俟

ssu^b (reflect, think) 思

su (custom) 俗

sui yu tz'u pa wang^a pu yi^c yi 雖由此霸王不異矣

ta (extend) 達

tao (path, the Way) 道

te^a (virtue, power) 德

te^b (get, do well, understand) 得

t'i (body) 體

t'ien (Heaven) 天

t'ien ming[a] (Decree of Heaven) 天命
t'ien dao 天道
tsai (in, lie with, up to) 在
tsai wo 在我
tsai wai 在外
ts'ai (endowment, talent) 才
ts'e yin (commiseration) 惻隱
tsun (to honor) 尊
ts'un (preserve) 存
ts'un hsin[a] 存心
ts'ung (follow, obey, come from) 從
ts'ung ch'i[b] pai yü[a] wai 從其白
　　於外
tuan (germ, beginning) 端
t'uan shui (whirling water) 湍水
t'ui (extend) 推
tung (move) 動
t'ung ch'i 同耆
t'ung jan 同然
t'ung mei 同美
t'ung t'ing 同聽
tzu (oneself) 自
tzu yung 自用
tz'u[a] (decline, words, teachings) 辭
tz'u[a] ch'i[a] 辭氣
tz'u[a] jang 辭讓
tz'u[b] (secondary, follow) 次

wai (external, outside) 外
wang[a] (true king) 王
wang[b] (forget) 忘
wei[a] (act, do) 爲
wei[a] chi[a] (for oneself) 爲己
wei[a] jen[b] (for others) 爲人
wei[b] (describe as, regard as) 謂
wei[c] (false appearance, conscious
　　activity) 僞
wen ch'i[b] feng erh yüeh[b] chih[g]
　　聞其風而悅之
wo (I, me) 我
wu[a] (things) 物
wu[b] (aversion) 惡

wu ch'ih chih[g] ch'ih wu ch'ih yi
　　無恥之恥無恥矣
wu shih[a] (not causing things to
　　happen) 無事
wu ti (without enemy, invincible)
　　無敵
wu wei[a] (non-action) 無爲
wu wei[a] ch'i[b] so pu wei[a], wu yü[b]
　　ch'i[b] so pu yü[b] 無爲其
　　所不爲、無欲其所不欲
wu wei[a] erh wu pu wei[a]
　　無爲而無不爲
wu yi[a] wu ming[a] 無義無命

yang (nourish) 養
yao (what is important or
　　essential) 要
Yao Shun hsing[a] che yeh
　　堯舜性者也
Yao Shun hsing[a] chih[g] yeh
　　堯舜性之也
yen (words, speech, teachings,
　　doctrines) 言
yi[a] (propriety, righteousness)
　　義
yi[a] hsi 義襲
yi[b] (good form) 儀
yi[c] (surprising, different) 異
yi[c] hu (how strange) 異乎
yi[c] yü[a] pai ma chih[g] pai yeh wu
　　yi yi[c] yü[a] pai jen[b] chih[g] pai
　　yeh 異於白馬之白也
　　無以異於白人之白也
yi[d] (one) 壹
yi[e] (contribute to) 益
yi an she chi wei[a] yüeh[b] che yeh
　　以安社稷爲悅者也
yi li chia jen[a] 以力假仁
yi li fu jen[b] 以力服人
yi shan fu jen[b] 以善服人
yi shan yang jen[b] 以善養人
yi te[a] fu jen[b] 以德服人

yi te^a hsing jen^a 以德行仁
ying (respond) 應
yu (worry, concern) 憂
yu hsing^a shan yu hsing^a pu shan
   有性善有性不善
yu jen^a yi^a hsing 由仁義行
yu shih^a (causing things to happen)
   有事

yü^a (pertaining to, being drawn
   to) 於
yü^b (desire) 欲
yüeh^a (simple, what is important
   or essential) 約
yüeh^b (take pleasure in, moved
   by) 悅
yung (courage) 勇

Bibliography

Section 1 of this Bibliography lists editions of early Chinese texts cited in the text and notes; Section 2, commentaries on the *Meng-tzu* and other premodern Chinese texts; Section 3, translations of the *Meng-tzu*; Section 4, secondary sources. The following abbreviations are used in the Bibliography:

CTCC   Chu-tzu chi-ch'eng 諸子集成
HY   Harvard-Yenching Institute Sinological Index Series
KHCPTS   Kuo-hsüeh chi-pen ts'ung-shu 國學基本叢書
SKCS   Ssu-k'u ch'üan-shu 四庫全書
SPPY   Ssu-pu pei-yao 四部備要
SPTK   Ssu-pu ts'ung-k'an 四部叢刊

Early Chinese Texts

Chuang-tzu 莊子. All references are to chapter and line numbers in the HY ed.

Han-fei-tzu 韓非子. All references are to chapter, paragraph, and clause numbers in Chou Chung-ling 周鐘靈, Shih Hsiao-shih 施孝適, and Hsü Wei-hsien 許惟賢, comps., *Han-fei-tzu so-yin* 韓非子索引. Beijing: Chung-hua shu-chü, 1982.

Hsün-tzu 荀子. All references are to chapter and line numbers in the HY ed.

Huai-nan-tzu 淮南子. All references are to volume, page, and line numbers in the SPPY ed. Also consulted: Chung-fa Han-hsüeh yen-chiu so 中法漢學研究所, comp., *Huai-nan-tzu t'ung-chien* 淮南子通檢. Shanghai: Shang-hai ku-chi ch'u-pan-she, 1986.

Kuan-tzu 管子. All references are to volume, page, and line numbers in the KHCPTS ed. Also consulted: Wallace Stephen Johnson, comp., *Kuan-tzu yin-te* 管子引得 (English title: *A Concordance to the Kuan Tzu*). Taipei: Ch'eng-wen ch'u-pan-she, 1970.

Kuo-yü 國語. All references are to volume, page, and line numbers in the *T'ien-sheng-ming-tao-pen* 天聖明道本, ed. Also consulted: Chang Yi-jen 張以仁, comp., *Kuo-yü yin-te* 國語引得. Taipei: Chung-yang yen-chiu-yüan, Li-shih yü-yen yen-chiu-so, 1976.

Lao-tzu 老子. All references are to chapter numbers in Jen Chi-yü 任繼愈, trans., *Lao-tzu hsin-i* 老子新譯. Shanghai: Shang-hai ku-chi ch'u-pan-she, 1978.

Li-chi 禮記. All references are to volume, page, and line numbers in the SPPY ed. Also consulted: HY.

Lieh-tzu 列子. All references are to volume, page, and line numbers in the SPTK ed.

Lü-shih ch'un-ch'iu 呂氏春秋. All references are to volume, page, and line numbers in Hsü Wei-yü 許維遹, comp. *Lü-shih ch'un-ch'iu chi-shih* 呂氏春秋集釋. Beijing: Shang-wu yin-shu-kuan, 1955. Also consulted: Michael Carson, comp., *A Concordance to the Lü-shih ch'un-ch'iu*. San Francisco: Chinese Materials Center, 1985.

Lun-yü 論語. All references are to book and passage numbers in Yang Po-chün 楊伯峻, trans., *Lun-yü i-chu* 論語譯注. Beijing: Chung-hua shu-chü, 1980. Also consulted: HY.

Meng-tzu 孟子. All references are to book and passage numbers (with book numbers 1A–7B substituted for numbers 1–14) in Yang Po-chün 楊伯峻, trans., *Meng-tzu i-chu* 孟子譯注. Beijing: Chung-hua shu-chü, 1984. Also consulted: HY.

Mo-tzu 墨子. All references are to chapter and line numbers in the HY ed.

Shang-chün-shu 商君書. All references are to page and line numbers in the CTCC ed.

Shang-shu 尚書. All references are to page and line numbers of the text in James Legge, trans., *The Shoo King*. Hong Kong: London Missionary Society, 1865. Also consulted: Ku Chieh-kang 顧頡剛, comp., *Shang-shu t'ung-chien* 尚書通檢. Shanghai: Shang-hai ku-chi ch'u-pan-she, 1990.

Shen-pu-hai 申不害. All references are to page and fragment numbers in Herrlee G. Creel, *Shen Pu-hai: A Chinese Political Philosopher of the Fourth Century B.C.* Chicago: University of Chicago Press, 1974.

Shen-tzu 慎子. All references are to page and fragment numbers in P. M. Thompson, ed. *The Shen Tzu Fragments*. Oxford: Oxford University Press, 1979.

Shih-ching 詩經. All references are to ode and section numbers in Yang Jen-chih 楊任之, trans., *Shih-ching chin-i-chin-chu* 詩經今譯今注. Tientsin: Tien-chin ku-chi ch'u-pan-she, 1986. Also consulted: HY.

Tso-chuan 左傳. All references are to page and line numbers of the text in James Legge, trans., *The Ch'un Ts'ew with The Tso Chuen*. Rev. ed. Taipei: Wen-shih-che ch'u-pan-she, 1972. Also consulted: HY.

Commentaries on the Meng-tzu and Other Pre-Twentieth Century Chinese Texts

Unless otherwise indicated, all references are to the book and passage numbers (with book numbers 1A–7B substituted for numbers 1–14) of the *Meng-tzu*, trans. Yang Po-chün (see above under *Meng-tzu*).

Chang Shih 張栻. *Meng-tzu shuo* 孟子說.

Chao Ch'i 趙岐. *Meng-tzu chang-chih* 孟子章指.

——. *Meng-tzu chu* 孟子注.

Chao Shun-sun 趙順孫. *Meng-tzu tsuan-shu* 孟子纂疏.

Chiao Hsün 焦循. *Meng-tzu cheng-i* 孟子正義. References to longer passages are to volume, page, and line numbers in the SPPY ed.

Chu Hsi 朱熹. *Chu-tzu yü-lei* 朱子語類. All references are by page numbers to *Chu-tzu yü-lei*. Beijing: Chung-hua shu-chü, 1986.

——. *Meng-tzu chi-chu* 孟子集註.

——. *Meng-tzu huo-wen* 孟子或問. References to longer passages are to volume, page, and line numbers of the text in the *Chu-tzu i-shu* 朱子遺書.

Hsü Ch'ien 許謙. *Tu Meng-tzu ts'ung-shuo* 讀孟子叢說.

Hu Ping-wen 胡炳文. *Meng-tzu t'ung* 孟子通.

Hu Yü-huan 胡毓寰. *Meng-tzu pen-i* 孟子本義. Taipei: Cheng-chung shu-chü, 1958.

Huang Tsung-hsi 黃宗羲. *Meng-tzu shih-shuo* 孟子師說. All references are to volume, page, and line numbers in the SKCS ed.

Juan Yüan 阮元. *Hsing-ming ku-hsün* 性命古訓.

P'ei Hsüeh-hai 裴學海. *Meng-tzu cheng-i pu-cheng* 孟子正義補正. Taipei: Hsüeh-hai ch'u-pan-she, 1978.

Shuo-wen chieh-tzu 說文解字.

Su Che 蘇轍. *Meng-tzu chieh* 孟子解.

Sun Shih 孫奭. *Meng-tzu chu-shu* 孟子注疏.

Sung Hsiang-feng 宋翔鳳. *Meng-tzu Chao-chu pu-cheng* 孟子趙注補正.

Tai Chen 戴震. *Meng-tzu tzu-i shu-cheng* 孟子字義疏證. All references are to section numbers (with text divided into 43 sections) in *Meng-tzu tzu-i shu-cheng*. 2d ed. Beijing: Chung-hua shu-chü, 1982.

Ts'ai Mu 蔡模. *Meng-tzu chi-shu* 孟子集疏.

Wang Ch'ung 王充. *Lun-heng* 論衡. All references are to page and line numbers in the CTCC ed.

Wang En-yang 王恩洋. *Meng-tzu shu-i* 孟子疏義. Taipei: Hsin-wen-feng ch'u-pen-kung-ssu, 1975.

Wang Fu-chih 王夫之. *Tu Ssu-shu ta-ch'üan shuo* 讀四書大全說. All references are to page numbers in *Tu Ssu-shu ta-ch'üan shuo*, vol. 2. Beijing, Chung-hua shu-chü, 1975.

Wang Pang-hsiung 王邦雄, Tseng Chao-hsü 曾昭旭, and Yang Tsu-han 楊祖漢. *Meng-tzu i-li shu-chieh* 孟子義理疏解. Yung-ho, Taiwan: O-hu yüeh-k'an tsa-chih-she, 1983.

Wang Yang-ming 王陽明. *Chuan-hsi-lu* 傳習錄. All references are to passage numbers, following the numbering in Wing-tsit Chan, trans., *Instructions for Practical Living and Other Neo-Confucian Writings by Wang Yang-ming*. New York: Columbia University Press, 1963.

Yü Yüeh 俞樾. *Meng-tzu ku-chu tse-ts'ung* 孟子古注擇從.

——. *Meng-tzu p'ing-i* 孟子平議.

——. *Meng-tzu tsuan-i nei-wai p'ien* 孟子續義內外篇.

Yü Yün-wen 余允文. *Tsun-Meng-hsü-pien* 尊孟續辨. All references are to volume, page, and line numbers in the SKCS ed.

————. *Tsun-Meng-pien* 尊孟辨. All references are by volume, page, and line numbers in the SKCS ed.

Translations of the Meng-tzu

Unless otherwise indicated, all references are to the book and passage numbers (with book numbers 1A–7B substituted for numbers 1–14) of the *Meng-tzu*, trans. Yang Po-chün (see above under *Meng-tzu*).

English translations

Chai, Ch'u, and Winberg Chai, eds. and trans. *The Sacred Books of Confucius and Other Confucian Classics*. New York: Bantam Books, 1965.

Chan, Wing-tsit, comp. and trans. *A Sourcebook in Chinese Philosophy*. Princeton: Princeton University Press, 1963, chap. 3.

Dobson, W. A. C. H., trans. *Mencius: A New Translation Arranged and Annotated for the General Reader*. Toronto: University of Toronto Press, 1963.

Giles, Lionel, trans. *The Book of Mencius* (Abridged). New York: Dutton, 1942.

Lau, D. C., trans. *Mencius*. London: Penguin, 1970.

Legge, James, trans. *The Works of Mencius*. 2d ed. Oxford: Clarendon Press, 1895.

Lyall, Leonard A., trans. *Mencius*. London: Longmans, Green, 1932.

Ware, James R., trans. *The Sayings of Mencius*. New York: New American Library of World Literature, 1960.

Modern Chinese translation

Yang Po-chün 楊伯峻, trans. *Meng-tzu i-chu* 孟子譯注. Beijing: Chung-hua shu-chü, 1984.

Japanese translations

Hattori Unokichi 服部宇之吉, trans. *Kokuyaku Mōshi* 國譯孟子. *Kokuyaku Kambun taisei* 國譯漢文大成. vol. 1. Tokyo: Kokumin bunko kankōkai, 1922.

Kanaya Osamu 金谷治, trans. *Mōshi* 孟子. 2 vols. Tokyo: Asahi shimbunsha, 1955, 1956.

Uchino Kumaichirō 内野熊一郎, trans. *Mōshi* 孟子. *Shinshaku Kambun taikei* 新釋漢文大系, vol. 4. Tokyo: Meiji shoin, 1962.

Secondary Sources

Ames, Roger T. "The Mencian Conception of *ren xing*: Does it Mean 'Human Nature'?" In Henry Rosemont, Jr., ed., *Chinese Texts and Philosophical Contexts: Essays Dedicated to Angus C. Graham*, pp. 143–75. La Salle, Ill.: Open Court, 1991.

Bloom, Irene. "Mencian Arguments on Human Nature (*jen-hsing*)." *Philosophy East and West* 44 (1994): 19–53.

Boodberg, Peter A. "The Semasiology of Some Primary Confucian Concepts." *Philosophy East and West* 2 (1952): 317–32.

Chan, Wing-tsit. "The Evolution of the Confucian Concept *jen*." In Charles K. H. Chen, comp., *Neo-Confucianism, Etc.: Essays by Wing-tsit Chan*, pp. 1–44. Hong Kong: Oriental Society, 1969.

Chan, Wing-tsit, trans. & comp. *A Source Book in Chinese Philosophy*. Princeton: Princeton University Press, 1963.

Chao Chi-pin 趙紀彬. *Lun-yü hsin-t'an* 論語新探. 3 vols. Beijing: Jen-min ch'u-pan-she, 1976.

Ch'en Ta-ch'i 陳大齊. *Ch'ien-chien chi* 淺見集. Taipei: T'ai-wan Chung-hua shu-chü, 1968.

——. *Ch'ien-chien hsü-chi* 淺見續集. Taipei: T'ai-wan Chung-hua shu-chü, 1973.

——. *Hsün-tzu hsüeh-shuo* 荀子學說. Rev. ed. Taipei: Hua-kang ch'u-pan-pu, 1971.

——. *K'ung-tzu hsüeh-shuo* 孔子學說. 4th ed. Taipei: Cheng-chung shu-chü, 1969.

——. *Meng-tzu tai-chieh-lu* 孟子待解錄. 2d ed. Taipei: T'ai-wan shang-wu yin-shu-kuan, 1981.

——. *Meng-tzu ti ming-li ssu-hsiang chi ch'i pien-shuo shih-k'uang* 孟子的名理思想及其辯說實況. 4th ed. Taipei: T'ai-wan shang-wu yin-shu-kuan, 1974.

Ch'en T'e 陳特. "Yu Meng-tzu yü Yang-ming k'an Chung-kuo tao-te-chu-t'i che-hsüeh ti fang-fa t'e-hsing yü fa-chan" 由孟子與陽明看中國道德主體哲學的方法特性與發展. *Hsin-ya hsüeh-shu chi-k'an* 新亞學術集刊, 3 (1982): 37–51.

Cheng, Chung-ying. *New Dimensions of Confucian and Neo-Confucian Philosophy*. Albany: State University of New York Press, 1991.

Cheng Li-wei 鄭力為. *Ju-hsüeh fang-hsiang yü jen ti tsun-yen* 儒學方向與人的尊嚴. Taipei: Wen-chin ch'u-pan-she, 1987.

Chu I-t'ing 朱貽庭. "P'ing Yang-chu ho Yang-chu-hsüeh-p'ai ti jen-sheng che-hsüeh" 評楊朱和楊朱學派的人生哲學. *Chung-kuo che-hsüeh-shih* 中國哲學史, Dec. 1988, 40–44.

Creel, Herrlee G. *Chinese Thought from Confucius to Mao Tse-tung*. Chicago: University of Chicago Press, 1953.

——. *"What Is Taoism?" and Other Studies in Chinese Cultural History*. Chicago: University of Chicago Press, 1970.

Cua, Antonio S. "The Conceptual Aspect of Hsün Tzu's Philosophy of Human Nature." *Philosophy East and West* 27 (1977): 373–89.

——. "Confucian Vision and Human Community." *Journal of Chinese Philosophy* 11 (1984): 227–38.

——. *Ethical Argumentation: A Study in Hsün Tzu's Moral Epistemology*. Honolulu: University of Hawaii Press, 1985.

——. "Morality and Human Nature." *Philosophy East and West* 32 (1982): 279–94.

——. "The Quasi-Empirical Aspect of Hsün Tzu's Philosophy of Human Nature." *Philosophy East and West* 28 (1978): 3–19.

Eno, Robert. *The Confucian Creation of Heaven: Philosophy and the Defense of Ritual Mastery.* Albany: State University of New York Press, 1990.

Fingarette, Herbert. *Confucius: The Secular as Sacred.* New York: Harper & Row, 1972.

———. "The Problem of the Self in the *Analects.*" *Philosophy East and West* 29 (1979): 129–40.

———. "Response to Roger T. Ames." In Mary I. Bockover, ed., *Rules, Rituals and Responsibilities: Essays Dedicated to Herbert Fingarette,* pp. 194–200. La Salle, Ill.: Open Court, 1991.

Fu, Charles Wei-hsun. "Fingarette and Munro on Early Confucianism: A Methodological Examination." *Philosophy East and West* 28 (1978): 181–98.

Fu P'ei-jung 傅佩榮. *Ju-chia che-hsüeh hsin-lun* 儒家哲學新論. Taipei: Yeh-ch'iang ch'u-pan-she, 1993.

Fu Ssu-nien 傅斯年. *Hsing-ming ku-hsün pien-cheng* 性命古訓辨證. Taipei: Lien-ching ch'u-pan, 1980 [1938].

Fung Yiu-ming [Feng Yao-ming] 馮耀明. "Tang-tai hsin-ju-chia ti 'ch'ao-yüeh-nei-tsai' shuo" 當代新儒家的「超越內在」說. *Tang-tai yüeh-k'an* 當代 月刊, no. 86 (Apr. 1993): 92–105.

———. "Tang-tai hsin-ju-hsüeh ti 'che-hsüeh' kai-nien" 當代新儒學的「哲學」概念. In *Tang-tai hsin-ju-hsüeh lun-wen-chi: tsung-lun-p'ien* 當代新儒學論文集：總論篇, pp. 349–96. Taipei: Wen-chin ch'u-pan-she, 1991.

Fung Yu-lan [Feng Yu-lan] 馮友蘭. *Chung-kuo che-hsüeh shih* 中國哲學史. Rev. ed. Hong Kong: T'ai-p'ing-yang t'u-shu, 1970.

———. *Chung-kuo che-hsüeh shih: pu-p'ien* 中國哲學史：補篇. Rev. ed. Hong Kong: T'ai-p'ing-yang t'u-shu, 1970.

———. *Hsin-yüan-tao* 新原道. Hong Kong: Chung-kuo che-hsüeh yen-chiu-hui, 1977 [1944].

Graham, A. C. "The Background of the Mencian Theory of Human Nature." *Ch'ing-hua hsüeh-pao (Tsing Hua Journal of Chinese Studies)* 6 (1967): 215–71. Reprinted in idem, *Studies in Chinese Philosophy and Philosophical Literature,* pp. 7–66. Albany: State University of New York Press, 1990.

———. *Chuang Tzu: The Inner Chapters.* London: George Allen & Unwin, 1981.

———. "The Dialogue Between Yang Ju and Chyntzyy." *Bulletin of the School of Oriental and African Studies* 22 (1959): 291–99.

———. *Disputers of the Tao: Philosophical Argument in Ancient China.* La Salle, Ill.: Open Court, 1989.

———. *Later Mohist Logic, Ethics and Science.* Hong Kong: Chinese University Press, 1978.

———. "Relating Categories to Question Forms in Pre-Han Chinese Thought." In idem, *Studies in Chinese Philosophy and Philosophical Literature,* pp. 360–411. Albany: State University of New York Press, 1990.

———. "The Right to Selfishness: Yangism, Later Mohism, Chuang Tzu." In Donald Munro, ed., *Individualism and Holism: Studies in Confucian and Taoist Values,* pp. 73–84. Ann Arbor: University of Michigan, Center for Chinese Studies, 1985.

Hall, David L., and Roger T. Ames. *Thinking Through Confucius*. Albany: •
State University of New York Press, 1987.

Hansen, Chad. *Language and Logic in Ancient China*. Ann Arbor: University
of Michigan Press, 1983.

Harwood, Paul. "Concerning the Evolution and Use of the Concept of *t'ien*
in Pre-Imperial China." *Tung-hai hsüeh-pao (Tunghai Journal)* 31 (1990):
135-88.

Hou Wai-lu 侯外廬, Chao Chi-pin 趙紀彬, and Tu Kuo-hsiang 杜國庠.
Chung-kuo ssu-hsiang t'ung-shih 中國思想通史, vol. 1. Beijing: Jen-min
ch'u-pan-she, 1957.

Hsü Fu-kuan 徐復觀. *Chung-kuo jen-hsing-lun shih: hsien-Ch'in p'ien* 中國人性
論史：先秦篇. 2d ed. Taipei: T'ai-wan shang-wu yin-shu-kuan, 1975.

———. *Chung-kuo ssu-hsiang-shih lun-chi* 中國思想史論集. 4th ed. Taipei:
T'ai-wan hsüeh-sheng shu-chü, 1975.

———. *Chung-kuo ssu-hsiang-shih lun-chi hsü-p'ien* 中國思想史論集續篇.
Taipei: Shih-pao wen-hua ch'u-pan, 1982.

Hu Shih 胡適. *Shuo ju* 說儒. Taipei: Yüan-liu ch'u-pan, 1986 [1935].

Huang Chang-chien 黃彰健. "Shih Meng-tzu 't'ien-hsia chih yen hsing yeh
tse ku er i i' chang" 釋孟子「天下之言性也則故而已矣」章. In Chung-
hua ts'ung-shu pien-shen wei-yüan-hui 中華叢書編審委員會, ed., *Meng-
tzu yen-chiu-chi* 孟子研究集, pp. 111-24. Taipei: Chung-hua ts'ung-shu
pien-shen wei-yüan-hui, 1963. Revision of edition originally edited by
Yang Hua-chih 楊化之.

Huang Chün-chieh 黃俊傑. *Meng-hsüeh ssu-hsiang-shih lun* 孟學思想史論,
vol. 1. Taipei: Tung-ta t'u-shu, 1991.

———. *Meng-tzu* 孟子. Taipei: Tung-ta t'u-shu, 1993.

———. "'Rightness' (*i*) versus 'Profit' (*li*) in Ancient China: The Polemics
Between Mencius and Yang Chu, Mo Tzu, and Hsün Tzu." *Proceedings of
the National Science Council, ROC, Part C, Humanities and Social Sciences* 3
(1993): 59-72.

Isenberg, Arnold. "Some Problems of Interpretation." In Arthur F. Wright,
ed., *Studies in Chinese Thought*, pp. 232-46. Chicago: University of Chicago Press, 1953.

Ivanhoe, P. J. *Ethics in the Confucian Tradition: The Thought of Mencius and
Wang Yang-ming*. Atlanta: Scholars Press, 1990.

———. "Human Nature and Moral Understanding in Xunzi." *International
Philosophical Quarterly* 34 (1994): 167-75.

Jen Chi-yü 任繼愈. *Chung-kuo che-hsüeh fa-chan-shih: hsien-Ch'in* 中國哲學
發展史：先秦. Beijing: Jen-min ch'u-pan-she, 1983.

Knoblock, John. "Review of A. C. Graham *Disputers of the Tao: Philosophical
Argument in Ancient China*." *Journal of Asian Studies* 50 (1991): 385-87.

Knoblock, John, trans., *Xunzi: A Translation and Study of the Complete Works*, •
vol. 1, *Books 1-6*. Stanford: Stanford University Press, 1988.

Kupperman, J. J. "Confucius, Mencius, Hume and Kant on Reason and
Choice." In Shlomo Biderman and Ben-Ami Scharfstein, eds., *Rationality*

in Question: Eastern and Western Views of Rationality, pp. 119–39. Leiden: Brill, 1989.

Lai, Whalen. "Kao Tzu and Mencius on Mind: Analyzing a Paradigm Shift in Classical China." *Philosophy East and West* 34 (1984): 147–60.

———. "The Public Good That Does the Public Good: A New Reading of Mohism." *Asian Philosophy* 3 (1993): 125–41.

———. "*Yung* and the Tradition of the *shih*: The Confucian Restructuring of Heroic Courage." *Religious Studies* 21 (1985): 181–203.

Lau, D. C. "On Mencius' Use of the Method of Analogy in Argument." *Asia Major* 10 (1963). Reprinted in D. C. Lau, trans., *Mencius*, pp. 235–63. London: Penguin, 1970.

———. "Some Notes on the *Mencius*." *Asia Major* 15 (1969): 62–81.

———. "Theories of Human Nature in Mencius and Shyuntzyy." *Bulletin of the School of Oriental and African Studies* 15 (1953): 541–65.

Lau, D. C. trans. *Confucius: The Analects*. London: Penguin, 1979.

———. *Mencius*. London: Penguin, 1970.

Lao Ssu-kuang 勞思光. *Chung-kuo che-hsüeh shih* 中國哲學史, vol. 1. 2d ed. Hong Kong: Chinese University of Hong Kong, Chung Chi College, 1974.

Lee Ming-huei [Li Ming-hui] 李明輝. *Ju-chia yü K'ang-te* 儒家與康德. Taipei: Lien-ching ch'u-pan, 1990.

———. *K'ang-te lun-li-hsüeh yü Meng-tzu tao-te-ssu-k'ao chih ch'ung-chien* 康德倫理學與孟子道德思考之重建. Taipei: Chung-yang yen-chiu-yüan, Chung-kuo wen-che yen-chiu-so, 1994.

———. "Meng-tzu 'chih-yen-yang-ch'i' chang ti i-li chieh-kou" 孟子「知言養氣」章的義理結構. In idem, ed., *Meng-tzu ssu-hsiang ti che-hsüeh t'an-t'ao* 孟子思想的哲學探討, pp. 115–58. Taipei: Chung-yang yen-chiu-yüan, Chung-kuo wen-che yen-chiu-so, 1995.

———. *Tang-tai ju-hsüeh chih tzu-wo chuan-hua* 當代儒學之自我轉化. Taipei: Chung-yang yen-chiu-yüan, Chung-kuo wen-che yen-chiu-so, 1994.

Li Hsi 里西. "Shih 'jen, t'i ai yeh'" 釋「仁、體愛也」. *Chung-kuo che-hsüeh-shih* 中國哲學史, Apr. 1989, 49–51.

Li Tu 李杜. *Chung-hsi che-hsüeh ssu-hsiang chung ti t'ien-tao yü shang-ti* 中西哲學思想中的天道與上帝. Taipei: Lien-ching ch'u-pan, 1978.

Lin Yih-jing [Lin Yi-cheng] 林義正. *K'ung-tzu hsüeh-shuo t'an-wei* 孔子學說探微. Taipei: Tung-ta t'u-shu, 1987.

Lin, Yü-sheng. "The Evolution of the Pre-Confucian Meaning of *jen* and the Confucian Concept of Moral Autonomy." *Monumenta Serica (Journal of Oriental Studies)* 31 (1974–75): 172–204.

Liu Shu-hsien 劉述先. "The Confucian Approach to the Problem of Transcendence and Immanence." *Philosophy East and West* 22 (1972): 45–52.

———. *Ju-chia ssu-hsiang yü hsien-tai-hua* 儒家思想與現代化. Beijing: Chung-kuo kuang-po tien-shih ch'u-pan-she, 1992.

———. "Some Reflections on Mencius's Views of Mind-Heart and Human Nature." *Philosophy East and West* 46 (1996): 143–64.

———. "Yen-chiu Chung-kuo shih-hsüeh yü che-hsüeh ti fang-fa yü t'ai-tu"

研究中國史學與哲學的方法與態度. In Wei Cheng-t'ung 韋政通, ed., *Chung-kuo ssu-hsiang-shih fang-fa lun-wen hsüan-chi* 中國思想史方法論文選集, pp. 217–28. Taipei: Ta-lin ch'u-pan-she, 1981.

Metzger, Thomas A. "The Definition of the Self, the Group, the Cosmos, and Knowledge in Chou Thought: Some Comments on Professor Schwartz's Study." *American Asian Review* 4 (1986): 68–116.

———. "Some Ancient Roots of Modern Chinese Thought: This-Worldliness, Epistemological Optimism, Doctrinality, and the Emergence of Reflexivity in the Eastern Chou." *Early China* 11–12 (1985–87): 61–117.

Mou Tsung-san 牟宗三. *Chung-hsi che-hsüeh chih hui-t'ung shih-ssu-chiang* 中西哲學之會通十四講. Taipei: T'ai-wan hsüeh-sheng shu-chü, 1990.

———. *Chung-kuo che-hsüeh shih-chiu-chiang* 中國哲學十九講. Taipei: T'ai-wan hsüeh-sheng shu-chü, 1983.

———. *Chung-kuo che-hsüeh ti t'e-chih* 中國哲學的特質. 5th ed. Taipei: T'ai-wan hsüeh-sheng shu-chü, 1978.

———. *Hsin-t'i yü hsing-t'i* 心體與性體. 3 vols. Rev. ed. Taipei: Cheng-chung shu-chü, 1970.

———. *Ming-chia yü Hsün-tzu* 名家與荀子. Taipei: T'ai-wan hsüeh-sheng shu-chü, 1979.

———. *Yüan-shan lun* 圓善論. Taipei: T'ai-wan hsüeh-sheng shu-chü, 1985.

Munro, Donald J. *The Concept of Man in Early China.* Stanford: Stanford University Press, 1969.

Nivison, David S. "Critique of David B. Wong. 'Hsün Tzu on Moral Motivation.'" In P. J. Ivanhoe, ed., *Chinese Language, Thought and Culture: Essays Dedicated to David S. Nivison.* La Salle, Ill.: Open Court Press, 1996.

———. "Hsün Tzu on 'Human Nature.'" Unpublished paper, 1975.

———. "Investigations in Chinese Philosophy." Unpublished paper, 1980.

———. "Mencius and Motivation." *Journal of the American Academy of Religion,* Thematic Issues 47 (1980): 417–32.

———. "Motivation and Moral Action in Mencius." Unpublished paper, 1975.

———. "On Translating *Mencius.*" *Philosophy East and West* 30 (1980): 93–121.

———. "Philosophical Voluntarism in Fourth-Century China." Unpublished paper, 1973.

———. "Problems in Mencius, Part I." Unpublished paper, 1975.

———. "Problems in Mencius, Part II." Unpublished paper, 1975.

———. "Two Roots or One?" *Proceedings and Addresses of the American Philosophical Association* 53 (1980): 739–61.

———. "Weakness of Will in Ancient Chinese Philosophy." Unpublished paper, 1973.

P'ang P'u 龐樸. *Po-shu wu-hsing-p'ien yen-chiu* 帛書五行篇研究. 2d ed. Chi-nan: Ch'i-lu shu-she, 1988.

Richards, I. A. *Mencius on the Mind: Experiments in Multiple Definition.* London: Routledge & Kegan Paul, 1932.

* Rickett, W. Allyn, trans. *Guanzi: A Study and Translation*, vol. 1. Princeton: Princeton University Press, 1985.

———, trans. *Kuan-tzu*, vol. 1. Hong Kong: Hong Kong University Press, 1965.

Riegel, Jeffrey. "Reflections on an Unmoved Mind." *Journal of the American Academy of Religion*, Thematic Issues 47 (1980): 433–57.

Roetz, Heiner. *Confucian Ethics of the Axial Age: A Reconstruction Under the Aspect of the Breakthrough Toward Postconventional Thinking*. Albany: State University of New York Press, 1993.

Rosemont, Henry, Jr. "Review of Herbert Fingarette, *Confucius: The Secular as Sacred*." *Philosophy East and West* 26 (1976): 463–77.

Schwartz, Benjamin I. *The World of Thought in Ancient China*. Cambridge, Mass.: Harvard University Press, 1985.

Shun, Kwong-loi. "*Jen* and *li* in the *Analects*." *Philosophy East and West* 43 (1993): 457–79.

———. "Review of Robert Eno, *The Confucian Creation of Heaven: Philosophy and the Defense of Ritual Mastery*." *Harvard Journal of Asiatic Studies* 52 (1992): 739–56.

T'ang Chün-i 唐君毅. *Che-hsüeh lun-chi* 哲學論集. Rev. ed. Taipei: T'ai-wan hsüeh-sheng shu-chü, 1990.

———. *Chung-hsi che-hsüeh ssu-hsiang chih pi-chiao lun-wen-chi* 中西哲學思想之比較論文集. Rev. ed. Taipei: T'ai-wan hsüeh-sheng shu-chü, 1988.

———. "Chung-kuo che-hsüeh yen-chiu chih i hsin-fang-hsiang" 中國哲學研究之一新方向. In Wei Cheng-t'ung 韋政通, ed., *Chung-kuo ssu-hsiang-shih fang-fa lun-wen hsüan-chi* 中國思想史方法論文選集, pp. 123–39. Taipei: Ta-lin ch'u-pan-she, 1981.

———. *Chung-kuo che-hsüeh yüan lun: tao-lun p'ien* 中國哲學原論：導論篇. 3d ed. Hong Kong: Hsin-ya shu-yüan yen-chiu-so, 1978.

———. *Chung-kuo che-hsüeh yüan lun: yüan-hsing p'ien* 中國哲學原論：原性篇. Rev. ed. Hong Kong: Hsin-ya shu-yüan yen-chiu-so, 1974.

———. *Chung-kuo che-hsüeh yüan lun: yüan-tao p'ien* 中國哲學原論：原道篇, vol. 1. Rev. ed. Hong Kong: Hsin-ya shu-yüan yen-chiu-so, 1976.

T'ang Yi-chieh 湯一介. *Ju-tao-shih yü nei-tsai-chao-yüeh wen-t'i* 儒道釋與內在超越問題. Nan-ch'ang: Jiang-hsi jen-min ch'u-pan-she, 1991.

Ts'ai Hsin-an 蔡信安. *Tao-te chüeh-tse li-lun* 道德抉擇理論. Taipei: Shih-ying ch'u-pan-she, 1993.

———. "Ts'ung tang-tai hsi-fang lun-li-hsüeh kuan-tien lun Meng-tzu lun-li-hsüeh" 從當代西方倫理學觀點論孟子倫理學. In *Tung-hsi che-hsüeh pi-chiao lun-wen-chi* 東西哲學比較論文集, 2d series, pp. 403–14. Taipei: Chung-kuo wen-hua ta-hsüeh, Che-hsüeh yen-chiu-so, 1993.

Ts'ai Shang-ssu 蔡尚思. *K'ung-tzu ssu-hsiang t'i-hsi* 孔子思想體系. Shanghai: Jen-min ch'u-pan-she, 1982.

Ts'ai Shih-chi 蔡世驥. "Lun K'ung-tzu ti wu-wei ssu-hsiang" 論孔子的無爲思想. In Lo Tsu-chi 羅祖基, ed., *K'ung-tzu ssu-hsiang yen-chiu lun-chi* 孔子思想研究論集, pp. 289–94. Chi-nan: Ch'i-lu shu-she, 1987.

Ts'en I-ch'eng 岑溢成. "Meng-tzu 'chih-yen' ch'u-t'an" 孟子「知言」初探. *O-hu yüeh-k'an* 鵝湖月刊 4, no. 4 (Oct. 1978): 39–41.

———. "Meng-tzu Kao-tzu-p'ien chih 'ch'ing' yü 'ts'ai' lun-shih" 孟子告子篇之「情」與「才」論釋. 2 pts. *O-hu yüeh-k'an* 鵝湖月刊 5, no. 10 (Apr. 1980): 2–8; 5, no. 11 (May 1980): 7–13.

———. "'Sheng chih wei hsing' shih-lun" 「生之謂性」釋論. *O-hu hsüeh-chih* 鵝湖學誌 1 (1988): 55–79.

Tu Wei-ming 杜維明. *Confucian Thought: Selfhood as Creative Transformation.* Albany: State University of New York Press, 1985.

———. *Humanity and Self-Cultivation: Essays in Confucian Thought.* Berkeley, Calif.: Asian Humanities Press, 1979.

———. *Ju-chia ch'uan-t'ung ti hsien-tai chuan-hua* 儒家傳統的現代轉化. Beijing: Chung-kuo kuang-po tien-shih ch'u-pan-she, 1992.

———. *Way, Learning, and Politics: Essays on the Confucian Intellectual.* Albany: State University of New York Press, 1993.

Van Norden, Bryan W. "Mencian Philosophic Psychology." Ph.D. diss., Stanford University, 1991.

———. "Mengzi and Xunzi: Two Views of Human Agency." *International Philosophical Quarterly* 32 (1992): 161–84.

Waley, Arthur, trans. *The Analects of Confucius.* London: George Allen & Unwin, 1938.

———. "Notes on *Mencius.*" *Asia Major* 1 (1949–50): 99–108.

Wang Li-ch'ing 王禮卿. "Jen-nei yi-wai shuo chiao-ch'üan" 仁內義外說斠銓. *K'ung-Meng hsüeh-pao* 孔孟學報 5 (1963): 79–91. Reprinted in *Lun-Meng yen-chiu lun-chi* 論孟研究論集, pp. 353–69. Taipei: Li-ming wen-hua shih-yeh, 1981.

Wei Cheng-t'ung 韋政通. "Chung-kuo ssu-hsiang-shih fang-fa-lun ti chien-t'ao" 中國思想史方法論的檢討. In idem, ed., *Chung-kuo ssu-hsiang-shih fang-fa lun-wen hsüan-chi* 中國思想史方法論文選集, pp. 1–32. Taipei: Ta-lin ch'u-pan-she, 1981.

———. *Hsün-tzu yü ku-tai che-hsüeh* 荀子與古代哲學. 4th ed. Taipei: T'ai-wan shang-wu yin-shu-kuan, 1969.

———. "Wo tui Chung-kuo ssu-hsiang-shih ti chi-tien jen-shih" 我對中國思想史的幾點認識. In idem, ed., *Chung-kuo ssu-hsiang-shih fang-fa lun-wen hsüan-chi* 中國思想史方法論文選集, pp. 199–216. Taipei: Ta-lin ch'u-pan-she, 1981.

Wong, David. "Hsün Tzu on Moral Motivation." In P. J. Ivanhoe, ed., *Chinese Language, Thought and Culture: Essays Dedicated to David S. Nivison.* La Salle, Ill.: Open Court Press, 1996.

———. "Is There a Distinction Between Reason and Emotion in Mencius?" *Philosophy East and West* 41 (1991): 31–44.

———. "Universalism Versus Love With Distinctions: An Ancient Debate Revived." *Journal of Chinese Philosophy* 16 (1989): 251–72.

Wu K'un-ju 鄔昆如. "Hsien-Ch'in ju-chia che-hsüeh ti fang-fa yen-pien" 先秦儒家哲學的方法演變. *T'ai-da che-hsüeh lun-p'ing* 臺大哲學論評 14 (Jan. 1991): 55–71.

Yang Rur-bin [Yang Ju-pin] 楊儒賓. "Chih-li yü chien-hsing: lun hsien-Ch'in ssu-hsiang li ti liang-chung shen-t'i-kuan" 支離與踐形：論先秦思想裏的 兩種身體觀. In idem, ed., *Chung-kuo ku-tai ssu-hsiang chung ti ch'i-lun chi shen-t'i-kuan* 中國古代思想中的氣論及身體觀, pp. 415–49. Taipei: Chü-liu t'u-shu, 1993.

———. "Chih-yen, chien-hsing yü sheng-jen" 知言、踐形與聖人. *Ch'ing-hua hsüeh-pao* 清華學報 23, no. 4 (Dec. 1993): 401–28.

———. "Lun Meng-tzu ti chien-hsing kuan: yi ch'ih-chih-yang-ch'i wei chung-hsin chan-k'ai ti kung-fu-lun mien-hsiang" 論孟子的踐形觀： 以持志養氣爲中心展開的工夫論面相. *Ch'ing-hua hsüeh-pao* 清華學報 20, no. 1 (June 1990): 83–123.

Yang Tsu-han 楊祖漢. *Ju-chia ti hsin-hsüeh ch'uan-t'ung* 儒家的心學傳統. Taipei: Wen-chin ch'u-pan-she, 1992.

Yearley, Lee H. *Mencius and Aquinas: Theories of Virtue and Conceptions of Courage.* Albany: State University of New York Press, 1990.

Yü Ying-shih 余英時. *Nei-tsai ch'ao-yüeh chih lu* 內在超越之路. Beijing: Chung-kuo kuang-po tien-shih ch'u-pan-she, 1992.

Yüan Pao-hsin 袁保新. *Meng-tzu san-pien-chih-hsüeh ti li-shih hsing-ch'a yü hsien-tai ch'üan-shih* 孟子三辨之學的歷史省察與現代詮釋. Taipei: Wen-chin ch'u-pan-she, 1992.

Index of Passages in the 'Meng-tzu'

In this index, a "f" after a number indicates a separate discussion on the next page. A continuous discussion over two or more pages is indicated by a span of page numbers, e.g., "75–79." *Passim* is used for a cluster of references in close but not consecutive sequence.

Subject Index

In this index, a "f" after a number indicates a separate discussion on the next page, and an "ff" indicates separate discussion on the next two pages. A continuous discussion over two or more pages is indicated by a span of page numbers, e.g., "75–79." *Passim* is used for a cluster of references in close but not consecutive sequence.

Ability (*neng*), 35, 176, 188, 192, 254, 260; character and, 19, 22, 62, 120, 237; to change, 40, 214; to tell what is proper, 52, 71, 84, 148, 211; to act properly; 65; to adjust one's aim, 65, 68–69, 243; to be ethical, 138–39, 144, 174, 219, 230f; to practice *jen*ᵃ government, 139, 141, 219; and *k'o yi*, 191, 216–21 *passim*, 225, 230
Acceptance, *see Ming*ᵃ
Affairs, *see Shih*ᵃ
Ai (love, concern), 49–51, 64, 99–102, 145f, 165, 178, 239, 242f; *jen*ᵇ (for fellow human beings), 23, 132, 146; Mohist idea of, 31, 100; *wu*ᵃ (for things), 50; *ch'in* (for parents), 50, 63, 129–32 *passim*, 138, 145f, 156, 188–91, 217, 230; directed at the self, 100; for brothers, 106, 125, 145; Confucian idea of, 132–33, 240; for other members of one's own kind, 223, 225, 228
Ames, Roger T., 180f, 190. *See also* Hall, David L.

Analects, *see Lun-yü*
Analogy, 91, 99, 217, 219; military, 68; of archery, 68, 70, 122, 243; of water, 89f, 108, 213, 246; of willow, 88–90, 123, 211, 246; of taste, 136–37; vegetative, 137–38, 160, 183, 220; of the carpenter, 225
Ancestor, impersonating an, 84, 96, 107
Appropriateness, *see Yi*ᵃ
Archery, 59, 66, 178, 255. *See also under* Analogy
Aristotelian essence, 185

Bloom, Irene, 241, 256, 260
Body, *see T'i*
Boodberg, Peter A., 238f
Brother, 26, 101, 123, 125, 223; elder, 24, 57, 223f, 230, 243; younger, 24, 84, 95–96, 106–8, 230; obedience to elder, 63, 71, 120, 156–57, 243; respect for elder, 63, 84, 95f, 107, 138, 145f, 156, 188, 190, 217; child of elder, 127–28, 133, 145
Brotherhood, 106

ma Tzu, 32–33, 35, 216; criticism of, 69, 124, 216; teachings (*yen*) of, 116, 124, 166, 174

Mo-tzu, 74, 99f, 138, 175, 240, 260; on burial of parents, 29, 134; "Chien ai" chapter, 30, 52, 240; "Shang t'ung" chapter, 31ff, 240; on doctrines, 32, 116; "Ching shang" (chapter of *Mo-tzu*), 100; "Ching shuo shang" (chapter of *Mo-tzu*), 100; on Kao Tzu, 123–24; on *ch'ing*ᵃ, 184; on *jen*ᵇ, 190; on *li*ᵇ, 197; on neng, 216f; on *ming*ᵃ, 238; "So jan" chapter, 240

Mou Tsung-san, 236f, 262; on *hsing*ᵃ, 38, 181, 241, 246f, 256, 258ff; on *yi*ᵃ, 99, 249; on *t'ien*, 207, 259; on *ch'ing*ᵃ, 214–15, 260; on *ts'ai*, 218, 260

Mourning, 29, 32, 52, 223

Munro, Donald J., 71, 237, 239, 244, 261

Music, 27, 121, 184, 255

Natural course of things, 193–97 *passim*

Nei (internal, inside), 94, 102–3. *See also* Immanent dimension

Neng, see Ability

Nivison, David S., 98, 131, 134, 237, 247f, 252, 258; on Mohist thought, 34–35, 240–41, 251; on Kao Tzu, 116, 118, 123, 247, 250; on self-cultivation, 150–51, 253f

Non-action (*wu-wei*ᵃ), 27, 77, 120, 144, 195

North Sea, 217

O, *see* Evil

Obligations, 16–20, 235–40 *passim*

Office: responsibilities of, 53f; official rank, 61, 169, 200; attainment of, 78–79

Old person, 95, 101–6, 110f

Original goodness (*pen shan*), 188, 212, 259

Others, *see Jen*ᵇ

Overlord, *see Pa*

Ox, 49, 196; compassion for, 50, 64, 138–44 *passim*, 152, 189, 217; substituting a lamb for, 51, 64, 117; *chih*ᵃ *hsing*ᵃ, 91; *hsing*ᵃ of, 93, 99

Ox Mountain, 137

Pa (overlord), 72, 169f, 181, 183

Pai (white), 91–97 *passim*, 102, 104, 241, 247f

P'ang P'u, 203, 258

Parents, 30f, 50–52, 147f, 253; *ch'in ch'in*, 50–51, 146; relation to, 51–52, 57, 147; burial of, 52, 127–35 *passim*, 139f, 188; serving, 63, 71, 156f; bodies of deceased, 127, 129, 133f, 139–40, 145, 180; love for, 129f, 146, 188–91, 230

P'ei Hsüeh-hai, 188, 214, 253, 260

Pen (basis, root, original), 127, 129, 193

Perplexity, *see Huo*ᵃ

Persistence, 137, 155f, 174

Personal deity, 19, 78, 207ff

Petty person (*shao jen*ᵇ), 167, 186; *hsing*ᵃ of, 38, 90, 186, 256–57. *See also* Superior person

Physical form, *see Hsing*ᵇ

Pieh (discrimination), 30, 32, 35, 100, 127, 216f, 240

Po Yi, 57, 62, 66–71 *passim*, 171

Po-kung Yu, 72–75

P'o (oppress), 42–44

Political participation, 5, 45–46, 68f

Political thought: in early texts, 15–18; in the *Lun-yü*, 18–28 *passim*, 46, 162; in the *Mo-tzu*, 29; in Yangist thought, 45–47; in the *Meng-tzu*, 163–78 *passim*

Pre-Confucian thought, 14–28 *passim*

Predispositions: emotional, 218–21, 230; shared, 132f, 139, 147, 256;

Library of Congress Cataloging-in-Publication Data

Shun, Kwong-loi, 1953–
        Menicus and early Chinese thought / Kwong-loi Shun.
                p.   cm.
        Includes bibliographic references and index.
        ISBN 0-8047-2788-0 (cl.) : ISBN 0-8047-4017-8 (pbk.)
        1. Mencius.   2. Philosophy, Chinese — To 221 B.C.   I. Title.
B128.M324S48   1997
181' . 112 — dc20   96-12393
                                                                                          CIP

Year of original printing   1997

Last figure below indicates year of this printing

06   05   04   03   02   01   00

49727134R00192

Made in the USA
San Bernardino, CA
02 June 2017